How to Buy & Use Minicomputers & Microcomputers

by

William Barden, Jr.

Howard W. Sams & Co., Inc.
4300 WEST 62ND ST. INDIANAPOLIS, INDIANA 46268 USA

FIRST EDITION
SECOND PRINTING—1977

International Standard Book Number: 0-672-21351-6
Library of Congress Catalog Card Number: 76-19693

Printed in the United States of America.

Preface

The impact of the computer revolution has not yet been felt. It's true that our everyday lives have been radically changed by computerized billing, programmed education, computer traffic control, and the like, but the real computer revolution is still to come. It will be the minicomputer/microcomputer revolution. If the larger computers have influenced a great segment of our lives, the microcomputers will influence an even greater one. These physically small, dirt-cheap computers can be contained in applicances, automobiles, and small general-purpose systems.

This book discusses these smaller brethren of computers and shows how the reader can become a part of the revolution—how he can own and use a functioning computer system in his home to do a variety of practical or recreational tasks.

It doesn't take a mathematical or electronics genius to learn how to use and program one of these computers. Starting with a basic system, a beginner can learn by writing two- or three-step programs and rapidly work up to larger and more complicated functions. The beginner may then add to his basic system as his hobby (and pocketbook) grows. A minimum system is now in the $200 range.

The purpose here is to instruct the interested person in what computers are, how they perform their computing, and what tools are necessary to talk to all computers, especially the newer minicomputers and microcomputers. A detailed description of four low-priced minicomputers and many lower-priced microcomputers is included. Many examples of "real-world" connections to computers are given, as are short programs illustrating the programming of the computers both in the more rudimentary machine language and the BASIC language. Benchmark programs for every minicomputer or microcomputer discussed are provided for comparisons of one computer with another.

For the hobbyist or potential hobbyist, this book explains what computers are in the first chapter. Chapter 2 discusses how a computer can break down complex problems into single bits of data. The third chapter discusses minicomputer hardware—how a computer is physically put together to solve problems. The next chapter then covers the counterpart of hardware: computer software, or programs. It gives several examples of programs, including a complete BASIC program for playing tic-tac-toe with a computer. Chapter 5 discusses the devices that enable a computer to communicate with the outside world: peripheral devices. Several interface examples are provided, including a complete interface of a burglar alarm system to both a minicomputer and microcomputer. A reasonable approach to the selection of a computer system is handled in the next chapter. Chapter 7 presents goals and techniques to use in programming your computer to do the things you would like. The last two chapters provide detailed information on the currently available minicomputers and microcomputers so that a reader may determine which system offers the most advantages for his particular needs.

Credit for this book goes to many people, but a large portion of the total goes to my wife, Janet, who gave the most important contribution to any project—much encouragement.

WILLIAM BARDEN, JR.

ABOUT THE AUTHOR

William Barden, Jr., is currently a member of the Technical Staff of Development Laboratories, Inc., in Santa Monica, California. He has had 15 years experience in technical writing, computer programming, computer design, and computer systems design, mostly involving minicomputers. He has worked on 13 different computer systems and has written articles on computer and related equipment for various publications, including *Electronics World*. He is a member of the Association for Computing Machinery and the IEEE. His major interest is home computing systems. Other interests include mathematical games and sailing.

Contents

CHAPTER

1

Introduction to Computers, Minicomputers, and Microcomputers

This book has one goal—to give you the necessary background to buy and use your own computer system. No matter what type of computer system you acquire, whether it is a new or used minicomputer system with many devices attached to it, or a small microprocessor-oriented computer kit, two things are evident: You will be buying a system at a bargain price compared with that of computers of ten or even five years ago, and your computer system will be extremely powerful in terms of the number and speed of operations it can perform.

No longer are computers expensive. A completely functioning computer kit that can perform hundreds of thousands of operations per second can be purchased for only several hundred dollars; an elaborate system with the same computing power of a $100,000 system ten years ago can be purchased for the cost of a medium-priced new car. A smaller system with about the same computing power that can run such programs as tic-tac-toe and "space war," play music, provide computer-aided instruction, and record weather data, among other things, can now be purchased for about $1500. A large system may be built up from the basic "central processing unit" price of several hundred dollars, with additional items added piece by piece as the user desires (and in pace with the contents of his pocketbook). Another alternative is a shared purchase of a computer system. Many high schools and computer hobbyists

Fig. 1-1. DEC PDP-8 minicomputer.

Courtesy Digital Equipment Corp.

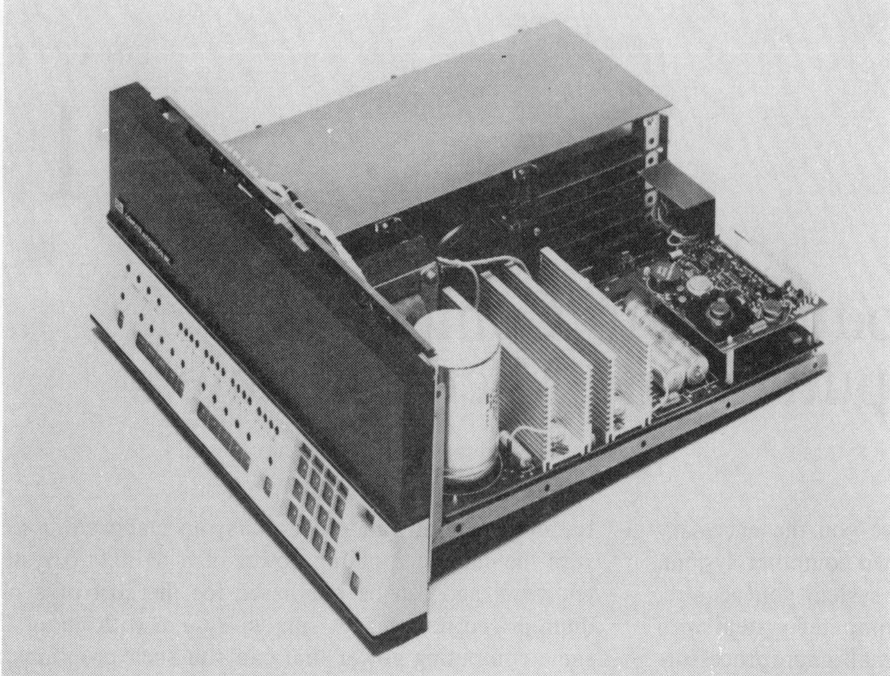

Courtesy Computer Automation, Inc.

Fig. 1-2. Computer Automation LSI-3/05 minicomputer.

have formed computer clubs with regular meetings and discussions, and, in some cases, with a central computer facility.

Fig. 1-1 shows a typical minicomputer system, an older Digital Equipment Corporation PDP-8 minicomputer with Teletype printer. The complete system can be purchased for about $1500, used. This purchase would include all operating software and everything needed to write and run various types of programs. Fig. 1-2 shows a new Computer Automation Alpha LSI-3/05 minicomputer, purchasable for under $3000, new with Teletype. Here, again, the purchase price would include basic software for generation of programs. A new MITS Altair 680 microcomputer system is shown in Fig. 1-3. A system in kit form with terminal and built-in cassette-tape input/output (I/O) secondary storage costs about $1500. This system is as versatile as the two previously mentioned and is representative of the new line of microprocessor-oriented kits or finished computers that are now being offered for hobbyists. The MITS kit includes utility software and a BASIC language capability.

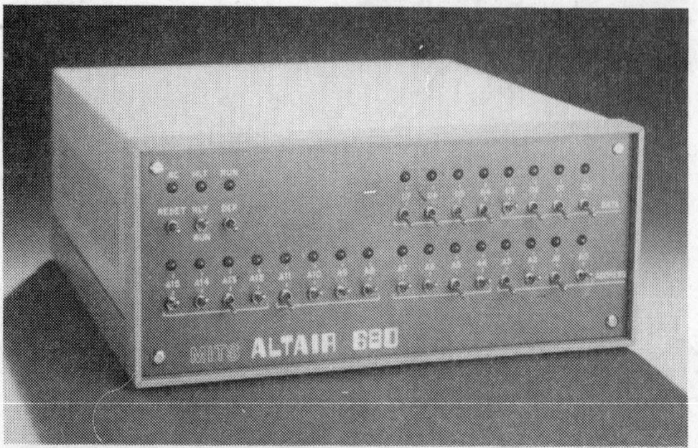

Courtesy MITS

Fig. 1-3. MITS Altair 680 microcomputer.

A SHORT HISTORY OF COMPUTERS

The ideas behind modern computers go back hundreds or even thousands of years. The abacus, after all, is a digital computer, and it is a very efficient one at that. The French mathematician Blaise Pascal constructed a type of calculator in 1642 that could add and subtract numbers. In the early 1800s an Englishman, Charles Babbage, developed what was then called "Babbage's Folly," a forerunner of today's modern computer. Interestingly enough, Babbage's ideas were valid and included many features found in computers today; the problem at the time was achieving tolerances too fine for the existing machine tools.

The modern computer was developed over a period of about 35 years, starting with a relay-type computer built by Bell Telephone Laboratories in 1940. The first general-purpose computer was developed jointly by Harvard University and International Business Machines Corporation. Early machines literally occupied rooms. The first commercially available computer, the Sperry Rand Univac, appeared in 1952. Its size was very impressive, as the basic components of the machine were vacuum tubes similar to the ones found in television receivers of the time. With the advent of the transistor, computers shrank in size to somewhat more reasonable levels. In place of the large vacuum-tube

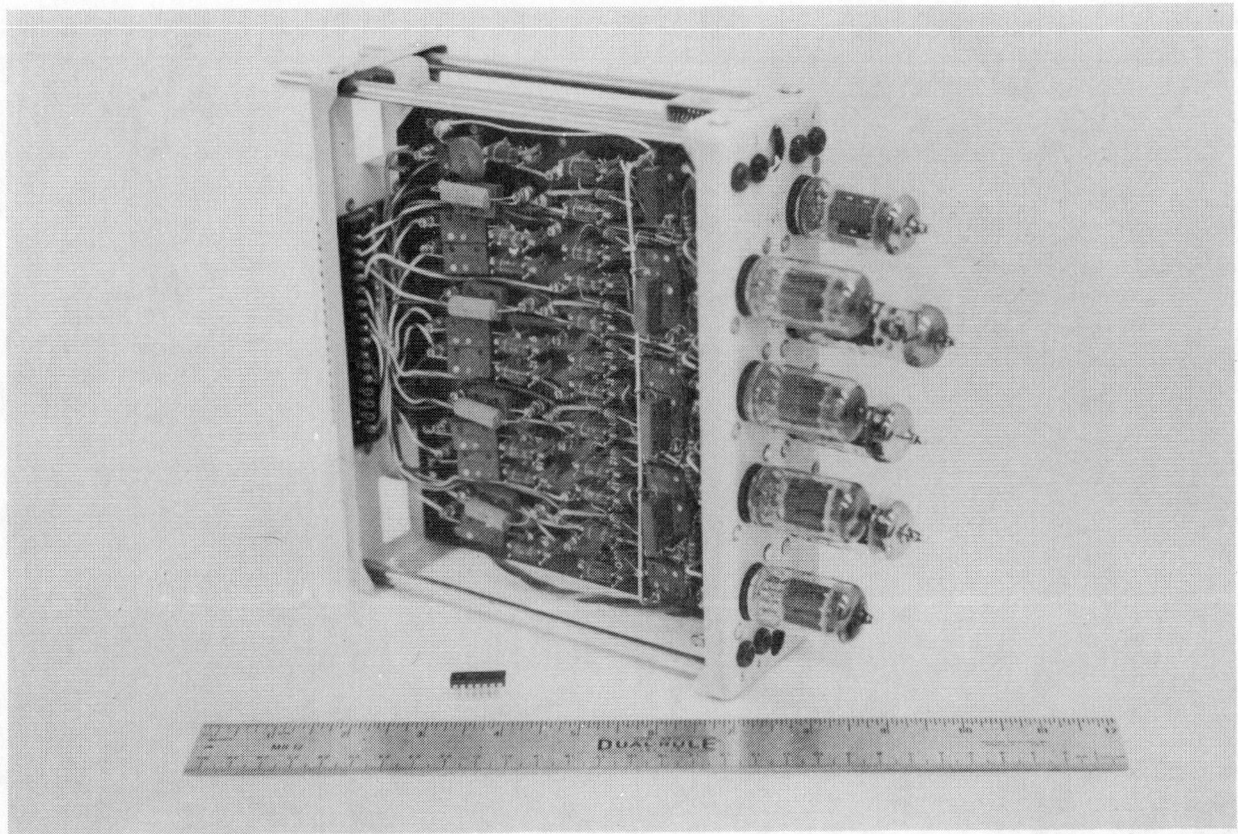

Courtesy Steven DeGarmo

Fig. 1-4. Vacuum-tube unit vs LSI storage device.

"flip-flop" storage device of Fig. 1-4, the transistorized unit was able to perform the same function at one-tenth the size.

By the late 1960s, advances in electronics technology had replaced the "discrete" components of transistors, resistors, and capacitors with a small-scale integration (SSI) "chip." (The word *small* refers to the chip having a small number of components packed into the chip, possibly only dozens!) Then it became truly feasible to have a desk-top computer, and equipment such as the Digital Equipment Corporation PDP-8 minicomputer began to appear. Rapid advancements in integrated circuits made the "small" in SSI become "large," and large-scale integration (LSI), packing thousands of transistors in a chip about ⅜ inch by ¾ inch, became commonplace, along with smaller, more powerful computers. The chip in Fig. 1-4 contains eight flip-flops.

The near-ultimate advance in microelectronics technology came in the early 1970s when integrated-circuit manufacturers started producing complete "microprocessor" computer circuits on a chip of less than a square inch. These chips were almost as powerful as their predecessor computer circuits and required a lot less space and power. Since the chips were manufactured in production quantities, the prices became extremely low, in some cases making available a completely functioning computer for a few hundred dollars per unit. Fig. 1-5 illustrates the Intel 8080 CPU chip (a central processing unit chip) that replaces possibly 200 small-scale and medium-scale integration chips. Indeed, much of the cost now in microcomputer systems is not in the chips themselves, but in packaging, power supplies, and other support items. Often, the cost of peripheral equipment, such as Teletypes, line printers, and card readers, far exceeds the cost of a minicomputer or microcomputer system.

The next advancement will undoubtedly bring still less expensive and more powerful microprocessor chips and a parallel development of inexpensive peripheral devices. More and more people will be able to afford computer systems, and those systems will far surpass their predecessors in the functions they can perform and the speed at which they can be executed.

USES OF MINICOMPUTERS

Minicomputers and microcomputers are used in so many different applications that it would be impossible to list all of them. One of the more fascinating uses is the implementation of electronic Ping-Pong or other types of electronic games. In this example, a microprocessor chip set is a computer chosen or "dedicated" to

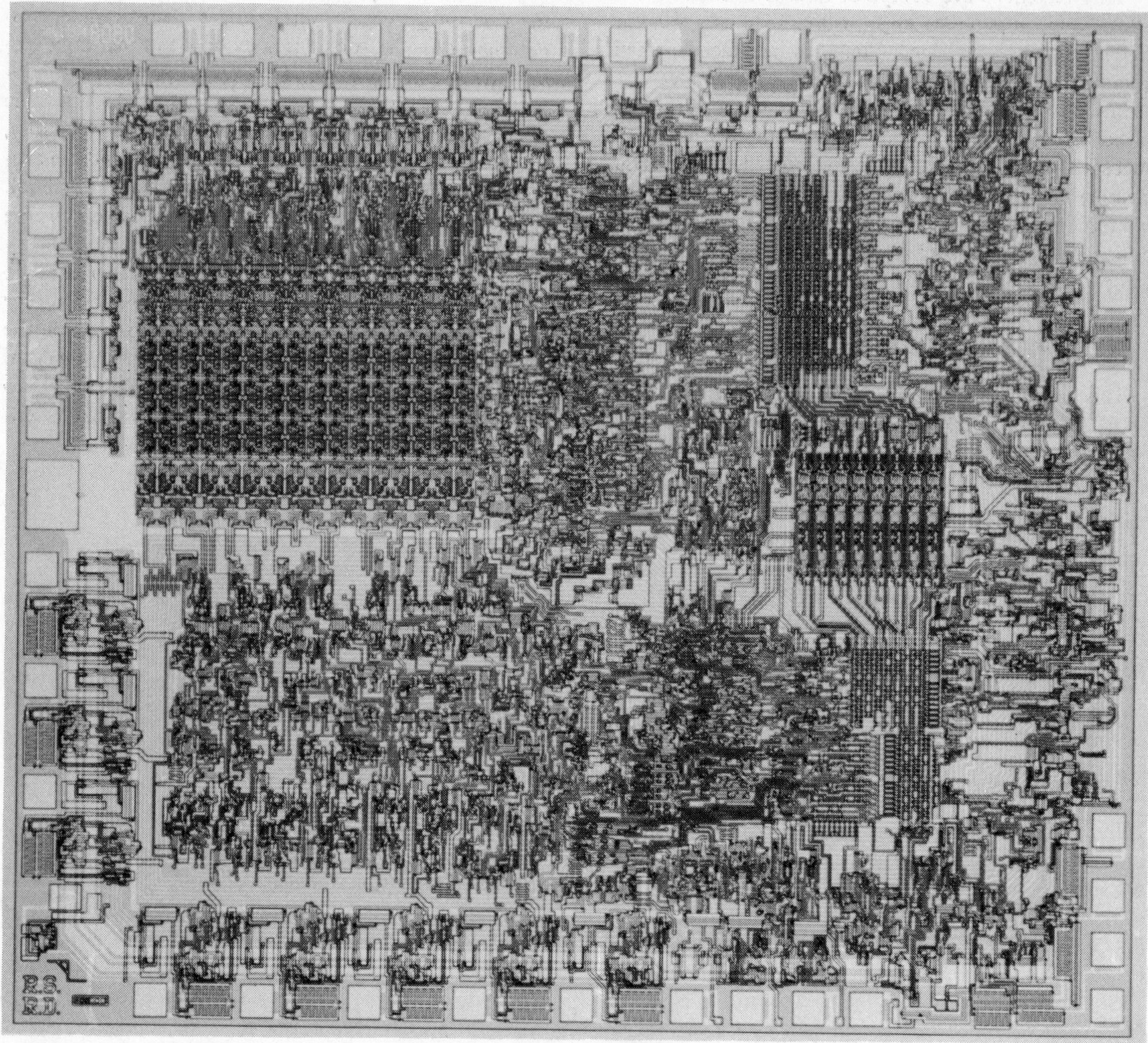

Courtesy Intel Corp.

Fig. 1-5. Intel 8080 CPU chip.

control the game. Traffic light controllers are another example of current uses of microprocessors. One microprocessor chip set can replace a great deal of mechanical and electromechanical equipment controlling traffic at intersections.

Minicomputers are widely used in scientific applications to record the results of experiments and to control precision scientific equipment. In one example, a minicomputer precisely positions a large deep-space tracking antenna for receiving space probe communications. Other minicomputers filter and process the data as they are received from the probe, and control the transmission of commands to the space vehicle.

Business applications, once exclusively the realm of larger computers, such as the IBM 360, are being performed more and more by minicomputers. Billing, accounts receivable, inventory control, and report generation can all be performed by an "in-house" minicomputer or microcomputer rather than a larger computer system that has to share its resources with many other users.

Commercial applications are numerous. Many newspapers have a number of on-line cathode-ray tube (crt) displays on which editors and reporters can enter stories or on which clerks can input classified advertisements. The news stories are then automatically composed and typeset on an automatic typesetting machine that is itself controlled by an integral minicomputer. The classified ad output also is sorted and printed by means of the minicomputer controller.

Only recently have computer hobbyists been able to afford minicomputer systems for their own uses at home. Hobbyists have done such things as interfaced a minicomputer to an electronic organ and programmed it to read music, compiled their own stock market programs to beat the market (one probably hears only about the successes in this application), and recorded continuous weather data on a computer system. Really, the uses are limited only by the user's imagination. Use your imagination, with the help of this book, to discover and develop your own applications for a minicomputer.

ORGANIZATION OF THIS BOOK

This book is divided into two basic parts. The first part, Chapters 1 through 7, tells the reader how minicomputer hardware and software work, describes the various types of peripheral devices available, outlines the necessary steps in purchasing a minicomputer system, and provides some hints on how to program a system for your application. The second part, from Chapter 8 on, describes in detail the currently available microcomputer and minicomputer systems. Incidentally, the dividing line between "minicomputers" and "microcomputers" is becoming more and more hazy; this book treats a *minicomputer* as being an inexpensive (costing up to a few thousand dollars), physically small, general-purpose computer, while a *microcomputer* is taken as a minicomputer having a microprocessor chip or chips as its central processing unit. Almost all of the general material in this book applies to both types of systems, and the word "minicomputer" will be used to apply to both minicomputers and microcomputers unless otherwise indicated.

CHAPTER 2

Minicomputer Basics

Robert Benchley, the humorist, once said that he was certain he could build a bridge if someone would just tell him the first step. Computers are a somewhat similar problem. Given a computer that calculates checking account balances, processes "real-time" data from space to construct images of Mars, or controls a paper mill, one wonders: "How would I go about designing and constructing it?"

COMPUTER PROBLEM SOLVING

Every problem can be broken down into a number of tasks or jobs to be performed. In the case of a paper mill, for example, there are many tasks required to produce nicely cut white paper at the end of a paper machine. Lumber must be sent to the mill. It must be "debarked." The stripped log must be put into a chemical solution that will "digest" or break down the log. The paper pulp must be mixed into a solution of water and pulp. This must then be spread thin and be rolled, pressed, and dried into paper. The continuous strip of paper must then be cut and packaged for sale.

Each of these tasks can be broken down further into subtasks. The task of cutting the continuous strip of paper might be divided into adjusting the speed of the machine, adjusting the cutting knives, stacking the paper as it is cut, determining when the stack is high enough that it can be hauled away and a new one started, and so forth.

By this time you know what is coming next. The subtasks can be further subdivided. Determining the final height of the paper stack can be accomplished by making certain the paper is stacking properly, by calibrating the height of the stack against a measure, and by detecting and avoiding paper jams.

Many complicated problems of this type can be broken down into a long list of steps. With computers, the levels of the tasks are simply much lower. It is very difficult to build an efficient paper stacker, but at least the problem appears to be solvable when it is broken down in this way:

1. Put a zero into a counter that counts the number of sheets of paper in a stack.
2. Start the paper machine.
3. Each time a sheet of paper is cut, add one to the count of sheets.
4. Multiply the count of the number of sheets by 0.020 inch (the thickness of a single sheet).
5. If the result from Step 4 is greater than 20 inches, go to Step 6; otherwise go to Step 3.
6. Stop the paper machine (in our simple case), haul away the stacked paper, and go back to Step 1.

Obviously, even the above example will not give us a very efficient paper mill (it does not provide for detecting paper jams, for example), but it does illustrate how a problem can be broken down into small steps. The question arises: "How small should the steps be?" It may be cheating somewhat to say that the six steps involve operations that at first glance appear to be *possible* to implement in some type of machine or computer. On the other hand, it is hard to imagine more basic operations than zeroing out a count, or adding one to a count, or multiplying two numbers. Let us assume for a moment that this level is the one for which we are striving to invent a machine—the level of adding, or subtracting, or multiplying two numbers. Notice also that Step 5 involves a comparison between two numbers, and a very important step of decision making rests on the results of that comparison ("Go to Step 6 *if* . . .").

IMPLEMENTING A SOLUTION TO A PROBLEM

Now that we have some idea of what we want to do in basic operations (even if only a hazy one), which piece of machinery can implement it? A mechanical machine could add two numbers and perform the level of operations described above, but mechanical machines have a tendency to be rather slow. What electrical machine could perform our operations? For a reader with an electronics background, the idea of adding two numbers by adding voltages might appear to be one solution.

An amplifier with two inputs might produce a larger and larger output voltage for larger and larger "sums" of input voltages. This approach is actually used. Since each of the input voltages is an "analog" of a number value, a computer that adds two numbers in this fashion is called an *analog computer*. Analog computers are perfectly feasible and in use today. However, they have several disadvantages. They are not conveniently set up to perform operations, and their accuracy is not good enough to avoid errors such as a two-cent error in a checking account balance. Is there another electrical device that can add two numbers? The answer is that there is, but the device is not very obvious. Don't feel too badly about not knowing the answer, however. It took centuries to arrive at what some people would accept as a simple solution.

Because of the nature of electronic devices, adding two numbers in analog fashion is not very accurate. Electrical components have a tendency to "age" and change their "characteristics" from one week to the next. If we added values of 1.23 volts and 2.38 volts today and got 3.61 volts, tomorrow we might get 3.60 volts. Obviously we need a device that will come up with the same value today, tomorrow, and a week from now.

BINARY DEVICES

One such electrical device is a switch. A switch is either off or on. It can represent one of only two values, a one or a zero, and a switch is therefore a two-state, or *binary* ("bi"=two), device. Although only two states can be represented by a switch, the condition of the switch is fairly certain (unless the switch is faulty)—much more so than the condition of a ten-state (or decimal) device where state 0 is 0 volt, state 1 is 0.1 volt, 2 is 0.2 volt, and so forth. One-tenth volt today may be two-tenths tomorrow, and there is that intolerable error again.

Given a binary device such as a switch, or flip-flop, or magnetic core (all explained in more detail later), how can we represent, say, 12,578 with something that can hold only a "0" or a "1"? One way would be to have at least 12,578 devices. This is not too efficient, to say the least. An alternative is to "weight" each device so that the first represents "1," the second "2," the third a higher value, and so forth. Although the weighting could be a 1-2-2-4-6-10 weighting, or some other set, a very efficient weighting is by powers of 2. As a matter of fact, weighting in this fashion is *most* efficient and parallels our standard decimal system. In our decimal system, the number 123 actually means $(1 \times 10^2) + (2 \times 10^1) + (3 \times 10^0)$, or $100 + 20 + 3$ (any number to the zero power is always 1). A weighting by powers of 2 means that successive devices represent the numbers $2^0, 2^1, 2^2, 2^3, 2^4, \ldots$, or (written without exponents) 1, 2, 4, 8, 16, ...

BINARY NUMBERS

Let us take a number, say 12,578, and see how a set of binary devices can represent that number. The number 12,578 can be represented as $(1 \times 8192) + (1 \times 4096) + (0 \times 2048) + (0 \times 1024) + (0 \times 512) + (1 \times 256) + (0 \times 128) + (0 \times 64) + (1 \times 32) + (0 \times 16) + (0 \times 8) + (0 \times 4) + (1 \times 2) + (0 \times 1)$. Note that 8192, 4096, 2048, 1024, . . . , are decreasing powers of 2 down to 2^0, or 1.* In our powers of 2 weighting scheme, a series of lights could represent 12,578 as shown in Fig. 2-1.

* A table of positive and negative powers of 2 is given in Appendix A, on p. 209.

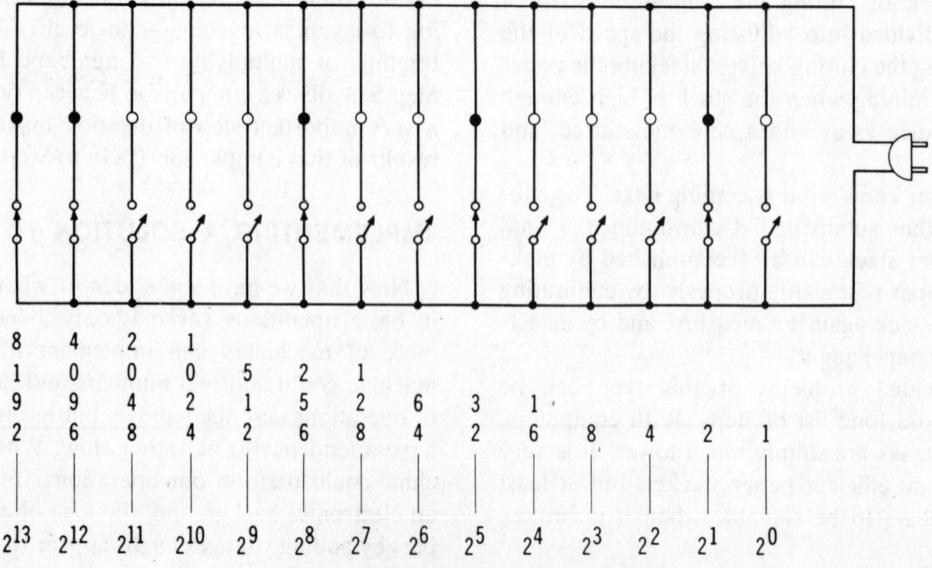

Fig. 2-1. Sample binary representation.

With some study of Fig. 2-1, one can see that numbers from 0 to 16,383 (all switches on) can be represented. In fact, for a given number of lights and switches, the maximum number that can be represented is 2 raised to the power of that number minus one, or $2^n - 1$. For example, with two lights, $2^n - 1 = 2^2 - 1 = (2 \times 2) - 1 = 4 - 1 = 3$. For three lights, $2^3 - 1 = 7$. For ten lights, the maximum number that can be held is $2^{10} - 1 = (2 \times 2 \times 2 \times 2 \times 2 \times 2 \times 2 \times 2 \times 2 \times 2) - 1 = 1023$, represented by all ten lights being on. Note that the maximum number that can be held is one less than the *total* number of combinations that can be held. For example, three switches can hold a maximum number of 7 but have a total of eight distinct combinations of lights. This is shown in Fig. 2-2, where three lights are used to represent the decimal numbers from 0 to 7; here 7 is the maximum number, but there are eight combinations.

NUMBER	LIGHTS		
0	○	○	○
1	○	○	●
2	○	●	○
3	○	●	●
4	●	○	○
5	●	○	●
6	●	●	○
7	●	●	●

Fig. 2-2. Three-element binary device.

Adding and Subtracting Binary Numbers

Just as we can add, subtract, multiply, or divide using the decimal system, a computer uses the binary system implementation to perform these arithmetic operations. As an example, suppose we have two decimal numbers that are to be added, 23_{10} and 18_{10}. (We will use a subscript of "10" to represent the decimal number system and a subscript of "2" to represent the binary number system—otherwise, numbers such as 11_{10} and 11_2 would be ambiguous.) In decimal addition, we know that 3 and 8 equal 11, so we mark down a "1" and "carry" a 1. Now we add 2 and 1 and the carried 1 to get 4 (see Fig. 2-3).

```
STEP 1:  23      STEP 2:   1
         18               23
        (1)1              18
                          41
```

Fig. 2-3. Decimal addition.

To add in binary, we first have to convert the two operands to binary numbers. Thus, 23 is 16 + 4 + 2 + 1, all powers of 2. Ranking these in order, we get $(1 \times 2^4) + (0 \times 2^3) + (1 \times 2^2) + (1 \times 2^1) + (1 \times 2^0)$, or 10111_2. Also, 18 is 16 + 2, or $2^4 + 2^1$, giving us 10010_2. Now we can add the two binary numbers. In Step 1 of Fig. 2-4, 1 and 0 gives 1. Next, 1 and 1 is 10_2, where we have a carry into the next power of 2 position (remember, only two states are possible in a binary device, 0 or 1). So, 0 is written down and 1 is carried to the next position (Step 2). The carry, 1, and 0 here give a sum of 10_2 again, so we must write down a 0 and carry a 1 again (Step 3). The final answer is shown in Step 4. To double-check the answer, we can reconvert the binary number back to decimal. Thus, $101001 = 2^5 + 2^3 + 2^0 = 32 + 8 + 1 = 41_{10}$.

Subtraction of binary numbers is very much like addition except that we have a "borrow" instead of a carry. The borrow works the same way that it does in decimal subtraction, except that instead of borrowing ten, two is borrowed. To subtract 23 from 41, we have the steps shown in Fig. 2-5. First, 1 from 1 is easy—we get a 0 (Step 1). Now what is 1 from 0? Just as we subtract a 9 from a 2 in decimal by borrowing a ten, we have to borrow here. So, 1 from a borrowed 10_2 is 1 (Step 2). But wait a minute, we did not have a 1 in the next position to borrow! Here, again, just as we continue borrowing in a decimal number, we borrow in binary (Step 3). Our borrowed 1 from the fourth place becomes a 0, and we have the partial answer of 0010. Completing the subtraction, the final result is shown in Step 4.

Binary Multiplication and Division

Fortunately for most of us, except the most dedicated computer freaks, multiplication or division in binary is not really necessary. It is possible, of course, to build up multiplication tables for binary numbers (such as $10_2 \times 11_2 = 110_2$), but it is usually much simpler to convert to decimal numbers, multiply or divide, and reconvert the final result to a binary number. Many computers do not have instructions that multiply or divide as part of their "instruction repertoire." The multipli-

```
STEP 1:  10111   STEP 2:  10111   STEP 3:  10111   STEP 4:  10111
         10010            10010            10010            10010
             1             (1)01           (1)001         (1)01001
```

Fig. 2-4. Binary addition.

Fig. 2-5. Binary subtraction.

cation and division, rather than being done in computer hardware, is done in "software" as a 10- or 12-step program. Multiplication is accomplished in the software by a sequence of shifting and addition; division is performed by a series or shifts and subtractions. This will be covered later.

Double-Dabble

A very easy way to convert a binary number to its decimal equivalent is to use a method called *double-dabble*. In this method, we work on a binary number from left to right, taking the first binary digit, or *bit* (*b*inary dig*it*), and multiplying it by 2 to give a partial result. The partial result is now added to the next bit, the result of that is multiplied by 2 and added to the next bit, and so forth. Here is how it works. Take the

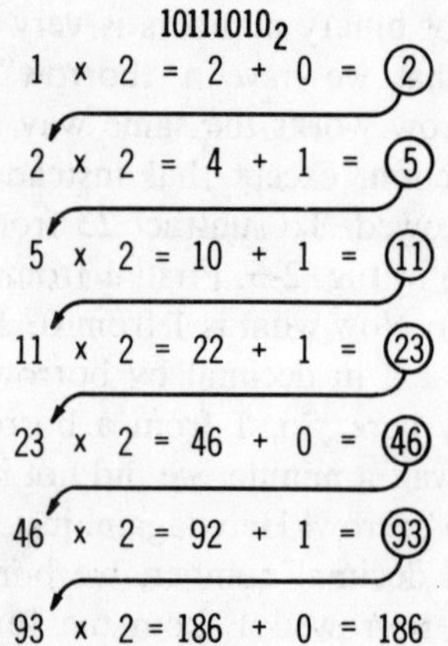

Fig. 2-6. Double-dabble with 10111010_2.

binary number 10111010_2, for example. Using double-dabble and starting from the left, we have the process shown in Fig. 2-6. The answer of 186 can be verified by using our old method to get $2^7 + 2^5 + 2^4 + 2^3 + 2^1 = 128 + 32 + 16 + 8 + 2 = 186$.

Converting From Decimal to Binary

Unfortunately, to convert from decimal to binary it is necessary to use a more tedious procedure. To convert, divide the number by 2 and record the remainder. Divide the quotient (result) by 2 and record the remainder again. Stop when the quotient is zero. Fig. 2-7 shows the procedure in converting the decimal number 186.

The remainders, *in reverse order*, give the answer of 10111010_2. Another way to convert is simply to take the largest power of 2 that will "go" into the number or "residue." In the previous example, 186 is larger than

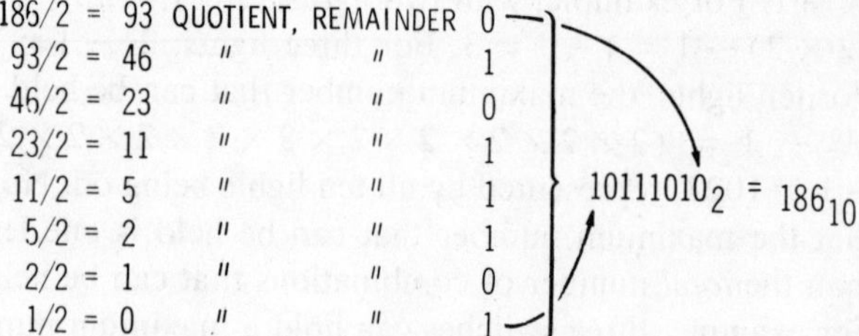

Fig. 2-7. Decimal-to-binary conversion.

128 but smaller than 256, so subtract 128 from 186, leaving a residue of 58. Then, 32 but not 64 can be subtracted, leaving 26. Next, 16, 8, and 2 are subtracted, leaving 0. The numbers 128, 32, 16, 8, and 2 are 2^7, 2^5, 2^4, 2^3, and 2^1, respectively. Ordering the powers of 2, we get 10111010_2. Proficiency at this method, however, takes a little time, so don't be dismayed if this approach doesn't seem convenient at first.

Two's Complement Binary Numbers

There is one more thing to know about the binary number system before we have adequately covered it in respect to minicomputers. Almost all minicomputers represent negative numbers by a method called *two's complement* representation. To negate a positive binary number to two's complement form, change all ones to zeros, change all zeros to ones, and add one to the result. Strange, you say? Well, there is a very good reason for the two's complement form, but it is related to hardware again. It is easier for most hardware to operate if both positive and negative numbers are in two's complement form than if each number has a sign and magnitude. Suppose, for example, that we made all binary numbers eight bits long, with seven bits of magnitude, and the leftmost bit a sign bit. The sign bit would be a 1 if the number were negative and a 0 if the number were positive. Then, +23 and −18 would be represented as shown in Fig. 2-8. If the computer were to add

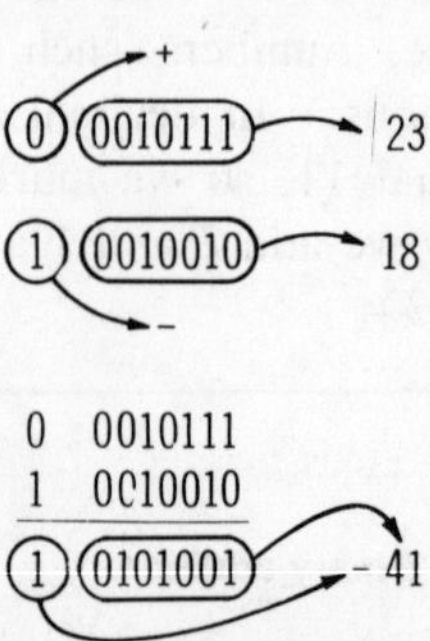

Fig. 2-8. Sign, magnitude addition (*incorrect*).

these two numbers directly, the result would be −41 as shown in the same figure, obviously the wrong answer.

With two's complement implementation, however, adding directly would give the correct answer. Remember the rules: If the number is positive, put a 0 in the sign bit and leave the number alone. If the number is negative, change all ones to zeros, all zeros to ones, and add one. If the number is to be eight bits long, remember to "extend" zeros left to begin with, into unused bit positions: 101_2 becomes 00000101_2, for example. In the example of Fig. 2-8, +23 becomes 00010111_2 and −18 is converted to two's complement form as shown in Fig. 2-9. Now we can add just as the computer does. Note that since only eight bits can be held in the result, the "most significant" bit is lost (or dropped in the "bit bucket" on the floor, an imaginary container that holds all sorts of computer garbage). The answer is +5, just as it should be. The two's complement method may seem a cumbersome way to represent negative numbers, but it is much simpler from a hardware designer's standpoint than implementing computer hardware to do a sign and magnitude addition—to check the sign, add or subtract the two numbers on the result of the comparison, restore the sign of the result, and so forth.

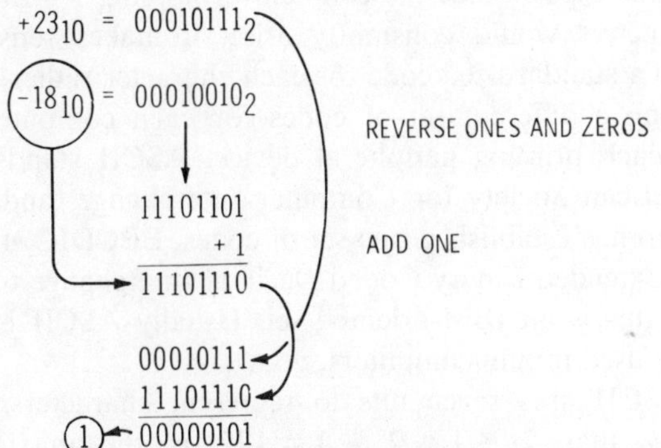

Fig. 2-9. Two's complement addition.

FLOATING-POINT NUMBERS

Now we have 99 percent of what we need to know about binary numbers in minicomputers. Another type of representation of numbers commonly found in minicomputers is floating-point numbers, which are described in Appendix E. It is important to know this only if it is desirable to operate with numbers representing millions or larger or very small numbers, or if one wants to get intimately familiar with the "internals" of a FORTRAN compiler program.

OCTAL AND HEXADECIMAL NUMBERS

There are two other number systems that a minicomputer user must know about: octal and hexadecimal. Actually, for any given minicomputer, only one system

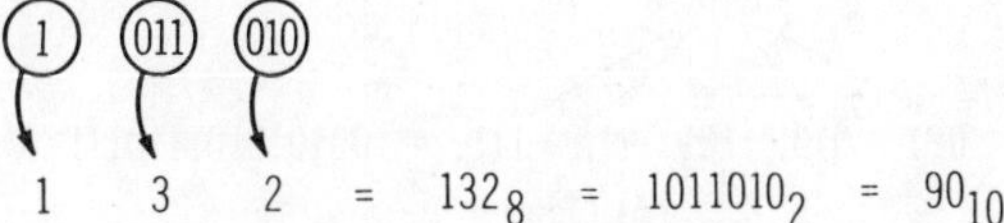

Fig. 2-10. Binary-to-octal conversion.

is used. Octal and hexadecimal are simply ways to shorten binary number representation. It would be very tedious to write out long strings of 1's and 0's to represent data for 100 different values. If those values were each 16 bits long, 1600 characters would be involved. Using octal representation, however, about 600 characters would be written, and hexadecimal would shorten the string to 400 characters.

For octal (or "eight") data representation, three binary digits make up one octal digit. Since three bits can hold values of 0, 1, 2, 3, 4, 5, 6, or 7, octal digits include only these values. To write a binary number in octal, divide the binary number into groups of three, starting from the right. The binary number 01011010 would be divided into (01) (011) (010), for example. Now convert each group to its corresponding octal digit. Fig. 2-10 illustrates the conversion for 01011010_2. The binary number becomes 132_8 in octal, or base 8. The positional notation is similar to binary or decimal, so $132_8 = (1 \times 8^2) + (3 \times 8^1) + (2 \times 8^0) = 64 + 24 + 2 = 90_{10}$. Writing in octal requires about one-third the number of characters to express a long string of binary data. It is not exactly one-third since consecutive 16-bit values are expressed as values of six octal digits, the most significant octal digit being only a one or a zero.

For hexadecimal ("hex" = 6, "decimal" = 10), or base 16, representation, four bits are converted to one hexadecimal digit. In four bits, one can express up to $2^4 - 1 = 15_{10}$, so how do we express 10, 11, 12, 13, 14, and 15? We could use arbitrary symbols such as *, !, x, @, &, and " for these digits, but it is a lot more convenient to use something easier to remember, so the alphabetic characters A, B, C, D, E, and F have come to represent 10 through 15, respectively. To convert from binary to hexadecimal, divide the binary number into groups of four binary digits, starting from the right. For 1011010, Fig. 2-11 shows the conversion. Here again, the positional notation is the same, and we have $(5 \times 16^1) + (10 \times 16^0) = 80 + 10 = 90_{10}$.

Don't bother about converting from hexadecimal to octal and vice versa—you will never need to. To convert from octal or hexadecimal values to binary, write down binary digits in groups of three or four in order corre-

(101) (1010)

5 A = $5A_{16}$ = 1011010_2 = 90_{10}

Fig. 2-11. Binary-to-hexadecimal conversion.

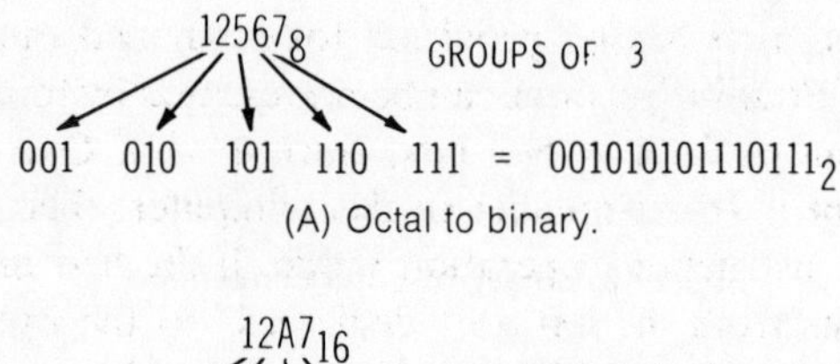

(A) Octal to binary.

```
12A7₁₆      GROUPS OF 4

0001 0010 1010 0111 = 0001001010100111₂
```

(B) Hexadecimal to binary.

Fig. 2-12. Converting from octal or hexadecimal to binary.

sponding to the octal or hexadecimal digits. Two sample conversions from octal and hexadecimal to binary are shown in Fig. 2-12.

To convert from octal and hexadecimal to decimal, the same double-dabble method as described previously

```
1735 = ?10

  1 x 8 = 8 + 7 = (15)
 15 x 8 = 120 + 3 = (123)
123 x 8 = 984 + 5 = 989₁₀
```

(A) Octal double-dabble.

```
1A2₁₆ = ?₁₀

 1 x 16 = 16 + A = (26)
26 x 16 = 416 + 2 = 418₁₀
```

(B) Hexadecimal double-dabble.

Fig. 2-13. Octal and hexadecimal double-dabble.

can be used. To convert, take the leftmost digit, multiply by 8 or 16, add the next digit, multiply that sum by 8 or 16, and so forth. Fig. 2-13 shows an example for both octal and hexadecimal. It is also possible to convert from decimal to octal or hexadecimal by the divide

```
989₁₀ = ?₈

989/8 = 123  QUOTIENT, REMAINDER 5
123/8 = 15   QUOTIENT, REMAINDER 3     1735₈
 15/8 = 1    QUOTIENT, REMAINDER 7
  1/8 = 0    QUOTIENT, REMAINDER 1
```

(A) Decimal to octal.

```
418₁₀ = ?₁₆

418/16 = 26  QUOTIENT, REMAINDER 2
 26/16 = 1   QUOTIENT, REMAINDER 10    1A2₁₆
  1/16 = 0                       1
```

(B) Decimal to hexadecimal.

Fig. 2-14. Decimal-to-octal and decimal-to-hexadecimal conversion.

and save remainders technique. (In fact, both double-dabble and the save remainder technique work for any number base.) Fig. 2-14 shows the save remainder technique for two examples, conversion from decimal to octal and to hexadecimal.

Appendix B gives conversions between octal, binary, hexadecimal, and decimal numbers up to decimal 255.

ASCII AND EBCDIC

Binary numbers in minicomputers do not have to represent absolute values. They may also represent a string of bits or groups of bits where each group, or "field," stands for a certain function. Furthermore, groups of bits may represent codes of various types. Two examples of "coded" data that appear in minicomputers are so-called ASCII ("Ask-e") and EBCDIC ("Ib-see-dick") data. Both types of data represent alphabetic, numeric, and special characters, both with different codes.

You might well imagine that a computer would have to hold data representing the digits 0–9, the alphabet A–Z, and such symbols as @, #, and ?, since one of the chief uses of computers these days is to print reports of various types. Since the problem of holding a string of characters would constantly arise, it makes sense to have a standardized code for each character rather than having a different set of codes for each computer or for each printing peripheral device. ASCII stands for *A*merican *S*ociety for *C*omputer *I*nterchange, and this group has established one set of codes. EBCDIC stands for *E*xtended *B*inary *C*oded *D*ecimal *I*nterchange *C*ode, and this is an IBM-oriented set. Usually ASCII is the code used in minicomputers.

ASCII uses seven bits to represent characters. We know that $2^n - 1 = 2^7 - 1 = 127$ is the maximum count that can be held in seven bits. Counting 0, therefore, 128 different codes can be held in seven ASCII bits. An "A," for example, is 1000001_2; a space, 0100000_2. An eighth bit is almost always added as the most significant bit and is set to a constant 1 or 0 or used to represent the "parity" of the character, a check bit that is set to a 1 or 0 depending upon the total number of ones or zeros in the code. EBCDIC uses eight bits for alphanumeric or special characters and can therefore represent 256 different combinations of codes for 256 unique characters. A complete list of ASCII and EBCDIC codes appears in Appendices C and D.

Many minicomputers use "words" of eight or sixteen bits. When a string of ASCII or EBCDIC characters appears, one character fits nicely in eight bits, and two in sixteen. In the ASCII case, a 16-bit binary number holding two characters may be separated into two groups of eight bits, the upper bit of each group ignored, and the two seven-bit values looked up in the conversion chart to find the ASCII characters. A 16-bit value of 0100000100100000_2 would become 1000001_2 and 0100000_2, which would decode to the characters "A" and "space."

Notice that in the foregoing discussion the codes used, whether ASCII or EBCDIC, are usually not related to computer hardware. The computer does not know that 1000001_2 represents "A." It is only the computer software that recognizes the combination of bits as an "A" and prints out that letter. (However, the peripheral device usually *does* recognize, or decode, the combinations into characters.)

OTHER GROUPS OF BITS

Just as seven bits may represent an ASCII character, other groups or "fields" of bits may represent different things in a minicomputer. Suppose, just for the sake of discussion, that we have an extremely simple computer that can only add, subtract, multiply, and divide. (This is not only a simple computer but an unworkable one besides, as it has no provision for input and output of data.) Four instructions can be represented by four codes that can be held in two bits, since $2^2 = 4$. One of the fields of a 16-bit number in this computer, then, might be the instruction "operation" code. If the first and second bits from the left are "dedicated" to the operation code field, the 16-bit number for a divide instruction might appear as $11XXXXXXXXXXXXXX_2$, where 11 is the code for divide, and $XXXXXXXXXXXXXX_2$ is probably dedicated to defining other functions associated with the divide instruction (for example, where to place the result, where to find the divisor, and so forth). If the operation codes for add, subtract, and multiply were 0, 1, and 2, respectively, an add, subtract, and multiply would be represented by $00XXXXXXXXXXXXXX_2$, $01XXXXXXXXXXXXXX_2$, and $10XXXXXXXXXXXXXX_2$. Instruction formats are covered in detail in the next chapter. For the moment, however, just remember that binary numbers in a computer represent many other things besides absolute numbers or character codes.

CHAPTER

3

Minicomputer Hardware

A minicomputer system is made up of "hardware" and "software." Software is made up of all documentation, program listings, program code, and similar items. Hardware is the more tangible part of a computer system—the "hard" part that sits there for all to see—the chassis that contains the computer, input/output devices such as a Teletype or card reader, power supplies, and the like.

BASIC COMPONENTS

Computer systems obviously vary in size and complexity. A minimum configuration would be something similar to that of Fig. 1-1, a box or "chassis" that contains the minicomputer proper and a Teletype or some type of input/output terminal. This system has all that is required to create computer programs, save them (in this case on paper tape), and run or execute them. More elaborate systems, such as a system used in a business with ten programmers or so, might look like Fig. 3-2. This system includes a minicomputer (or two), a terminal, an additional "memory" for the computer, a secondary slower memory called a "disc drive," magnetic tape transports (similar to a large home tape recorder), and a large line printer. Larger systems than this are quite common–some have a dozen minicomputers connected together and a room full of peripherals.

Although a system may consist of several types of input/output devices, as mentioned above, the central part of any system is the minicomputer proper. The minicomputer is the controller: the device that starts, monitors, and controls all of the component parts of the

Fig. 3-1. DEC PDP-8 minicomputer system.

Courtesy Digital Equipment Corp.

Courtesy Digital Equipment Corp.

Fig. 3-2. A larger minicomputer system—Digital Equipment Corporation XVM System.

system. This chapter will consider the minicomputer or microcomputer alone. Input/output devices or "peripheral" devices will be treated in more detail in Chapter 5.

Fig. 3-3 shows a minicomputer connected to a single Teletype with a breakdown of the parts of the minicomputer. This is a typical minicomputer or microcomputer in that the manufacturer has created basically an empty box with a front panel, connectors for plugging in printed-circuit boards, and a power supply capable of supplying power to any boards that are plugged into the connectors. In this simple case, one board shown is the main portion of the computer, the "central processing unit" (or CPU); another shown is a memory board; and a third is the board that controls data exchange be-

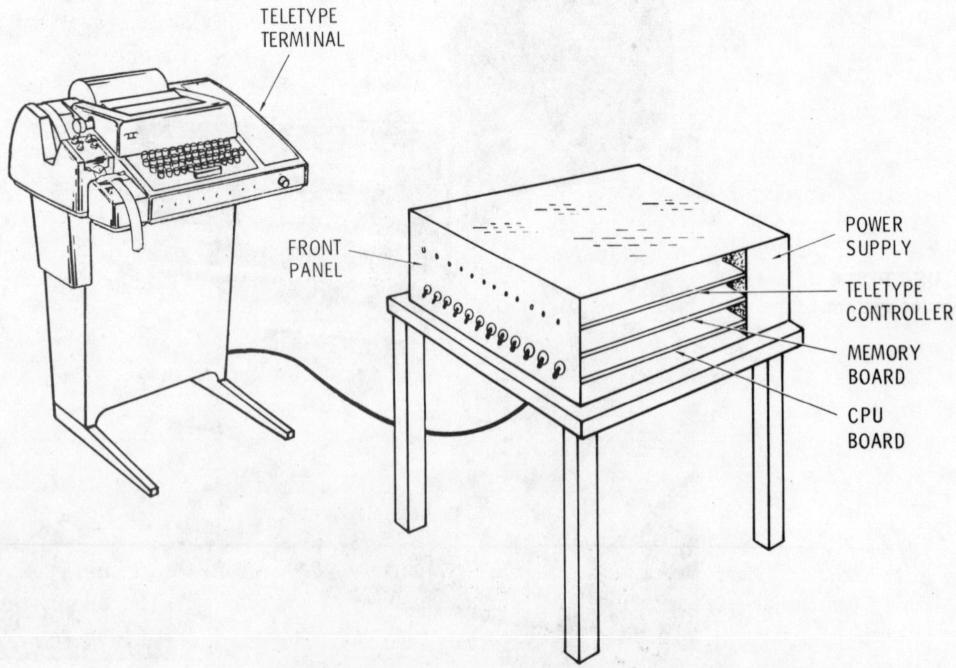

Fig. 3-3. Minicomputer component parts.

tween the CPU and Teletype. The manufacturer has made the minicomputer in this fashion so that various configurations can be created by customers buying additional memory boards, "controller" boards, and other options. (With computers, as well as with many other consumer items, the customer gets stung on the "whitewalls.")

Functionally, all minicomputer systems can be shown as in Fig. 3-4, which is very much like Fig. 3-3 except for the secondary memory. There are always a CPU, a memory, and input/output devices, and sometimes there are secondary storage devices such as disc drives or magnetic tape units.

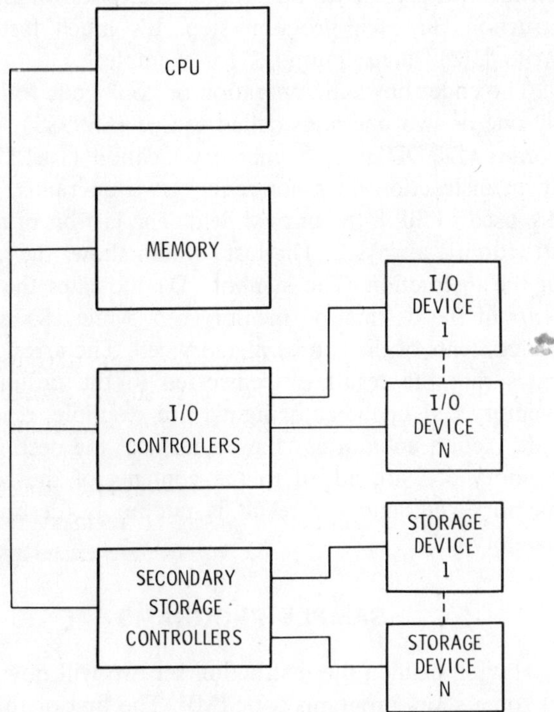

Fig. 3-4. Functional block diagram of minicomputer system.

A RUDIMENTARY COMPUTER

Since the CPU is the heart of the system, it requires a great deal of our time and analysis. Suppose once again that we wanted to implement a computer to perform certain basic operations such as addition and subtraction. Knowing a little bit more about binary devices and the binary numbering system, we will design a rudimentary computer. Since every computer has a name and since this is a very simple computer, let's call it "SIMP" for *Si*mple *M*ultipurpose *P*rocessor.

It seems reasonable to be able to add and subtract binary numbers with SIMP. These two functions are two instructions. Since multiplication and division can be implemented in software, we will forget about these latter two functions. As mentioned earlier, a series of program steps requires a means to "jump over" a number of steps to alter the sequence of instruction execution. In the paper mill example of Chapter 2, we could not keep piling up sheets of paper in the stacker forever. We needed a means to compare the height with a predetermined value and take some other action when the result of the comparison indicated the paper was stacked over the limit. This requires a "compare" instruction and a "jump if" instruction. For convenience, we'll also add an "unconditional jump" instruction, one that always jumps. Since we eventually want to output data to the outside world from the computer, we will also implement an "output" instruction and, of course, an "input" instruction. Another useful instruction, although not absolutely necessary, is a "stop" instruction to stop the machine.

Our SIMP computer now has these instructions: add, subtract, compare, jump, jump if, input, output, and stop. To further define these instructions we will have to know a little about the memory of the computer. Memory cells are very similar to post-office boxes. Post-office boxes are numbered in sequence on the outside of the box. We will number our memory cells from 0 to 63, a total of 64 memory cells, each one holding 16 bits of data. When we talk about the contents of memory cell 17, we may visualize a post-office clerk going over to box number 17 and withdrawing a post card with a 16-bit value printed on it. We are usually interested in the contents of the box, rather than the box number itself. We could have made each memory cell eight bits wide, as is typical of microcomputers, but we'll leave it at 16 bits. A memory of 64 cells is not huge, but it is sufficient for our simple programs. We chose 64 because it is a power of 2. We could have used 56 or 77, but powers of 2 generally are easier to implement in hardware and require less complicated design.

Now we can proceed with our basic computer implementation. Further defining the add instruction, we will say that an *add* takes the contents of one memory cell, adds them to the contents of another memory cell, and replaces the contents of the last memory cell with the new value. *Subtract* works in the same fashion, except that the first cell's contents are subtracted from the second cell's contents. *Compare* compares the contents of one memory cell with the contents of a second memory cell. If the contents are equal, a "flag" is set. If unequal, the flag is reset. The flag in this case will be a binary device such as a flip-flop that holds either a 1 (set) or a 0 (reset). The flag can be tested by a "jump if" instruction.

Before defining the jump and jump if instructions, the question arises of how the machine performs these series of steps or instructions. The 64 memory cells contain either data values or instructions (or nothing meaningful if a cell is not used). The data values might be used by add or subtract instructions, or for comparisons.

Cells might also be set aside, or reserved, for the results of operations. If there were no pieces of data or reserved cells in memory, there would be room for 64 instructions. If there were instructions in locations 0 through 23, there obviously could be no data in these locations at the same time. To simplify things, let's set down a rule that data will be stored only in locations 32 through 63, and instructions will be stored only in locations 0 through 31. There is no reason that the reverse could not be true, or that instructions and data could not be intermixed. We will also say that when the computer is started, it begins by retrieving the contents of location 0, assumes that it is an instruction, and performs the operation. It then goes to the next instruction, performs it, and so forth.

The only time the CPU alters its sequence of instructions is when it encounters a *jump* or *jump if* instruction. It then goes to the memory cell specified by the jump and starts sequential operation from that cell. If the flag is set (1), the jump if causes the same action as a jump instruction. If the flag is not set (0), the jump if causes no action, and the next instruction in sequence is executed.

The *input* instruction causes the contents of 16 switches on the front panel of the computer to be put into a specified memory cell. The *output* instruction causes the contents of a specified memory cell to be displayed on 16 lights on the front panel. *Stop* halts the computer, but the CPU will continue with the next instruction in sequence when a "continue" switch is pressed.

Having specified the operation of SIMP, instruction words can now be defined. We know that it takes three bits to hold eight different codes, so we will use the first three bits of the 16 bits in each instruction word to define the operation. This field will be called the *operation code.* That leaves 13 bits. There are 64 memory cells, and it takes another six bits to specify 64 different

Table 3-1. SIMP Computer Instruction Set

Instruction	Mnemonic	Code	Action
Add	ADD	000SSSSSSDDDDDD0	(D) + (S) → D
Subtract	SUB	001SSSSSSDDDDDD0	(D) − (S) → D
Compare	COM	010SSSSSSDDDDDD0	Set flag if (S) = (D)
Jump	JMP	011000000LLLLLL0	Go to location L
Jump If	JMI	100000000LLLLLL0	Go to location L if flag
Input	INP	101000000DDDDDD0	(Switches) → D
Output	OUT	110000000SSSSSS0	(S) → Indicator lights
Stop	STP	1110000000000000	Stops computer
		OP, FIELD 1, FIELD 2, ALWAYS 0	

values. Furthermore, two cells have to be specified for some instructions such as add and subtract. We will use the first six bits after the operation code as a "source" memory cell specifier, and the next six bits to specify the "destination" memory cell. We have now used $3 + 6 + 6 = 15$ bits out of a possible 16 in an instruction word. One bit, the least significant, will not be used for instructions but, of course, can be used in data values.

Table 3-1 now shows the instruction set of our basic SIMP computer. In this table, the first column shows the instruction and the next the mnemonic for that instruction. The mnemonic is simply a memory device to avoid having to write the whole description of the instruction for each program step. It's much faster to write "JMI" than "jump if," for example.

The code shows the operation or "op" code followed by one or two operands called source (SSSSSS), destination (DDDDDD), or memory location (LLLLLL). If an instruction does not require two operands, zeros are used to fill in the unused field. The last bit of an instruction is always 0. The last column shows the action of the instruction. The symbol (D) indicates the *contents* of the destination memory cell, while (S) means the contents of the source memory cell. The arrow indicates that the result is transferred to the destination memory cell or indicator lights. For example, read the Add Action column as "the contents of the destination memory cell are added to the contents of the source memory cell, and the result is put in the destination memory cell."

SAMPLE PROGRAMS

Having defined the instruction set, we will now look at some short programs for SIMP. The first of these is a short program to add the numbers from 0 to 100, display the results on the indicator lights, and stop. Table 3-2 lists the program. The table shows the locations 0 through 35 in the first column. However, since 0 through 8 are used for the program and 32 through 35 are used for data, only those are shown. The remaining locations could have anything in them. The Contents column shows the actual locations after "loading" memory with the program. Note that locations 32 and 33 are zeroed by the program and could be anything after the load. The next column shows the mnemonic, and the next shows the one or two operands in decimal. A Remarks column explains what is being done.

The program starts executing instructions at location 0. The CPU "fetches" the data of 0010100000100000_2, looks at the first three bits, and decodes them as a subtract instruction. It then gets the contents of memory location 32, gets the contents of location 32 again (computers are usually dumb enough not to recognize

Table 3-2. SIMP Program Number 1

Location	Contents	Instruction	Operands	Remarks
0	0011000001000000	SUB	32,32	CLEAR RESULTS
1	0011000011000010	SUB	33,33	CLEAR NUMBER
2	0001000011000000	ADD	33,32	
3	0001000101000010	ADD	34,33	ADD 1 TO NUMBER
4	0101000011000110	COM	33,35	COMPARE TO END
5	1000000000001110	JMI	7	JUMP IF END
6	0110000000000100	JMP	2	GO FOR NEXT N
7	1100000001000000	OUT	32	OUTPUT RESULT
8	1110000000000000	STP		STOP
32	xxxxxxxxxxxxxxxx			HOLDS RESULT
33	xxxxxxxxxxxxxxxx			NUMBER
34	0000000000000001			ONE
35	0000000001100101			101 (DECIMAL)

that it is the same location), subtracts the second operand from the first, and stores the result of 0 in memory location 32. Subtracting any number from itself always produces 0, so that is one way of clearing a location to hold the current results of adding 0 + 1 + 2, and so forth. Note that to execute this one instruction the CPU had to go to memory four times—once to "fetch" the instruction, twice to get the two operands, and once to store the result. The first three accesses were memory "reads," and the next access was a memory "write."

The CPU then adds one to a "program counter" register (initially set to 0) which points to the next instruction at location 1. The program counter is normally incremented by one during each instruction's execution, except in the case of jump instructions. The instruction at location 1 is now executed by the CPU. This instruction zeros out location 33 in the same fashion as the first instruction. The program counter is then incremented by one again, and the instruction at location 2 is fetched.

The instruction at location 2 adds the contents of location 33 to the contents of location 32 and stores the result in location 32. Since (33) = 0 and (32) = 0, the result of 0 is stored in location 32. The next instruction executed (location 3) adds the contents of location 33 to the contents of location 34 (a "1") to get a result of 1, which is then stored in location 33 in preparation for adding 1 (we have already added 0).

The next instruction (location 4) compares the current value of the number in location 33 with the value 101_{10}. If the current value of (33) is not 101, it must be less than 101 and the addition process should continue. If the current value *is* 101, all numbers from 0 to 100 have been added and the addition should stop. The flag is set if the values are equal. Since they are not at this point, the flag is reset (0).

The instruction at location 5 causes the CPU to examine the flag. Since it is not set, the "if" condition is not satisfied and the program counter is incremented once more. The next instruction in sequence at location 6 causes the operand of "2" to be put into the program counter of the CPU. The CPU now goes blindly on its way, fetching the instruction at location 2, which repeats the next add of 1 to the partial result. Locations 2 through 6 are a *loop;* the program loops back to repeat the addition, bumps the number to be added, tests for an end condition, and continues. After 101 loops (remember, 0 was added, in addition to 1 through 100), the new value to be added will give 101 and the flag is set by the compare instruction at location 4. When the JMI instruction at location 5 is executed, the CPU senses the flag is set and moves the operand of "7" into the program counter. The next instruction executed is at location 7 and causes the result of the total addition to be displayed on the 16 indicator lights. The program counter is then incremented, and the STP instruction at location 8 stops the computer from execution.

If you understand this short program on our mythical computer, you have learned many of the important concepts relating to minicomputers. Remember, most of these concepts evolved over a number of years and some were quite profound during the 35 years or so that the modern digital computer was being developed.

Since we have talked about a "software" multiply routine, let's discuss how this might be implemented using our SIMP computer. One way is to try and follow the same procedure as we do in decimal multiplication, that is, taking one digit at a time and multiplying it by the multiplicand. The same approach can be followed in a binary multiplication, taking one bit at a time and multiplying it times the multiplicand. A much simpler approach, however, is to simply add the multiplicand a number of times equal to the multiplier. For example, 15×3 can be found by adding 15 three times: $15 + 15 + 15 = 45$. The same method works in binary, of course, $1111 + 1111 + 1111 = 101101_2$. The program for this is shown in Table 3-3. It multiplies two positive 16-bit numbers.

Assuming that the program has been loaded into memory, the computer starts operation at location 0. The contents of location 0 are an input instruction, which reads the settings of the 16 front-panel switches. (Because we have constructed the program to read the multiplier first, we know that the multiplier will be put into location 32.) The program counter is incremented by 1, and the instruction in location 1 is fetched. This is a STP instruction which halts the computer. A stop here is necessary to enable us to put the value of the multiplicand into the front-panel switches. Having done that, we can press the continue switch on the front panel, and the computer bumps the program counter to location 2 and continues. The instruction at location 2 reads (inputs) the multiplicand from the switches and stores it into location 33. The next instruction at location 3 clears (zeroes) location 34. Location 34 is used as a "working" location to hold the additions of the multiplicand. Note that locations 32 through 34 have now been "initialized" to three new values and could have held any values previously. The COM instruction at location 4 sets the flag if the multiplier is 0. The multiplier is being decremented by one for each addition to count the number of additions. Unless the multiplier was 0, the flag is reset (0) and the JMI at location 5 causes no action. The ADD instruction at location 6 adds the multiplicand to the working result. One is then subtracted from the multiplier by the SUB instruction at location 7, and the program jumps back to location 4 by the JMP at location 8. After the multiplicand has been added the number of times corresponding to the multiplier, the multiplier is at 0 and the COM instruction at location 4 sets the flag, causing the JMI instruction at location 5 to load 9 into the program counter. The CPU now jumps to location 9, where the result in location 34 is displayed on the control-panel lights. The CPU stops when it reaches location 10. You may want to actually try this program on paper as shown in Fig. 3-5. This figure lists the sequence of execution and all results, intermediate or final. Note that the result is valid for a 0 multiplier. The result is invalid for a result greater than 65,535, since only a number equal to or less than that

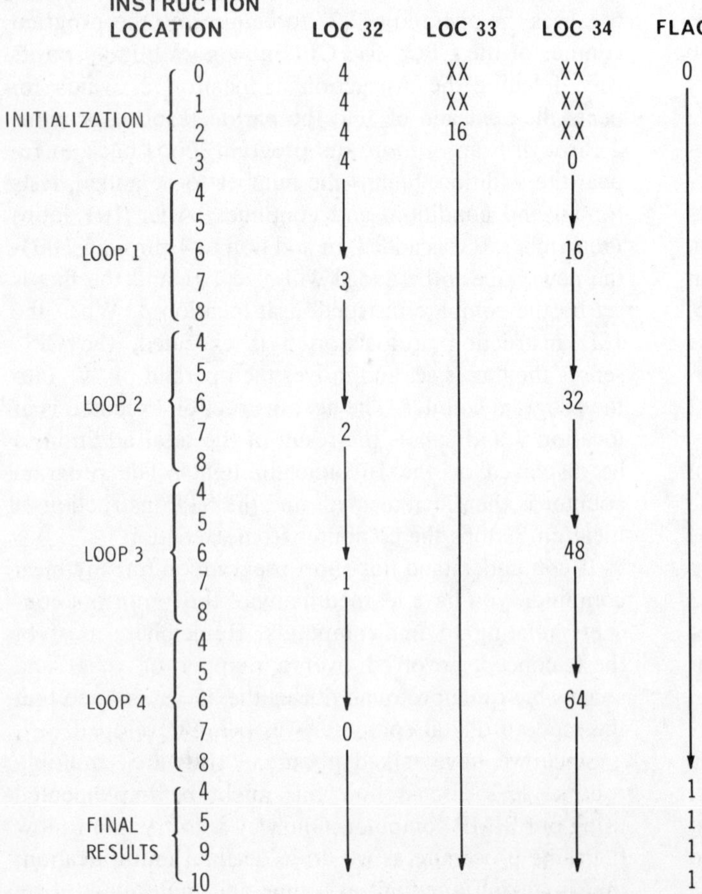

Fig. 3-5. SIMP program number 2 execution for 16 × 4 = 64.

Table 3-3. SIMP Program Number 2

Location	Contents	Instruction	Operands	Remarks
0	1010000001000000	INP	32	GET MULTIPLIER
1	1110000000000000	STP		
2	1010000001000010	INP	33	GET MULTIPLICAND
3	0011000101000100	SUB	34,34	CLEAR RESULT
4	0100000001000110	COM	32,35	COMPARE FOR END
5	1000000000010010	JMI	9	GO IF DONE
6	0001000011000100	ADD	33,34	ADD MULTIPLICAND AGAIN
7	0011001001000000	SUB	36,32	MULTIPLIER — 1
8	0110000000001000	JMP	4	GO FOR NEXT ADD
9	1100000001000100	OUT	34	DISPLAY RESULT
10	1110000000000000	STP		STOP
32	xxxxxxxxxxxxxxxx			HOLDS MULTIPLIER
33	xxxxxxxxxxxxxxxx			HOLDS MULTIPLICAND
34	xxxxxxxxxxxxxxxx			HOLDS RESULT
35	0000000000000000			ZERO
36	0000000000000001			ONE

number can be displayed on the front-panel lights. (The 16-bit result in this case is "unsigned.")

CPU INSTRUCTION IMPLEMENTATION

The instruction set of our SIMP computer used two binary devices in the CPU: a flag flip-flop and a "register" called the program counter. The program counter was initially reset to 0 to point to the first instruction and was incremented by one for the next instruction or loaded by an operand during a jump or conditional jump when the condition was met. The program counter could be a set of six flip-flops similar to the flag flip-flop, with some additional logic circuitry to increment the count by one at certain times.

The sequence of execution of one instruction in the SIMP CPU goes somewhat like this:

1. Fetch the instruction pointed to by the program counter.
2. Add 1 to the program counter.
3. Read the source memory location specified by the instruction's first operand field, or don't read anything if this field is not used for the instruction.
4. Read the second operand from memory, if required.
5. Perform the operation.
6. Write the results of the operation into memory, if required.
7. Go to Step 1 unless this was a STP instruction.

You can see that there is a sequence of steps not unlike a program that is implemented in the hardware of the CPU. Typically each instruction execution (all seven steps) might take from 1 to 6 microseconds (millionths of a second) in a minicomputer. A "synchronous" type computer CPU would always execute the seven steps even if, for example, there were no operand to access from memory (JMI instruction). For this type of computer, all instruction execution times would be the same. A "nonsynchronous" type of minicomputer would execute only those CPU steps (or "phases") necessary to perform the instruction. The JMI instruction would perform only Steps 1, 2, 5, and 7, bypassing three memory accesses. (Step 5 for the JMI would replace the incremented contents of the program counter with the instruction operand.)

CPU REGISTERS

The most time-consuming part of the CPU's instruction implementation was and is memory access. It is much faster to store into a hardware register like the program counter than to read or write from memory. Modifying the program counter in a typical minicomputer might take only 100 nanoseconds (100 billionths of a second), but a memory access might take 1200 nanoseconds (1200 billionths, or 1.2 millionths of a second).

One and two-tenths millionths of a second may not seem like a great deal of time. However, since billions of instructions may be executed in typical programs, a much more efficient computer would be one that kept memory accesses to a minimum.

Modern minicomputers reduce the number of memory accesses by providing a number of registers in the

CPU similar to the program counter. These registers are used to hold temporary or intermediate results. The number of registers varies from 1 to 16, or may even be several banks of 16. In the programs of Tables 3-2 and 3-3, no memory accesses during the loop would have been needed at all if registers had been used. The running result could have been held in one register while a second register could have held the current number. The registers in the CPU are usually eight bits in microcomputers and sixteen bits in minicomputers and hold binary values in two's complement form. That is, a positive number is held as $0XXXXXXXXXXXXXXX_2$ with the most significant bit a 0, and a negative number has the most significant bit set with the two's complement number calculated as in Chapter 2.

Modern minicomputers also have another problem related to memory. The more memory accesses needed to get an instruction, the slower the instruction execution time. If a memory is made up such that one access can read eight bits, then an instruction word that takes up sixteen bits is going to require two memory accesses during the CPU's fetch cycle. The problem, then, becomes to pack as much information as possible into each instruction word. The next question is, "'How much is enough?"

ADDRESSING MEMORY

A basic question related to the preceding problem is the amount of memory that must be addressed or identified. If every computer program could be put into 256 16-bit words of memory, there would be no problem, for 256 words could be addressed by 8 bits ($2^8 = 256$). A compromise solution adopted by most minicomputer manufacturers is to make the maximum memory size 32,768 16-bit (or 8-bit) words, and by others to make the upper limit 65,536 words. Both of these values can be held in 16 bits. As a matter of fact, 32K or 64K (where K stands for 1024) is usually quite adequate for most programs. A good programmer would be hard pressed to write a program large enough to fill 64K in several years. Since addressing 64K directly takes 16 bits, how can we address memory and still have a short instruction word?

"Long" Instructions

There are two basic schemes for doing this. The first scheme used by Interdata and Varian says, "The heck with it, let's make some instructions equal to 32-bit lengths. That way we can fit the operation code, register code, and other things in the first 16-bit word and use the second word to address 65,536 words of memory." In this case, fetching the instruction requires two memory accesses, each having a 16-bit value. However, each manufacturer has "short" instructions of only 16 bits (1 memory access) which are used for certain types of instructions (for example, instructions that involve CPU register-to-register operations). The Interdata Models 6 and 7 (and others), for instance, have a 16-bit AHR instruction, which stands for *A*dd *H*alfword *R*egister. Interdata's "halfword" is 16 bits long, or two 8-bit bytes. It appears in Fig. 3-6. In this instruction the $(R1) + (R2) \rightarrow R1$, where R1 and R2 are two of the sixteen possible CPU registers. Four bits define R1 ($2^4 = 16$), four bits define R2, and eight bits define a large set of operation codes of which $0A_{16}$ happens to be AHR ($0A_{16} = 00001010_2$). The AHR instruction is a "short" instruction requiring one memory access to fetch the instruction and no memory accesses to add the operands; they are all in CPU registers.

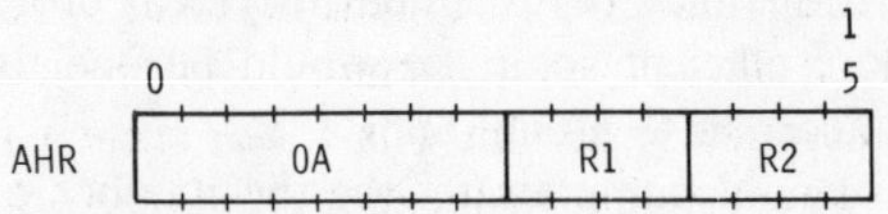

Fig. 3-6. Register-to-register instruction.

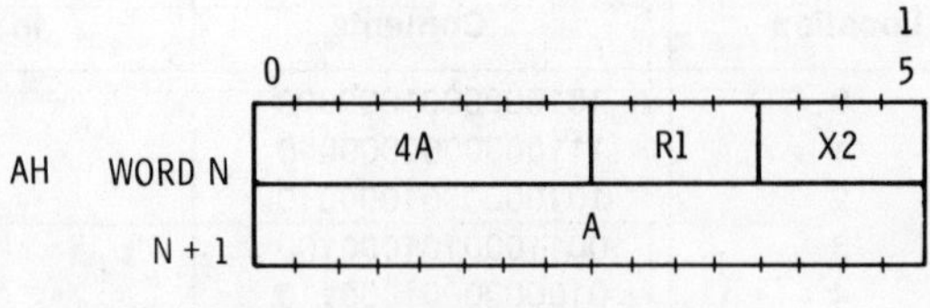

Fig. 3-7. "Long" instruction.

The AH instruction is a "long" instruction. It takes 32 bits and two memory accesses and is shown in Fig. 3-7. The first field of $4A_{16}$ is the operation code for *A*dd *H*alfword. Register R1 is the destination CPU register. Register X2 is the CPU "index" register used to modify the address. For the moment assume it is 0, specifying no "indexed" addressing. Address A is a 16-bit value specifying a memory address of the source operand. In the AH instruction the $(A) + (R1) \rightarrow R1$. (This assumes no indexing, which we shall investigate later.) Note that the instruction is really very similar to our SIMP computer, except that the destination is a CPU register, and the operation code field is much larger. Note also that the bits in each word of the AH and AHR instructions are numbered from left to right, 0 through 15. Some manufacturers use 0–15 left to right, but many use 15–0 left to right. The order 15–0 may make a little more sense, since 2^0 is the rightmost bit, but whichever method is used, it will be used consistently in all of that manufacturer's literature.

"Short" Instructions

Data General Corporation's Nova computer use only 16-bit words for instructions. At first glance, it is hard to see how 32,768 16-bit words can be addressed by a 16-bit instruction that must use some bits for operation

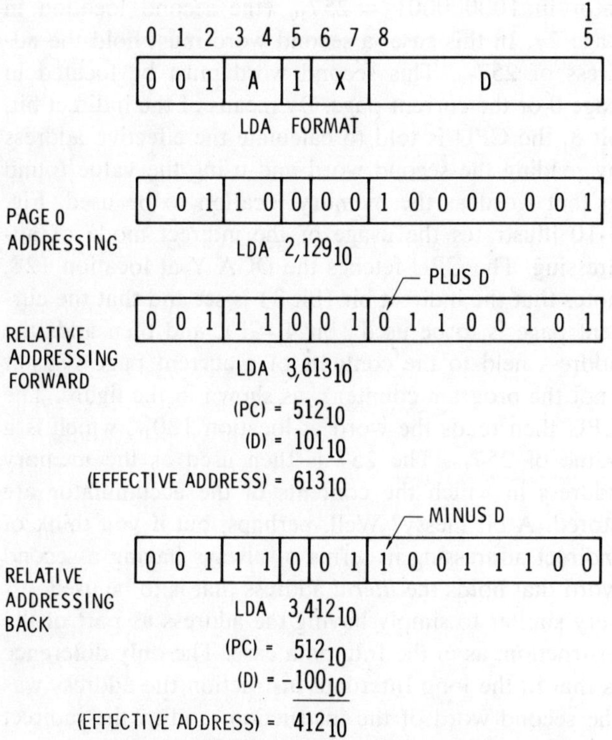

Fig. 3-8. Page 0 and relative addressing.

codes and other functions. Let's look at a typical Nova instruction to see what is done. In the Nova series, the LDA (*L*oad *A*ccumulator) instruction appears as shown in Fig. 3-8.

The "accumulator" is another term for CPU register —it is still a 16-bit general-purpose register as described previously. Since the Nova series has four registers, a field of two bits ("A") designates which register is to be loaded from memory. Loading is nothing more than moving the 16-bit contents of a memory cell to the register. Bits 0, 1, and 2 specify the operating code, and here they are 001_2 to denote an LDA.

Page 0 Addressing

When bits 5, 6, and 7 are all 0's, the memory address is equal to the binary value in the "D" or displacement field. To load accumulator 2 from memory location 129_{10}, then, the instruction would look like the second portion down of Fig. 3-8. Note that the maximum memory address that can be specified in this "addressing mode" is 11111111_2, or 255_{10}. The first 256 locations (including 0) are called *page 0,* or sometimes *0 page* by Data General and by other manufacturers who use this scheme. The 0 page may be larger than 256, or it may be smaller, but 256 is typical.

Relative Addressing

When bit 5 is a 0 and bits 6 and 7 are 01_2, another type of addressing mode is implemented by the Nova CPU. This mode is called *self-relative* or *relative addressing*. In this mode, the current contents of the CPU program counter are added to the contents of the D field. The result of this addition is called the *effective address.* It defines the memory location to be used in loading the accumulator. Suppose that at location 512_{10} in a Nova program, we wanted to load accumulator 3 with the contents of memory location 613_{10}. The LDA instruction would look like the third part of Fig. 3-8. The CPU in fetching the instruction would note the addressing mode as "relative" and calculate the effective address by adding 512_{10} and the D field, treated as an 8-bit *signed* value. What happens if the sign of D (bit 8) is negative? In this case, the effective address is "back" of the current location. If at location 512_{10} we wanted to load accumulator 3 with the contents of 412_{10}, the LDA would appear as shown in the fourth part of Fig. 3-8. Note that the D field value had to be "sign-extended" by the CPU to correctly represent a -100_{10} in 16 bits.

Using the relative mode and the eight bits of the displacement field, it is possible to address backwards $10000000_2 = 128_{10}$ locations and forward $01111111_2 = 127_{10}$ locations from the current instruction. Since the current instruction moves around to any place in memory, the range of 128 back to 127 forward is called a *floating page* to differentiate it from the fixed page 0. Many other manufacturers use this concept of a floating page since most of the time a program is addressing memory close to the current instruction. Fig. 3-9 shows the floating-page and page 0 concept.

Indirect Addressing

As handy as the floating page idea is, there comes a time when a program has to address a location beyond the floating page and not in page 0. The Nova and any other minicomputers that have only a 16-bit (or one-word) instruction set must then use a technique which is known as *indirect addressing* (bit 5 in the Nova LDA instruction).

To illustrate indirect addressing, let's use a PDP-8 instruction, DCA Y (*D*eposit and *C*lear *AC*). The PDP-8 in its various models uses a 12-bit instruction word and 12-bit two's complement data words. The DCA Y is shown in Fig. 3-10. The function of the DCA is to take the contents of the accumulator—the main CPU register—and store them in the specified memory location. (Incidentally, the accumulator is cleared in the process, which is not usually the case in other minicomputers.)

The address field of this PDP-8 instruction specifies $2^7 = 128$ locations which define a "page." This page, however, does not "float" but remains fixed. There is a maximum of 32_{10} pages in memory. When bit 4 is 0, page 0 is specified; when bit 4 is 1, the current page is indicated. Suppose that at location $10000000_2 = 128_{10}$ (the start of page 1), it is required to store the accumu-

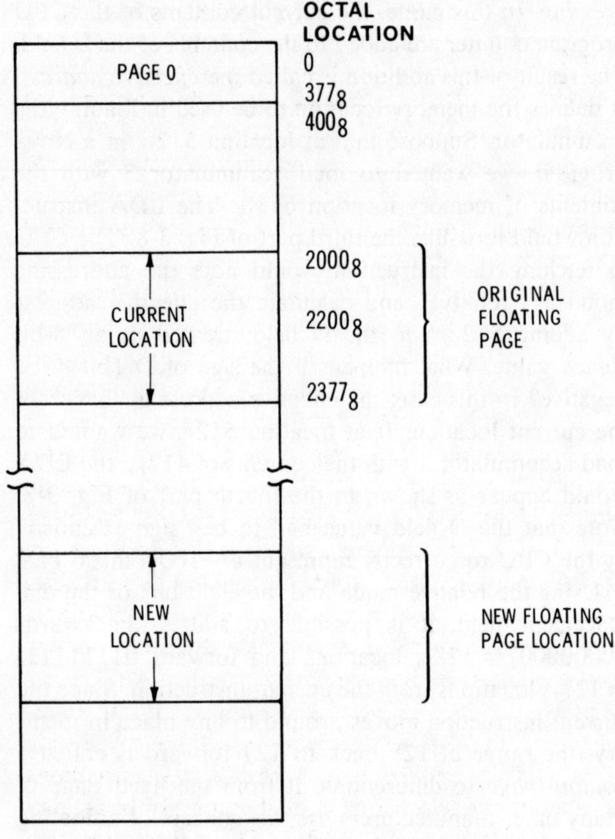

Fig. 3-9. Floating-page addressing.

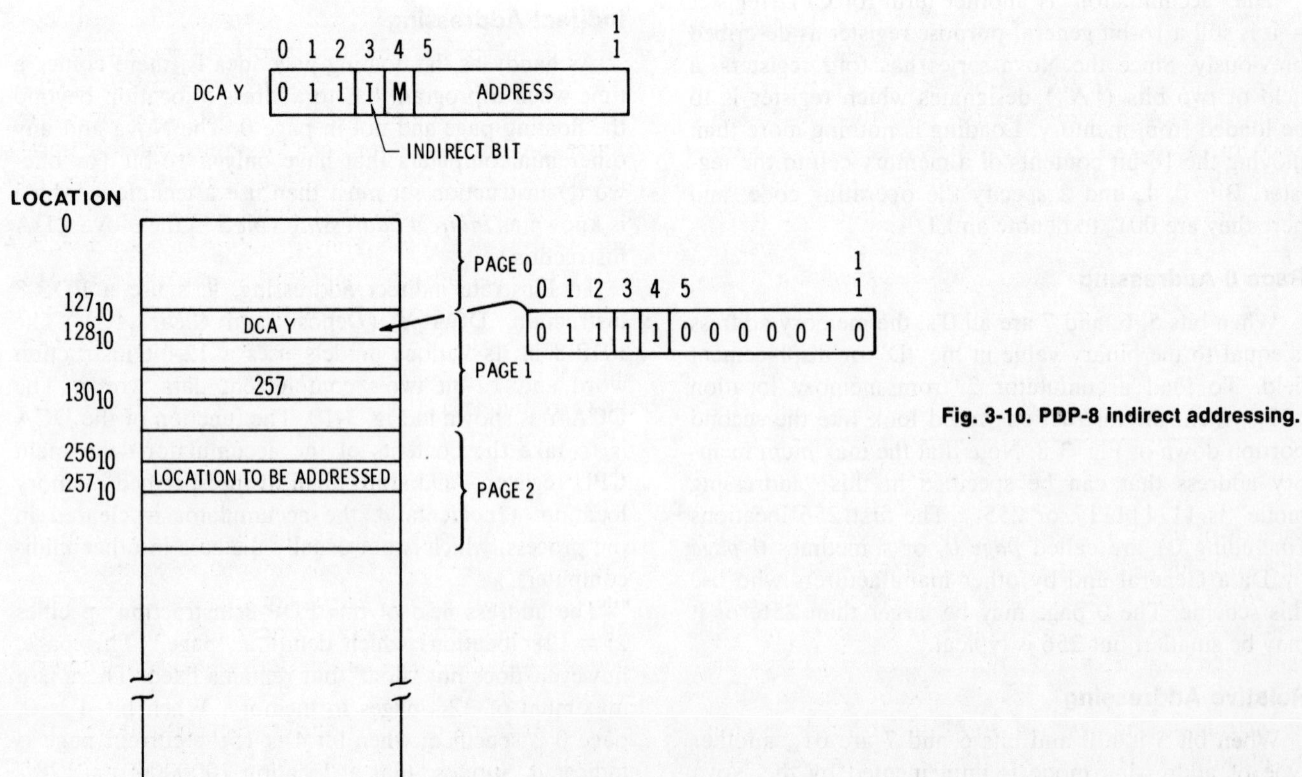

Fig. 3-10. PDP-8 indirect addressing.

lator in $100000001_2 = 257_{10}$ (the second location in page 2). In this case, a second word must hold the address of 257_{10}. This second word must be located in page 0 or the current page. By means of the indirect bit, bit 3, the CPU is told to calculate the effective address by reading the second word and using the value found in that word as the memory location to be used. Fig. 3-10 illustrates the usage of the indirect mode of addressing. The CPU fetches the DCA Y at location 128, notes that the indirect bit (bit 3) is set and that the current page is to be used (bit 4 = 1), and then adds the address field to the contents of a current page register (not the program counter), as shown in the figure. The CPU then reads the word at location 130_{10}, which is a value of 257_{10}. The 257 is then used as the memory address in which the contents of the accumulator are stored. A bit messy? Well, perhaps, but if you think of indirect addressing in terms of always having a second word that holds the *literal* address that is to be used, it's very similar to simply having the address as part of the instruction, as in the Interdata case. The only difference is that in the long Interdata instruction the address was the second word of the instruction, and in the indirect case the second word was somewhere else in memory.

Indexing

The Nova indirect addressing is similar to the PDP-8 case except that here the instruction may be indirect to a larger page 0 or indirect to a second word somewhere within the floating page. What about the other addressing modes in the Nova? There are two additional modes: when bits 6 and 7 are set to 10_2 and 11_2. In both cases, they specify *indexed* addressing. In indexed addressing, the effective address is calculated by adding the contents of an index register to the displacement, or D, field. The index register is nothing more than accumulator 2 (bits 6, 7 = 10_2) or 3 (bits 6, 7 = 11_2). If accumulator 2 held 1008_{10} and the program required the value at location 1020_{10} to be loaded into accumulator 1, the instruction would appear as shown in Fig. 3-11. The CPU would then add AC2 to 12_{10} to get 1020_{10}, read the contents of location 1020_{10}, and store

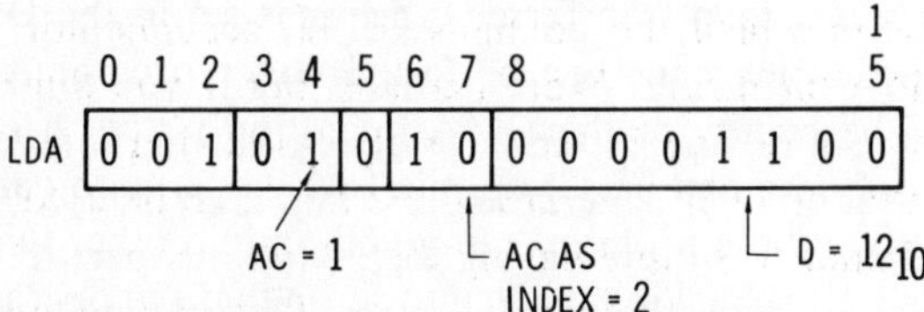

Fig. 3-11. Indexed addressing.

the contents in accumulator 1. Why have this addressing mode at all? It may not be apparent right now, but it makes programming a great deal more efficient. Chapter 4 gives illustrations of programming methods and illustrates the uses of indexing.

Immediate Addressing

Another mode of addressing does not really address a memory location at all. In the *immediate* mode, a data value within the instruction word is used in the function of the instruction. For example, the Intel 8080 chip (used in the MITS Altair 8800 and other microcomputers) has an number of immediate instructions. An ADI (*Add Immediate* to A) instruction is shown in Fig. 3-12. Here the CPU takes the second byte of the instruction and, treating it as an operand, adds it to the

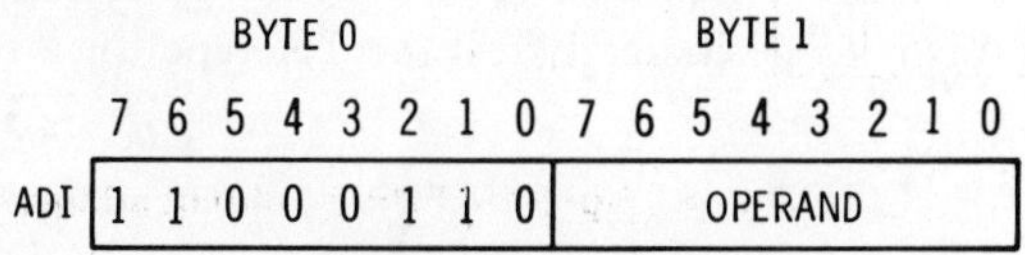

Fig. 3-12. Immediate addressing.

contents of the A accumulator. Most immediate instructions will be working with eight-bit values usually treated as signed seven-bit values specifying operands from −128 to +127. Immediate instructions are efficient when they are used in minicomputers, as only one access (of the instruction word) must be done to obtain the instruction and operand. In the microcomputer case, the machine still makes two one-byte accesses, but it does eliminate a possible three-byte "long" instruction.

DATA WORD FORMATS

Up to this point in the chapter we have seen how instruction sets of minicomputers are determined by the number of registers and "architecture" of the CPU and by memory addressing requirements. Another factor that helps define the instruction set is the requirement for data word formats. Most minicomputers use 16-bit data words, while microprocessor hardware uses 8-bit data words. Eight bits allow for incrementing counts for loops and holding ASCII data quite well, but they are generally too short to be useful in arithmetic computations. (As a result, they are "linked" together in microcomputer software to obtain the necessary precision.) Even 16-bit words, though, are inadequate for programs that require operands larger than ±32,767 (maximum count in 16 bits with a sign bit). On the other hand, 16 bits can be a nuisance when two ASCII characters are "packed" into a 16-bit word. Unpacking or retrieving one or the other may require "masking" off one after a shifting operation and may consume three or four instructions on some minicomputers.

Because of varying data requirements, some minicomputers, such as the Interdata series, try to provide several types of data formats. Interdata has instructions that operate on bytes (8 bits), halfwords (16 bits), and floating-point numbers (32 bits). Their instruction formats are a 16-bit instruction word (one memory access) and a 32-bit instruction word (two memory accesses). Other manufacturers provide only 8-bit or 16-bit data and require the user to write software that provides more bits for greater precision. Probably one extreme of this approach is a microprocessor chip such as Intel's 4040, which is oriented towards four-bit data slices. Of course, any size data word can be implemented in software regardless of what the basic hardware limitation is. Even a microprocessor built around the Intel 4040 chip can implement 32-bit floating-point instructions in software; however, the price paid for this implementation is increased software execution time. Instead of a one-instruction Interdata AE Floating-Point Add, software in another computer may take 60 instructions to perform the same function.

I/O REQUIREMENTS

Another factor influencing instruction sets of minicomputers is the requirement for input/output (I/O). There are two basic types of communication between input/output, or peripheral devices, and the CPU or memory—multiplexer bus transfers and direct memory accesses (DMA).

The first type of I/O transfer, the multiplexer bus, transfers 8 or 16 bits of data from a CPU register to an I/O device or from the I/O device to the CPU register.

The terminology *multiplexer bus* is used because there is one set of bus lines that are used to "multiplex" communications between many devices and the CPU. Transfers are slow-speed transfers and are usually limited to an instruction loop that first tests whether the I/O device is "ready," transfers the data, and then loops back to test the device again. The reason the device may not be ready is that some devices, such as a Teletype Keyboard Printer Model ASR-33, can only accept data at very slow rates. The ASR-33, for example, accepts data at the rate of 10 characters per second. While this is 120–words-per-minute typing rate, it is extremely slow to a computer that executes up to a million instructions per second. During the transfer of a string of characters to a Teletype, most of the time is devoted to waiting for the teletype to become "ready," that is, to go through its 100-millisecond (100 thousandths of a second) cycle with each character before the next can be transmitted. Multiplexer bus transfers are usually performed for slow-speed devices that are byte-oriented. Communication from the CPU to various devices can be "interleaved" a byte or word at a time. Typical devices that would use multiplexer bus I/O would be a line printer and paper-tape reader. An example of the instruction loop for output to a Teletype is shown in Fig. 3-13, implemented for a Nova series minicomputer.

The second type of I/O transfer is for high-speed devices and is called a *direct memory access,* or DMA for short. For some devices, DMA transfers are necessary because the data transfer rates are too high for a software loop to keep up with. For example, the transfer rate to a magnetic disc (an I/O device with the recording medium consisting of a magnetic disc revolving at about 1800 rpm) is about 600,000 8-bit bytes per second. If the software had to get the next byte, check for an end condition, output the byte to disc, test for ready and loop back, it might take ten instructions, limiting this loop to 100,000 bytes per second, a rate incompatible with disc speed. Another strong reason for DMA is that the DMA can be started and the CPU can go on with normal instruction execution while the transfer of data occurs. Transfers to and from high-speed devices are generally performed, then, over DMA, a direct port to memory. The DMA "controller," a piece of hardware usually separate from the CPU, is given the starting address of the data—the number of bytes or words to be transferred—and then it transfers the data independent of the CPU. The DMA accomplishes this by "cycle-stealing" from the CPU. When the high-speed I/O device is ready for the next byte or word of data, it "steals" a slice of time from CPU instruction execution and accesses memory to read or write the data. It then releases the CPU to continue normal instruction execution; the CPU is not even aware that it has been inhibited from executing the current instruction. When the data transfer is complete (when the complete block of data has been transferred), a flag is set in the DMA channel which can then be tested under program control. The beauty of the DMA operation is that a large block of data can be set up, the DMA operation can be started, and the program can go off and do other things, periodically checking the flag to sense that the operation is done (or using an interrupt as described in the following section).

INTERRUPTS

Both the multiplexer bus and DMA operations may be under control of an *interrupt* system. Suppose that a program is running in a computer that executes 100,000 instructions a second. If a string of ten characters has to be output to a 10-character-per-second Teletype printer, the operation will take 10/10, or 1, second. The actual number of instructions needed to output the ten characters will be on the order of 40 or 50 (get next character, test ready, output character, loop back—for ten characters). Obviously for $100{,}000 - 40 = 99{,}960$ instruction times, the program has been "waiting" for the Teletype to become ready. It would be very convenient to enable the program to solve other problems or perform other operations during this "dead" time. One way to do this is to periodically test the Teletype for a ready

```
GETCH:   LDA     0,@PNTR    ;LOAD CHARACTER            }
         MOV     0,0,SNR    ;GO TO "OUTP" IF NOT 0     } PORTION TO GET AND
         JMP     DONE       ;FOUND 0- DONE             } TEST NEXT CHAR
-------------------------------------------------------
OUTP:    SKPBZ   TTO        ;SKIP IF TTY NOT BUSY      }
         JMP     .-1        ;GO BACK TO OUTP           } ACTUAL OUTPUT
         DOAS    0,TTO      ;OUTPUT ONE CHARACTER      } PORTION
         JMP     GETCH      ;GO FOR NEXT CHARACTER     }
DONE:
           ~
```

Fig. 3-13. Teletype output loop.

condition after performing a certain number of other instructions. It becomes tedious to count instructions in this fashion, though; a better scheme would be to have some external stimulus tell the program that the Teletype has received the character and printed it and is ready for the next character, or that a DMA transfer of 1000 words has been completed to a magnetic tape, or that a card reader has finished reading a card. An interrupt does exactly that. If an I/O device is set up to interrupt the CPU, an interrupt signal will be detected; the normal instruction execution will be inhibited, and the CPU will transfer control (by loading the program counter) to a special software interrupt routine.

How does the CPU do this? It depends upon the type of minicomputer. For some minicomputers, an interrupt will cause the program counter to be loaded with the contents of memory location 0 before the next instruction is executed. The *current instruction location* might be saved in location 1. At the end of the interrupt routine, the program counter is effectively reloaded with the "current" instruction location in location 1 and the program continues where it left off. The interrupt routine first of all saves all registers and "status" in special locations so that they can be restored at the end of the interrupt processing. The routine then asks, under program control, who interrupted, and why. After finding out the source of the interrupt, the routine than takes special action dependent upon the type of interrupt. At the end of the processing, the routine restores any registers and status flags and then executes a special "return form interrupt" instruction to return control to the interrupted program as previously discussed.

A more sophisticated type of interrupt structure might cause a branch to a different location for each type of interrupt. An interrupt from a Teletype might go to location 100, an interrupt from a DMA might go to location 102, and so forth. This scheme is called *vectored interrupts.*

Since many I/O devices might be running simultaneously in a large system, an interrupt from one might interrupt the interrupt-processing routine of another, if the second interrupt was of a higher "priority" than the first.

Take the example of a minicomputer controlling a pickle-canning operation shown in Fig. 3-14. At time $t = 0$, a payroll program is running. At A, a priority 2 interrupt is received. Priority 2 has been assigned to a sensor checking brine salinity. The salinity check routine is then entered (A to B). At B, a higher-priority interrupt caused by temperature control of the brine is received. After completing the B to C portion of the temperature control routine, an interrupt at C signals a jar count is needed and the jar count routine is entered (C). After the number of jars has been totaled, the temperature routine is reentered (D). At the end of the routine, with the brine temperature firmly recorded, the salinity check is reentered (E). After further processing, a priority 6 interrupt is received (pickle-slicer is jammed!). The interrupt processor outputs a message to the only human in the entire pickle-canning complex, and the pickle slicer is cleared. The salinity check is reentered (G), completed (H), and the payroll program is resumed.

Although the above is a tongue-in-cheek example, it is certainly representative of the complexity of even a somewhat small minicomputer process control system and well within the capabilities of a small minicomputer's interrupt structure.

TYPES OF INSTRUCTIONS

We have seen that the instruction sets of any minicomputer are very much related to the "architecture," memory size, data word formats, and I/O requirements of the computer system. In a simple computer such as the PDP-8, the instruction set may consist of about 32 instructions; in an Interdata 7/16, the instruction set may encompass 113 instructions. Every manufacturer, of course, would like to include a statement such as this in its advertising literature, The Mark VIII minicomputer has a powerful instruction set of 3020 instructions. In fact, the actual number of instructions is very hard to compare from one computer to another. There may be no appreciable difference from one instruction with bit 13 set and one with bit 13 reset, and yet these are two more "powerful instructions." All minicomputers and microcomputers, however, have about the same types of instructions, and comparisons may be made based on the general types available. These types, loosely grouped, are:

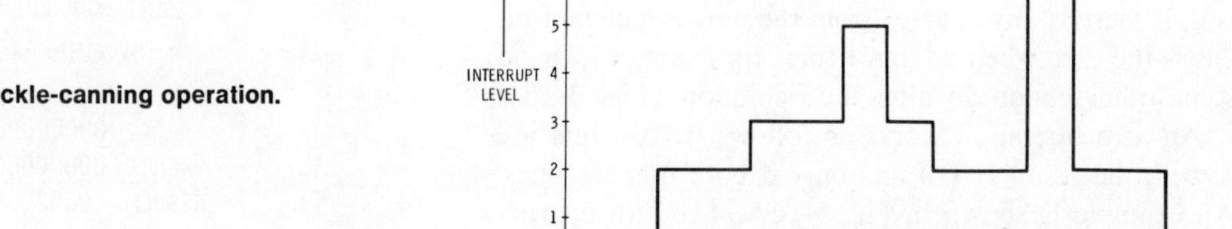

Fig. 3-14. Interrupt-driven pickle-canning operation.

- Memory Reference instructions.
- Branch (or Jump) instructions.
- Arithmetic and Logical instructions.
- Compare instructions.
- Input/Output instructions.
- Special instructions.

Memory Reference instructions are simply that. A CPU register is loaded from memory, or the contents of a CPU register are stored somewhere in memory. Sometimes only an 8-bit byte is loaded or stored, as in the Interdata LB (*L*oad *B*yte) or STB (*St*ore *B*yte) or the Intel 8800 LDA (*L*oa*d* *A* Direct) or STA (*St*ore *A* Direct). Sometimes as many as sixteen 16-bit registers are loaded, as in the Interdata LDM (*L*oad *M*ultiple). A Memory Reference of this type normally takes one memory cycle for the instruction fetch (two if a long instruction) and one memory access for each load. Sometimes an instruction of this type will increment or decrement the memory cell's contents, test the results, and jump on the results of the test, as in the Nova DSZ (*D*ecrement and *S*kip if *Z*ero). An instruction of this type would take three memory cycles, one for the fetch, one for the contents to be read and tested, and one for replacing the contents.

Branch or Jump instructions always include a simple JMP or BR which causes an unconditional jump to a specified location. The PDP-8 SKP (*Skip*, Unconditional) is this type of instruction. There are always many conditional branches that test the condition of one or more flags. The flags have usually been set as a result of a previous arithmetic, input/output, or other type of operation. A flag might indicate a comparison, for example. The Motorola MC6800 microprocessor instruction BMI (*B*ranch if *Mi*nus) branches if the N flag on the CPU chip is set. The Interdata BXLE (*B*ranch on Inde*x* *L*ow or *E*qual) instruction branches to a given location if the content of the first index register (CPU register) is less than or equal to the content of a second CPU register, a fairly sophisticated branch.

Arithmetic and Logical instructions include not only add and subtract, but logical and shift operations as well. Add and subtract operate the way described previously. Sixteen-bit or 8-bit two's complement signed operands are added or subtracted. Both the operands are usually found in CPU registers (assuming the computer has more than one). A flag may be set if the result is 0, if there is any "carry" from the most significant bit (as is the case when adding 1 to 1, for example), or on some other condition after the operation (Fig. 3-15).

An AND operation works as follows. If two bits are ANDed, the result is 1 if and only if both bits are ones. An example is shown in Fig. 3-16A. The AND instruction is used to mask off certain fields. If there are two ASCII characters packed in a 16-bit word, for example,

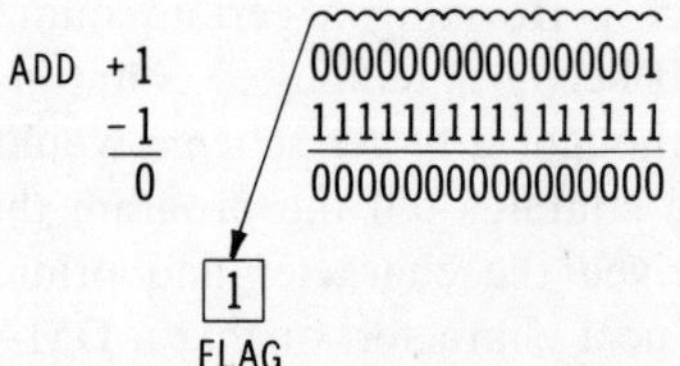

Fig. 3-15. Carry to flag operation.

the AND operation which is shown in the second part of Fig. 3-16B will "pass" only the second (rightmost) character.

The OR operation produces a 1 in the result if there is at least a 1 in either operand, or both (see Fig. 3-17A). An OR instruction is used to set certain bits as flags or to merge data. An XOR, or EXCLUSIVE OR, operation produces a 1 in the result if and only if there is a

```
       0000000000000011
AND    0000000000000101
RESULT 0000000000000001
```

(A) Example of AND operation.

```
    0011000100110010  ASCII "1," "2"
AND 0000000011111111  MASK
    0000000000110010  ASCII "2"
```

(B) Making left field with AND operation.

Fig. 3-16. AND operation and example.

0 and 1 or 1 and 0 in the same bit positions of two operands. If both bits are ones, or if neither is a one, a zero is produced in the result (see Fig. 3-17B). The XOR operation is not used as frequently as the AND or OR, but might be used to alternate a value between 1 and 0, for example. Actual examples of these instructions are the MOS Technology MSC6502 microprocessor instructions AND, ORA, and EOR.

If the preceding arithmetic instructions are performed between two CPU registers, they require only one memory access to fetch the instruction. Most minicomputers and microcomputers have a bevy of other "register-to-register" instructions related to the above, such as incrementing a register, decrementing a register, negating a register's contents (making a positive number negative, and vice versa), zeroing a register, and so forth. These

```
       0000000000000011
"OR"   0000000000000101
RESULT 0000000000000111
```

(A) OR operation.

```
       0000000000000011
"XOR"  0000000000000101
RESULT 0000000000000110
```

(B) XOR operation.

Fig. 3-17. OR and XOR operations.

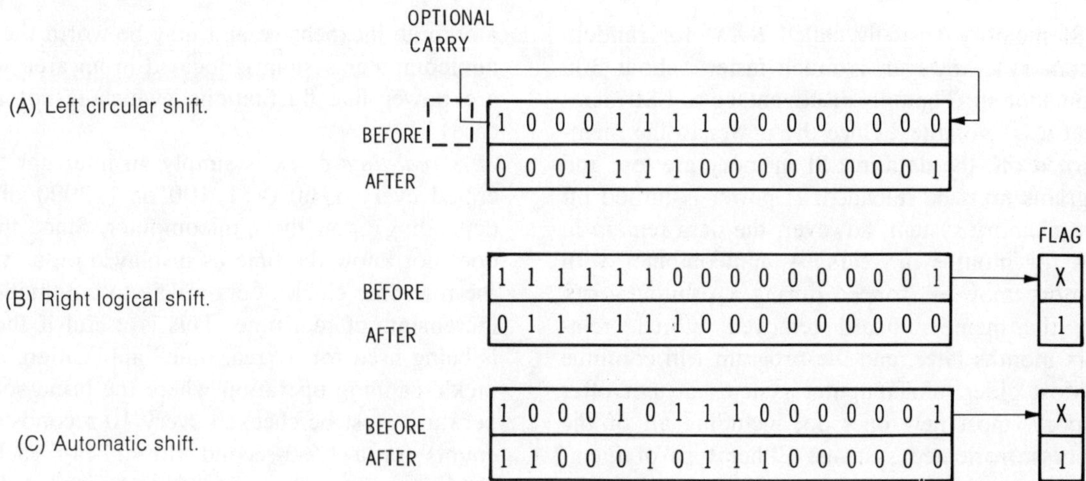

Fig. 3-18. Shift operations.

functions are things one usually gets for free with the hardware of the CPU.

Another type of Arithmetic and Logical instruction is a *shift.* There are three types of shifts, but not all minicomputers implement all types. All three types usually involve one CPU register, although "double" shifts are sometimes provided (two registers at once) or the result of the shift may be transferred to a second register. A *circular shift* rotates the register contents, sometimes through a carry flip-flop. (See Fig. 3-18A.) A *logical shift* drops bits off one or the other end into a flag which can then be tested by a branch instruction (Fig. 3-18B). An *arithmetic shift* extends the sign bit for a right shift and sets a flag (Fig. 3-18C). Note that shifting one bit position to the right divides the original number by two and that shifting one bit to the left multiplies the number by 2. Shifting more bit positions (BP) multiplies or divides by corresponding powers of 2, as illustrated in Fig. 3-19. Some minicomputers can shift only one bit position for each shift instruction, while others can shift *n* times. Up to 16 shifts may be performed on the Computer Automation LSI-3/05, for example, and the Fairchild F8 microprocessor can perform shifts of one or four bit positions.

When a minicomputer has Compare instructions (they may be implicit in other arithmetic instructions by setting flags), the contents of two registers are compared, and the results of the comparison set specific flags for equality, high, low, and so forth.

Input/Output instructions either set up I/O transfers via the multiplexer bus or the DMA. Typically, in the former case a CPU register is loaded with eight bits or a word of data, and an "output" or "input" I/O instruction is executed to effect the transfer. The instruction usually contains an 8-bit I/O device code to designate the I/O device involved. Most of the device codes are preassigned (Teletype = 02_8, for example). In a microcomputer the I/O device code may actually be a 16-bit address preassigned to an I/O device. In the DMA case, as mentioned previously, a start address is sent to the DMA channel (or controller) via a single instruction, the number of words to be transferred is sent by a second, and the operation is started by the third.

Special instructions include such instructions as those to control interrupts, automatic program load (loading of a small "bootstrap" program), or special hardware options (memory "mapping," floating-point, power-fail, and so forth).

MEMORY

In the early days of computers, memory was a very expensive commodity. At this time, core memory is relatively inexpensive—about 2¢ per bit from the computer manufacturer. Its very existence is being threatened by LSI memory chips, however, which are now less expensive than core memory and will become even less expensive in years to come. Core memories are binary devices, and there is a small core for each bit of data. A 16-bit memory word has 16 cores associated with it. When the core is "read," a one changes to a zero and the data must be restored by rewriting the bit. This slows up the cycle somewhat since each memory cycle has to include a "restore" portion, even though the data are available earlier. Minicomputer core memories operate from about 600 nanoseconds to 3 microseconds with about 1 microsecond being typical. Core is almost never offered with microcomputer systems.

BEFORE	$00000011_2 = 3$		BEFORE	$11110100_2 = -12$
SHIFT LEFT 1 BP ←	$00000110_2 = 6$		RIGHT 1 BP →	$11111010_2 = -6$
SHIFT LEFT 1 BP ←	$00001100_2 = 12$		RIGHT 1 BP →	$11111101_2 = -3$

Fig. 3-19. Multiplication and division by shifting.

An LSI memory (usually called *RAM* for random access memory), however, is much faster—about 300 nanoseconds or so. The only disadvantage to LSI memory is that it is "volatile." Once the power to the memory is turned off, the data in LSI memory are lost and any programs must be reloaded. If power is turned off on a core memory system, however, the data remain in the cores for months or years. A minicomputer with core memory may be stopped during a printout on a Teletype, the memory board removed, stored, reinstalled six months later, and the program will continue typing! Most older minicomputer systems do not offer LSI memory; most new ones do, including all of the microprocessor-oriented systems. Either type of memory is adequate, although the trend will continue to be toward LSI.

SPECIAL HARDWARE FEATURES

Besides the basic hardware in the architecture of the CPU, LSI or core memory, and controller for peripheral devices, a number of special options are available from minicomputer manufacturers and for some microcomputers.

One of these options is *power-fail safe*. Power-fail safe saves the program if line power to the computer should be cut off or if the level of the ac line power should drop beyond a certain point. Once the power is restored, the program continues from the interrupted point. The power failure is really a special interrupt that causes a "vector" to a power-fail safe routine where the contents of volatile CPU registers and flags are placed in selected core locations. When power comes up, the registers and flags are restored. Power-fail safety is usually quite inexpensive and may be worth the cost if the minicomputer system is located in an area where there are power line fluctuations (which is not usually the case).

A *real-time clock* is simply an interrupt that is generated every 1/60 or 1/100 or 1/2000 of a second, depending upon the minicomputer. Since the program does not know the time as displayed on a "real" clock, the real-time clock offers a way to automatically count increments of real time. This is useful if the computer is being used for a "real-time" application, such as the pickle-canning operation where the brine solution temperature must be checked every 10 seconds or so (600 counts for a 1/60-second clock). For each real-time clock interrupt, the count is incremented and a comparison to 600 is made—if the reading is 600 or greater, a temperature check is made. A real-time clock option, like the power-fail-safe option just discussed, is relatively inexpensive.

Hardware *multiply and divide* is frequently offered as a special option "unbundled" from the basic computer. It is usually quite expensive and is probably not worth the cost in small minicomputer configurations since a multiply and divide can easily be implemented in software.

Other options include such items as memory mapping (control of partitions of memory), a second DMA channel, writable control store (WCS)–a dedicated piece of hardware memory that could be used to implement superfast short programs or instructions that are often used—and others. Unless you have some special-purpose requirements or can purchase these options in used equipment at little extra cost, they are usually not worth the extra price.

CHAPTER

4

Minicomputer Software

Unlike computer hardware, computer software cannot be easily separated into functional blocks such as CPU, memory, and secondary storage. Computer software encompasses all programs that are usable by the computer in question, and ranges from the simplest ten-instruction program to large operating systems for the computer that took five or six man-years to write. This chapter will deal with the most common types of software that would normally be required for a computer system, including assemblers, compilers, support programs, and applications software. Chapter 7 is also concerned with software but covers programming techniques and methods.

MACHINE LANGUAGE

The most basic type of software is machine language code. Machine language is exactly what we used for the programming examples in our SIMP computer, the combination of binary ones and zeros making up a complete program. Refresh your memory by looking at the instruction set of the SIMP computer in Table 3-1 of Chapter 3. Although we used some convenient mnemonics such as "JMP" for a jump instruction, ultimately we had to say, "Well, let's see, a jump instruction is of the form 011 000000 LLLLLL 0, so we'll write down that value for location 20. Now it looks like we'll have to jump to location 30 at this point, so LLLLLL = 30 and we can write 011 000000 011110 0 for a jump to 30." Furthermore, we had to do the same thing for all of the instructions in the program, "assembling" the instructions in the proper format, one after another. Now this is a perfectly feasible thing to do. As a matter of fact, this is exactly what was done in the early days of programming. Assembling instructions by hand does lead to some interesting problems, however. Suppose that we had assembled a 30-instruction program for the SIMP computer in locations 0 through 29_{10}. There would probably be four or five JMP or JMI instructions in the program with a location specified in each similar to that shown in Fig. 4-1.

Since very few programs work the first time, it's highly likely that we would have to change some "code" to correct errors we had made. In a more extreme case, we might even have to insert four or five instructions at some point in the program. If, in this example, we had to insert five instructions directly after location 1, all of the remaining 28 instructions would have to be "moved down" as shown in Fig. 4-2; the JMP 10 at location 5 would now be at location 10, the JMI at 12 would now be at location 17, and the JMP at 13 would now be at location 18. Notice, though, that the addresses specified in the three instructions are no longer valid, viz, "10" should be "15," "15" should be "20," and

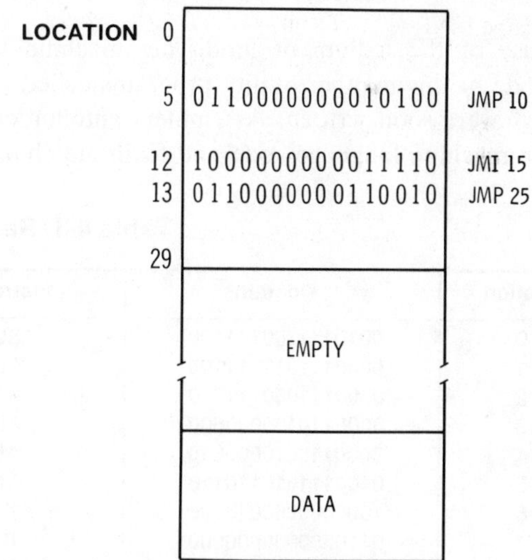

Fig. 4-1. Sample program number 3.

"25" should be "30." To correct the program after inserting the five instructions, it would be necessary to go back and change the LLLLLL fields of each JMP or JMI instruction. In our simple case, only three instructions were involved, but in typical cases on a minicomputer as many as one out of two instructions might have to be redone. For a 30-instruction program, this is not too time-consuming, but imagine the work involved for hundreds of instructions. Would you bet that the aver-

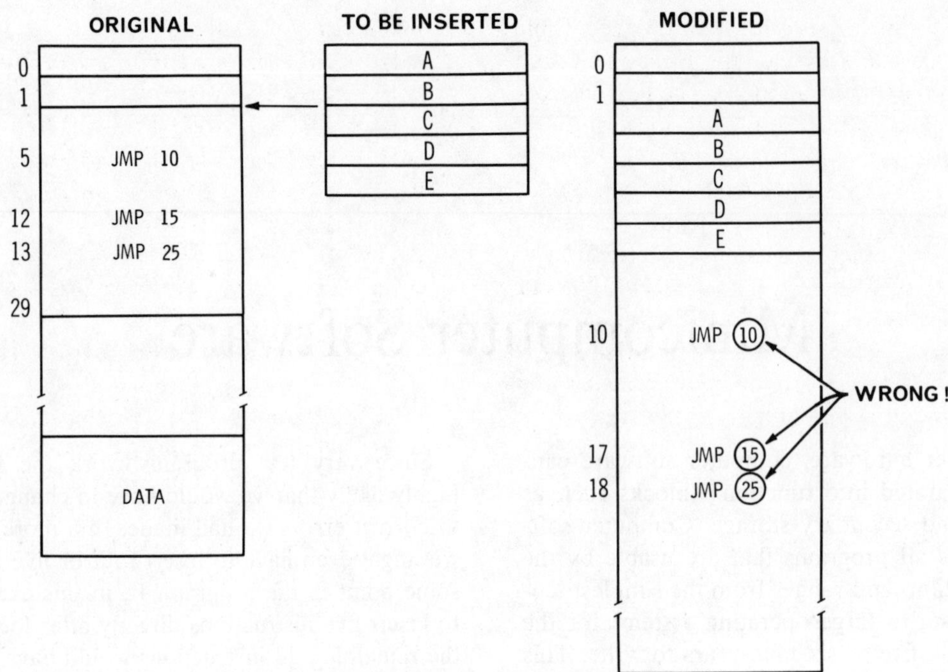

Fig. 4-2. Program modification without assembler.

age programmer can modify four hundred instructions in this fashion and not make an error?

ASSEMBLERS

Because of the tedium of modifying machine language code in this manner, utility programs called "assemblers" were soon written. Assemblers automatically *assemble* machine language code and facilitate changes to the programs. Instead of laboriously hand-coding four hundred instructions, a programmer could now feed in his program to the computer and moments later the assembler program could print out four-hundred neatly generated instructions, with no errors in operation codes or addresses.

Let's see how this works. Using the SIMP computer again, we will illustrate the assembly process with a short program to put a "30" in location 30, a "31" in

Table 4-1. Sample Program Number 4

Location	Contents	Instruction	Operands	Remarks
0	0010111100111100	SUB	30,30	ZERO TO LOCATION
1	0000111010111100	ADD	29,30	CURRENT LOCATION VALUE
2	0000111000111010	ADD	28,29	BUMP LOCATION VALUE
3	0000110100000000	ADD	26,0	BUMP SUB 30,30
4	0000110010000010	ADD	25,1	BUMP ADD 2,30
5	0100111010110110	COM	29,27	COMPARE
6	1000000000010000	JMI	8	GO IF DONE
7	0110000000000000	JMP	0	GO FOR NEXT STORE
8	1110000000000000	STP		STOP
↓	↓			↓
25	0000000000000010			2
26	0000000010000010			BUMPS EACH OPERAND BY 1
27	0000000001000000			64
28	0000000000000001			1
29	0000000000011110			30
30	XXXXXXXXXXXXXXXX			DON'T CARE
↓	↓			↓
63	XXXXXXXXXXXXXXXX			DON'T CARE

location 31, and so forth, up to location 63 (see Table 4-1). This program starts by clearing location 30 and then adding 30 to the 0 in location 30. The next instruction (at 2) then changes the 30 to 31 in location 29 in preparation for the next store into location 31. Now we have a subtle step. The instruction at location 3 adds 0000000010000010_2 to the instruction at location 0, changing it to SUB 31,31. Let's examine that carefully. Originally in location 0 there was a 0010111100111100_2, meaning "SUB 30,30." Adding the value at location 26 results in 0010111110111110, or SUB 31,31! There is no reason why we cannot treat an instruction like any other item of data and that is just what we have done in this case. The next instruction, at location 4, adds $2 = 10_2$ to the ADD 29,30 in location 1, changing it to ADD 29,31 in the same fashion. The two instructions have now been set up to store a 31 in location 31. After a compare at location 5 for the last address to be changed, the program jumps back to location 0 to effect the change. After each store, the program modifies the instructions at locations 0 and 1, ending when the value in location 28 is 64 (flag is set and JMI causes jump to location 8 for a stop).

Now let's see how this program would be input to an assembler. Since an assembler program is a rather large program, typically 2000 to 8000 instructions, and since our SIMP computer has a memory size of 64 words, it is evident that we cannot run the assembler program in the SIMP computer. Usually the assembler *is* run in the same computer, but in this case we will have to "cross-assemble"—that is, run an assembly program in another computer to assemble instructions for the first computer, in this case our SIMP machine.

The assembler program accepts "lines" of assembly language instructions. Each line defines one instruction, with an operation code ("SUB"), operands ("30,30"), and comments ("ZERO TO LOCATION"). In this case, let's assume that the lines of assembly language are going to be entered on a Teletype keyboard. The Teletype works similarly to an ordinary typewriter except that each character is sent to the computer. In this case, the assembler program "reads in" each line of characters, and after all lines have been input, it spews out a listing of machine language code that can then be loaded into the SIMP computer.

To input our program, the assembler might type out an "INPUT?" command to the Teletype and await our lines of characters defining the program. We would then type in the characters shown in Fig. 4-3.

Several problems are immediately obvious. First of all, we see from Table 4-1 that locations 9 through 24 are "don't care" locations. We don't care what values are to be in them. We could write 16 lines of zeros, but it is much more convenient to tell the assembler that the next set of lines are to be assembled for locations starting at 25. We do this by a "pseudo-op," which is simply a way of telling the assembler that this is not a line that will generate an instruction but is a line that informs the assembler of some condition or command. The ".LOC XXX" pseudo-op will cause the assembler to assemble the next line at location XXX. In our case, we would write ".LOC 25" and also add a ".LOC 0" at the beginning, just in case the assembler does not know enough to start at location 0 (see Fig. 4-4).

```
INPUT?
SUB   30,30   ZERO TO LOCATION
ADD   29,30   30+I TO LOCATION
ADD   28,29   BUMP LOCATION VALUE
ADD   26,0    BUMP  SUB 30,30
ADD   25,1    BUMP  ADD 29,30
CMI   29,27   COMPARE
JMI   8       GO IF DONE
JMP   0       GO FOR NEXT STORE
STP           STOP
```

Fig. 4-3. SIMP assembler input—Part 1.

Note that in Fig. 4-4 the two .LOCs have been added and two new pseudo-ops have also been added. The first of these, ".DATA," instructs the assembler that the following operand is an item of data rather than an instruction. The second, ".END," instructs the assembler that this is the end of assembler "source" input statements and tells the assembler to start assembling the statements into machine code. After a slight pause (computing), the assembler now outputs a listing of the machine language code for each location, the location address, and the entire source statement, as shown in Fig. 4-5. Note that the locations on the listing are in octal numbers (first column) along with the assembled

```
INPUT?
.LOC 0
SUB   30.30   ZERO TO LOCATION
ADD   29,30   30+I TO LOCATION
ADD   28,29   BUMP LOCATION VALUE
ADD   26,0    BUMP SUB  30,30
ADD   28,1    BUMP ADD  29,30
CMI   29,27   COMPARE
JMI   8       GO IF DONE
JMP   0       GO FOR NEXT STORE
STP           STOP
.LOC   25
.DATA 2
.DATA 130
.DATA 64
.DATA 1
.DATA 30
.DATA 0
.END
```

Fig. 4-4. SIMP assembler input—Part 2.

```
                SIMP ASSEMBLY LISTING        PG 1
                        .LOC      0
000     027474   SUB      30,30     ZERO TO LOCATION
001     007274   ADD      29,30     30 + I TO LOCATION
002     007072   ADD      28,29     BUMP LOCATION VALUE
003     006400   ADD      26,0      BUMP SUB 30,30
004     007002   ADD      25,1      BUMP ADD 2,30
005     047266   COM      29,27     COMPARE
006     100020   JMI      8         GO IF DONE
007     060000   JMP      0         GO FOR NEXT STORE
010     160000   STP                STOP
                 .LOC     25
031     000002   .DATA    2         2
032     000202   .DATA    130       BUMPS EACH OPERAND BY 1
033     000100   .DATA    64        64
034     000001   .DATA    1         1
035     000036   .DATA    30        30
036     000000   .DATA    0
                 .END
```

Fig. 4-5. SIMP assembler listing.

instructions or data (second column). The resultant output of the assembler could now be keyed into the computer, and the program could be run—we have eliminated the tedious process of hand-assembling the program. Any changes to the program can now be made by inserting, modifying, or deleting source language lines (in practice this is done easily by an "edit" program rather than by retyping, as we shall see later).

Is there anything we could do to make the assembly process even more efficient and useful? We have the assembler automatically changing an ADD instruction to a 000 SSSSSS DDDDDD 0 instruction, where SSSSSS and DDDDDD are source and destination memory locations. We are still forced to define the source and destination memory locations by numeric values, however. Suppose we let the assembler define those numeric values for us; let the assembler keep track of where those values are. To do this, we must give each memory location that is *referenced* a name or symbol as shown in Fig. 4-6. Note that in the figure we can mix numeric ref-

```
        .LOC    0
START   SUB     30,30         ZERO TO LOCATION
        ADD     VALUE,30      30+I TO LOCATION
        ADD     ONE,VALUE     BUMP LOCATION VALUE
        ADD     BUMP,0        BUMP   SUB 30,30
        ADD     TWO,1         BUMP   ADD 29,30
        COM     VALUE,END     COMPARE
        JMI     DONE          GO IF DONE
        JMP     START         GO FOR NEXT STORE
DONE    STP
        .LOC    25
TWO     .DATA   2
BUMP    .DATA   0'202'
END     .DATA   64
ONE     .DATA   1
VALUE   .DATA   30
        .END
```

Fig. 4-6. Symbolic addressing.

erences to locations, such as "SUB 30,30" and "symbolic" references such as "ONE." How does the assembler know what location "ONE" refers to ? The answer to this is that the assembler generates a table of symbols with addresses, called a *symbol table,* which it can refer to in assembling the instructions. To do this, the assembler must make two "passes" through the source code. The first pass enables the assembler to construct the symbol table, and the second pass is used to assemble the instructions and generate the listing.

If we type on the Teletype the statements shown in Fig. 4-6, the assembler has produced a symbol table that looks somewhat like Table 4-2 after the first pass. For each symbolic name of a location, the assembler has put the corresponding location next to it which it

Table 4-2. Assembler Symbol Table

Bump	26
Done	8
End	27
One	28
Start	0
Two	25
Value	29

computed simply by counting source lines and by setting the count to a new value when the .LOC pseudo-op was encountered. On the second pass which now occurs, the assembler reads the source statements once more, assembles the instructions, and substitutes the numeric location value for the symbol. For example, "ADD VALUE,30" becomes "ADD 29,30" or 000 011101 011110 0_2. The resultant output listing is the same as the previous listing (Fig. 4-5) except that the source listing now includes the symbolic names of the locations (Fig. 4-7) and the symbol table is listed after the regular assembly listing as a convenience to the user. By listing symbolic references to locations, the symbolic assembler eliminates one more tedious task for the programmer—the task of keeping track of where data or instructions are located. For the most part, the listing shown in Fig. 4-7 will be very similar to the listing for any minicomputer or microcomputer assembly. The locations and instructions may be in hexadecimal, and there will be differences in format, but most listing will closely resemble the figure.

If you have been following this discussion closely, several questions may have arisen. First of all, how about that second pass? Must I type in the source program again? The answer is no. In larger systems, the assembler will save the source statements as they are read in on magnetic tape or disc and will automatically reread them for the second pass. Since we are considering using a Teletype as our input device in this case, we would probably first of all punch a paper tape of the input lines. If the paper-tape punch on an ASR-33 (Automatic Send-Receive) Teletype is turned on while the keyboard is being used, a punched tape similar to that of Fig. 4-8 is produced. This paper tape has eight bit positions across the width of the tape, representing seven data bits for one ASCII character and an eighth bit that is generally unused. There are ten "frames" per lateral inch and are therefore ten characters per inch. Fig. 4-8 shows the input source line "START SUB 30,30 ZERO to location CR LF" on a section of the tape. Once the tape has been generated "off-line" (not under computer control), it can be input twice to the assembler, once for each pass. The paper tape also provides a convenient way of editing lines in this small configuration, as a new tape may be produced from any part of an old tape by using the paper-tape punch and paper-tape reader together and merging new data from the keyboard at the same time (see Chapter 5 for more on I/O devices).

The second question that may have occurred is: "What about errors?" Suppose "ADE" was typed instead of "ADD." The assembler, like most other programs, cannot detect even an obvious error like the substitution of "ADE" for "ADD" and therefore will give a diagnostic error indication on the listing. The diagnostic will also show errors for such things as improper format, invalid data values, or many other conditions. These diagnostics generally are a great help in assembling a program, since they immediately flag trouble areas which can be corrected and reassembled. Table 4-3 shows a representative set of diagnostics for the SIMP assembler.

Table 4-3. SIMP Assembler Diagnostics

Code	Meaning
C	Invalid Operation Code
D	Duplicate Symbol
E	Data Error
N	Invalid Number of Arguments
U	Undefined Symbol

LOADER PROGRAMS

In the preceding discussion we have been speaking of assembly listings, and the implication has been that the assembled instruction from the listing can be keyed into the computer from the front panel and the program can then be run. Obviously there is an easier way. The assembled instruction set of the program (that is, the second column of machine language instructions in Fig. 4-7) not only can be printed on a listing but can be

```
                    SIMP ASSEMBLY LISTING                  PG 1

                        .LOC    0
000    027474   START   SUB     30,30        ZERO TO LOCATION
001    007274           ADD     VALUE,30     30 + I TO LOCATION
002    007072           ADD     ONE,VALUE    BUMP LOCATION VALUE
003    006400           ADD     BUMP,0       BUMP   SUB 30,30
004    006202           ADD     TWO,1        BUMP   ADD 29,30
005    047266           COM     VALUE,END    COMPARE
006    100020           JMI     DONE         GO IF DONE
007    060000           JMP     START        GO FOR NEXT STORE
010    160000   DONE    STP
011                     .LOC    25
031    000002   TWO     .DATA   2
032    000202   BUMP    .DATA   0'202'
033    000100   END     .DATA   64
034    000001   ONE     .DATA   1
035    000036   VALUE   .DATA   30
036    000000           .DATA   0            NOT REALLY NECESSARY
                        .END
```

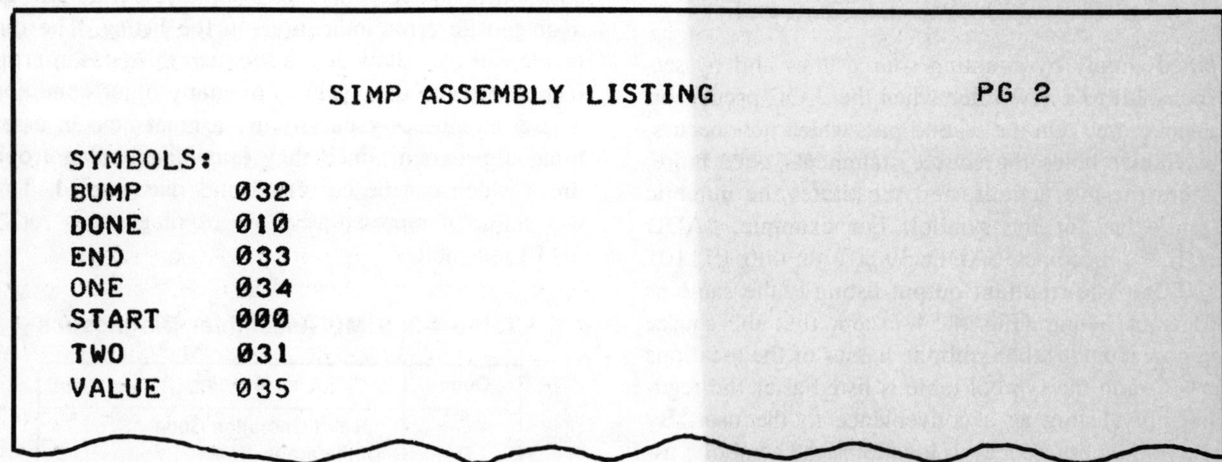

```
                    SIMP ASSEMBLY LISTING                  PG 2

SYMBOLS:
BUMP      032
DONE      010
END       033
ONE       034
START     000
TWO       031
VALUE     035
```

Fig. 4-7. Complete SIMP assembler listing.

punched onto paper tape. The paper tape can then be loaded into the computer by the Teletype under control of another program called a *loader program*.

The assembler for our SIMP computer might punch an object tape as shown in Fig. 4-8 for the program we have been discussing. The data are grouped in "blocks" on the paper tape and are in binary, rather than ASCII, as in the case of the source program. (See Fig. 4-9, where octal notation, e.g., 100001_8, is used to avoid long binary numbers.) Each block consists of four header

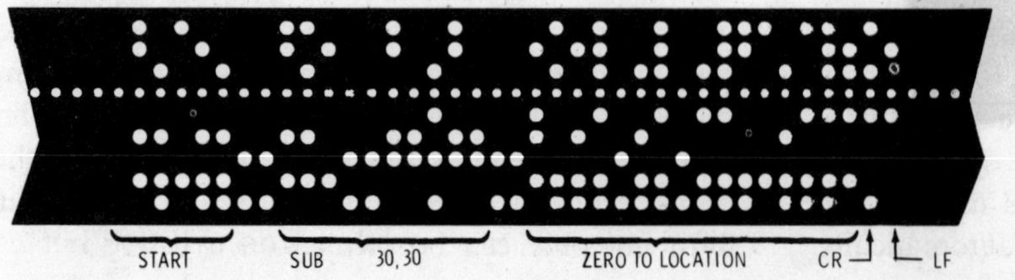

Fig. 4-8. Paper-tape assembler input.

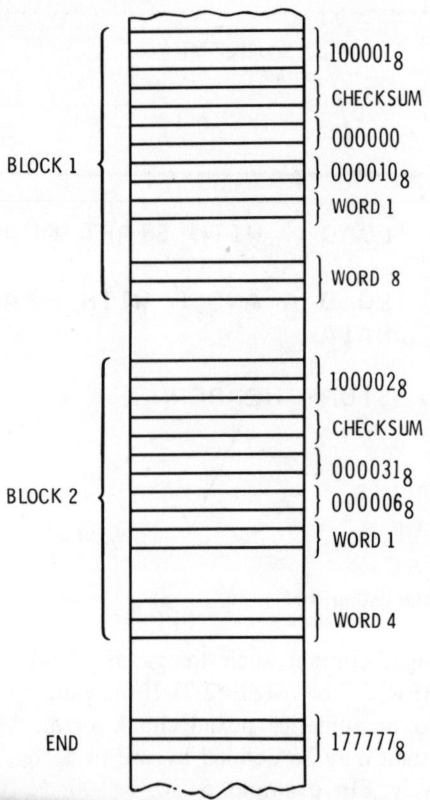

Fig. 4-9. Assembler object output.

words (eight 8-bit bytes). The first word represents the block sequence number, starting with 1. The second word is a *checksum* word that is a check on the data in the block. Checksums are usually obtained by adding (or exclusive-ORing) each byte of data. As each byte is read, the loader will calculate the checksum and compare it with the checksum in the block. If they match, the data have been read correctly. The third header word of the block is the starting address at which the data stored in the block are to be stored. (Note that the first block informs the loader to start at location 0, and the second indicates location $31_8 = 25_{10}$.) The fourth word is the number of words of data in the remaining part of the block. Blocks are separated by nulls (no punches) which the loader ignores. The end of the object tape is indicated by all ones punched in the tape. This example of an object tape is similar to the output of many simple assemblers.

The loader program will load the object tape by automatically reading paper tape from the Teletype. Ignoring nulls, it searches for the first nonzero byte. When it reads the two-byte value 100001_8, it compares the sequence number with the previous (0), reads the checksum, reads the location, and finally reads the number of words to follow. As each subsequent word is read, it is stored in the proper location and a location counter is bumped by one. When the number of words specified in the fourth header word have been read, the checksum from the tape is compared with the "running" checksum and, if they match, the second block is read in and the same process is repeated. The load is terminated by reading the third block with a sequence number of all ones.

MOTOROLA MC6800 ASSEMBLER

This section will illustrate a representative assembler for microcomputer systems by describing the cross-assembler produced by Motorola for its MC6800 Microprocessor. The MC6800 is used in the Altair 680 Microcomputer, the Sphere I Microcomputer System, and others. The assembler could be used to assemble code for these systems, assuming one had access to a time-sharing terminal or a larger computer system in which to run it.

The format for the assembler listing is shown in Fig. 4-10. The first column consists of a five-digit source statement line number. This is simply a sequential line number count in decimal. The next four digits are in hexadecimal and represent the instruction address (program counter) of the assembled program. Since the MC6800 microprocessor accesses instructions and data by byte locations, these addresses represent the byte locations. They increase by 1, 2, or 3, depending upon the length of the instructions and data. The next six digits represent either an instruction in hexadecimal, or data, or an operand for a pseudo-op. If the instruction is a one-byte instruction (for example, an "INX" instruction that increments a hardware register), only the one byte of hexadecimal 08 is printed, and the program counter (or instruction address) is advanced by 1. If the instruction is a two-byte instruction such as "ADDA #25" (add 25_{10} to the contents of accumulator A), two bytes—in this case hexadecimal BB19—are printed, and the instruction address is advanced by 2. If the instruction is a three-byte instruction such as LDAB COUNT (Load accumulator B with the contents of memory location "COUNT"), three bytes—here B6 XXXX, where XXXX is the address of COUNT—are printed and the instruction address is advanced by 3. Certain pseudo-ops may also be printed and may advance the instruction address as described below.

The next four fields are an "image" of the source statement as originally input by the user or programmer. Notice that these are what we would expect: a "label" for a location, an operation that describes the instruction, an operand field that describes the operand of the instruction or pseudo-op, and a comments field for programmer comments.

Labels may be up to six characters long and any alphanumeric combination (starting with an alphabetic character) except A, B, and X (A, B, and X refer to hardware registers). Operands consist of the 72 mne-

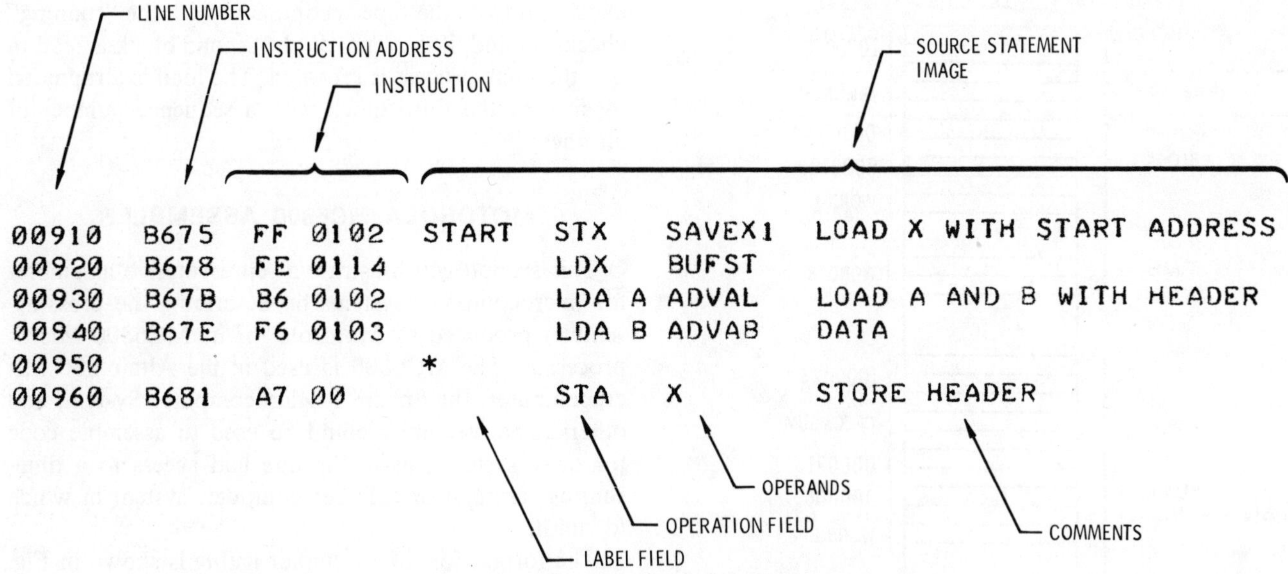

Fig. 4-10. Motorola MC6800 assembler listing.

monics corresponding to instructions, or 12 pseudo-ops shown in Tables 4-4 and 4-5. Operands are made up of numeric values, labels, or expressions such as "START +END." (Most assemblers provide some limited operations for expressions such as addition(+), subtraction (−), multiplication(*), or division(/) so that operand fields might contain such things as "END-START," "NUMBER/2," or "SIZE*2.") If the value in the operand field is numeric, hexadecimal, octal, binary, or ASCII, data may be defined by use of $, @, %, or ., respectively. For example, $100, @100, %100 represent 100_{16}, 100_8, and 100_2, respectively, and .A repre-

Table 4-4. Motorola MC6800 Instruction Mnemonics

Add	ADDA	Incre-	INC	Store	STAA	Jump	BRA
	ADDB	ment	INCA		STAB		BCC
	ABA		INCB	Subtract	SUBA		BCS
	ADCA	Load	LDAA		SUBB		BEQ
	ADCB		LDAB		SBA		BGE
AND	ANDA	OR	ORAA		SBCA		BGT
	ANDB		ORAB		SBCB		BHI
Bit	BITA	Push	PSHA	Trans-	TAB		BLE
Test	BITB		PSHB	fer	TBA		BLS
Clear	CLR	Pull	PULA	Test	TST		BLT
	CLRA		PULB		TSTA		BMI
	CLRB	Rotate	ROL		TSTB		BNE
Compare	CMPA		ROLA	Stack	CPX		BVC
	CMPB		ROLB		DEX		BVS
	CBA		ROR		DES		BPL
Comple-	COM		RORA		INX		BSR
ment	COMA		RORB		INS		JMP
	COMB	Shift	ASL		LDX		JSR
	NEG		ASLA		LDS		NOP
	NEGA		ASLB		STX		RTI
	NEBG		ASR		STS		RTS
Decimal	DAA		ASRA		TXS		SWI
Decre-	DEC		ASRB		TSX		WAI
ment	DECA		LSR			CC	CLC
	DECB		LSRA				CLI
XOR	EORA		LSRB				CLV
	EORB						SEC
							SEI
							SEV
							TAP
							TPA

Table 4-5. Motorola MC6800 Cross-Assembler Pseudo-Ops

Pseudo-Op	Description
ORG	Assign program origin
EQU	Equate a symbol
FCB	Form constant byte
FCC	Form constant characters
FDB	Form double constant byte
RMB	Reserve memory bytes
END	Define end of source program
MON	Return to console
NAM	Name the program
OPT	Assembler options
PAGE	Top of form
SPC	Vertical spacing

sents 1000001_2, the ASCII representation of the letter *A*. A decimal value has no prefix. Another special prefix is a # (pound sign) representing the immediate mode of addressing where the data are held in the instruction itself. If, for example, accumulator A is to be loaded with 25_{10}, the immediate instruction LDA A #25 would generate the instruction $861E_{16}$ where $25_{10} = 19_{16}$, and the data can be said to be in the instruction word itself, or "immediate." The complete hardware and instruction set of the MC6800 are covered in Chapter 8, so let's go on with the pseudo-op functions.

The first pseudo-op is always required and is our old friend "END," marking the end of the source program. The "EQU" pseudo-op stands for "*EQU*ate" and assigns a value to a symbol. It is a common pseudo-op in almost all assemblers. If, somewhere in our program, we had the source line "A EQU 123" and later an "LDAA #A" was used, the "LDAA #A" would be identical to an "LDAA #123." Equates are useful for assigning symbols to numeric values, which are difficult to remember. ("SPACE" makes much more sense than 00100000_2, for example.) The "FCB," or "*F*orm *C*onstant *B*yte," pseudo-op generates a byte of data for each operand in its operand field. A source statement of "SYMBOL FCB 3,5,16" would generate three bytes of data of 0003, 0005, and 0010 (hexadecimal), which would be listed in column 3 of the listing; the program counter would then be advanced by 3. The "FCC," or "*F*orm *C*onstant *C*haracters," pseudo-op assembler directive would do the same thing, only with character data. The source statement of "SYMBOL FCC THIS IS A MESSAGE" would generate 17 bytes corresponding to the ASCII characters THISbISbAbMESSAGE, where "b" stands for blank or space characters. Obviously, FCC is useful for generating messages that could be output from the program.

The pseudo-op "FDB," "*F*orm *D*ouble Constant *B*yte," is similar to the FCB directive, but a 16-bit value (two bytes) is generated for each operand and the program counter is advanced by two times the number of operands. A source statement of "SYMBOL FDB 1234, 567" would generate four bytes as follows: 04, D2, 02, 37 (hexadecimal). Taken together, the first two equal 1234_{10} and the next two equal 0237_{10}. Pseudo-op FDB is useful for generating data values larger than eight bits when data must be greater than 255_{10}. (The largest value in eight bits is 255_{10}.) The "MON" pseudo-op is a special one for the Motorola system and returns control to the system monitor. The "NAM" pseudo-op allows the user to "*NAM*e" his program. This name will then be printed out at the top of each page of the listing. The "OPT" pseudo-op is another special command unique to this assembler; it allows the user to define the assembler output options such as long format listing, suppression of error messages, and the like. The "ORG" pseudo-op is identical with ".LOC" of our SIMP assembler. It defines the address at which the program counter is to be set. If no ORG appears, the assembler assumes that the program is to be assembled starting at location 0.

"PAGE" advances the assembler to the top of the next page. A PAGE pseudo-op is useful for appearance's sake in long listings where a user might want to put each "routine" on a separate page or all data constants on one page. An "RMB," or "*R*eserve *M*emory *B*ytes," is somewhat similar to the ORG directive in that the program counter is "bumped" by the number of bytes specified in the operand field. If, for example, a source line of "LIST RMB 30" was input, the program counter would be advanced by 30. The RMB is used to set aside "blocks" of memory which may be used during execution of the program as tables or other types of working storage. The last pseudo-op is the "SPC" directive, or "*SP*a*C*e Lines," which causes a number of lines to be skipped. The number is contained in the operand field. Here again, as in the case of the PAGE, the SPC enables the user to control the output format of the listing.

The object output of the assembler described above can be a paper tape with an object code as described earlier. In this case, the resultant object code is even less sophisticated than the object format described for our SIMP system.

HIGHER-LEVEL LANGUAGES

Assembly language was quite an improvement over the machine language hand-translation process. At best, however, assembly language is still quite a chore. To write a 1000-step program requires writing at least 1000 source statements, assembling the program, executing the program, detecting errors in the program during execution (no, Virginia, not too many programs run the very first time), reassembling the program after changes, and so forth. An easier, more efficient way to code programs was sought. Instead of writing virtually at the "machine level," wasn't it possible to write in something that was closer to English? One of the first "higher-level" languages was FORTRAN (*FOR*mula *TRAN*slator), written by IBM in 1956. Now instead of a programmer having to "LDA O,CONST" (Load accumulator with the contents of a location called "CONST"), he could write "A=CONST" and accomplish the same thing, or more. Furthermore, it was more than a one-for-one translation. In place of possibly one hundred instructions in assembly language, the programmer could now write "C=SQRT(A**2−B**2)," corresponding to $C = \sqrt{A^2 - B^2}$. Naturally those 100 instructions would be used, but the "compiler" program would compile (as opposed to assemble) them automatically. Other compilers for other higher-level languages appeared over the years—COBOL for business applications (*CO*mmon *B*usiness *O*riented *L*anguage), PL/1 (*P*rogramming *L*anguage 1), and BASIC (*B*eginner's *A*ll-Purpose *S*ymbolic *I*nstruction *C*ode), to mention a few. All of these had one thing in common: They freed the programmer from writing code at almost a machine language level. Naturally, since one seldom gets something for nothing, the user of a higher-level language pays in two areas.

Programs executed from a higher-level language run more slowly than their pure assembly-language coded counterparts, due to some redundancy in compiled instructions and system overhead. The programs generally take up more memory space than a comparable pure assembly-language coded program. Except for specialized systems where speed of operation is important (real-time control, for example), a higher-level language is an extremely good way to program. In the general case, a programmer using BASIC can write and "debug" a program many times faster than one using assembly language; the difference in execution speeds of the resulting program would probably not be noticeable, especially if the system being used relies on Teletype for input and output operations. Most of the time the program will be "waiting" on the Teletype to finish with the last character—it would be "I/O bound." Since BASIC is a common language at present, and since it is offered with most microcomputer systems such as the Altair 8800, let's look at the BASIC language and how it operates, then examine FORTRAN briefly. These languages are usually offered in most of the minicomputer systems.

BASIC Language

The original BASIC language was developed at Dartmouth College. BASIC, as the name implies, is indeed one of the easiest languages to learn and use. BASIC programs are made up of numbered statements, numbered consecutively between 1 and 9999. Numbers may be skipped, but the number of each new statement must be greater than the last. An example of a BASIC program is given in Fig. 4-11 and duplicates the first program on our SIMP computer to add the numbers from 0 to 100. This program sets a value called "A" to 0 in statement 100. Statements 120 through 140 define a loop to add the numbers. Statement 140 is the same as a "jump if" instruction to jump back to the start of the loop if I is less than the value of 102. If I is 102, then statement 150 is executed to output or print the value of A. The loop will be executed 101 times. Since the value of I will vary from 1 to 101, the value of (I−1) will vary from 0 to 100 and A will vary as follows: 0, 1, 3, 6, ...

```
100  LET A= 0
120  FOR I=1 TO 101
130     LET A=A+(I-1)
140  NEXT I
150  PRINT A
160  END
```

Fig. 4-11. BASIC program number 1.

There are 17 BASIC statement types shown in Table 4-6. Not all of them would have to be used in every program, of course.

The first statement type is an END statement. A program must be terminated by an END, just as an assembly source input was terminated by an END pseudo-op. A STOP statement halts execution of a program at some point. Depending upon the system, a message similar to "STOP AT XXXX" will be printed out for a STOP, where XXXX is the statement number. The program can then be resumed by typing a "run" command of some type. STOP is used to alert the user of some error or abnormal condition such as invalid input

Table 4-6. BASIC Statement Types

Statement	Description
END	Terminates source input
STOP	Stops program execution
LET	Assigns a value to a variable
DATA	Defines block of data
READ	Reads from block of data
RESTORE	Resets data block pointer
GOTO	Transfers control
IF-THEN	Conditionally transfers control
FOR	Sets up a loop
NEXT	Defines end of loop
DIM	Allocates space for an array
REM	Defines remark or comment
GOSUB	Transfers control to subroutine
RETURN	Returns control to calling program
DEF	Defines a function
INPUT	Enables input of variables
PRINT	Enables printing of variables and text

data, or it might be used in program debugging to let the user know he has executed the program down to a certain point. Note that the END and STOP are completely different in function: STOP is a "dynamic" command used while executing the program, and END simply marks the end of the program.

We have seen an example of the LET command in the sample program. LET assigns a value to a variable. Variable names are either a single letter from *A* through *Z* or a single letter followed by a single digit, such as A5, Z2. In our example, we set variable A equal to 0 by "LET A=0." The second time a LET statement was used, A was set to "A+(I−1)," an expression. In an expression, BASIC can indicate addition by the use of a plus (+) sign. For example, "LET G=A+3" sets variable G to the value of A plus 3. A minus (−) sign enables subtraction in the same manner. "Let Z2=Z1−C" sets variable Z2 to the difference of Z1−C. Multiplication is designated by an asterisk (*). "LET H=Z1*Z2" sets variable H equal to the product of Z1 and Z2. Division is designated by a slash (/). "LET A=1/Z" sets variable A to the reciprocal of Z or one divided by the value of Z. The last "operator" is an up arrow (↑). (Yes, there is an up arrow on a Teletype, or if it isn't marked on a key, it should be–it's the "shift" N key.) The statement "LET A=B↑2" sets variable A to the value of B squared. "LET Z1=Z2↑3" sets Z1 equal to Z2 cubed. Note that variables raised to a noninteger power are also valid. "LET Z1=Z2↑1.2" is quite all right, and if the expression worries you, forget it—you'll probably never use a similar expression.

Now that you know the arithmetic operators +, −, *, /, and ↑, let's look at some expressions. "LET A=B*2+I/3" uses multiplication, addition, and division. Wait a minute, though. Do we want to divide B*2+I by 3, or divide I by 3? There is an order of precedence in such an expression. The order is shown in Table 4-7. Using these rules, B would be multiplied by 2, I would be divided by 3, and then the two answers would be added. If the order of precedence confuses you, use parentheses. Expressions within parentheses are always evaluated first; so, that eliminates ambiguities within a long expression. "LET A=(B*2+I)/3" results in the expression (B*2+I) being evaluated first, and the result is then divided by 3. Note that more than one level of parentheses may be used. "LET A=(((B*2+1)))/3" is perfectly valid (but a little stupid), and "LET Z1=((Z1/2)*3)+4" results in Z1/2 being multiplied by 3 and this result being added to 4 to define a new Z1.

Table 4-7. BASIC Expression Evaluation Priority

Order	Description
1	Move through expression from left to right
2	Evaluate innermost parentheses
3	Perform all exponentiation
4	Perform all multiplication and division
5	Perform all addition and subtraction
6	Go to next innermost parentheses and repeat 3 through 6 until done

The DATA statement of Table 4-6 does what the name implies. It defines a block of data. The statement "100 DATA 2.3,5.6,3,5,−2" defines a single block of data with the value of 2.3, 5.6, 3, 5, and −2 in that order. More than one DATA statement defines more data for that *single* data block. If we have three DATA statements at three separate locations as shown in Fig. 4-12, the resulting data block would have the values shown. Normally, DATA statements would appear at the beginning of the program and would be consecutive statements.

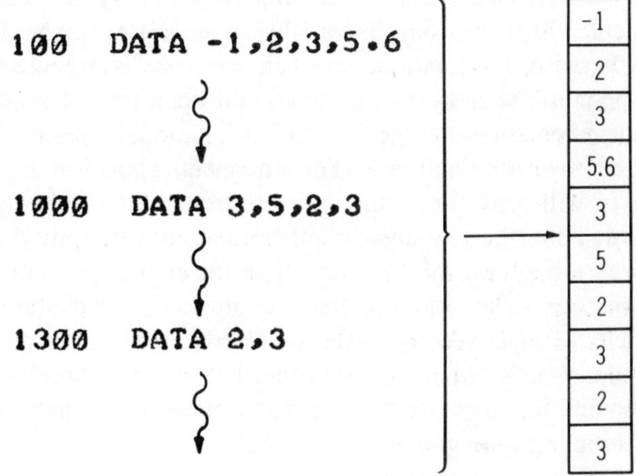

Fig. 4-12. DATA example.

The READ and RESTORE statements are closely aligned with the DATA statement. The READ statement "reads" data from the data block. For example, "1400 READ X,Y,Z" in Fig. 4-12 would set X, Y, and Z equal to −1, 2, and 3, respectively. Each successive READ statement reads the next value from the data block. The data block may be thought of as having a pointer that is "bumped" by a one each time a value is READ. After being bumped, the pointer points to the next value. It is possible to READ beyond the end of the block. The statements in Fig. 4-13 do that. There are three data items and six reads. In this case, the system will print an "out of data" message during program execution. The data block pointer may be reset with a RESTORE statement. The statements in Fig. 4-14 result in the pointer being reset after two reads. No "out of data" message would result.

```
100 DATA 0,0,1,5.6
200 READ X,Y
300 READ Z1,Z2,Z3,Z4
```

Fig. 4-13. Out of data example.

```
100  DATA  0,0,1,5.6
200  READ  X,Y
250  RESTORE
300  READ  Z1,Z2,Z3,Z4
```

Fig. 4-14. RESTORE example.

The GOTO statement is similar to a jump or "branch" instruction in assembly language. It unconditionally transfers control to another statement. The statement "200 GOTO 300" would result in a jump over statements 220 through 260 in the example of Fig. 4-15.

The IF-THEN statement is another way to alter the sequence of instructions in a BASIC program. It is similar to a conditional jump in assembly language. The IF-THEN is sometimes expressed as IF-GOTO. The two statements are identical. The statement "100 IF A=B THEN 200" causes a jump (or GOTO) to statement 200 if and only if variable A equals variable B. Otherwise, the next statement in sequence is executed. The equal sign (=) is a "relational operator" relating one expression to another. Other relational operators are shown in Table 4-8. The statements shown in Fig. 4-16 will result in all the numbers from 0 to 100 being added together, a slightly different approach from the program of Fig. 4-11. Note that the two expressions compared may be just that—expressions. The statement "100 IF(A−1)=(B+2) THEN 200" is permissible. Watch out for expressions that are too complex, though, for the system in use may not be able to handle a long string of items.

Table 4-8. IF-THEN Relational Operators

Operator	Meaning	Use
<	Less than	M<N
<=	Less than or Equal to	M<=N
=	Equal to	M=N
>	Greater than	M>N
>=	Greater than or Equal to	M>=N
<>	Not Equal to	M<>N

The example of Fig. 4-16 uses a loop from statement 130 through 160. Another way of implementing a loop is with the FOR statement. We saw the use of this in Fig. 4-11. The FOR statement is of the form "FOR X=START TO END STEP INCREMENT," defining a starting value, an ending value, and an increment. The statement "120 FOR I=1 TO 101 STEP 1" is identical

```
100  LET A= 0
120  LET B= 0
130  IF B=101  GOTO  180
140  LET A=A+B
150  LET B=B+1
160  GOTO  130
180  PRINT A
200  END
```

Fig. 4-16. BASIC program number 2.

to "120 FOR I=1 TO 101"; the STEP is used only if the increment is something other than a value of 1. "120 FOR I=2 TO 102 STEP 2" would result in values of I = 2, 4, 6, 8, . . . , 102. Let's use that example to add all even numbers from 2 to 102. This is shown in Fig. 4-17. The NEXT statement simply takes the program back to statement 120 for the next increment of I. Note that in the FOR statement the start and end expressions may again be exactly that—simple expressions. The statement "FOR I=(A−1) TO (B+100) STEP 2" would probably be valid. Why probably? Well, under certain conditions the loop might never end. If a loop is defined by "FOR I=2 to 100 STEP 3," there is some question about the outcome, because the value

```
100  LET A= 0
120  FOR I=2 TO 102 STEP 2
130    LET A=A+I
140  NEXT I
150  PRINT A
160  END
```

Fig. 4-17. BASIC program number 3.

of 100 is never matched, only I = 98 and 101. The FOR statement is a powerful statement because it enables "nested" loops. The nesting may be generally done to four levels. A four-level nested loop is shown in Fig. 4-18. The lines defining the loops do not cross. The NEXT statement for the last "FOR VARIABLE" must be encountered before a NEXT statement for another variable. Fig. 4-19 shows an example of incorrectly nested loops.

The DIM (*DIM*ension) statement is a statement similar to the DATA statement in that it is "nonexecutable." Instead of defining data, however, the DIM statement defines the places *for* the data. The data are filled in by other statements in the program. One- and two-dimensional arrays may be reserved by the DIM state-

```
200  GOTO  300
220  READ X,Y
240  PRINT X,Y
260  GOTO  400
300  PRINT "THIS IS A GOTO EXAMPLE"
```

Fig. 4-15. GOTO example.

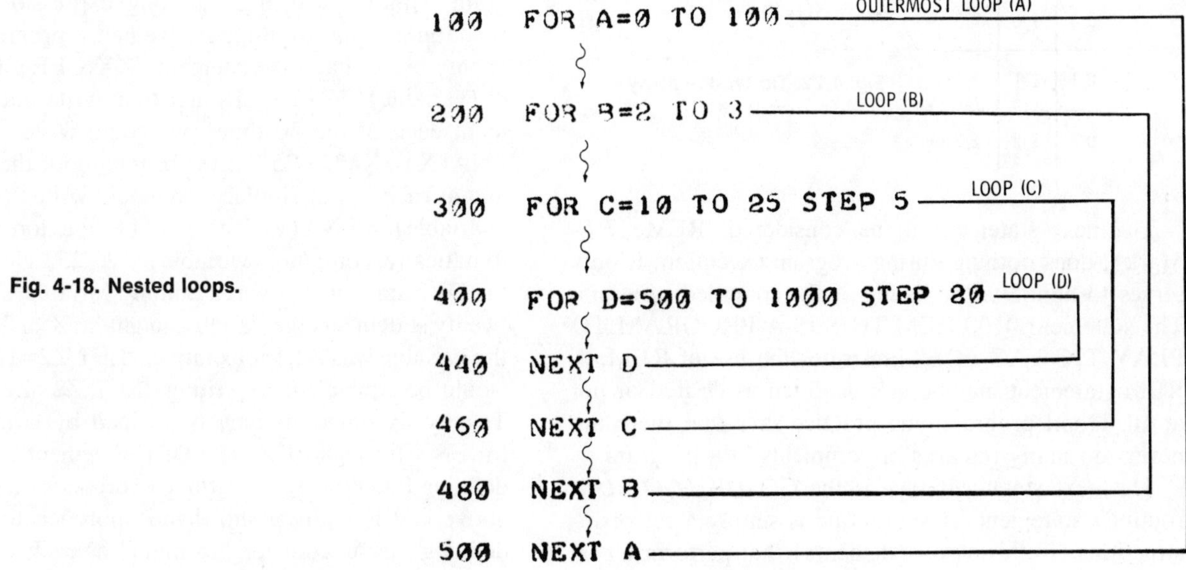

Fig. 4-18. Nested loops.

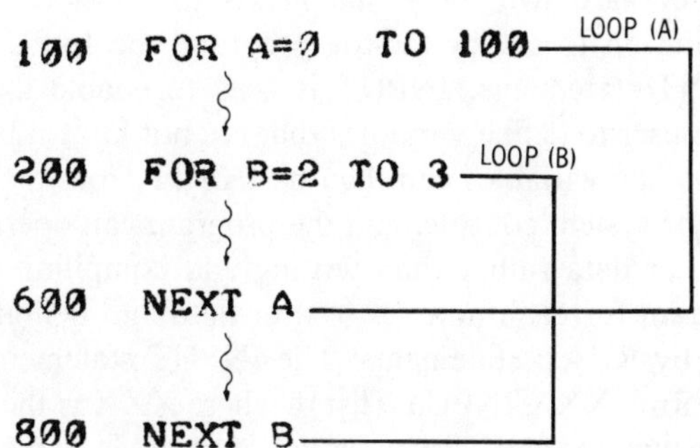

Fig. 4-19. Incorrectly nested loops.

ment. A one-dimensional array is nothing more than a list of items. The statement "10 DIM A(4) simply reserves five "elements" for a list of items called A, as shown in Fig. 4-20. (The first element is numbered 0.) The five elements are not filled in as of yet. To reference the elements of this one-dimensional array, parentheses and a number are used, the number representing the number of the item from the start of the array. The statement "100 LET A(2)=3," for example, stores a 3 into the third element of the array. The statement "200 LET B=A(2)" sets B equal to the contents of the third element of array A.

Two-dimensional arrays are a little harder to visualize. Fig. 4-21 shows a two-dimensional array named Z2. The array is a 4 by 9 array and may be thought of as a

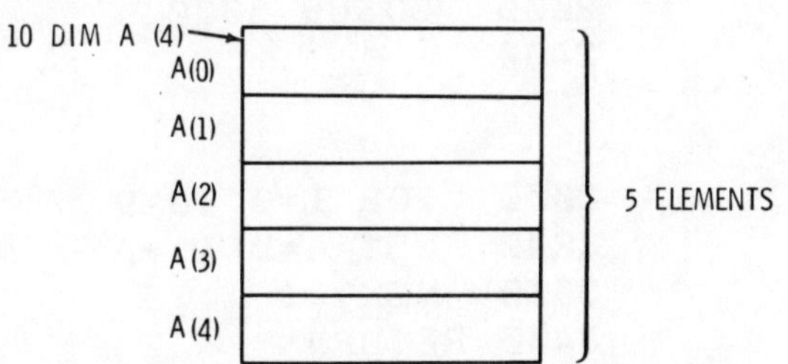

Fig. 4-20. DIM Allocation, one-dimensional.

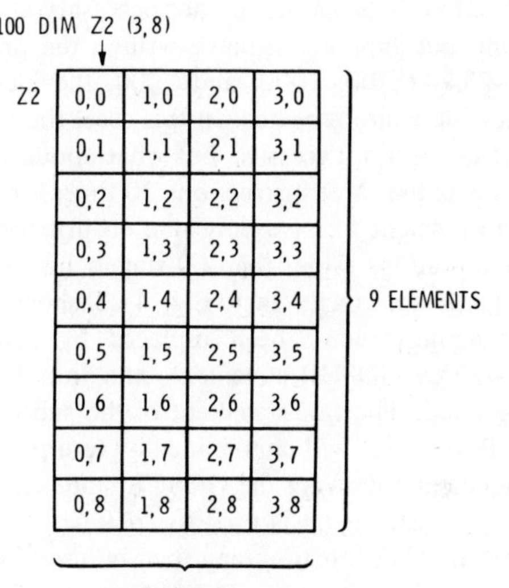

Fig. 4-21. Two-dimensional array.

rectangular "matrix." The total number of elements is $4 \times 9 = 36$. To address any element, parentheses and two values are used. The statement "100 let A=Z2 (1,5)" sets variable A to the value found in the (1,5)th element of the array. By the way, note that arrays may be and usually are addressed by variables such as in "100 LET A=Z2(I,J)" where I and J define the horizontal and vertical elements of array Z2. As an example of the use of arrays, let's define an array for a tic-tac-toe game (we'll end the discussion of BASIC with a program to *play* tic-tac-toe as a reward for sitting through all of this). Tic-tac-toe is played with nine squares as shown in Fig. 4-22. We have a choice of a nine-element one-dimensional array or a 3×3 two-dimensional array. We'll choose the 3×3 and define it by "100 DIM S(2,2)," where S is the name of the array. The center square of the tic-tac-toe matrix can now be referenced by S(1,1).

S

0,0	1,0	2,0
0,1	1,1	2,1
0,2	1,2	2,2

Fig. 4-22. Tic-tac-toe array.

The next statement to be considered, REM (*RE*-*M*ark), does nothing during program execution; it only serves to annotate the listing of the compiled program. The statement "100 REM THIS IS A PROGRAM TO PLAY TIC-TAC-TOE" illustrates the use of REM. A REM statement may be used as often as desired or not at all. Good programming practice says that there are never too many remarks or comments in a program.

The next statement type is the GOSUB (*GO SUB*-routine) statement. A subroutine is simply a set of instructions (in this case, statements) that perform a certain function. Subroutines are not necessary at all in any program, but suppose we have written the program in Fig. 4-23. At 700, 1000, and 2000, the identical instruction steps are repeated. In this case, the number of statements are not excessive, but what about a program that repeats the three instructions 20 times? Wouldn't it be more efficient to have only one occurrence of those three instructions rather than 60 statements? A subroutine lets us do exactly that. Fig. 4-23 shows how the nine statements have been replaced by seven statements—three GOSUB statements and four in the subroutine itself. The last statement of the subroutine is a RETURN which will automatically return control to the statement following the GOSUB statement.

The DEF statement is used to *DEF*ine a function in a program. That function may then be used in the program without rewriting the long expression that the function is equal to. Suppose we had a program that at twenty places had the statement "XXX LET (variable) = (variable)**2+25." Rather than write out the statement each of the 20 times, we could write "100 DEF FNA(X)=X**2+25" at the beginning of the program, and at each of the 20 places we could write "XXX LET (variable) = FNA(variable)." The function would automatically compute (variable)**2+25. Note that in the DEF statement X was a dummy variable, since in the twenty statements the variable might be X or Y or Z1. If the variable was Z2, for example, "LET Z2=FNA(Z2)" would be equivalent to writing "LET Z2=Z2**2+25." Twenty-six functions may be defined by writing DEFs for FN*A* through FN*Z*. The DEF statement is useful for defining functions for repetitive expressions like the one above and is really a shorthand approach to explicitly defining the function or "formula" at each occurrence.

There are two more statements to consider before moving on to the tic-tac-toe program, the INPUT and PRINT statements. INPUT is used to enable the program user to define variables that are not known beforehand. The variables can then be INPUT from the Teletype or system console, and the program can operate on the user data rather than writing and compiling a new program for each new set of user data and defining the data by READ statements. The INPUT statement is of the form "XXX INPUT (list)" where XXX is the statement number and (list) is a list of variable names. For example, "100 INPUT X,Y,Z" would provide for an input of three variables, X, Y, and Z. When the program was executed, the system would probably type the "prompt" character (?) when the statement was encountered, and wait for the user to type three data

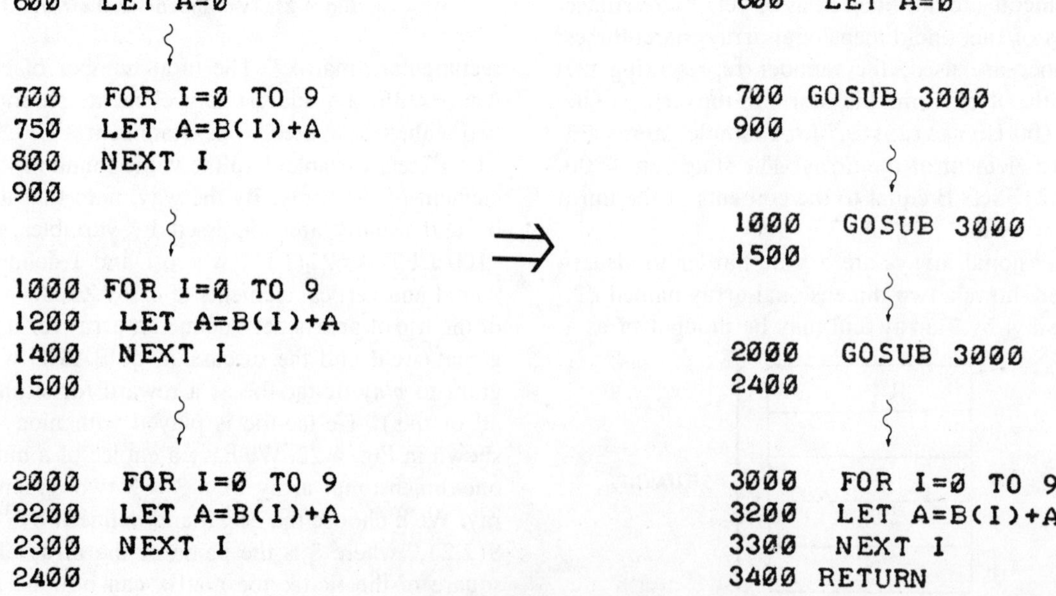

```
600   LET A=0
        ⁝
700   FOR I=0 TO 9
750   LET A=B(I)+A
800   NEXT I
900
        ⁝
1000  FOR I=0 TO 9
1200  LET A=B(I)+A
1400  NEXT I
1500
        ⁝
2000  FOR I=0 TO 9
2200  LET A=B(I)+A
2300  NEXT I
2400
```

⇒

```
600   LET A=0
700   GOSUB 3000
900
        ⁝
1000  GOSUB 3000
1500
        ⁝
2000  GOSUB 3000
2400
        ⁝
3000  FOR I=0 TO 9
3200  LET A=B(I)+A
3300  NEXT I
3400  RETURN
```

Fig. 4-23. Subroutine use.

```
100  REM  PROGRAM TO ADD ALL NUMBERS FROM A TO B
120  LET T= 0
140  PRINT "INPUT A,B"
150  INPUT A,B
155  IF A<> 0 GOTO  160
157  LET A=1
160  FOR I=A TO B
170     LET T=T+I
180  NEXT I
190  PRINT T
200  END
```

Fig. 4-24. BASIC program number 4.

items. The user would then type the three values, separated by commas, for example, 3.5, 4, 9.4. Naturally, the user must not type too many values or too few, or the system will respond with the appropriate error message. As an example of the INPUT statement, let's look at a program to add the numbers from A to B where A and B are user-defined (see Fig. 4-24). The message "INPUT A,B" is printed out and the system then types "?." The user would reply with two values and execution would then continue with the total (T) being printed after the termination of the addition loop (160-180).

We have been using the PRINT statement all through this discussion of BASIC. By now it is obvious that a statement such as "100 PRINT "ANSWER" " will print the text "ANSWER" and the statement "200 PRINT X" will print the value of X. If X is an integer or contains six digits or less, it will be printed in the form 12345.67, preceded by a minus sign if the number is negative. A real or integer number that requires more than six digits (dependent upon the system) will be printed out in "exponential" form. This is somewhat similar to scientific notation. In scientific notation, a very large or very small number may be represented by a number between 1 and 10, multiplied by a power of 10. (See Table 4-9.) In exponential notation, the "E" replaces 10 and the number that follows represents the power of ten. In scientific calculations, this representation automatically keeps track of the decimal point. In the computer case, it eliminates printing long numbers like .000000123 or 1,234,777,000,000. (Most BASIC systems can hold only six decimal digits anyway, so "significance" beyond that is lost. The number 1,234, 567,891 becomes 1,234,570,000.)

The PRINT statement allows more than one variable to be printed. A "100 PRINT A,B,C,D" prints the values of the variables A, B, C, and D. Text may be interspersed with the variables as in "250 PRINT "VALUE OF A IS: ,"A, "VALUE OF B IS: ,"B," in which case the line printed will be "VALUE OF A IS:," followed by the value of variable A, followed by "VALUE OF B IS:," followed by the value of variable B. The list may be not only variables, but also expressions. For A = 2,

Table 4-9. Scientific and Exponential Notation

Number	Scientific	BASIC Form
1	1×10^{0}	1
.0234	2.34×10^{-2}	.0234
−.00045	-4.5×10^{-4}	−.00045
23456	2.3456×10^{4}	23456
−123,456,789	$-1.23456789 \times 10^{8}$	−1.23457E + 8
1,000,000,000,000,000	1.0×10^{15}	1E + 15
.0000000345	3.45×10^{-8}	3.45E − 8

the statement "300 PRINT A,A↑2,A↑3" prints "2 4 8." The PRINT statement in addition gives the user some format control capability. If the items in the list to be printed are separated by commas, each item will be printed at a predefined "tab" position. If the items are separated by semicolons, only a single space will be printed between items. The statement "400 PRINT A;B;C" prints "AAAA BBBB CCCC," for example. If the last item of the list has no semicolon or comma, the next PRINT will print on the next line. If the last item of the list has a semicolon or comma after it, line spacing is not done.

There is one more group of items that most BASIC systems provide: standard functions. Certain mathematical functions may be "precanned" and available to the user. The statement "200 LET Y=SIN(X)" uses one of these, the sine function. Other available functions are given in Table 4-10.

Table 4-10. BASIC Functions

Function	Description
SIN(X)	Sine of *x*, *x* in radians
COS(X)	Cosine of *x*, *x* in radians
TAN(X)	Tangent of *x*, *x* in radians
ATN(X)	Arctangent of *x*, *x* in radians
LOG(X)	Natural logarithm of *x*
EXP(X)	e^{x}
SQR(X)	Square root of *x*
ABS(X)	Absolute value of *x*
INT(X)	Greatest integer not larger than *x*
RND(X)	Random *x* between 0 and 1
SGN(X)	Algebraic sign of *x*

BASIC is usually supplied in two forms with a minicomputer system. The first is an "interpretive" BASIC. The user enters statements and is prompted by the system. If he makes an error, the system tells him as he is entering the statement. He can then retype the statement. At any time the user can run the program, stop execution, or list the program from the keyboard. This type of system is highly interactive as far as communication between system and user, and it is ideal for running most BASIC programs. The second type of BASIC is one in which the user must "compile" the program, load the object code, and execute. Although this is faster in execution than an interpretive BASIC, it is much more time-consuming for program preparation.

Now that we have looked at BASIC statements, let's look at a tic-tac-toe program. Fig. 4-25 shows an actual sample execution of such a program. The "*READY" indicates that the interpretive BASIC control program is waiting for the next command. The "RUN" is supplied by the user and starts execution of the program, which has already been loaded into the computer. After the "RUN," all printed output is generated as a result of program execution. The first item printed is the title, "TIC-TAC-TOE." The next item printed is the tic-tac-toe matrix with the identifiers for the nine squares. The next line is "CHOOSE X." After printing this, the program waits (via an INPUT statement) for the user to choose any square that has not been used. The first chosen was square 1. An "X" for the user was put into square 1, and the program put a "0" into its choice, the center square. The matrix was then printed. After printing, the prompt line "CHOOSE X" was printed again and the sequence repeated. This time the user chose square 4 and the machine blocked with a choice of square 7. The next move found the user rashly choosing square 8. The program replied with square 3 and printed out a rather unsporting message along with the final matrix. The game is then started again (not shown).

The program for tic-tac-toe is shown in Fig. 4-26. It is not represented to be the most efficient tic-tac-toe program in existence, but is simply a sample of what can be done in a short program. As a matter of fact, the program can sometimes be beaten. The program starts at statement 5. The first part, part A, clears a nine-element matrix (one-dimensional) to all zeros (statements 15–40) and then prints out the matrix numbers by statements 60–100.

Statements 102–170 (part B) find the user's first choice. Subroutine 1000 returns to statement 120 the user's choice in variable A. If the user has chosen the center square (5), A=5 and the program goes to 145 to choose either square 1 (S0) if square 1 is free or square 3 (S2) if square 1 is already used. If the user has not chosen the center square, statements 130 and 140

```
* READY
RUN
TIC-TAC-TØE
MATRIX:  1 * 2 * 3
        ***********
          4 * 5 * 6
        ***********
          7 * 8 * 9

CHØØSE X
? 1
 X *   *
***********
   * 0 *
***********
   *   *

CHØØSE X
? 4
 X *   *
***********
 X * 0 *
***********
 0 *   *

CHØØSE X
? 8
I WIN! HA! HA! HA!

 X *   * 0
***********
 X * 0 *
***********
 0 * X *
```

Fig. 4-25. Tic-tac-toe program output.

are executed and the program puts a "0" in the center. Note that squares 1 through 9 correspond to S0 through S8, respectively, and that no X or 0 has a value of 0: an X is 1, and a 0 is 7. At 160 the matrix with a 0 and X is printed by subroutine 2000. The subroutine returns to statement 180.

Part C, statements 180 through 610, is the "main loop" of the program. The sequence of steps to be followed is:

1. Get user input (180–200).
2. Test whether user has won. If so, print a message and restart (210–270).
3. Test if any squares remain unfilled. If not, it's a draw—print message and restart (271–279).
4. Test if user has two squares in any row, column, or diagonal. If so, put a "0" in unused square and then test for a computer win. If computer has won, print message and restart (280–340).

```
5   REM TIC-TAC-TØE PRØGRAM
10  DIM S[8]
15  REM CLEAR SQUARES
20  FØR I= 0 TØ 8
30    LET S[I]= 0
40  NEXT I
50  PRINT "TIC-TAC-TØE"
60  PRINT "MATRIX:  1 * 2 * 3"
70  PRINT "         ***********"
80  PRINT "          4 * 5 * 6"
90  PRINT "         ***********"
100  PRINT "          7 * 8 * 9"                PART A
------------------------------------------------------------
102  REM FIND USER CHØICE
110  GØSUB  1000
120  IF A=5 GØTØ  145
130  LET S[4]=7
140  GØTØ  160
145  IF S[ 0]<> 0 GØTØ  158
150  LET S[ 0]=7
155  GØTØ  160
158  LET S[2]=7
160  REM PRINT MATRIX
170  GØSUB  2000                              PART B
------------------------------------------------------------
180  REM MAIN LØØP
190  REM GET USER INPUT
200  GØSUB  1000
210  REM TEST USER WIN
220  GØSUB  4000
230  IF R<> 0 GØTØ  271
235  PRINT
240  PRINT "YØU WIN, YØU CHEAT!"
250  REM PRINT MATRIX                         PART C
260  GØSUB  2000
270  GØTØ  15
271  LET A= 0
272  FØR I= 0 TØ 8
273    IF S[I]<> 0 GØTØ  275
274    LET A=1
275  NEXT I
276  IF A=1 GØTØ  280
277  PRINT
278  PRINT "DRAW"
279  GØTØ  250
280  IF R<>2 GØTØ  380
290  LET S[B]=7
300  REM TEST MACHINE WIN
310  GØSUB  4000
320  IF R<>1 GØTØ  350
330  PRINT
335  PRINT "I WIN! HA! HA! HA!"
340  GØTØ  250
350  REM PRINT MATRIX
360  GØSUB  2000
370  GØTØ  190
```

Fig. 4-26. BASIC program number 5 tic-tac-toe.

```
380  IF R<>3 GØTØ  410
390  LET S[B]=7
400  GØTØ  330
410  IF S[4]<> 0 GØTØ  440
420  LET S[4]=7
430  GØTØ  350
440  IF S[ 0]<> 0 GØTØ  470
450  LET S[ 0]=7
460  GØTØ  350
470  IF S[2]<> 0 GØTØ  500
480  LET S[2]=7
490  GØTØ  350
500  IF S[6]<> 0 GØTØ  530
510  LET S[6]=7
520  GØTØ  350
530  IF S[8]<> 0 GØTØ  560
540  LET S[8]=7
550  GØTØ  350
560  LET I=1
570  IF S[I]<> 0 GØTØ  600
580  LET S[I]=7
590  GØTØ  350
600  LET I=I+2
610  GØTØ  570
```

SUBROUTINE 1000

```
1000  REM RØUTINE TØ READ USER INPUT
1010  PRINT
1020  PRINT "CHØØSE X"
1030  INPUT A
1040  IF S[A-1]= 0 GØTØ  1080
1050  PRINT
1060  PRINT "HUH?"
1070  GØTØ  1020
1080  LET S[A-1]=1
1090  RETURN
```

SUBROUTINE 2000

```
2000  REM RØUTINE TØ PRINT MATRIX
2010  PRINT
2020  FØR I= 0 TØ 6 STEP 3
2030    FØR J= 0 TØ 2
2040      LET K=I+J
2050      LET B=S[K]
2060      IF B<> 0 GØTØ  2090
2070      PRINT "   ";
2080      GØTØ  2130
2090      IF B<>1 GØTØ  2120
2100      PRINT " X ";
2110      GØTØ  2130
2120      PRINT " Ø ";
2130      IF J=2 GØTØ  2150
2140      PRINT "*";
2150    NEXT J
2160    PRINT
2170    IF I=6 GØTØ  2190
2180    PRINT "***********"
2190  NEXT I
```

Fig. 4-26. BASIC program number 5 tic-tac-toe. (Cont'd.)

```
2200   RETURN
4000   REM RØUTINE TØ TEST MATRIX. ØN RETURN (R)=0 USER WINS.
4010   REM =1 MACHINE WINS.=2 USER HAS TWØ IN LINE.=3 MACHINE
4020   REM HAS TWØ IN LINE.=4 NØ LINE WITH TWØ.
4030   LET V=3
4040   GØSUB  5000
4050   IF R<>V GØTØ  4110
4070   LET R= 0
4080   RETURN
4110   LET V=21
4120   GØSUB  5000
4130   IF R<>V GØTØ  4160
4140   LET R=1
4150   RETURN
4160   LET V=14
4170   GØSUB  5000
4180   IF R<>V GØTØ  4200
4185   LET R=3
4190   RETURN
4200   LET V=2
4210   GØSUB  5000
4220   IF R<>V GØTØ  4250
4230   LET R=2
4240   RETURN
4250   LET R=4
4260   RETURN
5000   REM RØUTINE TØ TEST LINES FØR VALUE V
5005   LET F= 0
5010   LET E=2
5020   LET I=1
5030   GØSUB  6000
5040   IF R<>V GØTØ  5070
5060   RETURN
5070   LET F=3
5080   LET E=5
5085   LET I=1
5090   GØSUB  6000
5100   IF R<>V GØTØ  5110
5105   RETURN
5110   LET F=6
5120   LET E=8
5125   LET I=1
5127   GØSUB  6000
5130   IF R<>V GØTØ  5140
5135   RETURN
5140   LET F= 0
5150   LET E=6
5160   LET I=3
5170   GØSUB  6000
5180   IF R<>V GØTØ  5190
5185   RETURN
5190   LET F=1
5200   LET E=7
5205   LET I=3
```

SUBROUTINE 4000

SUBROUTINE 5000

Fig. 4-26. BASIC program number 5 tic-tac-toe. (Cont'd.)

```
5210  GØSUB  6000
5220  IF R<>V GØTØ  5230
5225  RETURN
5230  LET F=2
5240  LET E=8
5245  LET I=3
5250  GØSUB  6000
5260  IF R<>V GØTØ  5270
5265  RETURN
5270  LET F= 0
5280  LET E=8
5290  LET I=4
5300  GØSUB  6000
5310  IF R<>V GØTØ  5320
5315  RETURN
5320  LET F=2
5330  LET E=6
5340  LET I=2
5350  GØSUB  6000
5370  RETURN
-----------------------------------------------------
6000  REM RØUTINE TØ ADD LINE
6010  LET R= 0
6020  FØR J=F TØ E STEP I                         SUBROUTINE
6030     LET R=R+S[J]                                6000
6040     IF S[J]<> 0 GØTØ  6060
6050     LET B=J
6060  NEXT J
6070  RETURN
6080  END
```

Fig. 4-26. BASIC program number 5 tic-tac-toe. (Cont'd.)

5. Test if computer has two squares in line. If so, fill in the third and go to print "win" message, etc. (380–400).
6. Since neither computer nor user has taken two squares at this point, put a "0" in square 5 (center), a corner square, or an "inside" square in that order. Then go back to print the matrix and wait for the next user move (410–610).

Part C may be defined further by a description of the three subroutines, 1000, 2000, and 4000. Subroutine 1000 reads an input of 1 to 9. If the indicated square is in use, the subroutine prints "HUH?" and goes back to 1020 to ask for further input. If the square is not in use, a 1 (X) is put into it. Subroutine 2000 prints the matrix, printing an "X" for a 1, a "0" for a 7, or a blank for a 0. Subroutine 4000 tests the matrix and returns a variable R to indicate a user win (R=0), a machine win (R=1), a user line with two X's (R=2 and B= blank square number), a computer line with two 0's (R=3 and B=blank square number), or no line with two or more X's or 0's (R=4). To do this, subroutine 4000 uses two additional subroutines, 5000 and 6000. Subroutine 5000 tests any row, column, or diagonal for a specified total. The total, V, represents three X's (V=3), three 0's (V=21), two 0's (V=14), or two X's (V=2). The conditions are tested in that order. Subroutine 5000 does the actual addition for the eight possible lines and returns a total in R. Subroutine 6000 is called by subroutine 5000 to add the three squares of each of the eight possible lines (three rows, three columns, and two diagonals).

It may not be immediately obvious by glancing at the program what each routine does and how it does it, but this is a relatively complicated program. If you sit down and carefully follow each statement, you will see the flow. Record an imaginary game on paper and put down the values of each variable as you step through the program. Note that routine 5000 is not as complicated as it looks but is made up of eight calls to routine 6000, the calls representing the top line, middle line, bottom line, leftmost column, middle column, right column, left-to-right diagonal, and right-to-left diagonal, respectively. With a little bit of practice, you could be writing much more complicated programs than this.

FORTRAN and ALGOL

The two other popular languages available with some minicomputer systems (but not microcomputer systems, yet) are FORTRAN and ALGOL. The former is probably as widely used as BASIC. ALGOL, however, may sometimes be offered but does not have the large following of either BASIC or FORTRAN. For this reason, only FORTRAN will be discussed here. References to ALGOL texts are presented in Appendix F.

FORTRAN was first developed by IBM for their 704 computer and was available in 1956. There are several types of FORTRAN available for some minicomputer systems, labeled FORTRAN II, FORTRAN IV, FORTRAN V, and so on. Generally the power and flexibility of the FORTRAN package increases with the model number. FORTRAN II is a subset of FORTRAN IV, for instance. FORTRAN is usually offered as a two-pass compiler; that is, a program must be compiled and the output of the compiler must then be assembled. It is seldom offered as an interactive software package such as interactive BASIC. The following discussion of FORTRAN is meant to serve only as an introduction to the language. More detailed discussions may be found in the reference books listed in Appendix F.

A short sample program in FORTRAN is shown in Fig. 4-27. It is an example, once again, of a program to add the numbers from 0 to 100 and print out the total. In some respects, the statements are similar to BASIC. In place of "LET J=0," we have "J=0," but the meaning is the same. In place of "FOR I=1 TO 101 STEP 1," we have "DO 100 I=1,101" (all of the statements from the "DO" through the specified statement number will be performed in the loop). There is no "NEXT I" because the end of the loop has been specified by the statement number in the "DO" statement. The statement numbers do not have to be sequential as in BASIC; note the "50" after the "100" statement number. Comments are no longer "*REM*arks" but are specified by a "C" in column 1 of the source input. Probably one of the more important differences between FORTRAN and the interpretive BASIC packages is the flexibility of the I/O. The "WRITE" and "FORMAT" statements permit a great deal of general-purpose formatting and data representation. "Extended" BASIC packages, if available for a given minicomputer, however, usually offer as much in this area. The "WRITE" statement in the example states that a "write" will be done to device 3 (predefined by the user or system) according to the format of "FORMAT" statement 50 and with a list of variables as specified—variable I in this case. The "FORMAT" statement 50 specifies that the printer will first skip to the first line of the next page (1H1), then print the text "TOTAL= " and then output four digits of an integer variable called I (from the WRITE statement). A familiar "END" statement marks the end of the FORTRAN program.

Table 4-11 lists the types of FORTRAN statements. The first type of statement is an arithmetic assignment statement. These evaluate the expression on the right-hand side of the equation and store the result as the

```
C       THIS IS A SAMPLE PROGRAM
        J=0
        DO 100 I=1,101
        J=J+(I-1)
100     CONTINUE
        WRITE (3,50) I
50      FORMAT (1H1,7HTOTAL= ,I4)
        END
```

Fig. 4-27. FORTRAN program number 1.

Table 4-11. FORTRAN Statements

Type	Use	Example
arithmetic assignment	Computational	A=(I+J)*128
REAL	Defines a real number	REAL A,B
INTEGER	Defines integer number	INTEGER, A,BLK
END	Denotes end of program	END
STOP	Denotes last executable statement	STOP
PAUSE	Temporarily halts program	PAUSE 123
GOTO	Branching	GOTO 310
GOTO (n_1,n_2, . . . ,n_m)	"Computed" branching	GOTO (123,310,560,30), J
IF (A) n_1,n_2,n_3	"Computed" branching	IF (I—J) 130,140,150
DO n I=m_1,m_2,m_3	Loops	DO 125 I=1,31,5
CONTINUE	Dummy for DO	CONTINUE
DIMENSION	Defines arrays	DIMENSION A (3,5,7)
DATA	Initializes variables	DATA ANUM,BNUM/1.2,3.6/
READ (a,n) list	Read I/O	READ (3,125) AREA,SIZE
WRITE (a,n) list	Write I/O	WRITE (3,150) AREA,I,N
FORMAT	Defining output format	FORMAT (1h1,4HTEXT,I3 I3)
DOUBLE PRECISION	Defines higher-precision number	DOUBLE PRECISION SIZE,A
EQUIVALENCE (a,b), . . . ,(c,d)	Equates variables	EQUIVALENCE (ARRAY (2,3),Y)
ASSIGN i to m	Assigns statement number to variable	ASSIGN 125 TO INT
GOTO m_1	Assigned GOTO	GOTO INT

variable on the left-hand side. For example, "A=4.5" stores 4.5 into variable A. The expression "K=K+ (I*2)" multiplies the variable I by 2 and adds the value of variable K to the result. The result of that operation is stored as K. In general, unless otherwise defined by REAL or INTEGER statements, variable names beginning with I, J, K, L, M, or N are "integer" values and are held as straight binary numbers. Other variable names are treated as "real" values. "Real" here means "floating point." The important thing to remember is that integer values probably will hold only $\pm$ $32{,}767_{10}$, while real values will hold any number with some (very slight) inaccuracy in the digits. Integer variables are usually used for indexing ("DO I=1,70") or for variables that will remain small in magnitude. An arithmetic assignment statement uses arithmetic operators similar to those of BASIC. The only difference is exponentiation where the BASIC up arrow (↑) is replaced by two asterisks (**). However, the symbols +, −, *, and / still denote addition, subtraction, multiplication, and division. Parentheses may be used for clarity or to define the order of evaluation. The priorities of evaluation (left to right, exponentiation, multiplication and division, addition and subtraction) are approximately the same.

The END statement, as mentioned, denotes the end of the source input to the FORTRAN compiler. STOP is a statement that returns control to the operating system, if any. It is normally used as the last statement to be executed. A PAUSE statement causes the system to halt after typing "PAUSE XXXX," where XXXX is an optional statement number that may be specified.

The simple GOTO statement is exactly the same as a GOTO statement in BASIC. An unconditional branch is done to the statement number specified. A more complex form of the GOTO is the form "GOTO (n_1, n_2, . . . , n_m),I," where n_1 through n_m are statement numbers and I is an integer variable. If I=1, a GOTO n_1 is performed; if I=2, a GOTO n_2 is done; and so forth for I equal to succeeding integers.

The IF statement is somewhat analagous to a conditional branch. The form of the IF is "IF (A) n_1, n_2, n_3," where n_1, n_2, and n_3 are three statement numbers and A is a variable or expression. If the expression (A) is less than 0 (negative), a GOTO n_1 is performed. If (A) is equal to 0, a GOTO statement n_2 is performed. If (A) is greater than 0, a GOTO statement n_3 is done. The statement "IF (I−J) 100,150,50" would transfer control to statement 100 if I<J, to statement 150 if I=J, and to statement 50 if I>J.

The DO statement, as indicated, is similar to a BASIC FOR statement. The form is "DO n I=m_1, m_2, m_3" where m_1, m_2, and m_3 are constants or positive integer values, n is a statement number, and I is an integer variable. The statement "50 DO 105 IA=1,21,2" will execute all statements from 50 through 105 from variable IA=1 through IA=21 (10 steps of two) and then will execute the next instruction in sequence. DO statements, just like BASIC IF statements, may be nested, if the levels are nested properly and there is no crossing of boundaries. The statement following the DO loop must not be a GOTO or IF statement. If one of these two types is required, a dummy statement, CONTINUE, may be inserted to allow the normal sequencing through the loop.

The DIMENSION statement is similar to the BASIC DIM statement except that more than two-dimensional arrays may be used. A "150 DIMENSION A(3,3,3)" defines a 3 × 3 × 3 array (FORTRAN arrays start at 1 rather than 0 as in BASIC). Variables thereafter may be subscripted just as in BASIC. The statement "B=A (1,3,2)" would set variable B to the value found in cell (1,3,2) of array A, for example. The DATA statement is similar to the BASIC DATA, initializing data values at compile time.

Because I/O operations in FORTRAN are so versatile, the form of the I/O statements is somewhat complicated. A READ or WRITE statement is of the form "READ (a,n) list" or "WRITE (a,n) list." The "a" is usually an unsigned integer specifying the device number. The device number is preassigned by the system or may be reassigned by the user. Device number 3 could be Teletype keyboard, for example, and 5 could be a magnetic tape. The "n" is a FORMAT statement number in which the input or output format of the data is specified. "List" is a list of variables to be output. If we wanted to output three variables I, J, and A to Teletype, for instance, and the FORMAT statement defining the variables was at 105, the appropriate statement would read "WRITE (3,105) I,J,A." The FORMAT statement accompanying each READ or WRITE is of the form "FORMAT (c_1,c_2,c_3,...,c_n)" where c_1,...,c_n define a specification. The number of separate FORMAT specifications covers integers, double-precision numbers, real variables, fixed-decimal numbers, Hollerith (alphanumeric), blanks, literal text, carriage controls (line printer output), and other data types, each data type being represented by a letter such as *I* or *E*. A "FORMAT (F4.2,3X,F4.2)," for example, would output two variables (specified in the associated WRITE statement) in the form "1,23bbbl.23," where b represents a blank.

The above statements are the major FORTRAN statements. There are other FORMAT specifications, I/O statements ("REWIND"), subroutine calls ("CALL"), functions ("FUNCTION"), data definitions ("COMPLEX"), and other statement types that make FORTRAN a highly useful tool for mathematical problem solving at the expense of some study time and complexity in compiling and executing programs. If you are looking for a system to solve this type of problem efficiently, then the FORTRAN language may be your answer.

SUPPORT SOFTWARE

The assemblers, loader programs, and compilers discussed above are a portion of what is termed "support software" for a computer system. In addition to these programs, two other common support software packages are "editors" and "debug" programs.

A *source editor* is a software package that enables the source program to be changed for reassembly. The simplest editing process is via an ASR-33 Teletype. The source program on punched paper tape in ASCII format is edited "off-line" (not under computer control) by simultaneously reading the original paper tape and punching a new paper tape. Fig. 4-28A is a detailed drawing of a Teletype ASR-33. When the right-hand switch is in the LOCAL position, the Teletype is disconnected from any computer interface. The keyboard can now be used to print characters as keys are depressed. In fact, it is almost identical to operation of a typewriter in this respect. If the switch on the paper-tape reader portion is in the STOP position and the switch on the paper-tape punch portion is in the OFF position, the Teletype is essentially a typewriter.

If the paper-tape punch switch is set to ON and a key is depressed, a character will be simultaneously printed and punched. (This is the way the original ASCII source tape is produced for assembly.) If the paper-tape reader switch is set to START after a paper tape has been inserted into the reader assembly, the paper tape will be automatically read and printed on the keyboard. If the paper-tape punch switch is ON in this configuration, a new tape will be punched identical to the old. It is not too hard to see that characters or lines may be deleted from the original tape by reading and punching, stopping the read at the proper point, turning off the punch, reading the characters or lines to be deleted (and watching the keyboard to see what is being read), stopping the read, turning on the punch, and continuing. If characters are to be added, the process is similar except that the *reader* is turned off at a certain point, the characters to be added are typed from the keyboard, and the reader is once again turned on. Although the process sounds complicated, it is actually quite easy to edit a tape in this fashion. Fig. 4-29 shows a sample of this type of edit.

An editor program performs essentially the same function as an off-line Teletype. There are two types of editors in common use for minicomputers: *line editors* and *string editors.* Line editors add, delete, or modify (delete and add) source lines. String editors add, delete, or modify character strings.

Typically a line editor is loaded into the computer and started. The user then enters a string of edit commands (via the Teletype or system console in a small system). To delete lines, the command might be +23,25. Source lines 23 through 25 would then be deleted. (For a Teletype system, this would involve reading lines 23 through 25 but not punching them; the punch can be turned off or on under computer control). A command of +27,27 deletes line 27. A command of +50 reproduces (punches) all lines from the current line through line 50. An input line not prefixed by a "+" is added to the output tape as a new line. Table 4-12 shows an edit using a typical line editor program with a Teletype. A line editor, of course, could be used with more efficient peripherals (a magnetic tape, for instance), but the input reading and output writing actions are essentially the same.

A string editor works much the same as a line editor except that the commands specify character strings to be deleted or character strings with which to "position" the current character "pointer." Other commands may be used to insert characters, change characters, or search for character strings.

Probably the most useful program next to an assembler or compiler is a "debug" package. The "debugger" is loaded into memory along with the program to be debugged. "Bugs" are program problems, ranging from one instruction incorrectly coded to dozens of incorrect instructions. By using the debug package, sections of the program may be selectively executed, the contents of locations may be printed out and modified, and "patches" to existing code may be made.

While the above programs are the most common support programs, each computer manufacturer and some microcomputer manufacturers have many more programs available for either *support* or *application* programming. (Support is generally used to describe programs useful in program development—"tools" as it were; application programs are the actual programs that perform the desired application—like tic-tac-toe, for example.) Some of these are supplied with the hardware when a system is purchased new or used. Other software

Table 4-12. Line Editor Example

Input Tape			Output Tape	
Line Number	Contents	Commands	Line Number	Contents
12	~~SUB~~ 0,0 (DELETE; ADD)	+12,12	12	STA 0,K4
13	STA 0,K1	STA 0,K4	13	STA 0,K1
14	LDA 1,K2	+17,17	14	LDA 1,K2
15	BNE 1,1		15	BNE 1,1
16	JMP LOOP		16	JMP LOOP
17	~~LDA 1,K3~~	DELETE	17	LDA 2,K4
18	LDA 2,K4			

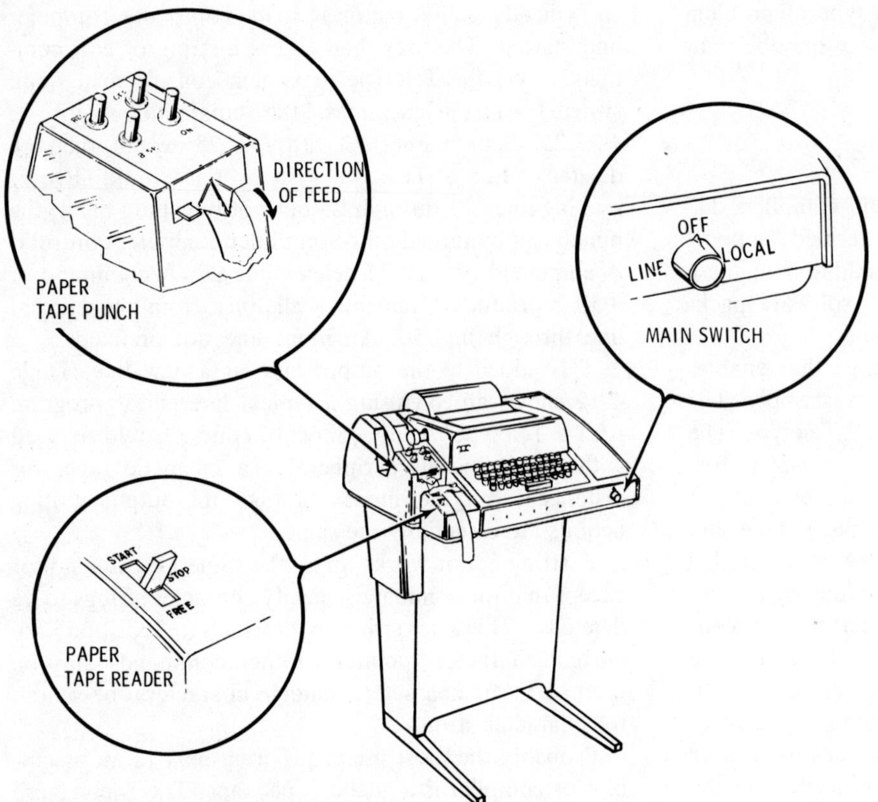

(A) Closeup of switches.

(B) Photograph of unit.

Courtesy Teletype Corp.

Fig. 4-28. Teletype Corporation ASR-33.

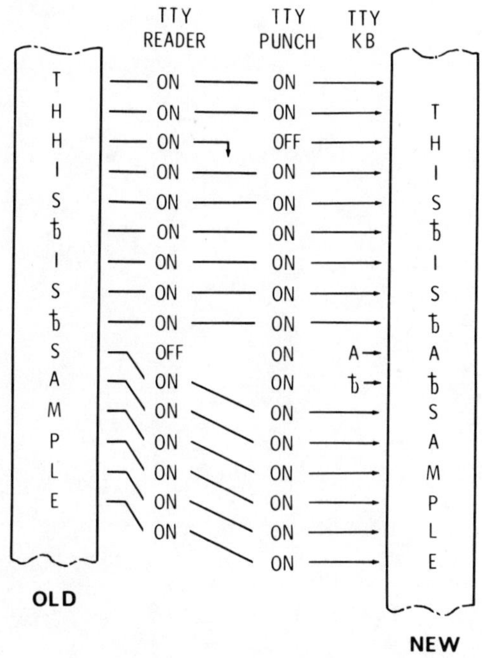

Fig. 4-29. Teletype editing.

is "unbundled" or separately costed from the hardware package. When software is supplied separately, the price is usually nominal—tens of dollars rather than hundreds.

OPERATING SYSTEMS

Most minicomputer manufacturers offer "operating systems" for their hardware. There is usually a great deal of difference between the operating systems designed for large-scale computer systems and those for minicomputer systems. Large-scale operating systems were designed to make more efficient use of expensive hardware. Rather than dedicating the entire system to one program, many programs are run simultaneously in a large system. The available memory is "partitioned" among these many users. Each user is allocated a "time slice" for program execution. When an I/O operation has to be performed, execution of the program initiating the I/O is suspended, since at that point the program is waiting on the I/O device to finish. The time required to wait for completion of I/O is enormously long compared with the speed of instruction execution; the time is better spent executing part of another user's program. Whenever an I/O operation is being performed, or whenever a user has had his "time slice," the next user's program is resumed at the point where it previously left off. Since there is normally a great deal of I/O activity in each program, most of the I/O wait time that would have been lost with only one program in memory is used by the execution of other programs. In this manner, the resources of an expensive computer system can be utilized most efficiently by many users. In addition to scheduling the various users for assembly, compilation, loading, and execution of programs, the operating system provides various utility (or support) functions such as saving programs in secondary storage, creating new "files" of data, or debugging aids.

Although minicomputer manufacturers are now becoming oriented towards competing with manufacturers of larger systems and are consequently developing operating systems more similar to large-scale systems, most existing operating systems (if they exist at all for some microcomputer systems) are primarily for single users (single programs). They do, however, offer a convenient way to tie assemblers, compilers, and utility software into one neat package in addition to providing "management" of data or program files. Unfortunately, to effectively use an operating system, one needs a disc or tape storage device to provide secondary storage of the operating systems and the user's files. The attractiveness of minicomputer operating systems can't be denied, but the question is largely an economic one—the peripheral hardware may well exceed the basic cost of the computer hardware and memory.

CHAPTER

5

Minicomputer Peripheral Devices

A minicomputer system in the simplest case is made up of a minicomputer with a Teletype ASR-33. There are even simpler microcomputers, as described in Chapter 8, but a microcomputer along with an ASR-33 is about the minimum practical system. Besides the Teletype, there are many other peripheral devices, however, that can be added to the system. These range in price from a hundred dollars to tens of thousands of dollars. Some of the devices are storage devices that retain programs or files of data. The paper-tape reader and punch on an ASR-33 read or punch paper tape that is in itself a storage medium. High-speed paper-tape readers and punches perform the same functions as Teletype paper-tape equipment, but at much faster speeds. The card reader is another type of I/O device that reads stored data. (High-speed card punches are so much out of the realm of minicomputers in price and use that they are not considered here.) Magnetic tape is used as a storage medium for a variety of tape drives, ranging from a very inexpensive audio cassette interface to a large computer-grade reel-to-reel tape machine. A relatively new type of storage device is the *disc file,* a rotating magnetic disc with a fixed or movable head to read the recorded data; an inexpensive version of this type of storage is a "floppy" disc. Another class of I/O devices print or display alphanumeric or other data. These range from an inexpensive KSR-33 Teletype (Teletype without paper-tape option) or "television terminal" to line printers that can print 20,000 characters per minute. Special-purpose peripheral hardware, such as modems, digital-to-analog converters, analog-to-digital converters, and others, is another class of devices. Finally, for a computer user who has some electronics knowledge, it is possible to build interfaces to existing equipment or to special-purpose equipment.

TELETYPES

The Teletype ASR-33 is such a standard piece of peripheral equipment in minicomputer and microcomputer systems that it has to be treated separately from other categories of I/O devices. Since an ASR-33 can be purchased new from Teletype Corporation, Skokie, Illinois, for about $1000 and since it offers almost every required function for a minicomputer system—printing, keyboard input, paper-tape punching and reading—it is the most cost-effective peripheral device around. Prices on a used ASR-33 are currently running about $750 with 30 days warranty. For a small fee, companies specializing in Teletype repairs and rentals will modify a Teletype to work with virtually any minicomputer. It may be necessary, however, to buy a "modification kit" from the computer manufacturer to interface the Teletype. These typically cost $100 to $200 and can be installed by the Teletype repair company. Teletypes purchased from the computer manufacturer are modified slightly to run with the computer, but one pays an enormous premium for that slight modification—ASR-33s from the manufacturer cost between $1750 and $2000. In some cases no modification is necessary.

The Teletype ASR-33 has a built-in tape reader and punch as described in Chapter 4. Another model, the KSR-33, has no paper-tape option but can only read from the keyboard and print. Data going to or from the Teletype are in "serial" form. Eleven bits of binary data make up one character of data; ASCII data are used. If no data are being sent from the computer to the Teletype, the data line is high or "marking" (1 bit). The first "space" bit starts the Teletype acquisition of data. The space bit lowers the line signal and effectively informs the Teletype that eight data bits are to follow. The eight data bits are then transmitted at evenly spaced intervals. Two "mark" bits complete the data transfer. Since ASCII code requires only seven bits to represent a character, the eighth bit is used for a "parity" bit. Typically this bit is always a one or zero in minicomputer systems, but it could be "odd" or "even" parity if the manufacturer desires. In odd parity, the parity bit is set to 1 if there are an even number of data bits and set to 0 if there are an odd number of data bits. In even parity, the parity bit is set exactly the opposite. Parity bits are used as a check on the validity of the data. Fig.

5-1 shows the transmission of the letter *Y* from the minicomputer to Teletype with even parity.

Transmission of data from Teletype to computer is the same except for direction. Here the minicomputer Teletype interface detects the first space (0) bit and reads in the serial data. Since the time interval between bits is 9.09 milliseconds (9.09 thousandths of a second), each character takes 11×9.09 ms $= 100$ ms to be received or transmitted by the Teletype. Ten characters can be transmitted by the Teletype in one second. For ten characters, $10 \times 11 = 110$ bits will be sent in one second. *Baud* is a term defined as transmission of data at a rate of one bit per second, so the Teletype is

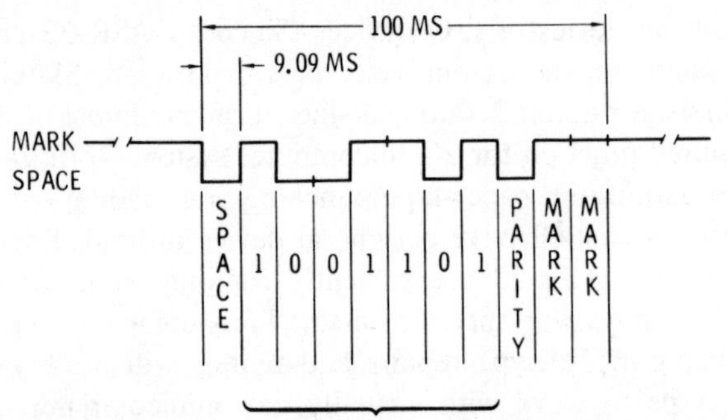

Fig. 5-1. Teletype serial data transmission.

sometimes referred to as a 110-baud device. Cathode-ray tube displays and other devices meant to be Teletype replacements vary from 110-baud, emulating the Teletype, to 9600-baud transmission rates. Data can usually be sent in both directions simultaneously—from minicomputer to Teletype and vice versa. This is *full duplex* transmission. Typically, data input from the Teletype will have to be "echoed" back from the computer, as the printer may operate only from the computer in the "LINE" mode. The sequence for inputing data from a Teletype after a key is pressed is this: The Teletype sends over 11 bits of data to the computer, the computer receives the data, the software outputs the same data received, the 11 bits are sent back to the Teletype printer, and the Teletype receives and prints the data. All of this happens so fast, of course, that it appears as if the user's depression of the key results in the printing of the character.

What happens between the serial data and the minicomputer? As you know, I/O is done in 8-bit (or sometimes 16-bit) bytes for devices on the multiplexer bus (non-DMA). In this case, the eight bits of serial data on input from the Teletype must be converted to a "parallel" 8-bit byte which is then sent to the CPU on eight data lines. Conversely, on output to the Teletype, eight bits of parallel data must be converted to eight bits of serial data, plus a leading space and trailing mark bits. The Teletype "controller" performs both input and output data conversions, in addition to possibly decoding commands (instructions) to turn the Teletype paper-tape reader or punch on or off. If this doesn't seen too complicated, you are right. Teletype controllers usually sell for only several hundred dollars or so, purchased new with the minicomputer or microcomputer. Physically they take up possibly one-fifth of a 15-inch plug-in board, leaving room for other options.

Teletype Corporation is not the only company manufacturing teleprinters. Many companies offer Teletype-like machines that are "plug-to-plug" compatible with a Teletype and can read and punch paper tape. There are even crt displays that are plug-to-plug compatible with a Teletype controller output.

Teletypes are not "cure-all" I/O devices. They are inexpensive and versatile, but since they are basically mechanical devices they are somewhat prone to mechanical failures. Fortunately, because they are popular devices, there are many companies in every large city that specialize in their repair. Inexpensive alternatives to a Teletype that you might consider are a television display and audio cassette, which are discussed later in this chapter.

HIGH-SPEED PAPER-TAPE EQUIPMENT

Teletypes are limited in speed to 10 characters per second on input or output. That may sound fairly fast, but think for a minute of the amount of time required to read in an assembler program on paper tape into a minicomputer using a Teletype paper-tape reader. A representative assembler might be 8000 bytes long, or contained on about 800 inches of paper tape. At 10 characters per second, it would take about 13 minutes to read in the tape. High-speed paper-tape equipment increases the reading speed to about 300 bytes per second, enabling the same 8000-byte program to be read-in in about 26 seconds. A high-speed punch, replacing the Teletype paper-tape punch, could punch at about 150 characters per second, 15 times faster than a Teletype. Fig. 5-2 shows a typical paper-tape reader and punch.

Unlike Teletypes, the high-speed reader and punch are parallel I/O devices. Usually one byte at a time is transferred from computer to punch or from reader to computer. Both the punch and reader are fairly simple devices. They only have to receive or transmit a byte, advance the tape one frame, and punch or read the next character. Because of these simple functions and because the data do not have to be converted from serial to parallel or the other way around, the controllers for punch and reader are usually less complicated than the Teletype controller. Many times they fit on the same "basic" I/O board as the Teletype controller in the computer system, and their prices are in the area of several hundred dollars apiece.

The cost of new punches and readers may be prohibitively expensive for a user interested in a very small system. A new punch with controller runs about $2000, and a new reader with controller about the same. If a used punch and/or reader are purchased with a controller for a specific minicomputer, the price drops drastically—each unit will probably cost less than half price. Surplus readers and punches, probably without controllers, are available from $50 and up. However, in the surplus equipment situation, be wary of the condition of the units. There are not many repairmen for this type of equipment except for the manufacturer itself. In addition, unless you can purchase exactly the same model as the minicomputer manufacturer uses with his equipment, the punch or reader may not work with the system.

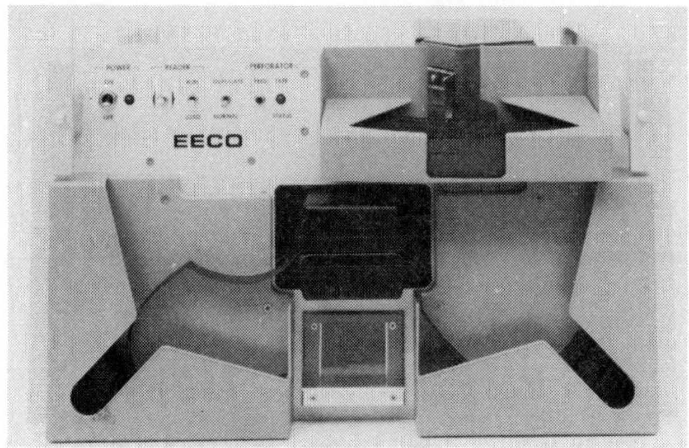

Courtesy EECO

Fig. 5-2. High-speed paper-tape equipment.

PUNCHED-CARD EQUIPMENT

In many larger computer installations, the storage medium for initial program development is the punch card. These installations have several *keypunches,* a rather large and complex machine that punches cards from an alphanumeric input at a keyboard. The cost of the keypunch, manufactured by IBM Corporation among others, far exceeds the cost of a small computer system. Keypunch services, however, will punch cards from your "coding sheets" at a cost of about a penny a card for unverified data (verification is entering the same data from a second machine called a verifier and detecting and correcting keypunch errors). The problem with having cards punched in this manner, though, is that there will almost certainly be keypunch errors that will require correction, necessitating another trip to the keypunch service. Although there are inexpensive hand punches available for correcting cards, constant trips to the keypunch service for the bulk of the cards may prove a little tedious. On the other hand, punched cards do offer some advantages. They are easily stored, they are "unit" records (one source line per card), and they are usable by any system with a card reader. A program can be edited by simply removing or inserting cards. If you are considering a system with card-reading capability, remember that some way of saving object programs and reading those programs and utility programs must be provided, and that means a supplement to the cards which may consist of paper-tape, magnetic-tape, or disc equipment.

The card medium is shown in Fig. 5-3. The card is 7⅜ × 3¼ inches and usually consists of 80 horizontal rows and 12 vertical columns. The 80 columns represent up to 80 alphanumeric and special characters, punched in Hollerith code. Binary data are punched by expensive card punches which will not be discussed here since their cost is prohibitive for any reasonable minicomputer system. As shown, numeric data are one punch, alphabetic data are two punches, and special characters are two or three punches in a column.

A typical minicomputer table-top card reader is shown in Fig. 5-4. Cards are fed from a card hopper; then they pass through the reading mechanism and fall into a card stacker. Sensing switches detect such conditions as hopper empty, stacker full, and card jams, and return the "status" to the card-reader controller and eventually to the minicomputer when a "read status" instruction is executed.

New card readers sold with the minicomputer are even more expensive than high-speed paper tape, costing in the neighborhood of $4500 with interface. The interface for the card reader is more complicated than any discussed previously because of the nature of card reading. To start the card in motion under a command from the computer, the card reader must sense that the stacker is not full, "pick" a card, detect the leading edge of the card, and "strobe" in each column of data at the proper time. The controller may operate under DMA, transferring the contents of the entire card to memory, or may operate a column at a time, putting the burden on the software to read in the next column and test for the column "ready" condition. Because of the complexity of the card-reader unit and the card-reader controller, this is not an inexpensive peripheral. Prices of used card readers and controllers for specific minicomputers are about 60 percent of the new cost. Surplus readers are available, but the same warnings apply. They are serviceable only by the manufacturer and may not be compatible with the minicomputer manufacturer's card-reader controller. Prices start at several hundred dollars for a used card-reader unit alone.

MAGNETIC TAPE EQUIPMENT

Magnetic tape equipment falls into four categories: reel-to-reel transports, cartridge equipment, cassette

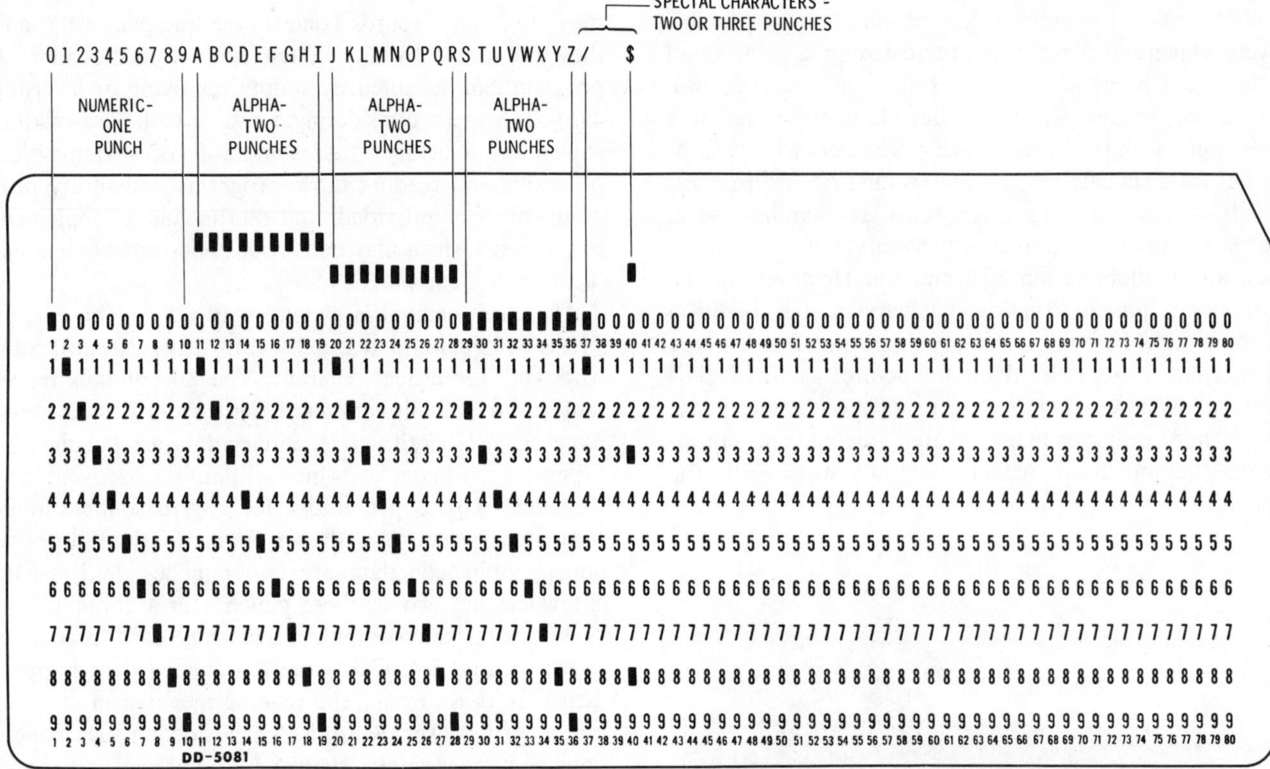

Fig. 5-3. Punched-card format.

Courtesy Decision Data, Inc.

Fig. 5-4. Card reader.

equipment, and audio cassette equipment, roughly in order of decreasing price.

The most attractive of these four types from the standpoint of storage, speed, and versatility is the reel-to-reel magnetic tape drive. A representative drive of this type is shown in Fig. 5-5. Tape feeds from a supply reel through a read "head" and onto the take-up reel. Tension arms (or vacuum columns) keep the tape from stretching or breaking while the tape is quickly brought up to speed. Tape speeds vary from 12.5 inches per second to over 100 inches per second on minicomputer-type drives. The tape is not free-running but is started under computer control and stops with each "record" read.

Courtesy Pertec Corp.

Fig. 5-5. Reel-to-reel magnetic tape transport.

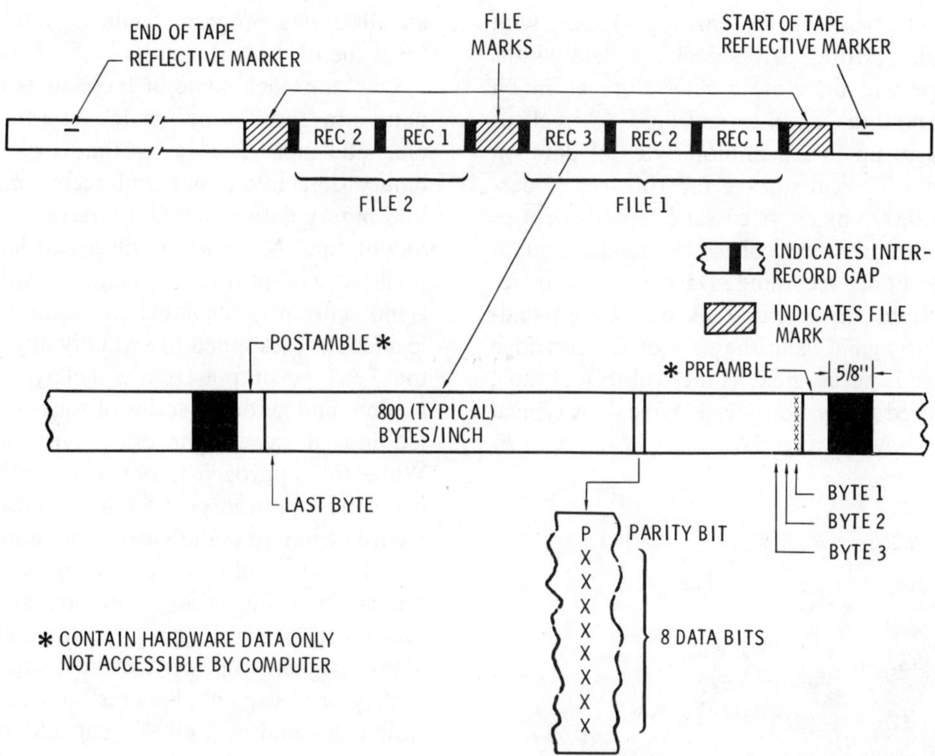

Fig. 5-6. Digital magnetic tape recording.

The tape medium is ⅝ inch wide and 1.5 mils (1.5 thousandths inch) thick, twice the width of that found in home audio equipment. Reel sizes range from 100 to 2400 feet. Data are written onto the tape in a series of records ranging in size from two bytes (16 bits) to 16,000 bytes or greater. From 556 to 1600 bits per inch (bpi) can be written on the tape, as shown in Fig. 5-6. The number of bits that can be written lengthwise is called the tape-writing *density*. The width of the data may be either six or eight bits, written on six to eight data "tracks," each track having an associated head to read or write the data. An additional track is used to write an odd or even parity bit, bringing the total number of heads and tracks to seven or nine. Seven-track magnetic tape transports are the older type; nine tracks are now provided with all minicomputer systems. The problem with seven-track units is that it takes three "frames" to represent 16 bits of data, whereas a nine-track unit can represent 16 bits in two frames. A nine-track transport with a recording density of 800 bpi (equivalent to 800 bytes per inch) requires 4000/800 = 5 inches to record a 4000-byte record. Each record is separated from other records by an interrecord gap (IRG) about ⅝ inch long. This IRG is required to provide some slack in which to start and stop the tape before reading and recording data. A special record, called a *file mark* or *end-of-file* (EOF), separates one file from another. A *file* is simply a collection of records used any way the programmer wishes. File one might be the source records of program number *n*, and file two might be the object records of program number *m*, for example. Since the IRG takes up a large amount of space (space enough to record 500 bytes per inch in a nine-track 800-bpi system), data are usually "blocked" into longer records. Ten lines of code might be contained in one record, for example, instead of ten unblocked records. Data on the tape may be ASCII, EBCDIC, or binary, and are solely a function of how the programmer writes the tape.

The magnetic tape controller is very complicated and consists of two parts: a "formatter" and a controller. The formatter does the actual job of recording and reading data to and from the tape, and the controller is the interface between the minicomputer and the formatter. The controller normally occupies one whole board in the minicomputer. Since both the formatter and the controller are complicated devices, the cost of reel-to-reel tape units is high, typically $5000 to $10,000 new, with controller. Used prices are 40 to 70 percent of new prices. Surplus prices range from $300 or so on up, for the transport and formatter alone. Typical prices of magnetic tape itself are on the order of $15 or so for a 400-foot reel.

Cartridge and cassette tape drives were originally made as inexpensive secondary storage devices to replace reel-to-reel magnetic tapes. Cartridge drives use a special type of cartridge similar to a home recording cartridge.

The number of tracks on the cartridge varies, with two being typical. Cartridge drives pack less data widthwise onto a tape and therefore cannot store as much data per given length as a reel-to-reel tape. (A reel-to-reel tape can store up to 2.6 million bytes of data on 100 feet of tape!) Typical storage for 100 feet of cartridge tape is 200,000 bytes. A cassette tape drive uses a tape cassette virtually identical to the standard audio cassettes used in home recording. Data are usually recorded on one track; a second track may be an "address" track. Here again, as in the case of the cartridge tape, data storage is not as great as the reel-to-reel tape, but several hundred thousand bytes is typical. A typical cassette drive is shown in Fig. 5-7.

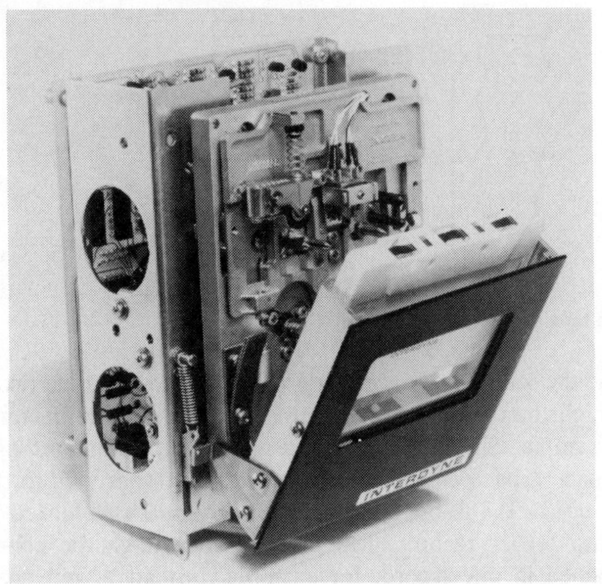

Courtesy Interdyne, Inc.

Fig. 5-7. Cassette digital tape recorder.

At this time most minicomputer manufacturers have a cassette drive available, and prices with controller run about $3000 for a single drive (one cassette) to $6000 (up to three cassettes). Used equipment is available at 40 to 60 percent of the new purchase price. Not much surplus equipment is to be found. Cartridges and cassettes cost from $8 to $15. In most cases the audio cassettes cannot be used.

If the above prices for magnetic tape equipment make you blanch, there is hope in sight. The MITS Altair 8800 microcomputer system offers an audio cassette interface for under $200 assembled. In addition, many other manufacturers offer this type of option for use with any computer system with a teletypewriter (tty) type of serial interface. The audio cassette interface will work with any (or most) audio cassette units used for home recording. It is essentially a paper-tape replacement and enables the reading and writing of data at rates up to 500 bytes per second. By using this option, an 8000-byte program could be loaded in 17 seconds for some of the faster units.

One approach some of these units take is to convert data into serial tones which are then recorded onto magnetic tape. The device that does the conversion of binary data into tones and reconverts the tones back into binary data is called a *modem,* for "*mo*dulator *de*-*m*odulator." Modems are discussed later in this chapter under special-purpose equipment. Although this option is not currently available for some systems, the basic idea could be applied to virtually any system by feeding the Teletype output from a Teletype controller into a modem and getting a series of tones out, which are then fed into a cassette or other type of audio recorder. While this approach is not as versatile as a computer magnetic tape transport (writing and reading successive records from an audio cassette is rather hard to accomplish), it does offer a convenient way of loading programs—one that is an order of magnitude faster than loading from a Teletype paper-tape reader.

All magnetic tape systems have one thing in common —they are "sequential-access" devices. If a file of data is near the end of a 400-ft magnetic tape, for example, it will take even the relatively fast 37.5 inch-per-second tape transport about two minutes to advance the tape from the beginning of the tape to the desired file. This period is eons by computer standards. To get around this sequential access of data, I/O devices with a "random access" were invented early in the game.

MAGNETIC DISCS

One of the first types of random-access devices was the magnetic drum. Magnetic drums were made up, literally, of a "drum" of magnetic material with read/write heads over a number of imaginary tracks, as shown in Fig. 5-8. The drum rotated at about 2000 revolutions per minute, or 33 revolutions per second, so that reading data from any point along the track was simply a matter of waiting 30 milliseconds maximum for that piece of data to come around. In place of sequential access, the drum became somewhat of a random-access device, since any track's worth of data could be retrieved rapidly.

Although drums are still being used, they have been replaced to a large extent by magnetic discs, which, as the name implies, are *discs* of magnetic material. To decrease the cost of the units and to increase the storage capacity, two heads were used on one or more *movable* arms, as shown in Fig. 5-9. Under software control, the arm can be rapidly positioned over the right track and the data read. Each disc is divided into two "surfaces." For a single disc (there are drives with ten discs), there are two surfaces: top and bottom. Each surface is divided into tracks, which are concentric circles around

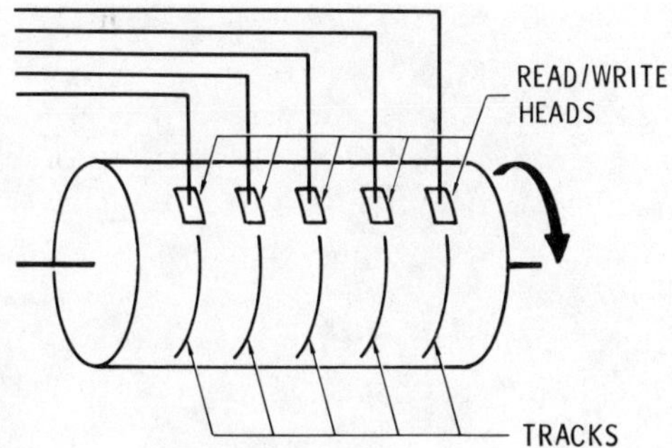

Fig. 5-8. Magnetic drum.

the surface's axis. Typically there are 200 or so tracks. Each disc is also divided into sectors. There are typically eight sectors per disc. Reading and writing are done a sector at a time. To read any sector, the disc is commanded via software to position the arm over the proper track, to enable either the top or bottom head, and to read the proper sector. The entire process of positioning and reading takes no longer than 100 milliseconds. One disc, which is usually removable, can hold about 2.3 million bytes.

As might be expected a disc drive, along with its associated controller, is one of the most expensive peripherals. New single disc drives with controller cost on the order of $10,000. Used equipment holds its value fairly well, being about half the new purchase price. A disc "pack" costs about $100.

Although the cost of new or used disc drives is probably prohibitive for most applications, a new type of disc using the same principles as above has become popular. This is the "floppy" disc, so called because the disc itself is flexible. The mechanics of the floppy disc drives are not as sophisticated as that of their larger brothers, and as a result the cost of drive and controller new is about $3000. One of the least expensive new drives is the drive for the MITS Altair 8800 computer system, costing about $2000. As of now, not too may used systems with floppy disc drives are available, but prices should be about one-half of new equipment as more manufacturers replace cassette equipment with floppy discs. Storage on the disc is about ¼ million bytes. Maximum access can run as high as 0.9 second, but typical track-to-track accesses would run about 100 milliseconds.

Floppy disc drives are very similar in appearance to their larger brothers but are physically smaller. Fig. 5-10 shows two floppy drives with a floppy disc cartridge to the side.

Floppy discs are an excellent reasonably low-cost replacement for all paper-tape-oriented equipment. If no hard copy (printed copy) of assemblies or reports is required, a floppy disc with the low-cost terminal discussed below would make for a versatile, low-cost minicomputer system.

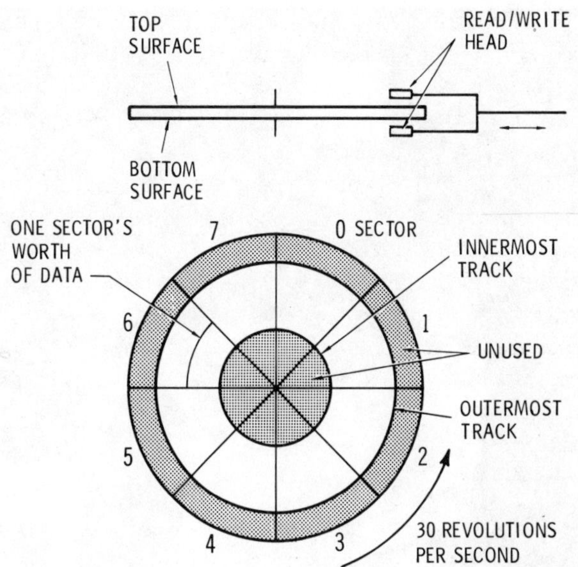

Fig. 5-9. Magnetic discs.

PRINTERS

In many applications, a hard copy is desired, whether it be a listing of a program or a printed report generated by the program. The obvious inexpensive solution, of course, is the Teletype once again. Teletypes produce a legible, pleasing copy on 8½-inch-wide paper (up to 72 characters in width) and any length (11-inch perforated paper is obtainable). Printing rates are 10 characters per second. To print an average listing of 500 lines (40 characters per line) takes about 35 minutes.

The next step up from a Teletype printer is one of the small printers that are plug-to-plug compatible with the Teletype. Here one doesn't have to worry about buying a special controller for the peripheral since the Teletype controller will suffice. Matrix-type printers print characters in a seven-by-nine matrix of dots. The resulting type is not as pleasing as a Teletype, but is quite legible. Fig. 5-11 shows a sample of copy produced by this type of printer. Printing rates run from 30 characters per second to 200 characters per second and beyond. Also available for some applications is a Selectric-type printer using a Selectric ball. The Selectric character code, however, is radically different from ASCII, and the unit will not be plug-to-plug compatible with a tty. Both types of printers start at about $2000 new, or about half that price used. Occasionally, surplus line printers appear. If they are tty compatible, they may be worth your while to buy if they are in reasonable condition.

There are many other types of line printers—chain printers, drum printers, and electrostatic types—but prices start at about $10,000 new. One pays for the much higher printing speeds of hundreds of lines per minute.

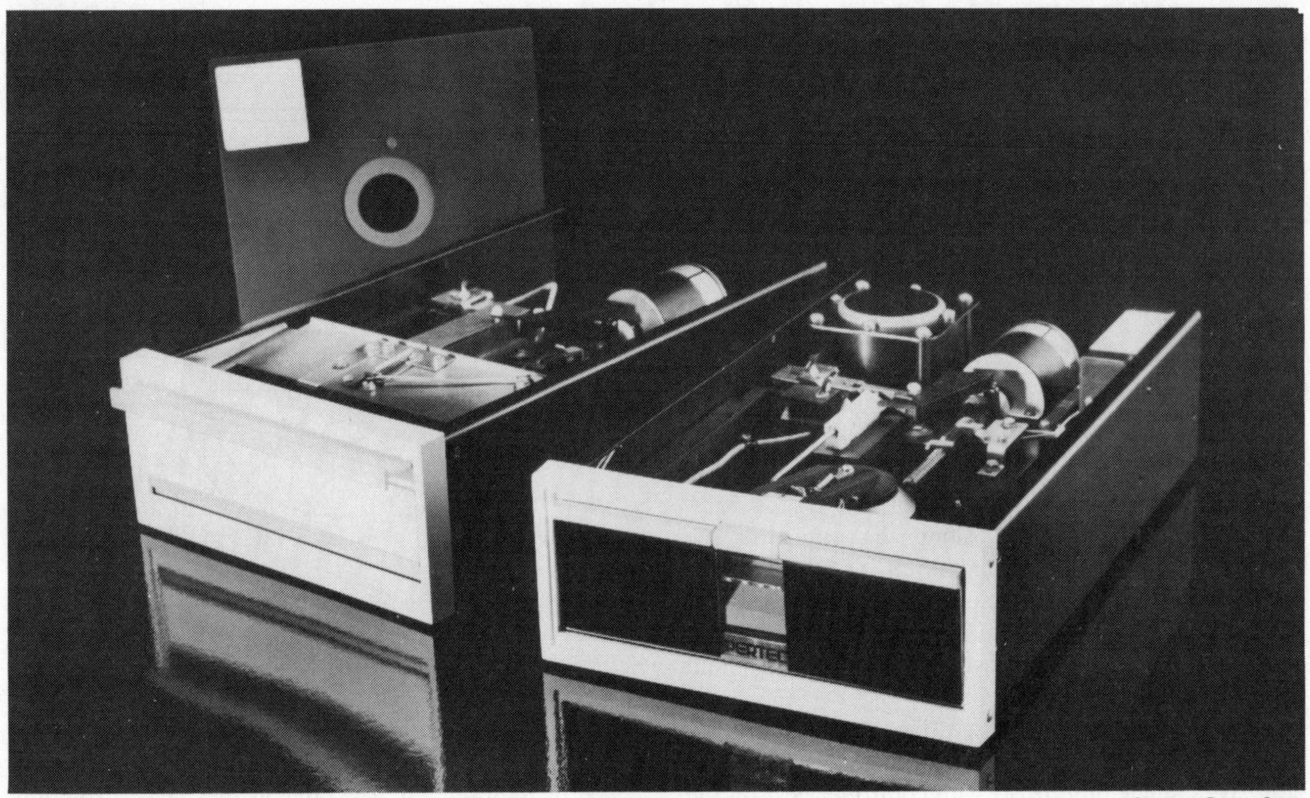

Courtesy Pertec Corp.

Fig. 5-10. Floppy disc drive and medium.

DISPLAYS

Where hard copy is not required, a crt (cathode-ray tube) or television display may be used. These are of two types: a display oriented towards lines of alphanumeric characters and a display of dot matrices. A third type, a "graphics" type display, is prohibitive in price and will not be discussed here. At the low end of the price scale is Southwest Technical Products CT-1024 Terminal System Kit (Fig. 5-12) which is made to work into a standard television set with very slight modifications. With tty compatibility options, the CT-1024 sells for about $230 in kit form. It displays 512 characters in 16 lines of 32 characters each.* Although 32 characters per line is somewhat of a handicap, it is certainly an inexpensive way to display data from a computer. Keyboard input to the computer is provided. Other companies provide similar types of displays at about the same price, many oriented toward the MITS Altair 8800 or 680 microcomputers. Cromemco offers a color matrix display designed to work into the MITS Altair 8800 microcomputer. Up to seven colors and black may be displayed on a 64 × 64 matrix in one mode, while a second mode provides for a 128 × 128 black and white display. A third mode is a high-speed (all modes work under DMA) 32 × 32 matrix for use in real-time display work.

* In each of two pages of memory, giving 1024 characters.

Displays that include a crt are, of course, higher priced, starting at about $1000. Almost all of the character-oriented displays are tty compatible, and some may operate at baud rates from 110 to 9600, if the rate is selectable in the computer's Teletype interface. Alphanumeric and special characters may be input from an integral keyboard; the number of characters displayed runs from about 512 to 1024 or more. Most of these displays will "roll" up as characters fill up the entire screen; the topmost line is pushed up and out of the screen and a new line is started on the bottom. Used displays are widely available and are about one-half the price of new displays.

MODEMS

Computer equipment for data communications includes controllers that will process high-speed data transfers along dedicated communication links, "conditioned" telephone lines (conditioned to eliminate noise sources), and unconditioned telephone (normal) lines. The equipment most interesting to the computer hobbyist is the low end of this equipment in speed and price. Normal phone lines may be used to transmit or receive data from a computer at rates up to 300 baud (300 bits per second). The device that accomplishes this is called a *modem* for "*mo*dulator-*dem*odulator." A modem is basically a very simple device in concept. If serial data

```
0048 F614 0034          JMP  GO250      GO250-NO!!
                *
                *
0049 FB8C 00D6  GO300   JST  *CSWRT     WRITE NEXT RECORD
004A 00BD               DATA GOLIST
004B F22D 0079          JMP  GO1000     GO1000-ERROR
004C F900       GO350   JST  DELAY:     WAIT
004D 000A               DATA 10         100 MSEC.
004E 0451               DATA 1105
004F B273 00C3  GO400   LDA  GOYC       INCREMENT LINE
0050 0B04               AAI  4          CT. BY 4
0051 9A71 00C3          STA  GOYC
0052 8A78 00CB          ADD  N0256      CHECK IF DONE?
0053 20E7 002C          JAM  GO200      GO200-NO,LOOP!!!
                *
0054 B288 00DD  GO490   LDA  GOMESB     PROVIDE DONE MESSAGE
0055 C416               LXP  22
0056 F900               JST  BEGIN:
0057                    DATA MESOUT
0058 0032               DATA 50
                *
0059 0110       GO500   ZAR             RESET BUSY
005A 9A60 00BB          STA  GOBUSY     FLAG
005B F900               JST  END:       RETURN TO THE EXEC.
```

Fig. 5-11. Matrix printing.

are input to a modem from, say, a Teletype interface, the modem will convert (modulate) the ones and zeros (marks and spaces) to two tones: one for "ones" and one for "zeros." The standards used to originate data are 2125 hertz (cycles per second) for a zero and 2225 hertz for a one. The tones are transmitted over the phone lines via a speaker next to the instrument's mouthpiece, and a "receive" modem at the other end reconverts (demodulates) the tones to marks and spaces.

Two Teletypes, therefore, could communicate over phone lines if there was a modem at each end. Fig. 5-13 shows transmission of two ASCII characters by this process. Note that the "bit" frequency is still 11 bits in 100 milliseconds, but that each character may be separated by varying time intervals dependent upon the operator's typing speed. Recall also that a "mark" is 2125 hertz and that a "space" is 2225 hertz.

By substituting computers for the Teletypes at either end, two minicomputers could transmit and receive data

Fig. 5-12. SWTP CT-1024 terminal.

Courtesy Southwest Technical Products

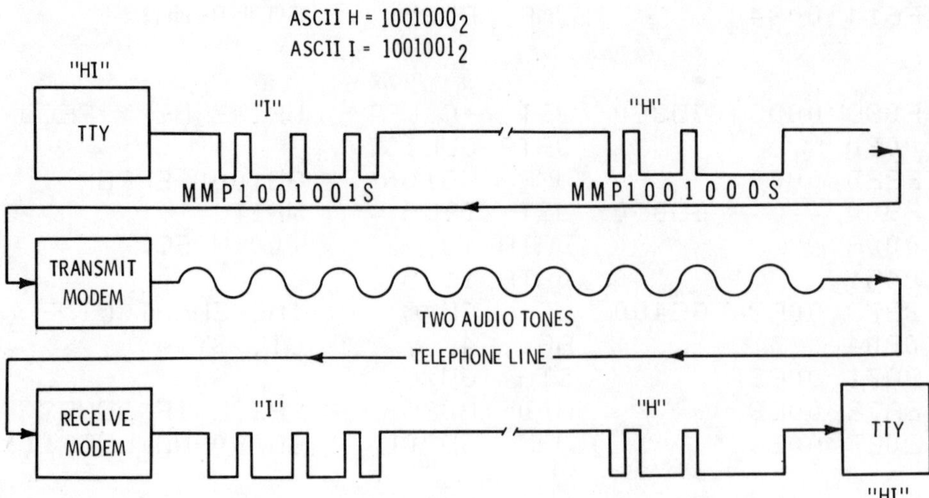

Fig. 5-13. Data communication by modem.

over ordinary phone lines. After all, the Teletype controller on each cannot differentiate between the output of a modem and the output of a Teletype. Another use for the modem is that of interface to an audio tape recorder used for secondary storage, as described earlier. Here again, the computer does not know whether it is getting data "real-time" or previously recorded. An inexpensive data recording device can be rigged by using a modem with almost any audio recorder. The faster the data are output to the tape, the more efficient the "packing density" of data on the tape will be. In this application, a 300+-baud modem could be used for a maximum transfer rate of 30 characters or more per second.

Because of advancements in LSI technology, a complete modem can now be put on a 24-pin chip. The required speaker, microphone, case, and so forth, bring the cost of a minimum "acoustic coupler" (modem with audio components) to about $150 for a 110-baud tty type. Used equipment is available, but it is not recommended since the newer, chip-oriented modems are probably much more reliable.

SPECIAL-PURPOSE EQUIPMENT

Besides the various types of peripheral devices mentioned above, every minicomputer manufacturer offers special-purpose interfaces to the minicomputer with which a user can connect the minicomputer to the real world. One common type of interface offers 16 "lines" or "discrete" outputs (or inputs). About the only restrictions on these are that the inputs and outputs must be binary ones or zeros at "TTL" (transistor-transistor logic) voltage levels—a nominal +5 volts for a one, and a nominal 0 volts for a zero. What the inputs and outputs represent is limited only by the user's imagination. Inputs might be switch closures for a burglar alarm system or fire detection system. Outputs might be relays to control sprinkler system valves. A board with 16 I/O lines such as this would typically run $500 or so new for a minicomputer though less for a microcomputer. (The same circuit can be designed and implemented by someone with electronics knowledge for much less—see the next section of this chapter.) Other special-purpose interfaces include analog-to-digital converters, which convert an external voltage level to parallel digital format, and digital-to-analog converters, which convert an output parallel digital value to an external voltage. The latter two devices are available in kit form for the MITS Altair 8800 microcomputer from various sources.

INTERFACING TO NONSTANDARD DEVICES

The remainder of this chapter is devoted to providing some information on interfacing surplus or home-brew equipment to a minicomputer or microcomputer. For those of you who will be using manufacturers' peripherals or used "standard" peripherals such as a Teletype, this section is not necessary. But if you have an old five-level Teletype or a surplus printer that you got for a bargain price, this section will give you some guidelines on how to go about interfacing your equipment.

All minicomputer manufacturers know that their equipment must be able to interface to the outside world for special applications. If the minicomputer does not have this capability or if the interface is made too difficult, the potential customer simply won't buy the equipment. For this reason every minicomputer and microprocessor manufacturer provides detailed "interface" manuals that give precise timing and even logic diagrams for the interface.

Digital Logic Elements

Minicomputer and microcomputer controllers are made up of logic elements that implement functions to be performed by the controller. The basic "building blocks" of these elements are the AND gate, OR gate, inverter, NAND gate, NOR gate, flip-flop, and one-shot. All of these devices are concerned with binary voltage levels. For a "1" level, the voltage input or output is typically +5 volts. For a "0" level, the voltage is typically 0 volts. These values are for TTL logic elements, which constitute most of the logic implementation of pre-1975 minicomputers. These values also represent a "positive-true" logic. If a "1" state was 0 volts and a "0" state was +5 volts, the logic would be "negative-true." In this discussion we will use positive-true logic, although both types might be present in one design.

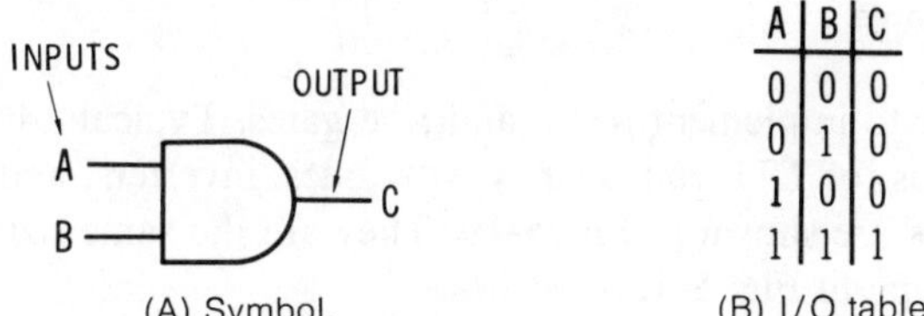

A	B	C
0	0	0
0	1	0
1	0	0
1	1	1

(A) Symbol. (B) I/O table.

Fig. 5-14. AND gate.

The AND gate is represented schematically in a "logic diagram" as shown in Fig. 5-14A. The AND gate functions as an AND instruction would—there is a "1" output if and only if both inputs are a "1." If neither are "1" or if only one input is a "1," the output is "0." How does the AND gate look in the real world? A TTL logic AND gate is shown actual size in Fig. 5-15. Four AND gates are in one package as shown. The "VCC" is the supply voltage of +5 volts, and "GND" is the ground return for power. More than two inputs may be used for the AND gate, but two and three are typical. If more than two are used, of course, the output is high only if all inputs are high.

The OR gate is analagous to the OR instruction. When one input *or* the other is "1," the output is "1." Fig. 5-16 shows the schematic representation of an OR gate.

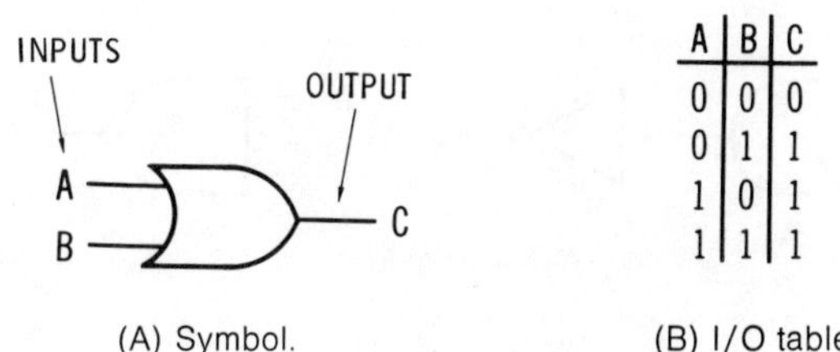

A	B	C
0	0	0
0	1	1
1	0	1
1	1	1

(A) Symbol. (B) I/O table.

Fig. 5-16. OR gate.

Here again, an OR gate may have more than one input, and the output is "1" if one or more inputs are "1."

An inverter is simply that. It inverts the logic signal. If the input is a "1," the output is a "0"; if the input is a "0," the output is a "1" (see Figs. 5-17A and 5-17B). Note that the circle at the output represents a low level, indicating that if signal A is applied, the output is $\bar{A}$, or "not A." "Not A" is the opposite of whatever signal A is. On a typical logic diagram, you may see a signal "DATA" input to an inverter in order to produce the signal $\overline{\text{DATA}}$. If signal DATA is true, signal $\overline{\text{DATA}}$ is false, and vice versa.

A buffer (Figs. 5-17C and 5-17D) does nothing "logically"; an input of "1" produces an output of "1" and a "0" produces a "0." However, it does "boost" the signal to enable the driving of more inputs.

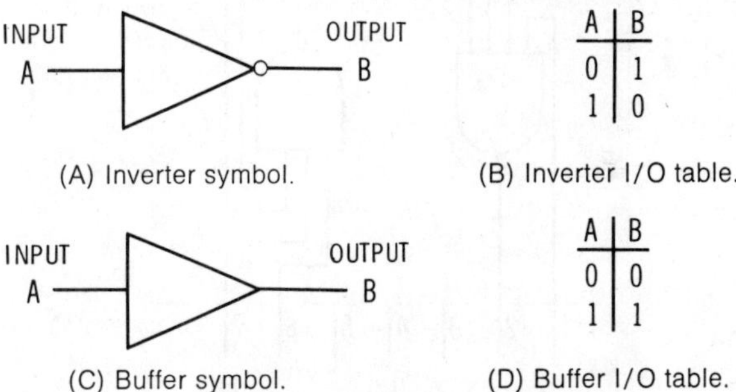

A	B
0	1
1	0

(A) Inverter symbol. (B) Inverter I/O table.

A	B
0	0
1	1

(C) Buffer symbol. (D) Buffer I/O table.

Fig. 5-17. Inverter and buffer.

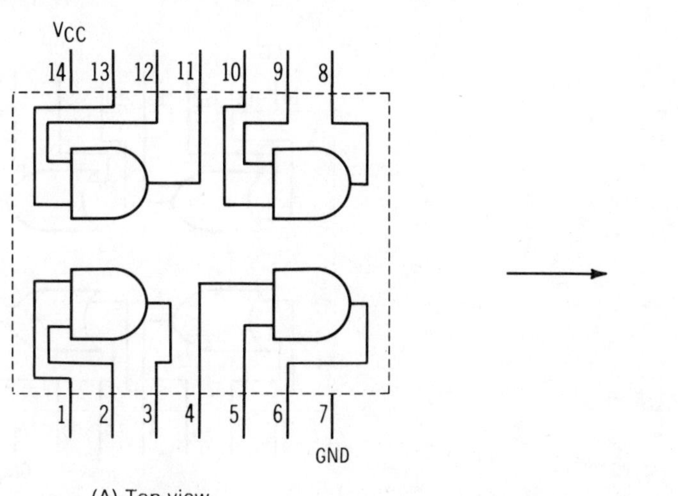

(A) Top view.

APPROXIMATELY 1/4" X 3/4"

(ACTUAL SIZE)

(B) Chip.

Fig. 5-15. TTL AND gate chip.

(A) NAND gate.

A	B	C
0	0	1
0	1	1
1	0	1
1	1	0

(B) NAND I/O table.

(C) NOR gate.

A	B	C
0	0	1
0	1	0
1	0	0
1	1	0

(D) NOR I/O table.

Fig. 5-18. NAND and NOR gates.

When an inverter is joined to an AND gate or OR gate, a NAND (*N*ot *AND*) or NOR (*N*ot *OR*) gate is produced, as shown in Fig. 5-18. For convenience, the NAND and NOR gates are shown with a circle at the output, indicating that when the gate performs the function, the output goes low. Why NAND and NOR gates? Because of the integration methods involved, it is easier and cheaper to implement NAND and NOR gates. Typical 14-pin chips for TTL NAND gates, NOR gates, inverters, and OR gates are shown in Fig. 5-19. They are the same size as the one in Fig. 5-15.

Suppose that we take what we have discussed so far and build a circuit to "decode" a binary value of 01010111 (87_{10}) for use in a controller to detect an

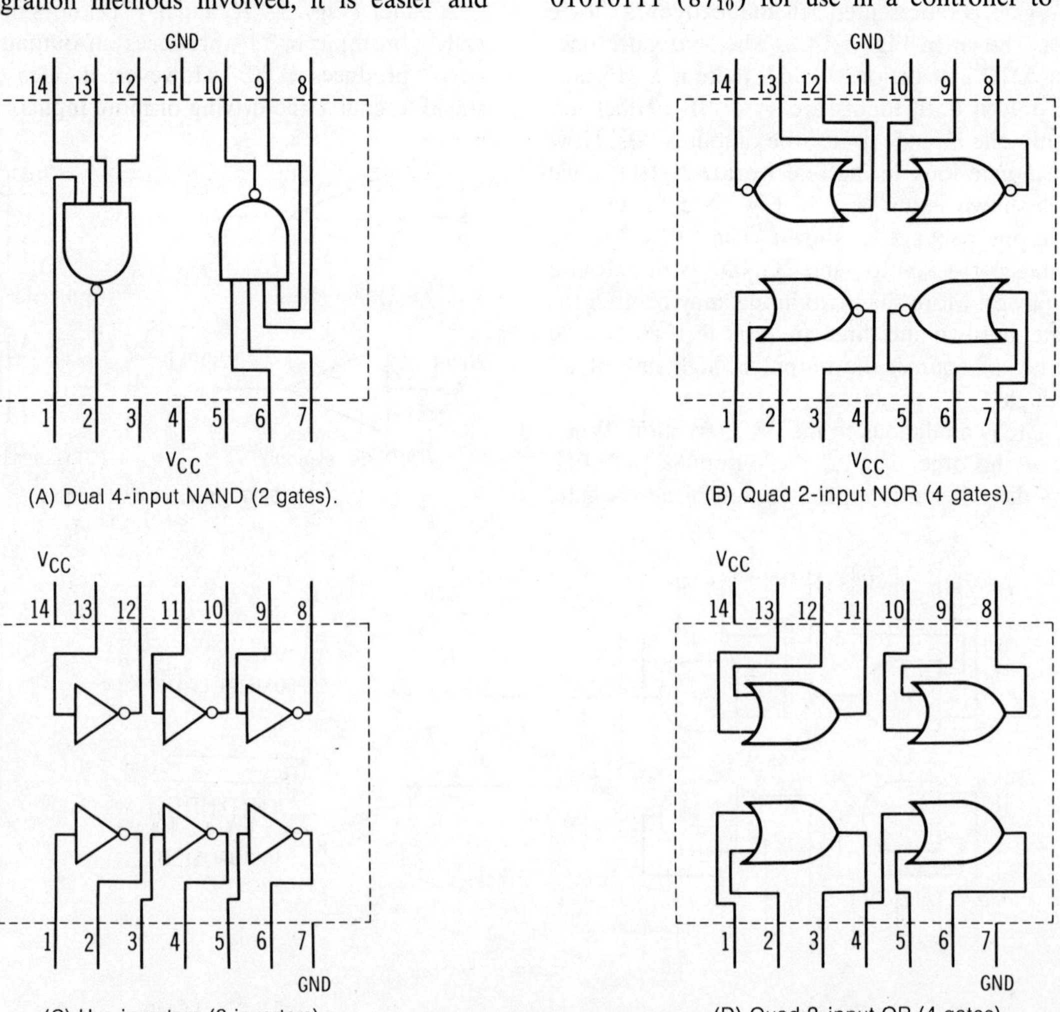

(A) Dual 4-input NAND (2 gates).

(B) Quad 2-input NOR (4 gates).

(C) Hex inverters (6 inverters).

(D) Quad 2-input OR (4 gates).

Fig. 5-19. Typical TTL packaging.

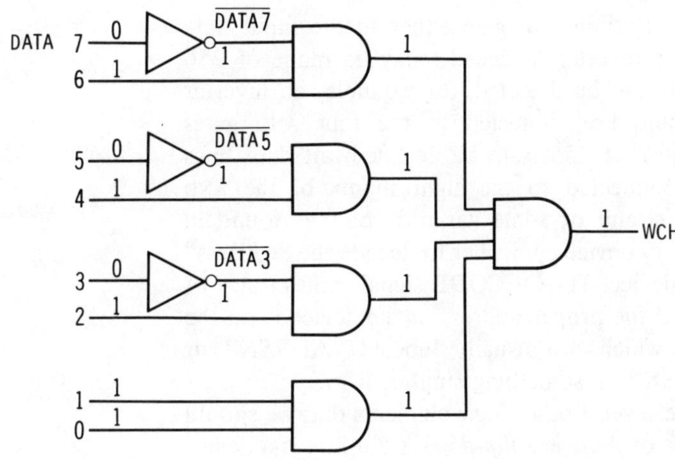

Fig. 5-20. ASCII "W" detect circuit.

DATA 7	$\overline{7}$	6	5	$\overline{5}$	4	3	$\overline{3}$	2	1	0	WCH
0	1	1	0	1	1	0	1	1	1	1	1
0	1	0	0	1	0	0	1	0	0	0	0
1	0	1	1	0	1	1	0	1	1	1	0

ASCII "W." The most significant bit will be called DATA7, and the least significant bit will be DATA0, with the bits in between labeled with their powers of two. We want an output called "WCH" for "W" character to go true when DATA6, DATA4, DATA2, DATA1, and DATA0 are true (1) and when DATA7, DATA5, and DATA3 are false (0). One way of implementing this is shown in Fig. 5-20. A truth table indicates the state of each signal in the circuit. Try using other values of DATA7 to DATA0 and you will see that only when the data are 01010111_2 will "WCH" come true. The circles around the signal names in Fig. 5-20 indicate which signals must be true for "WCH" to be true.

A generalized circuit to decode any value of eight bits from 0 to 255 is shown in Fig. 5-21. By connecting the

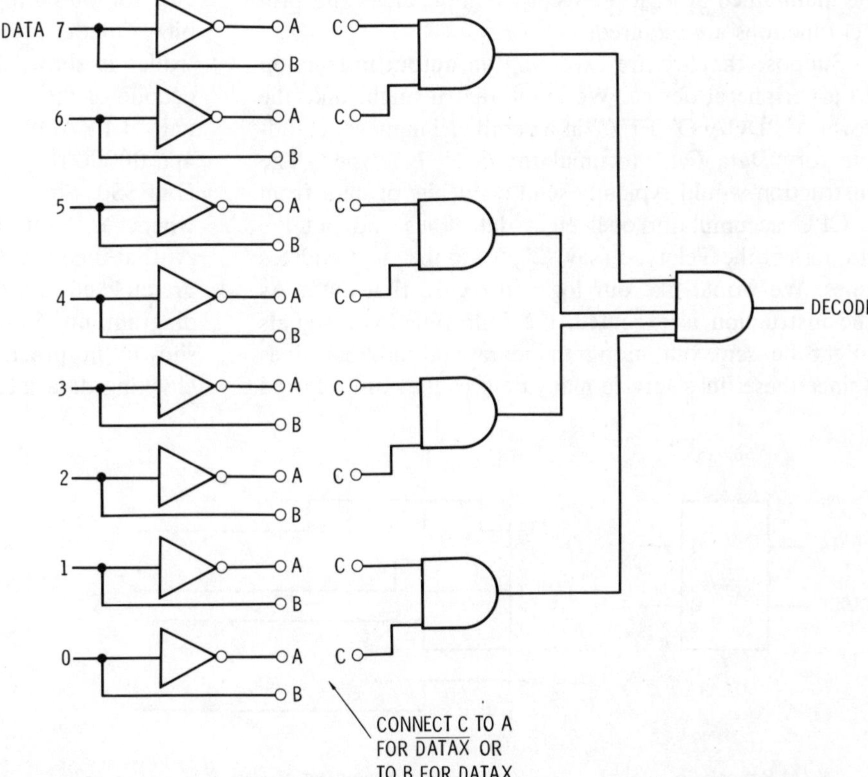

Fig. 5-21. Generalized 8-bit decode circuit.

input to the leading AND gate either to the input data line or to its inverter, a decode may be made of 256 values. If 0 is to be detected, for example, all inverter outputs would be connected to the four AND gates (eight inputs). If 255 is to be detected, all data lines would be connected to the eight inputs of the AND gates. This circuit or some variation of it is found in virtually every device controller to decode the "address" of the I/O device. The DECODE signal comes true (1) if and only if the proper address of the device is on the data lines, which are usually labeled "ADRSX" or "ADDRESSX" or something similar.

There are several other logic elements that we should look at. One of these is a *flip-flop*. A flip-flop is a device used to remember a 1 or 0 state. Once "set" ("1"), the flip-flop will hold that value until reset to a "0." The schematic representation for a simple flip-flop is shown in Fig. 5-22. This is a simple "D" flip-flop that records a data input when the "clock" signal makes a transition from a logic 0 to a logic 1. If the data input at that time is a 1, a 1 is recorded; if a 0, a 0 is recorded. When the clock rises to a 1 at time T_1, a 1 is recorded in the flip-flop. Note that the "true" output is labeled "Q" and that the false output is "not Q," or $\overline{Q}$. True and false outputs are usually provided with flip-flops. A "clear" input resets the flip-flop (Q=0) when a logic 0 is applied to the clear input at any time. The clock input is not involved in this "direct clear." Likewise, a "preset" input sets the flip-flop (Q=1) at any time when the preset is a logic 0. Obviously, then, both the preset and clear inputs must be maintained at logic 1 except when the clear and preset functions are required.

Suppose that we are executing an output instruction to a peripheral device. We know that it might take the form of "DOA O, TTY" in assembler language, standing for "*Da*ta *O*ut *A*ccumulator *O* to *T*ele*ty*pe." The instruction would typically send eight bits of data from a CPU accumulator over eight data lines and put the address of the Teletype (say "2") onto the eight address lines. We would like our logic to record that data. As the instruction is executed, the following logic signals might be sent out along the data and address lines (since these lines service many devices they are referred to as buses): a logic signal telling the peripheral device when an I/O address is present, a logic signal indicating when data for the device are present, and logic signals indicating what type of instruction is being executed (read, write, control, etc.). Fig. 5-23 shows a typical set of signals.

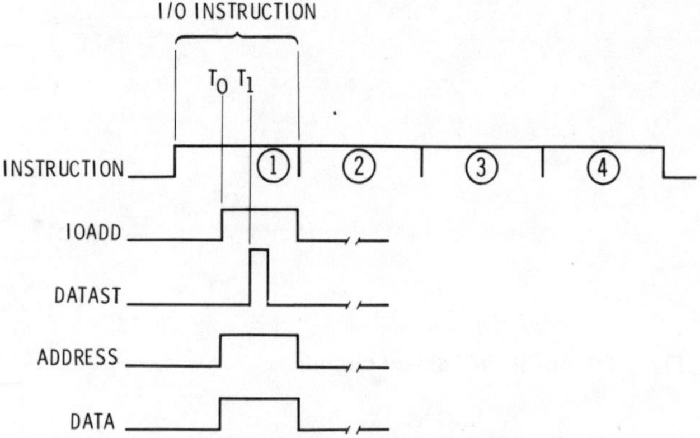

Fig. 5-23. Typical I/O interface signals.

INSTRUCTION indicates the current instruction being executed. Let's say our I/O instruction is executed at 1. At time T_0, IOADD comes high, indicating that an I/O address is on the ADDRESS lines. Also at this time, the device address (in this case 00000010_2) is put onto the eight ADDRESS lines, and the ASCII data for the Teletype are put on the eight DATA lines. To allow the lines to "settle" at time T_1, DATST (*data strobe*) comes up. DATAST is essentially a clock pulse that clocks the data into eight flip-flops. The complete circuit for outputing the ASCII character (or any eight bits of data) into the eight flip-flops of a Teletype controller is shown in Fig. 5-24. The upper portion is a decode of the Teletype address of $00000010_2 = 2$. Signal "TTYADD" comes true when "IOADD" is true and 00000010_2 is present on ADDRESS7 through ADDRESS0. Signal "CLKDAT" (*Clock Data*) goes true whenever the tty address is present and DATST is true. At that time the data on lines DATA7 through DATA0 are clocked into the D flip-flops D7 through D0. In this diagram no lines indicating a "read" or "write" are shown; in practice, these would be necessary before clocking data into the flip-flops.

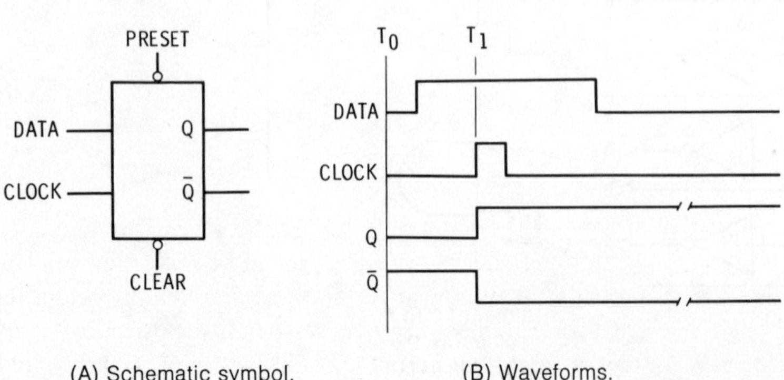

(A) Schematic symbol.

(B) Waveforms.

Fig. 5-22. D flip-flop.

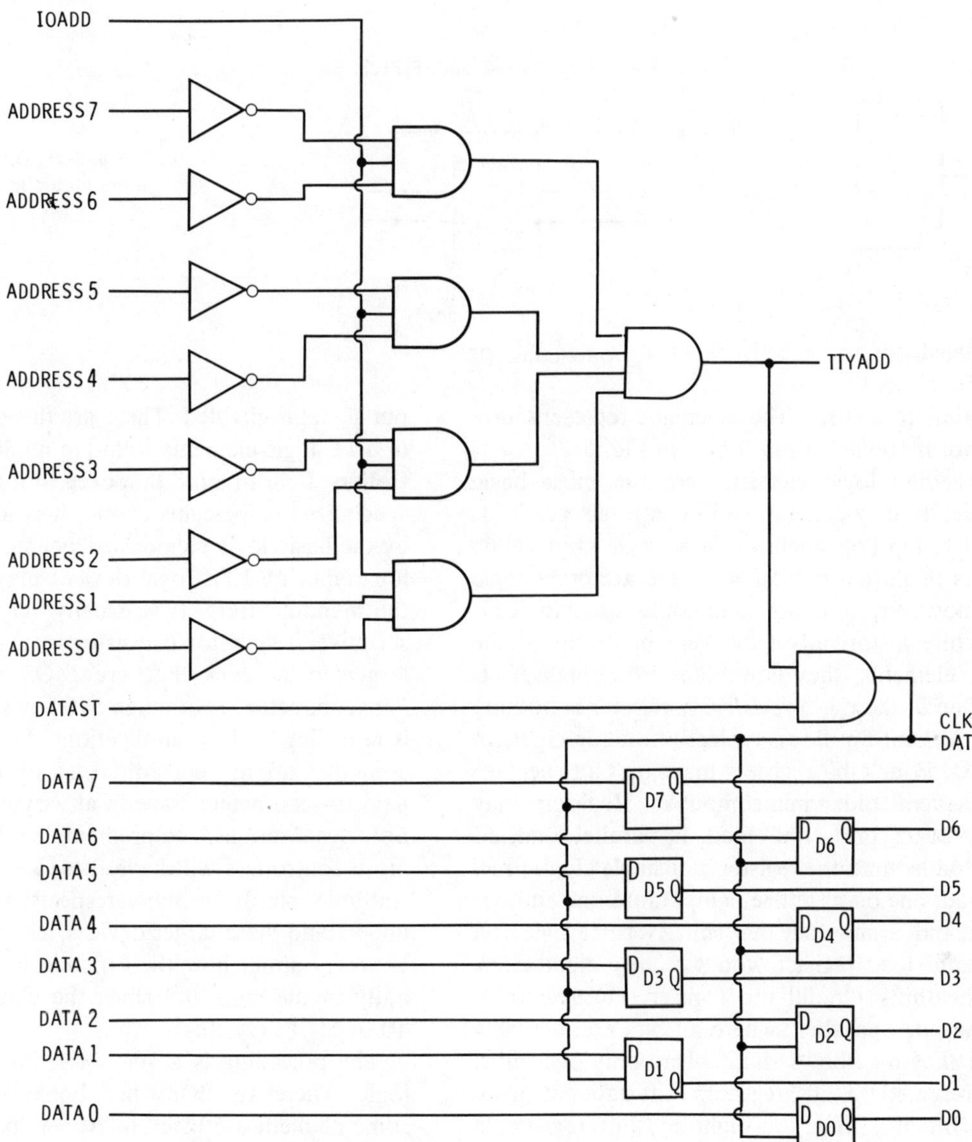

Fig. 5-24. I/O data output circuit.

The D flip-flop is one of several types of flip-flops. The other popular type is the *J-K flip-flop,* similar to the D type in that it has a Q and $\overline{Q}$ output, usually a preset or clear, and a clock, but different in that it has two inputs: a J and K. The schematic representation of a J-K flip-flop is shown in Fig. 5-25. When both inputs are logic 0, at the clock time nothing changes. If J is 1 and K is 0, the flip-flop is set similar to the D type. If J is 0 and K is 1, the flip-flop is reset. If both inputs are 1, the flip-flop "toggles"; that is, it changes to a 1 if it was a 0 and to a 0 if it was a 1. The J-K flip-flop may be used identically as a D type by grounding K. However, it may also be used in counters, as will be discussed later.

The last type of single logic element to be discussed in the *one-shot* or *monostable multivibrator.* Although the name is foreboding, the one-shot multivibrator is

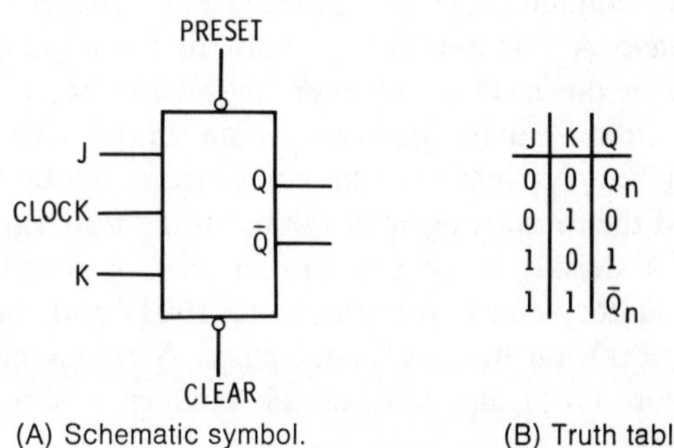

J	K	Q
0	0	Q_n
0	1	0
1	0	1
1	1	$\overline{Q}_n$

(A) Schematic symbol. (B) Truth table.

Fig. 5-25. J-K flip-flop.

simply a flip-flop that once set is reset automatically after a predetermined time that may vary from microseconds to milliseconds. The one-shot multivibrator is used for a number of purposes—one such purpose is to wait a safe time before clocking in data if the inputs

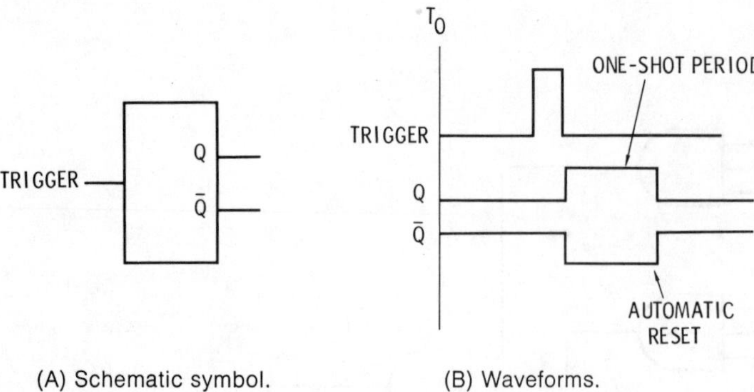

(A) Schematic symbol. (B) Waveforms.

Fig. 5-26. One-shot or monostable multivibrator.

take some time to "settle." The schematic representation of a one-shot multivibrator is shown in Fig. 5-26.

The preceding logic elements are the most basic types. Typically they come in from one to six per TTL chip; one J-K flip-flop might be in a single chip, while six inverters might be in another. There are other logic elements, however, that are commonly used in TTL circuits. While historically they were made up of the basic logic elements, they now come in a single TTL package. One of these is a *register*. A register is nothing more than several flip-flops, typically four or eight, in a single chip. Four 4-bit registers make up CPU accumulators in several older minicomputers. Registers may be parallel "load" or "serial" load. In parallel load, all inputs are loaded into the register at a single clock time. In serial load, one bit at a time is input into one end per clock time and a simultaneous shift is performed; an eight-bit serial load register would require eight clock times (eight shifts) to fill the register. Outputs from registers may be "parallel" where all bits are available at once, or they may be "serial," where only one bit at a time is presented. "Shift" registers shift data out or in, or both, a bit at a time. An eight-bit shift register, a standard TTL type, is shown in Fig. 5-27. Note that it is made up of the basic logic elements.

Another common type of advanced logic element is the *counter*. A counter does simply that—it counts pulses up or down. Some counters may be preset to a specified value. Binary counters count in binary. A four-bit binary counter would count from 0000_2 to 1111_2 and then restart again at 0000_2 on the next clock (pulse). A decade counter counts in tens. A four-bit decade counter counts from 0000_2 to 1001_2 and then resets to 0000_2 on the next count pulse. A representative counter, a TTL up/down decade counter, is shown in Fig. 5-28.

Other specialized types of chips have been developed. A *demultiplexer* effectively switches a single input to one of several outputs, depending on the state of address inputs. A *multiplexer* works the opposite—it switches one of several inputs to a single output, depending upon the state of the address inputs. A *comparator* compares two sets of inputs. If they are equal, an "equality" output signal is enabled. These are the more common types of TTL logic elements found in minicomputer I/O controllers. Bear in mind that even though the function of a specialized chip seems exotic, it is always implemented by the basic logic elements. Documentation for the various types of TTL logic devices may be obtained from the manufacturers. It is usually very complete and descriptive. Transistor-transistor logic is supplemented by larger logic chips that are MOS type (*M*etal-*O*xide *S*emiconductor). Although MOS is slower than TTL, it is replacing TTL in applications such as "asynchronous communications" controllers (a tty is an asynchronous device—characters come in at varying times; hence, it is not "synchronous," or predictable). Probably more and more controllers will have these large-scale chips (typically 48 pins). In many respects, it is much easier to understand these larger devices, since one does not have to worry about how the function is implemented internally in the chip and since the chip replaces possibly 40 or 50 TTL chips.

The preceding is a very brief introduction to digital logic. There are many fine books on the subject and some of them are listed in Appendix F. Because digital logic is "modular" and because everything is built up from the basic logic elements, it is fairly easy to learn and to reach the point where one is able to design and implement simple circuitry. For our purpose, i.e., interfacing peripheral equipment to a computer, the logic involved in most cases need not be too sophisticated, unless one is interfacing a disc or magnetic tape.

Simple Interface Examples

Let's take a look at a "real-world" example of a simple interface and discuss how to implement it on two computers, the Data General Nova series and a microprocessor (MPU) system that uses a Motorola MC6800 microprocessor chip. The device we wish to implement is one that will read eight switches representing "burglar" alarm type inputs from several different rooms of a home. We have run cabling as required to the eight switches and have brought the cables to a central point where the computer is located. The system is shown in Fig. 5-29. Note that some of the switches

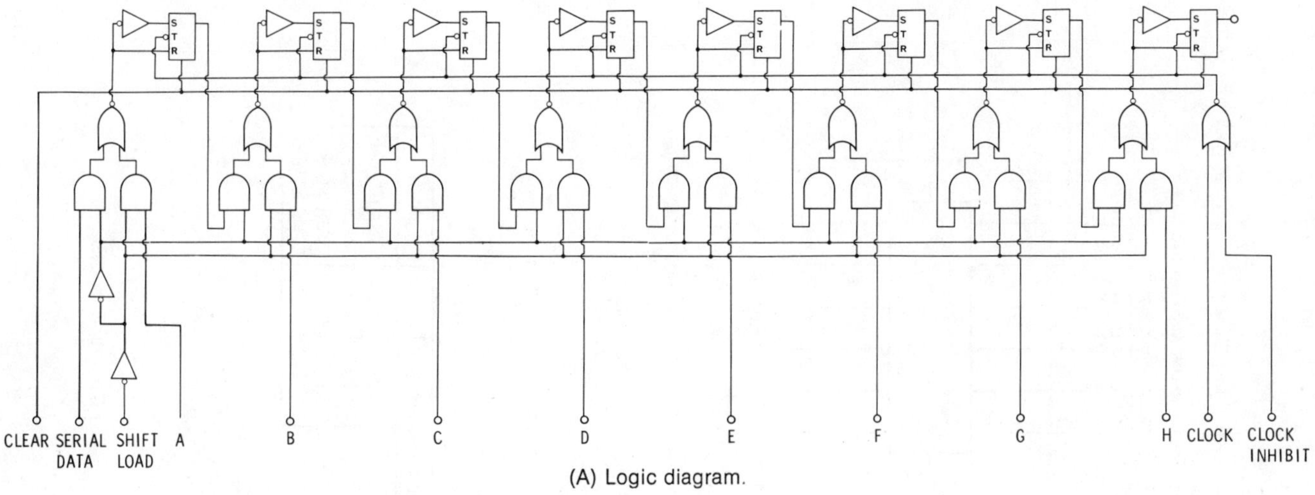

(A) Logic diagram.

DUAL-IN-LINE AND FLAT PACKAGE

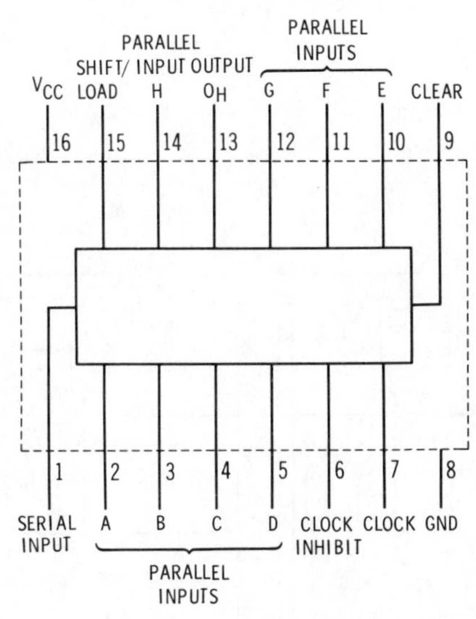

(B) Connection diagram.

SHIFT LOAD	FUNCTION
1	SERIAL IN SERIAL OUT
0	PARALLEL IN SERIAL OUT

(C) Truth table.

Fig. 5-27. TTL 8-bit shift register.

are normally closed (as, for example, to indicate a window closure). We want to be able to continuously monitor the state of the eight switches and detect closures or openings by our minicomputer program. We are never "writing" to this I/O device since that is meaningless, but will only be reading the device state.

The Data General Nova computer might be a Nova 1200, Nova 800, or Nova 2, to mention a few models. The publication providing interface information in this case is *How to Use the Nova Computers,* obtainable from Data General Corporation, Southboro, Massachusetts. A section in this book, entitled "Interfacing," has about 45 pages of information on how to interface to a Nova computer, and includes interface signals, connections, and logic diagrams for standard interfaces. First of all, we need a 15-inch × 15-inch printed-circuit board as described in the DGC manual. This can be obtained from DGC, or a similar board might be fabricated or picked up surplus. An alternative to a board might be to connect cable wires directly to the "backplane" of the computer—the backplane is the printed-circuit board with wire-wrap pins whose opposite side connects to the plugs for the various plug-in boards. Once we have the proper board, we have access to the "I/O bus" consisting of all interface signals. These signals are described in detail in the DGC manual and basically consist of 16 bidirectional data lines (data go either way for reads or writes), 6 device selection lines (for the device address), and 25 control lines.

Let's think a little about the logic of our interface. We need no registers to hold data but can simply sample the lines every time our program does a "DIA Y,XXX," which is a *D*ata *I*n *A*ccumulator instruction that transfers 8 (or 16) bits of data into CPU accumulator Y

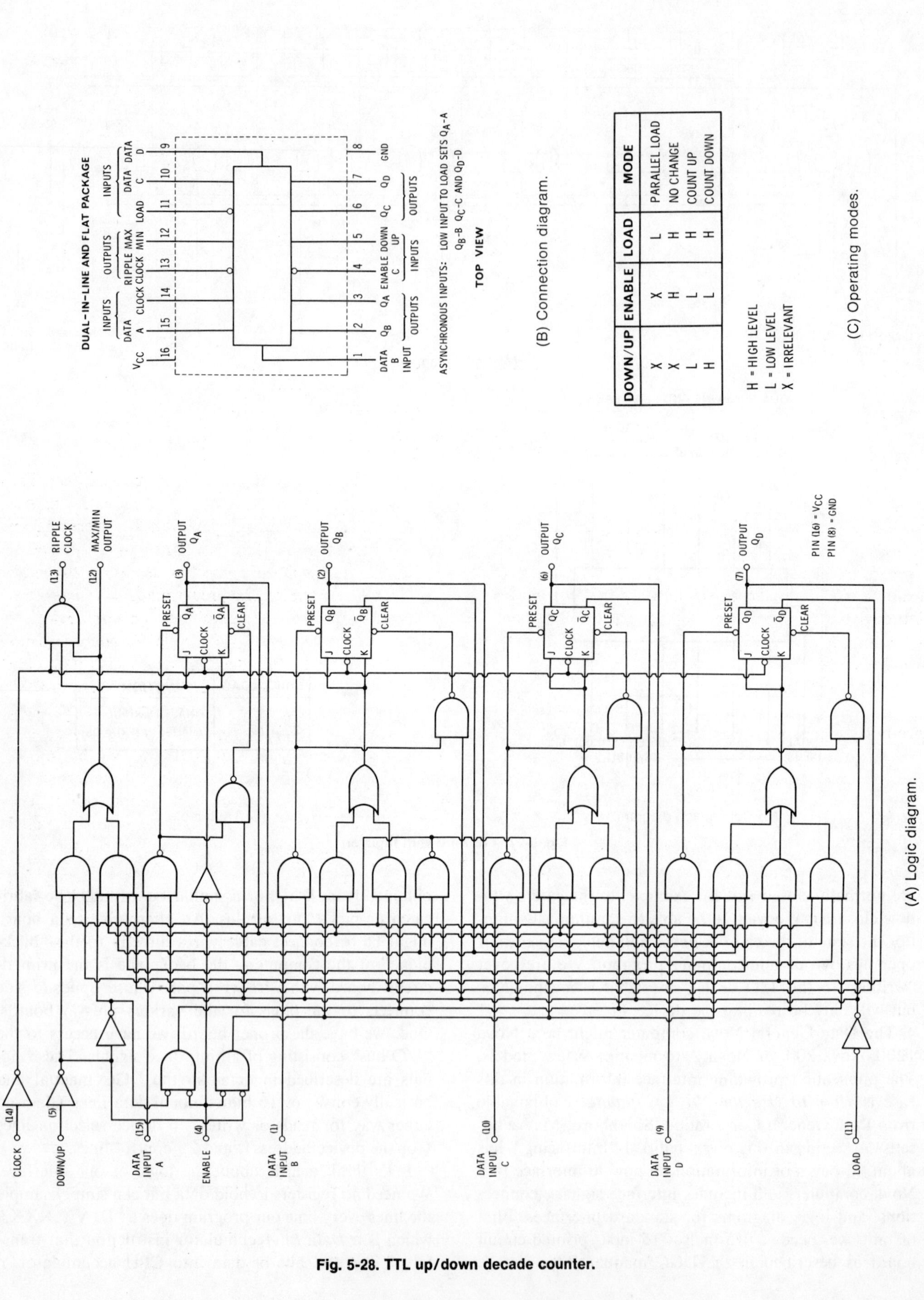

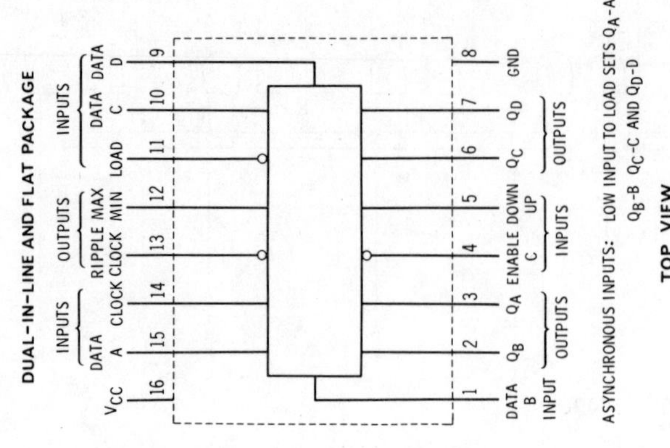

(B) Connection diagram.

DOWN/UP	ENABLE	LOAD	MODE
X	X	L	PARALLEL LOAD
X	H	H	NO CHANGE
L	L	H	COUNT UP
H	L	H	COUNT DOWN

H = HIGH LEVEL
L = LOW LEVEL
X = IRRELEVANT

(C) Operating modes.

(A) Logic diagram.

Fig. 5-28. TTL up/down decade counter.

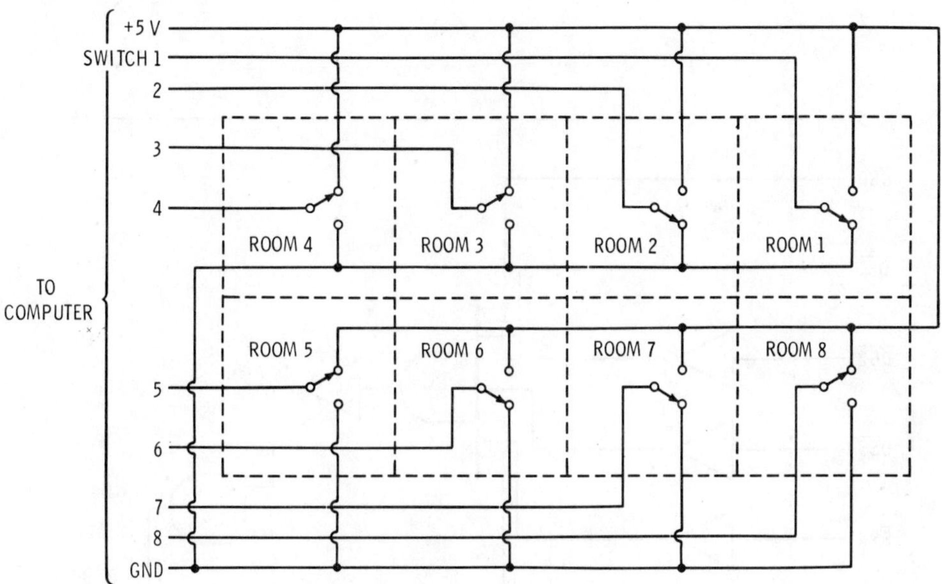

Fig. 5-29. Burglar alarm system.

(0–3) from device "XXX." We will assign our device address to be 16_8. This is "normally" used for a card reader, but our system has no card reader and this device address is available. Any device not used in the system can be used. There are 77_8 different addresses available (77_8 is dedicated to CPU special functions). Although we could use interrupts for our burglar alarm, they are not really necessary since we can read the switches every 1 second or so and get a sufficiently fast response to call the police. Also, there is no need for a DMA transfer of data. This is neither a high-speed device nor one that must transfer a large amount of data.

Let's go down the list of bus signals and see which ones are required. Lines DS0 to DS5 are device selection lines. When they have 16_8 on them, we will know that our device is being addressed. Lines DATA0 to DATA15 are 16 data lines. We will be using only eight —DATA7 through DATA15 to read our eight switches. Next are three signals generated from the CPU for *D*ata *O*ut *A*ccumulator instructions (DOA). Since we never write, these can be ignored. One of the three *D*ata *I*n *A*ccumulators is needed, the DIA. We will ignore the other two, DIB and DIC. Three other signals, STRT, CLR, and IOPLS, are generated by the CPU from an I/O instruction with certain bits set to start, clear, or pulse the I/O device. In our simple interface we need none of these. Two other signals, SELB and SELD, are concerned with "Busy" and "Done" flags for the device. Since our device is never busy (data are always available immediately), we can ignore these. Five other signals, RQENB, INTR, INTA, and MSKO, are concerned with interrupts. We are not using interrupts, so these can be ignored. The next eight signals, DCHR, DCHP, DCHA, DCHMO, DCHM1, DCHI, DCHO, and OVFLO, are for data channel (DMA) transfers. We are not doing this, so we will ignore these also. The last remaining signal is IORST, which is a "master clear" for all I/O devices generated by executing an "IORST" instruction. Here there is nothing to reset.

Looking further into the interface section of the manual, we find the timing for programmed I/O transfers. It appears in Fig. 5-30, simplified for our device. It appears that all we must do is decode our address (16_8) from DS0 through DS5, detect DATIA, and gate data onto DATA8 through DATA15 at the proper time.

The "device select" signal can be implemented as we have discussed previously. This is shown in Fig. 5-31. When DS5 through DS0 hold 010000_2, signal "DEVSEL" is enabled (comes true). Note that the signals on the bus are the false output of the address bits. The $\overline{\text{DEVSEL}}$ is ANDed with DATIA to give the signal $\overline{\text{DATAINA}}$. This signal, in turn, enables the output of the eight signal lines to data bus data lines $\overline{\text{DATA8}}$ through $\overline{\text{DATA15}}$. This is a complete logic diagram of the burglar alarm interface, but some additional circuitry might be required to provide noise protection and proper termination as per the DGC manual. It is an indication of how simply some devices can be interfaced, but admittedly is about the simplest case.

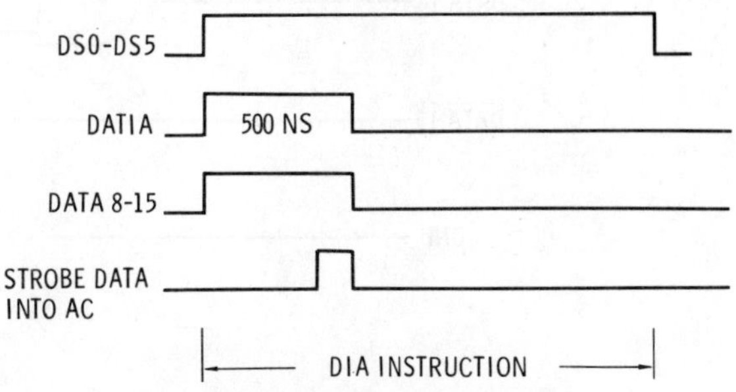

Fig. 5-30. Nova interface timing.

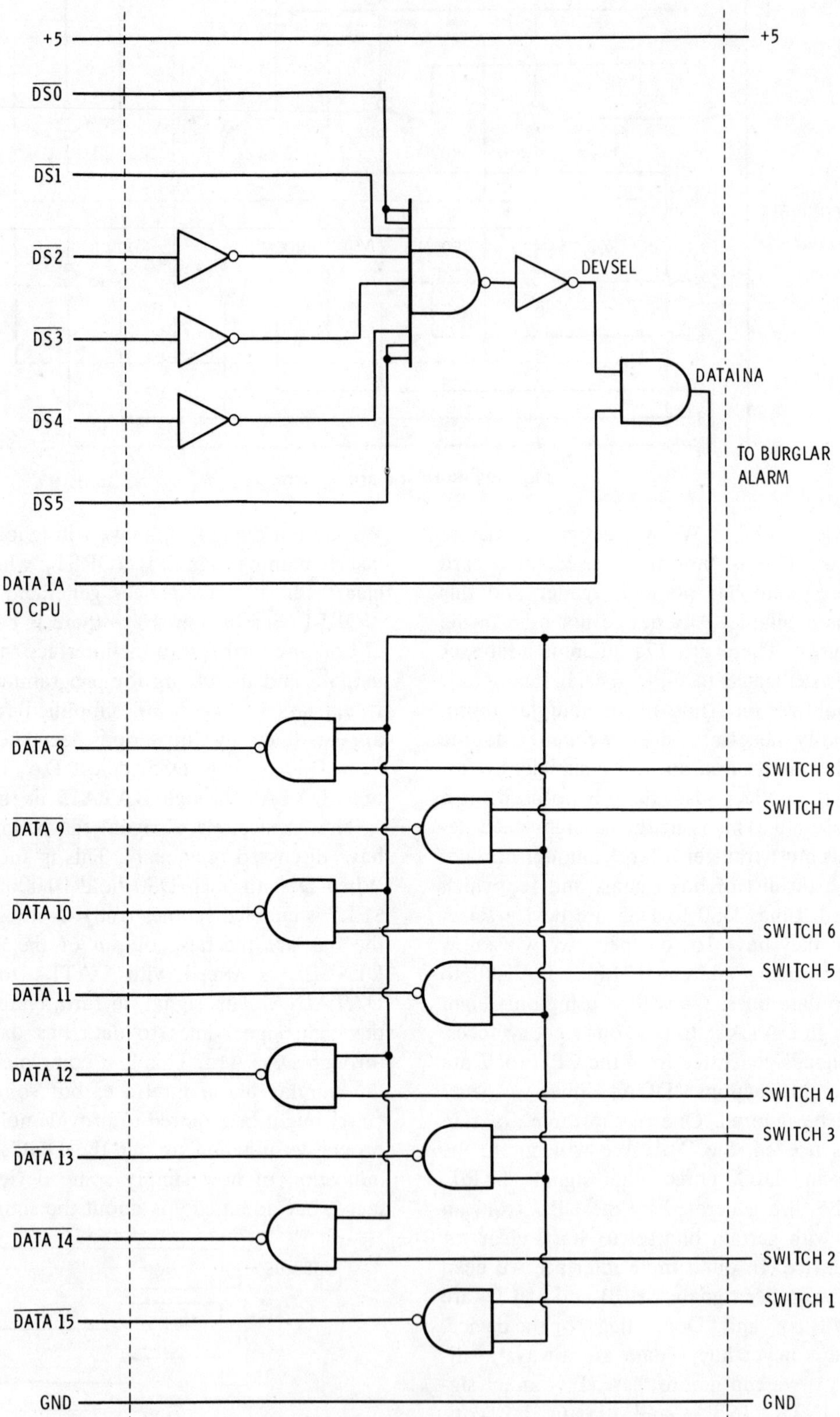

Fig. 5-31. Nova interfacing for simple device.

To use the interface, the Nova program would monitor the device by doing a "DIA 0,20" instruction every second or so. The state of the lines would be read into accumulator 0 of the CPU in the form XXXXXXXX 76543210 where X is "don't care" and 7–0 are the states of the eight switches. The eight bits of input could then be compared to the normal state, which is 00111001_2 (see Fig. 5-29). If there is a difference, a message could be printed on the Teletype indicating the room that is being burgled by a burglar or a cat.

Interfacing the same burglar alarm system to a microcomputer using the Motorola MC6800 microprocessor chip is somewhat different. Every microcomputer manufacturer may name signals differently, but the type and number of signals from the MC6800 chip itself are, of course, the same. There are two clocks, $\phi1$ and $\phi2$, externally supplied to the chip and probably on the CPU board. Sixteen address lines, A0 through A15, provide an address either for memory or for *peripheral I/O addressing.* Eight data lines, D0 through D7, are used to transfer data to or from the MPU (CPU) registers. A HALT signal stops MPU execution, but this does not concern us for our device. A Three-State Control (TSC) signal likewise is not a signal we are interested in, as it provides access to memory by devices other than the MPU for DMA purposes and we are not interested in that for this device controller. A Read/Write signal (R/W) signals memory and peripherals whether the MPU is in a read or write state. Valid Memory Address (VMA) is a signal that indicates if there is a memory or peripheral address on A0–A15. Data Bus Enable (DBE) controls the data bus lines D0–D7 for DMA operations; again, we are not interested. Bus Available (BA) indicates that the CPU is stopped—we are not interested in this signal either. Since we are not using interrupts for this device, the $\overline{\text{Interrupt Request}}$ ($\overline{\text{IRQ}}$) is not required; likewise for the $\overline{\text{Non-Maskable Interrupt}}$ ($\overline{\text{NMI}}$) signal. The last signal, $\overline{\text{Reset}}$, signals a power fail or initial start-up—another signal not required.

The signals involved, then, are $\phi1$, $\phi2$, R/W, A0–A15, VMA, and D0–D7. The relationship between them is given in the Motorola MC6800 Programming Manual and is shown in Fig. 5-32. When a read is being performed to address XXX_{16} and VMA is high, we can gate the data lines from the burglar alarm system to D0–D7. The circuit for doing this is shown in Fig. 5-33, and appears very similar to the Nova implementation.

Because there are no separate I/O address lines, the memory address must also address peripheral devices in the MC6800. This poses no special problems as long as a device address is a "nonexistent" memory address. If we assume that this system has only 40K of memory, then address $101XXXXXXXXXXXXX_2$ will never be used as a memory address and we can use it as a peripheral address instead. Here we decode only the most significant three bits (101) to produce a "DEVSEL" signal when VMA is also true. With the device selected and a read signal (write to the device is meaningless), DATAINA is true and gates the eight device lines to data lines D0 through D7. Executing a "LDAA" (*L*oad *A*ccumulator *A*) or a "LDAB" (*L*oad *A*ccumulator *B*) to a memory address of $101XXXXXXXXXXXXX_2$ will load the eight data bits representing the state of the eight burglar alarm lines into the appropriate MPU accumulator. Operation then proceeds as in the Nova

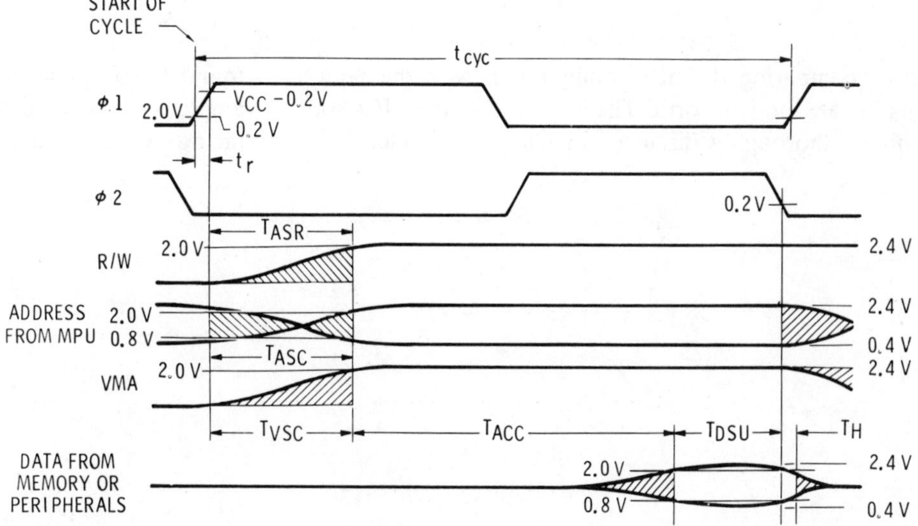

Fig. 5-32. MC6800 read data from peripherals.

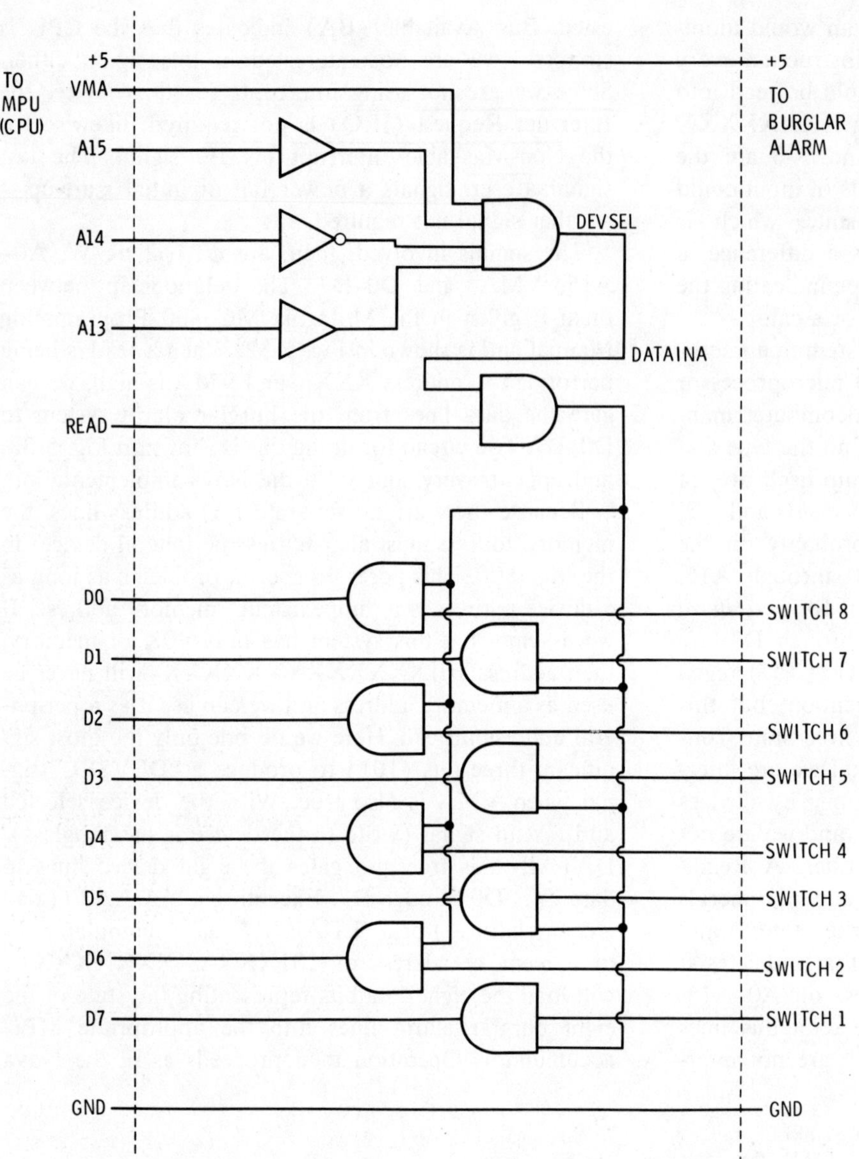

Fig. 5-33. Motorola MC6800 interfacing for simple device.

case, comparing the new configuration with the "normal" state, and so forth. The structure of the MC6800 will be thoroughly discussed in Chapter 8, since it is found in so many microcomputers, but this simple example is intended to show the similarities between interfacing devices in a minicomputer and microprocessor.

CHAPTER

6

How to Select and Buy a Minicomputer

This chapter discusses two questions. The first is: "How does one evaluate and select a minicomputer or microcomputer?" There must be a way to rationally select a computer system to perform your particular functions. Since you will be spending your hard-earned cash to purchase a computer system, you should get the best system for your dollar. Make no mistake, either, there are some "dogs" on the market today, both in the used minicomputer area and in the new microprocessor area. The second question is: "How does one buy the minicomputer selected?" There are some obvious and some not so obvious precautions to take in purchasing any type of computer equipment.

EVALUATING AND SELECTING

The selection of a minicomputer for your requirements breaks down into a number of factors. Let's look at some important groups of factors and then come up with selection criteria. The selection criteria will be based upon a number of factors. Each of these factors can be assigned a weight, which is really your personal preference for that factor. For example, if you have just inherited a small fortune, money may not be a factor at all, and the weight of that factor will be zero.

The first factor in our scheme is *speed* of the minicomputer. Minicomputers operate at memory cycle speeds of about 600 nanoseconds to 2 microseconds (0.6 to 2 microseconds), while microcomputers currently run at about 2 microseconds per cycle. However, the actual number of instructions per second that can be executed is a function not only of the memory cycle time but of the number of memory cycles or CPU cycles in an instruction. How do we evaluate the effective speed (instructions per second) of a minicomputer? Industry does it by running "benchmark" programs for various types of computers. These may be programs that are very similar to the actual type of programming that will be done with the system, but they may also be generalized programs. If, for instance, your programming is heavily computing (rather than I/O) oriented and a typical program will do a large number of operations with floating-point numbers, you would probably run a benchmark program with floating-point manipulations. If your system will be run for various types of problems—BASIC compilations, report printing, and some "number-crunching" program—you would run a set of generalized benchmarks for various machines. Benchmarks can be slanted towards the characteristics of a particular machine by orienting the program towards certain instructions in which the machine is efficient. Benchmark programs are also very much influenced by the skill of the programmer in utilizing the instruction set of the machine. In the Table 6-1, every attempt was made to be fair in the types of benchmarks. "Average" programming skill was assumed for a programmer who has been working as a programmer in assembly language on the selected machine for about one year. The benchmarks were generalized benchmarks of three short programs.

Benchmark I transfers 100 bytes of data from one block of memory to another, a very common operation in programming. Benchmark II converts from a six-digit ASCII octal value to a binary value of 16 bits. Benchmark III searches an 80-item string of characters for a given character. Table 6-1 shows the results in the

Table 6-1. Instruction Speed Benchmarks

Computer	Benchmark*			Average
	I	II	III	
8008-1 μp chip	69,215	1767.5	5542.5	25,762
8080 μp chip	7854	1018	3546	4139
MC6800 μp chip	3918	291	807	1672
F8 μp chip	5247	439	899	2195
MCS6502 μp chip	2604	447	440	1162
PDP-8/E	1158	125.8	668.8	651
Nova 800	688	58.8	252.6	334
CAI LSI-3/05 (core)	4006	339	1248.75	1865
Interdata 6/16	290.5	88.3	390.5	256

* Time in microseconds.

speed of each benchmark, the average speed, and the minicomputer or microprocessor chip involved.* (The average speed is somewhat misleading. It is only the average of these three benchmarks. Programs with a varied "mix" of operations would result in different averages.) In the case of microprocessors, specific microcomputers are not listed since the instruction speed is usually identical, because none of them modify the basic microprocessor chip itself. (In some cases, however, a "slow" clock frequency for the microprocessor is used in the microcomputer.) What is the significance of the instruction speed? Well, if you will never have any peripheral other than a Teletype and if all your programs will be heavily I/O oriented, any computer will do your job; your computer will be waiting on the Teletype most of the time. The weighting factor will be 0. If you will be doing almost no I/O and a great deal of number-crunching in BASIC, the weighting factor will be maximum, or 10. Don't forget that BASIC and FORTRAN compile or interpret speeds are a direct function of the instruction speeds.

The second factor is *peripheral availability*. If you want only a Teletype, forget this one—virtually every manufacturer offers a Teletype interface. If you eventually want a floppy disc, line printer, or something else, then look closely at what each system will offer. First of all, does the manufacturer offer the peripheral? If he offers it (in his sales literature), is it *really* designed, implemented, and available? How many have been sold? Are they all working well? What is the cost? If this is used equipment, is it available now and will it be available when you are ready to buy it? Most minicomputer manufacturers offer a larger number of peripherals at a slightly higher price than microcomputer manufacturers; get prices down in black and white.

Another factor is *support software*. What assemblers, loaders, and compilers are available? Are they released yet? If your interest is in FORTRAN only, microcomputers may not be a good choice, since most of them offer interpretive BASIC. If you are interested in maximum speed for real-time applications, an *interpretive* BASIC may not be sufficiently fast to control your DACs and it probably won't offer you a way to interface your equipment in software (to enable you to call an assembly-language driver for a DAC from a BASIC program, for example). How much memory must you have to run the assembler? BASIC? Other compilers? How much room is left for your source statements once you have loaded interpretive BASIC? And an important question for many people—is there a "user's group," an association of people with the same equipment who will trade programs for a common pool? A huge number of PDP-8 programs exist, for example, and there is probably going to be thousands of routines for the MC6800 and 8080-oriented microcomputer sets.

A fourth factor is *reliability*. Is your prospective purchase a third-generation minicomputer that is no longer being manufactured? If so, are you capable of repairing it, or can you find someone who is? What will he charge? If the minicomputer is still supported by the factory, how soon can they get a repairman out to you, and what is the cost? Typically, manufacturers charge for travel time to and from the repair site, and charge about $35 per hour for time spent at the site. An alternative might be shipping the unit to the factory for repair at a lower rate. What is the MTTR—the "mean time to repair"? In other words, how long will it take to fix it? Typically, several hours might be required. What is the MTBF—the "mean time between failures"? How long will the minicomputer or peripherals run before they fail? Typically, this may be a year for minicomputers and it probably will be even longer for microcomputers. The more mechanically complex the peripheral, the less the MTBF. You should think about how the necessary repair work will be done on a minicomputer and its peripherals.

Another factor is the *type of memory*. If you have only a Teletype and a CPU, do you want to reload a program every time you turn off the power? This would have to be done with a microcomputer RAM memory, but not with a minicomputer core memory where the loaded program remains in the core after powering down. If reloading the assembler or compiler each time (10 or 15 minutes worth of paper-tape reading) is not objectionable, fine. On the other hand, RAM memory prices will continue to come down, but core memory prices will probably remain pretty much where they are. In addition, RAM memory boards are less complex and easier to repair.

A factor often overlooked is *documentation*. What documentation is available? Is there complete documentation on every piece of hardware in the system? On every piece of software? Are the source listings supplied with any of the support software (typically they are not)? Is the material well written? This factor is particularly important in the case of used equipment where the manufacturer may be out of business. Without complete documentation, the equipment may be worthless.

Another factor related to the instruction set and architecture of the minicomputer is the *efficiency* of the system in use of memory. In other words, to perform a certain function, how much memory will be required? In one minicomputer system, all instructions may be 16-bit words; in another, 16-bit and 32-bit words may be used. Obviously, if all instructions require 32-bit instruction words, a lot of memory could be "eaten up" rapidly by the program. This factor was more important

* Appendix I gives the individual instruction times for each benchmark.

when memory was more expensive than it is now, but it is still a consideration. Representative efficiency in terms of the number of eight-bit bytes needed to implement the benchmarks discussed previously is given in Table 6-2 for various minicomputer and microcomputer systems.

The last and probably most important factor to most people is *cost*. Having considered all of the above factors, what is the final equipment configuration? How much memory will be involved, how many peripherals will be used, and what interface options will be required? Is the software included in the purchase price or is it "unbundled" (priced separately)? If you are considering a used minicomputer system and you are certain it is available, estimate the used cost at about 60 percent of the new purchase price.

Now make a list of all important factors. A sample list is shown in Table 6-3. Assign each factor an importance weight of 0 to 10 based on its impact to you. A factor that does not enter into the evaluation will be 0. Now list each system being considered by assigning a value of 0–10 to the factor. If a system is superfast, the "speed" value would be 10, for example. Multiply the factor value by the factor weight and add all subtotals. Also add all weights (column 2) and multiply the result by 10. This result is the "ideal" system for your needs—the closer a system comes to this ideal value, the closer it is to your needs.

In the example of Table 6-3, a total of eight groups were considered. Seven groups were given equal weights of 100 per group, except for cost. Cost was a very important factor and therefore given a weight of 200. Weights were then assigned to all factors within each

Table 6-2. Memory Storage Benchmarks

Computer	Benchmark* I	II	III	Average
8008-1 μp chip	41	39	25	35
8080 μp chip	17	26	18	20
MC6800 μp chip	33	38	16	29
F8 μp chip	20	37	13	26
MCS6502 μp chip	14	39	16	23
PDP-8/E	23	47	45	38
Nova 800	28	50	42	40
CAI LSI-3/05 (core)	34	36	24	34
Interdata 6/16	18	30	24	24

* Measured in number of eight-bit bytes required. PDP-8/E normalized to eight-bit storage.

Table 6-3. Evaluation Check List Example

Group	Factor	Wt	System A Value	Value X Wt	System B Value	Value X Wt
1	Speed	100	5	500	6	600
2	Teletype Available? Paper Tape Available? Mag Tape Available? Floppy Disc Available? Special Equip Available?	100	8	800	7	700
3	Assembler Available? Loader Available? Interpretive Basic Available? Two-pass Assembler Available? FORTRAN Available? Other Compilers Available? Applications Programs Available? User's Group?	100	8	800	5	500
4	MTTR MTBF Cost to Repair Repair Service Available?	100	8	800	8	800
5	Memory Volatility a Factor?	0				
6	Documentation	100	8	800	2	200
7	Memory Efficiency	100	6	600	7	700
8	Cost of Desired Equip Cost of Add'l Memory	200	6	1200	1	200
	TOTAL IDEAL SYSTEM (10 × WT)	800 8000		5500		3700

group. Some factors were meaningless and were assigned 0 weight. Values of 0–10 were then assigned for each factor for two computer systems, A and B. System A had a moderate computer speed, and a value of 5 was assigned for the speed factor, for example. System B was slightly faster and was given a value of 6 in the same category. Some questions that could be answered "yes" or "no" could be given values of 10 or 0, respectively. After all the "value × weight" figures had been calculated and added, it appeared that System A was closer to the ideal than System B. Naturally, the evaluation process takes some time and is not foolproof, but a systematic evaluation such as this may save a lot of headaches or surprises in the future after the system has been purchased.

BUYING A MINICOMPUTER SYSTEM

Once you have selected a system, the next step is to order and buy it. This really breaks down into three groups: buying a used minicomputer system, buying a new minicomputer system, or buying a microcomputer.

If you are buying a used system, you will be buying either from a private party or a computer broker. In either case, you must verify that the equipment is in good working order. With a computer broker, your payment will usually be held in escrow for a week or so while you check out the equipment. In the private party case, you might suggest that payment be made a week after the purchase, while you verify that everything works. How do you make sure that everything works? The manufacturer of every system has written diagnostics for each unit of the system. These normally would be supplied with the system in a loadable form (usually paper tape) along with operating instructions. Every diagnostic should be run after the system is set up. Several passes of each diagnostic should be performed. In the CPU diagnostic case, several passes are probably sufficient to verify that the CPU is good. Core memory diagnostics, however, should be run continually for several hours, if possible, to give the cores time to heat up (and fail). Diagnostics for disc or magnetic tape should be run with new disc packs or tape to eliminate errors caused by worn-out media. Don't be too surprised if you get "recoverable" errors on magnetic tape or disc, typically 1 or 2 per millions of bits written. (Recoverable errors are temporary errors that do not show up after the diagnostic retries.) If your system includes a Teletype, run the diagnostic and also try the Teletype in local mode. A good local mode test is to punch a tape with all characters terminated by a carriage return and line feed, and then read and simultaneously punch a new tape. The line will be repeated over and over. If the Teletype fails in local, consider having it serviced rather than sending it back—it may be worth it, since Teletypes do not run forever and only some cleaning of the distributor may be required.

Once you have verified that your system works, check off all items you have purchased. You should have all items, including loadable paper tapes (or other medium) of each piece of support software and documentation on the software. You should also have maintenance manuals for each piece of equipment and for the options, complete with logic diagrams and theory of operation manuals. If your documentation appears lacking, check with the computer broker—he may loan you missing tapes or manuals for your duplication, or supply copies for a nominal fee. If he does not have copies, you may be able to buy them from the manufacturer for a nominal fee, varying from several dollars on up to hundreds for specialized programs.

If you are ordering a new minicomputer system, make the delivery COD. This will normally be possible. Here, you should be very thorough in checking out the system when it arrives. The manufacturer will give you 30 or 90 days to verify that the equipment works. In this period, exercise it very thoroughly and leave the equipment on as much as possible to "burn it in." Far from being a superstition, this period of burn-in may show up some preliminary failures which can be repaired to result in a solid system. If failures do occur, immediately call the service department of the company and arrange for repair (at no charge to you). The same method of checkout using diagnostics should be followed as in the case of used equipment.

If the above procedures sound pessimistic to you, don't despair. Modern minicomputer systems are extremely reliable once they are burned-in and any manufacturing glitches (transients) have been removed. After all, though, it is your money and you should demand satisfaction from the beginning since you will be paying a premium for (infrequent) service calls later on.

If you are buying an assembled microcomputer rather than the kit type, the same guidelines apply as in the case of new minicomputers. Here, though, there may be a lack of diagnostics and you may have to provide your own simple programs to test the CPU, memory, and peripherals. If you are buying a kit, you are in another category. By the time you get done building it, you will probably be familiar enough with the computer to troubleshoot it yourself. An oscilloscope or at least a glomper-type LED display (a device that "glomps" on a chip and indicates the logic levels of the pins by LED lights) is a useful tool to have in debugging. You will probably also find a lot of advice available from others who have built the same kit, through computer clubs or the various publications devoted to computer hobbyists.

CHAPTER

7

Programming Your System

Before you start programming in earnest on your minicomputer system, you may want to think about programming goals. Maybe you simply want to "have fun" on the system, programming bits and pieces of different things. That's fine—it's a great way to learn. However, you may reach a point where that type of programming doesn't satisfy you any longer. You may start thinking in terms of some ambitious projects, such as the development of a music synthesizer program that not only can play music but can transpose keys and come up with random melodies, or you may plan a system to record and analyze weather data from windspeed, temperature, and humidity inputs, or you may want to develop a system to compute weather and amateur-radio satellite orbits and predict their locations.

BASIC GOALS

Any programming project larger than a few hundred lines of code probably is going to require some planning and some structuring of your programs to make the job easier. If you sit down and start writing code without preliminary planning you will probably end up doing twice the work regardless of whether you are writing assembly language code, BASIC, or FORTRAN.

In addition to planning your "super" project, you might also give some thought to "modularizing" your code so that you can build up a library of standard subroutines. Some of these undoubtedly could be used on your next project. For example, suppose that in several assembly language programs you print several types of reports. The first program generates, say, a report of all the high and low temperatures for the month, and the second program produces a report of selected stock prices. Each report is formatted; that is, there is a title and maybe a page number, several lines are skipped, several tabulated column headings such as "DATE," "HIGH TEMP," "LOW TEMP," or "STOCK," and "CLOSE" are printed, and then data in different formats are printed. In the case of a BASIC program, the formatting is easy, but in this assembly language case the program must keep track of the current line that is being printed, and at the end of the page it must skip lines to go to the top of the next page after bumping the line count. It must also skip so many lines after the page heading, tab to the proper position for column headings (write blanks), format certain data (put decimal points in temperature values or stock prices), and do a lot of things involved with formatting printing output. If you are going to produce many printed reports, all with different format requirements, it makes sense to write one general-purpose "report formatter" program (or routine or subroutine). By calling this routine with the proper code (jumping to it with a code value in a specified memory location, say), the report formatter would skip to the top of the next page (and update a page count, set the line count and character counts to 0), or position *n* character positions across the current line (and set character count to the updated value), or write a text string starting at a given address, or skip *n* lines. Once coded and debugged, this routine could be put in your library and reused each time a new program was written that called for report generation. The report formatter would be a standard "module."

Given enough general-purpose modules in a library, a great deal of coding can be eliminated for new programs in areas such as printing output, character string input, conversions from decimal to binary and binary to ASCII, floating-point operations, double-precision arithmetic operations, and many others. Naturally, something is lost in using precanned general-purpose routines. They are bound to be somewhat less efficient than routines coded specifically for the task at hand—they take more time and more instructions. However, if you can spare slightly more memory and a little more execution time, they are well worth your while. If you are buying a minicomputer system you will probably get a large number of the above-mentioned routines with the equipment; another possible source are user groups or computing-oriented magazines. In the worst case, of course, you will have to write and debug library routines only once.

What constitutes a good program? Sometimes a good program is like a parachute jump—if it works, it's good. There are probably four constraints commonly used in programming: size of the program, speed of operation of the program, time required to write the program, and time required to maintain the program.

Program size used to be very important when memory was expensive. Then it was imperative to write "tight code," using as little code as possible. Speed of the program is critical in real-time programming, where a system cannot waste a lot of time in "overhead" or separate tasks. Many time-critical programs cannot be written in FORTRAN, for example, because the degradation in time would be impossible to live with. The time required to write a program is probably the most important factor today. Labor time probably far exceeds the cost of additional memory and, in most cases, additional "CPU time" to run the programs. Program maintenance time is the last factor. If the code is too tight or too clever, or if the listing does not have a great deal of comments, the program may be impossible to maintain (correct or modify at some later date), even by the same programmer, who may have forgotten how clever he was! You will probably develop your own criteria and your own approaches for writing programs, but initially at least, take the middle road. Try to be logical but not too clever, try to write efficient code but don't worry about putting in a few extra instructions, plan the structure of the program carefully to reduce the time, and, most important, put in a lot of comments in the source code.

There are five general steps in implementing a large program: design, flowcharting, coding, debugging, and documentation. Opinions vary on the amount of time to be spent on each section, but most people seem to divide the total time into 50 percent for debugging and 50 percent for the other tasks. This large debugging period is probably common, as a result of insufficient time spent on design and flowcharting. The next sections outline each of the five tasks.

INITIAL DESIGN

As an example of the five tasks, let's design and implement a program to graph noontime temperature values for a month on a Teletype. We will do it in assembly language, although the same steps would be applicable in a higher-level language. Assume that the temperature values are recorded on paper tape in the format shown in Fig. 7-1. Data are in ASCII. A record for each day is separated from previous days by nulls (blank tape). Each day's record is in the form "DDMMYY±TTT," ten ASCII characters defining day (DD), month (MM), year (YY), and temperature (±TTT). The last record is not a valid record but has all nines (9999999999). This tape could have been generated by another program that read in temperature at noon from an ADC, converted the temperature to ASCII, and output it to the Teletype punch. Alternatively, the tape could have been manually prepared in the local mode of the Teletype. In the former case, both the "graph" program and the "data acquisition" program might operate under the same controlling program called the "executive," "supervisor," or "monitor," which would control the weather "system." By inputing an "ACQ" command (for *ACQ*uire), for example, the supervisor would transfer control to the portion of the system that reads in the temperature from the ADC and outputs the data to paper tape. At the end of that function, control would be returned to the supervisor. If the operator then input an "MTP" command (for *M*onthly *T*emperature *P*lot), the graph of monthly noontime temperature would be printed.

In any event, back to our program, the graph portion. Let's call it MTP for short. After the monthly data have been read in, a graph is produced on the Teletype. Since there are about 72 characters across a Teletype page, we should have plenty of room to print a maximum of 31 days horizontally (X-axis). We might consider printing a point every two character positions to make the graph more readable. Vertically we can print six

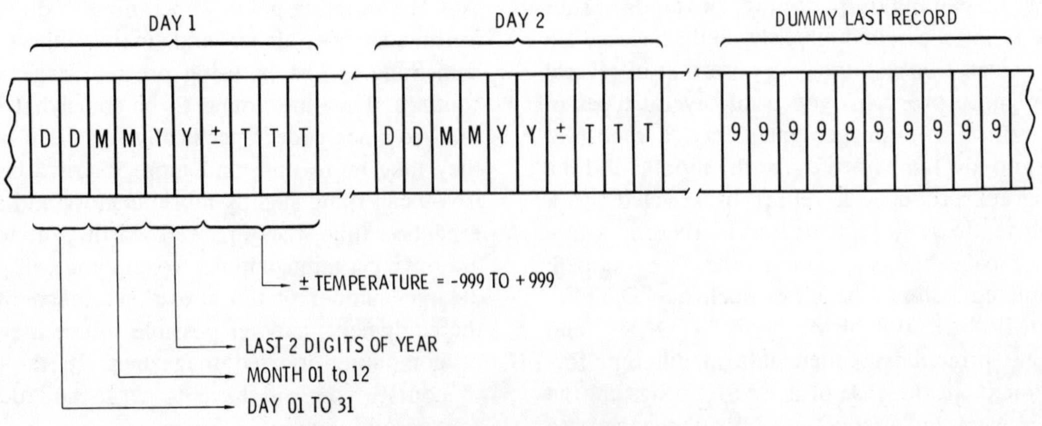

Fig. 7-1. MTP input format.

lines every inch. We have several choices in formatting the vertical scale. We can establish a range of, say, −50° to +150° and make the vertical distance some convenient size, say 10 inches. We would then have to convert each temperature value to binary and find the nearest temperature value on the vertical scale whose increments are 200°/[(6 × 10) + 1], or about 3.3°. We lose resolution, however, by using this method. If the temperature spread in the month was only 10°, only three lines of the graph (vertically) would be used, and it would be hard to distinguish between individual day's recordings. Another method might be to make the vertical scale in degree increments. That way each day's temperature could be represented by a vertical position on the graph. However, for a range of 200°, we would need 200/6 inches, or about 33 inches vertically of Teletype paper. A third approach is to make the increments 1°, but only over the range of temperatures for the month. If the monthly spread is 50°, then the vertical scale would be 50/6 = 8.3 inches. No resolution would be lost, and most monthly graphs would be of a reasonable vertical size. The format of this printout is shown in Fig. 7-2. The vertical scale should have a temperature indicated for each line, but only the highest and lowest have been shown.

Knowing what the input and output "formats" are, let's subdivide the program into the tasks required. First of all, we need a routine to read in the data. Since the

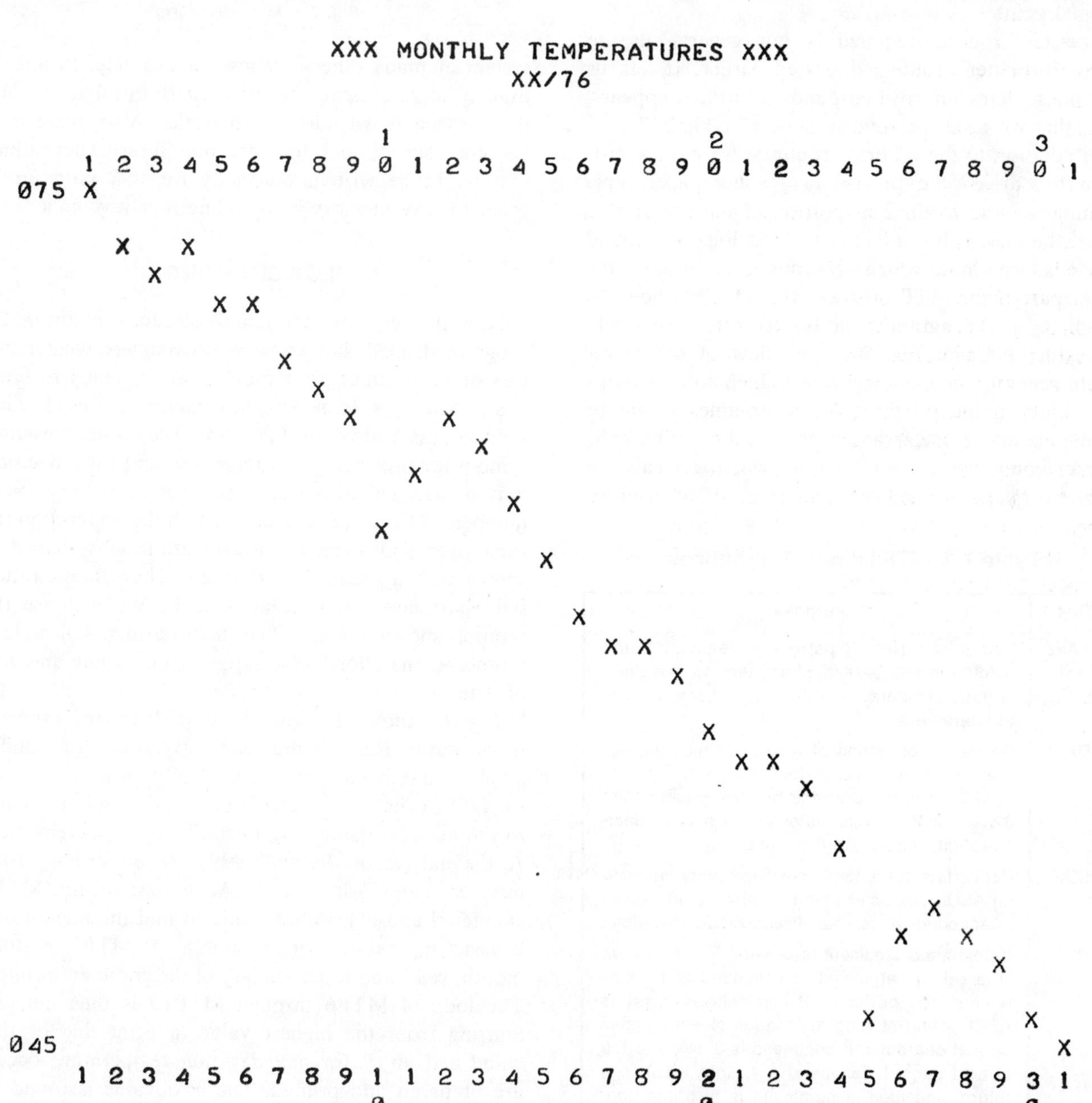

Fig. 7-2. MTP plot.

data records are separated by nulls, this routine should read in until a non-null character is read and should then read in ten characters. This could be a precanned routine, but we will assume that none exists. We will write one to read in a record, ignoring leading nulls and terminating on a null. The record size may be any length in the general case, so we will let the routine record and pass back the number of characters it has read. That way we can check for errors.

Next we need a routine to convert from ASCII temperature values to decimal and from decimal to binary. We will assume the ASCII to decimal to binary conversion routine exists for a string of up to five ASCII digits that define a decimal value of less than 32,768 with no decimal point.

The last routine required is our general-purpose "print formatter" routine discussed earlier. It lets us skip lines, character positions, and so forth. It appears, then, that we need the routines shown in Table 7-1.

In addition to these library routines, we need a program to "drive" the process of reading paper tape, printing, and so forth. This portion of the program is called the *driver*. It contains all of the logic not found in the subroutines, which, of course, constitutes the major part of the MTP program. If we look at how the complete MTP program would be structured, we would see something like Fig. 7-3. The flow of the driver would generally be from low core to high core. At various points in the program, the subroutines would be called. Naturally, the arrangement would differ with the type of computer. Lowest memory would typically be storage for variables and constants in an MC6800-based

Table 7-1. MTP Library Subroutines

Title	Purpose
RTAPE	Reads tape from Tty paper-tape reader, ignores leading nulls, passes characters to specified buffer, terminates on null, passes back number of characters read.
ADXBI	Converts from string of ASCII decimal characters to binary value. String terminated by null. If ASCII string represents number greater than 32,767 or if any character is not a valid decimal digit, results are incorrect.
BIXAD	Converts from a 15-bit positive binary value to an ASCII character string of form 12345, stored in specified buffer. No invalid results possible.
PRINT	If command argument is 0, skips N lines where N is second argument. If command is 1, skips N character positions. If command is 2, prints ASCII string starting at location N—terminates on null character. If command is 3, skips to top of next page. If command is 4, does a carriage return, line feed. If command is 5, prints contents of argument treated as a single, right-justified, ASCII character.

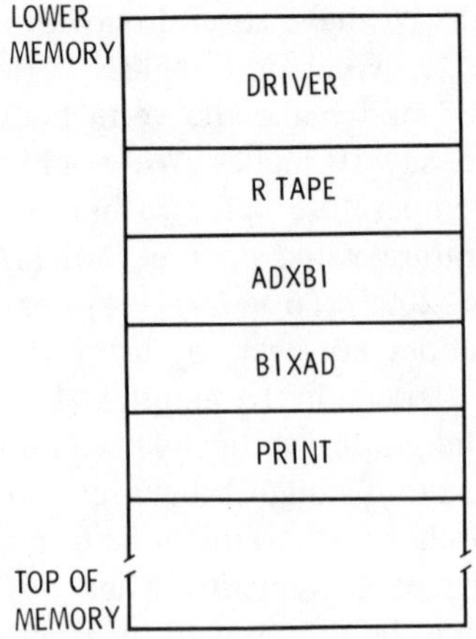

Fig. 7-3. MTP structure.

system or many other systems, for example. In an extremely large system, the driver portion might be further broken down into various tasks. Also, there may be other subroutines that are not library subroutines that might be written especially for this program in order to save memory by avoiding repetitive code.

FLOWCHARTING

Now that we have the coarse structure of the MTP program defined and know approximately what modules or subroutines are required, we are ready to flowchart. There is some standardization to flowcharting symbols, as shown in Fig. 7-4. The basic flowchart symbol for processing is a rectangle, and for a decision it is a diamond. On-page connectors are circles with numbers in them. (Corresponding circles connect on the same page.) Off-page connectors are usually shaped as shown with a number inside them. Here things rather fall apart and standardization ends. We will use the symbols shown in Fig. 7-4 for flowcharting. A flowchart represents the "flow" of a program in varying amounts of detail.

Fig. 7-5 shows the flow of the MTP program in very broad terms. Records are read and stored in a "buffer area" of the memory which is simply an area reserved for I/O. As each character is read and stored, a pointer to the next available byte in the buffer is incremented. At the end (record 9999999999), the buffer has (10 × number of days) bytes in it. At the last record, MTP3 is entered and a search is made to find the highest and lowest temperatures for the month. At MTP5 the title, month, year, and top boundary of the graph are printed. The loop of MTP6 through MTP10 is then entered. Starting from the highest value, a print line of that value and an *X* for any day that temperature occurs are prepared and printed. The next value is found by subtracting one degree, and the process is repeated for each value from high to low. After the last value is

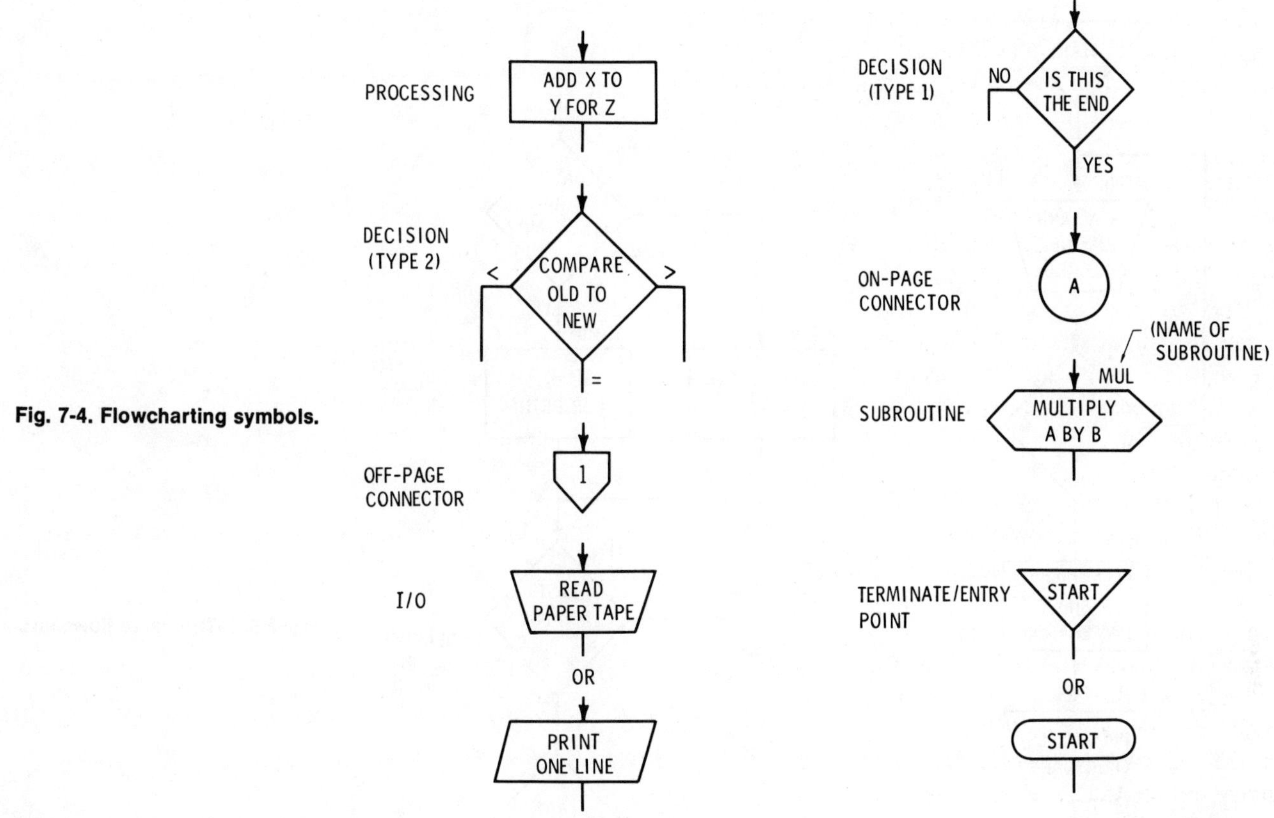

Fig. 7-4. Flowcharting symbols.

printed, the lower boundary is printed and the program is done.

Although the scheme in Fig. 7-5 appears reasonable, quite a few things are not defined, for example, the search for highest and lowest temperatures. We need the more detailed flowchart shown in Fig. 7-6, which expands Fig. 7-5. In the detailed flowchart, the paper-tape records are read into the buffer a record at a time. A "buffer pointer" points to the next 10-byte section of the buffer as a record is read. After the last record on the tape has been read, we have a buffer of from 28 records (February) to 31 records of 10 bytes each. Obviously, we must make certain that the memory area reserved for the buffer is at least $(31 \times 10) + 10 = 320$ bytes long. The appearance of the buffer after the last record (all 9s) has been read is shown in Fig. 7-7. Note that days can be found at BUFFER + 2, BUFFER + 12, BUFFER + 22, . . . , and that temperatures start at BUFFER + 6 and continue in BUFFER + 16, BUFFER + 26, ... By incrementing 10 bytes, we can "scan" down through the records very easily. The next thing to do after reading in the complete month's records is to find the highest and lowest temperatures. We do this by first setting "HIGH," the highest temperature, to −999 and "LOW," the lowest temperature, to 999. That way, after the first day's comparison we have HIGH and LOW equal to the temperature of the first day, which is correct. Now we scan the temperatures, starting at BUFFER + 6. As we scan, we convert the three ASCII bytes representing the day's temperature to a plus or minus binary value to facilitate comparison with HIGH and LOW. The conversion is done at MTP10 by ADXBI. Before each conversion is done, the three characters are moved to a small "working" area called TEMP that is seven bytes long, the last byte being a null. That way, routine ADXBI converts only the three bytes and terminates at the null byte. After conversion, the converted binary value is negated if the temperature was below zero. It is then compared to HIGH and LOW. If it is higher than HIGH, it becomes a new high. If it is lower than LOW, it replaces LOW. The buffer pointer is then bumped by 10 bytes to point to the next day's temperature, and we go back to MTP50 for the next conversion and comparison. When the first digit of the temperature is an ASCII "9," we know we have reached the end of the buffer. At that point we have the month's highest temperature in HIGH in binary and the month's lowest temperature in LOW in binary. We are now ready to print headers.

From MTP200 through MTP250, we make use of the PRINT routine to print the title. From MTP250 through MTP300, we print the month and year, arbitrarily picking up the month and year digits from the first record in the buffer. Next, in MTP310 through MTP400, we print the top heading of the graph, which lists the days of the month. At MTP410 we are ready to graph the month's temperatures. We use a location

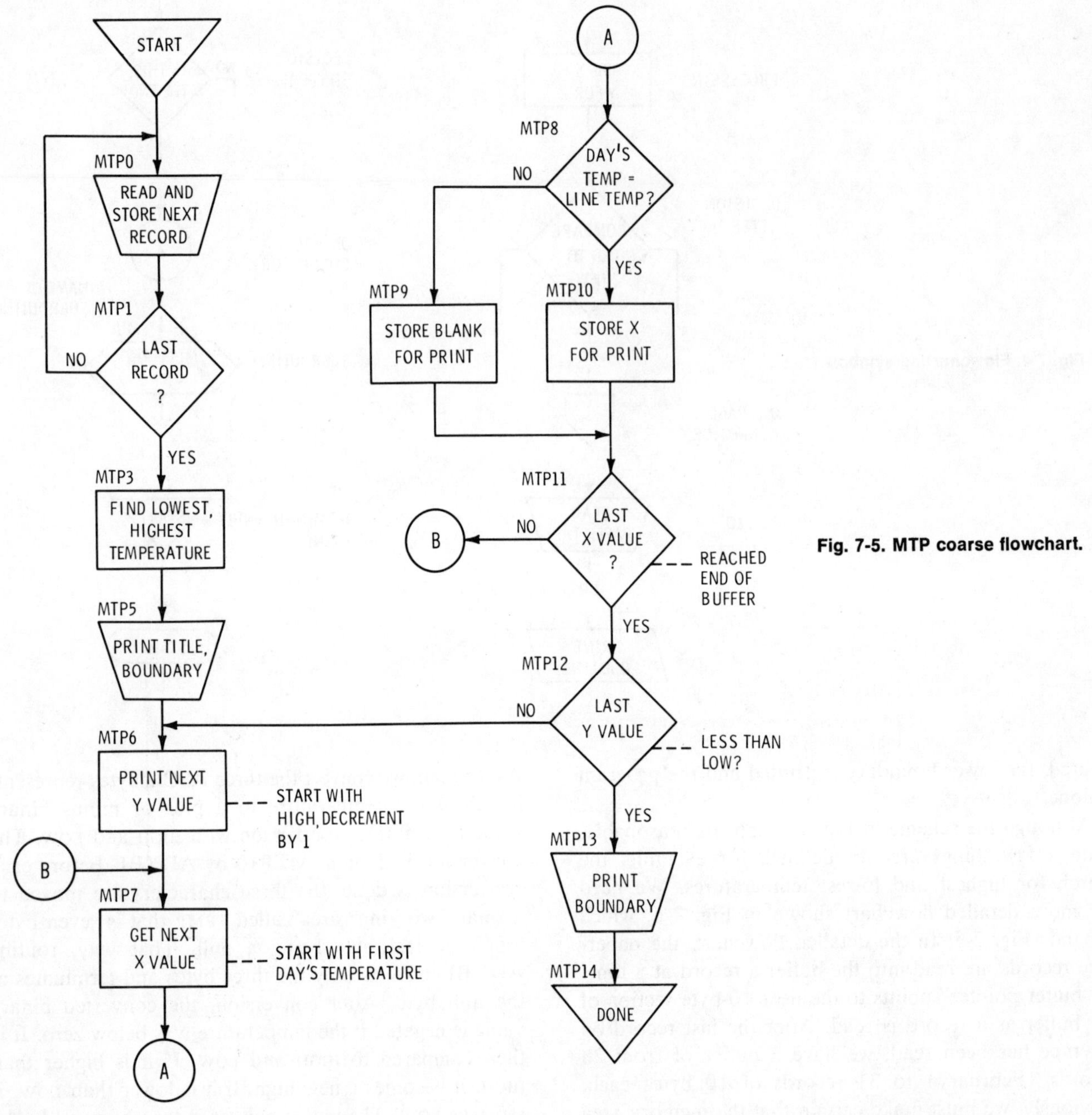

Fig. 7-5. MTP coarse flowchart.

called "WORK1" to hold the binary value of the current temperature. For each line, we convert WORK1 to ASCII using routine BIXAD (MTP450) and print the three ASCII digits (MTP460 through MTP500). In converting, we use the working area TEMP, again to hold the results of the conversion. Since up to six ASCII digits are possible from the conversion, TEMP must be six bytes long. We have added a seventh, a null, for printing results earlier.

Having printed the temperature value for the line, we go through the temperatures in BUFFER, starting at BUFFER + 6 (MTP550). For each temperature, we convert it to binary (MTP600 through MTP700) and compare it to WORK1. If they are equal, the day's temperature matches the line temperature, and we print an "X" and a blank. If they are not equal, we print two blanks. The buffer pointer is then bumped by 10 to point to the next day's temperature, and we continue the loop (MTP560 through MTP700). Note that as we continue scanning temperatures, we are automatically positioned under the proper day. If the day's temperature is "9999" (MTP580), we know that we have gone through the month's temperatures for the current vertical temperature line of the graph. We now decrement WORK1 by one degree at MTP800 and go back (5) to MTP420 to print the next line (loop MTP420 through MTP800). When, at MTP420, WORK1 is less than LOW, we know that we have printed the last temperature line and we can go to MTP900 to print the bottom boundary of the graph (MTP900 through MTP

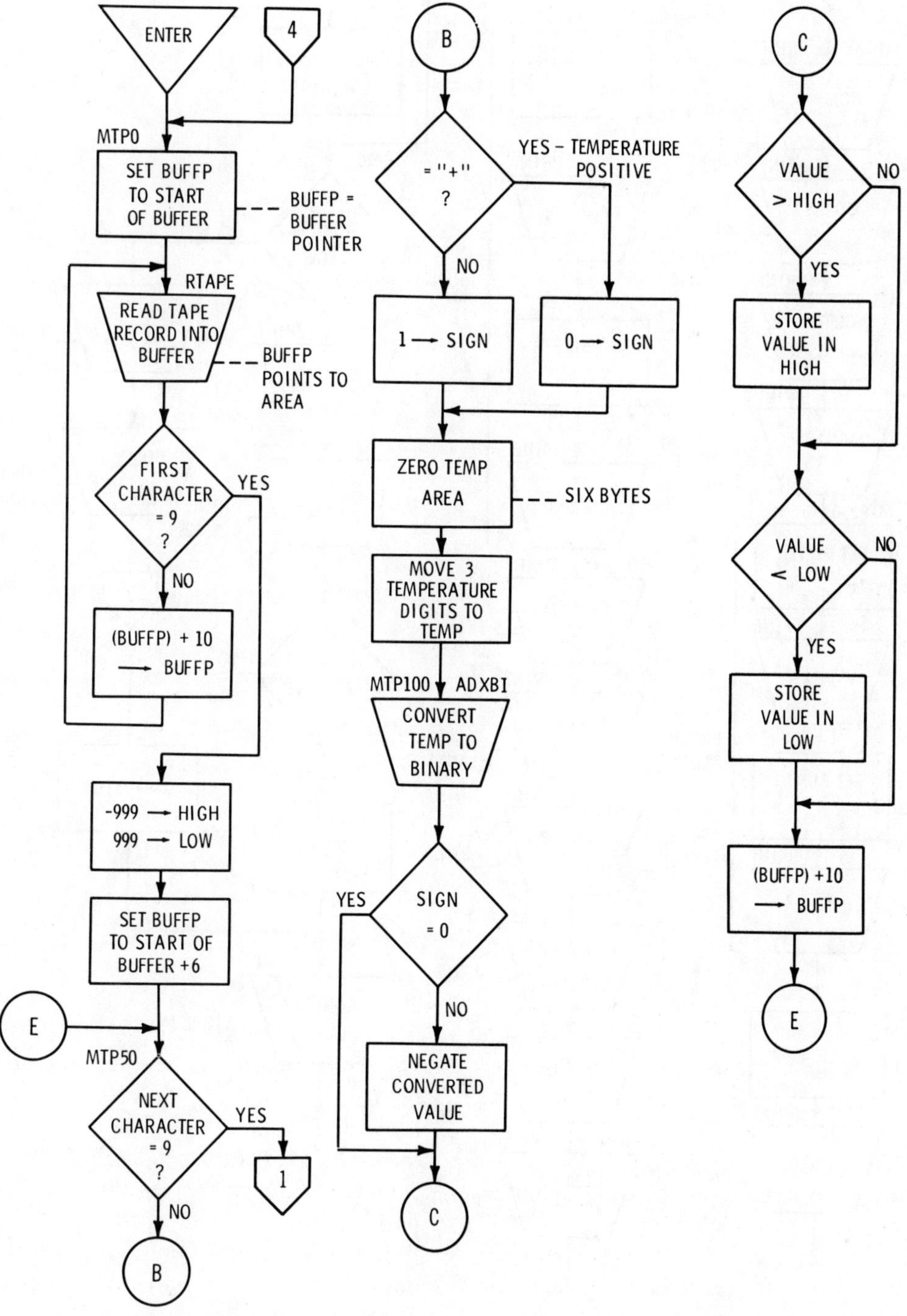

Fig. 7-6. MTP detailed flowchart.

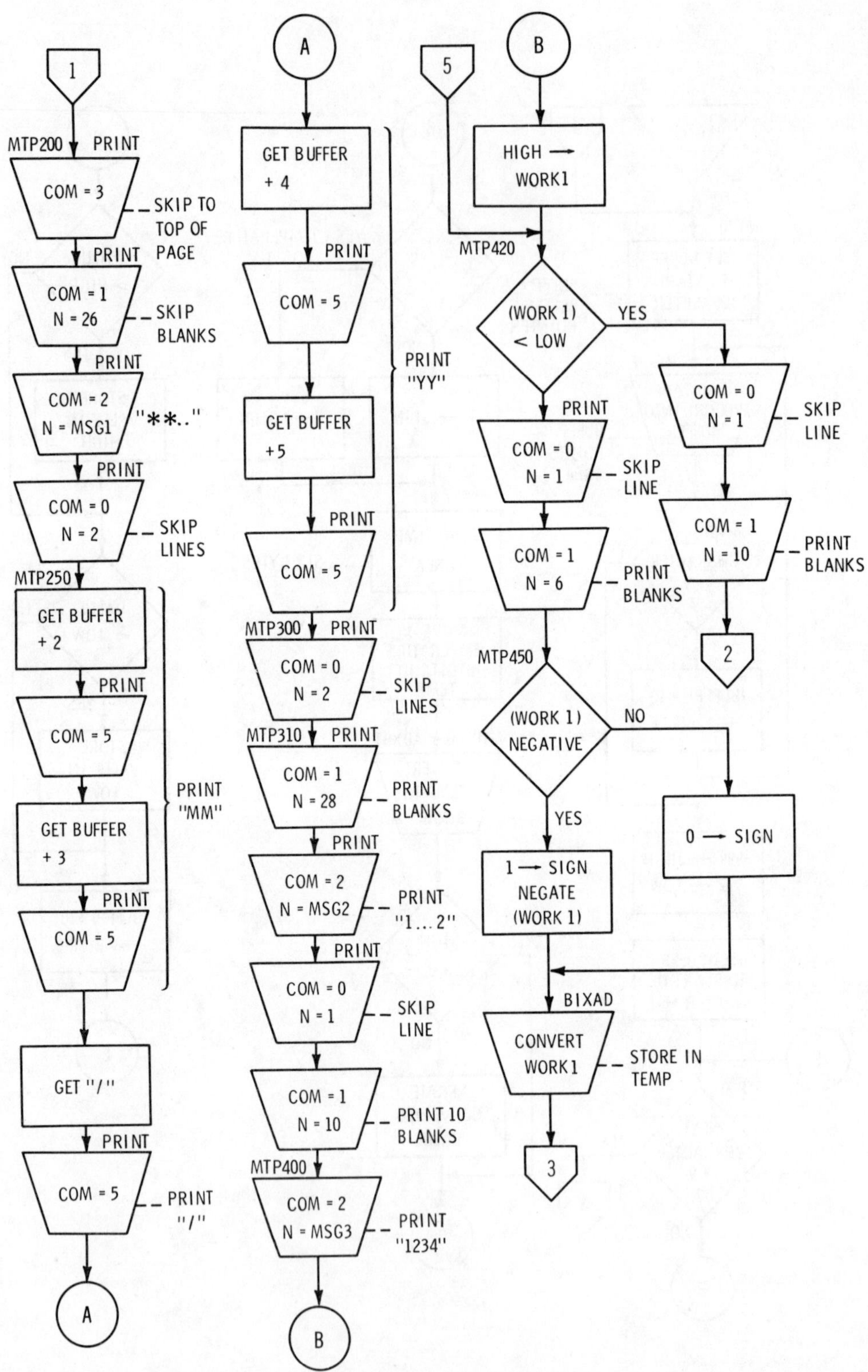

Fig. 7-6. MTP detailed flowchart. (Cont'd.)

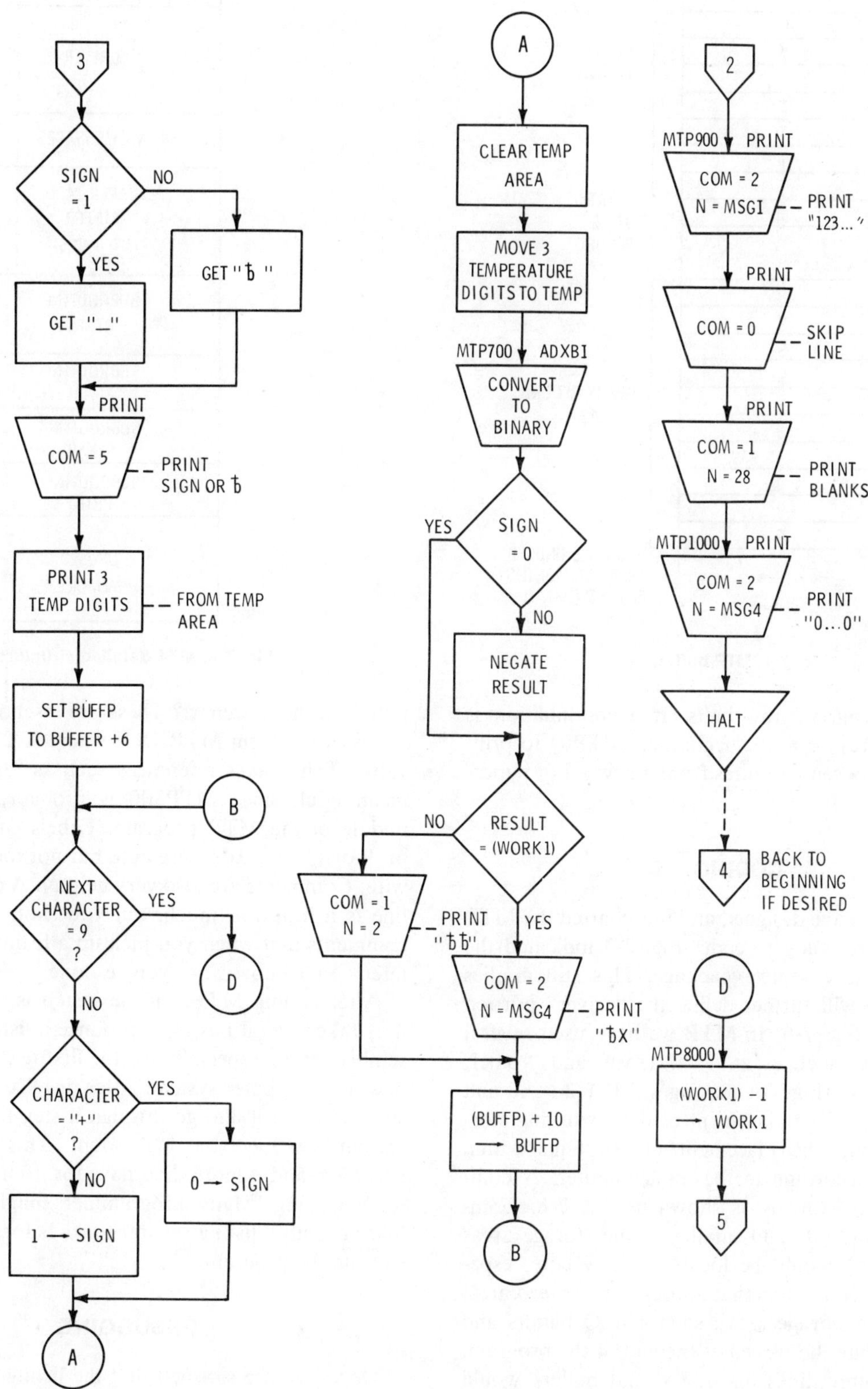

Fig. 7-6. MTP detailed flowchart. (Cont'd.)

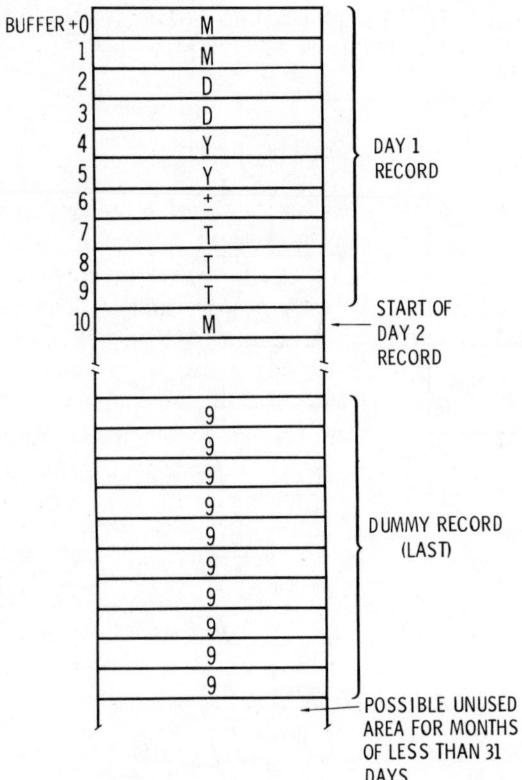

Fig. 7-7. MTP buffer.

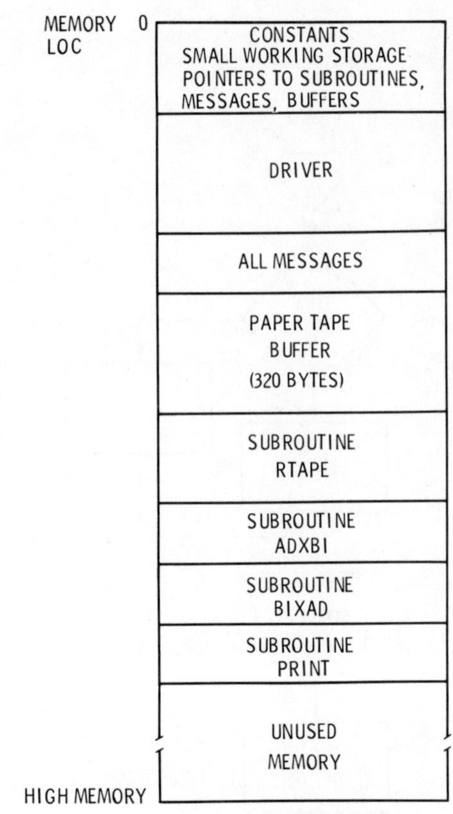

Fig. 7-8. MTP detailed structure.

1000). The program now halts. If a continuation is desired, it will restart at the beginning (MTP0) to print the next graph of temperatures from a new set of paper-tape records.

CODING

Now that we have designed and flowcharted the MTP program, we are ready to code. Fig. 7-3 indicated the structure for the complete package. This still applies except that we will further define the "driver" portion flowcharted in Fig. 7-6. In MTP we have used several storage sections, such as BUFFER, TEMP, and WORK1, and several text strings for messages ("0 1 2 . . ." and "0 . . . 0 . . .0"). The placement of these working storage sections and the placement of constants within memory vary according to the minicomputer. A common type of structure is as shown in Fig. 7-8. Commonly used constants and small working storage areas (such as TEMP) would be located in low core, especially for those computers that address a page zero area. Larger working storage areas, such as I/O buffers and text strings, would be placed at the end of the program. Linkages to subroutines, messages, and buffers would also be put in page zero or low core.

The actual coding of MTP is, of course, dependent upon the machine used. Some ground rules may help, however. Why not label locations with the same labels found on the flowchart? These are essentially sequential labels of the form MTPXXX where XXX is a numeric value. This makes references such as "JMP MTP500" meaningful, since MTP500 is probably about in the middle of the MTP program. Labels such as "BOMB" or "OOPS" or "BACK" are cute but not too easy to work with. Comments are also very helpful. A comment every line is a little too much, but you should have enough comments that when you pick up a listing three months later you'll know what you've done.

After coding MTP, the next step is to assemble. It may take several passes to produce a listing with no assembly errors, especially for the first few programs on a new minicomputer system. After this listing is produced, sit down with it and go through it step by step to make certain you have the logic right. This is called *desk checking,* and it more than pays for itself when it comes to debugging. Many programmers might go over the final assembly listing several times before attempting to execute the program.

DEBUGGING

Once you are satisfied that the listing is as error-free as possible, load the object of the program and prepare to debug. If you have a debug utility package, load it at the same time and use it to your advantage by setting breakpoints (debug detects when a specified location is executed) and by examining locations for proper results. If you have no debug package, it may prove helpful to "single-step" your computer through the program an instruction at a time, for those minicomputers that have that capability. (Obviously, this cannot be done too easily for a loop that is executed 32,000 times, however). It may also be beneficial to debug the program a section at a time, that is, to break the program into smaller portions, debug these portions, and then "put everything together" and continue debugging the whole program. Unless you are a super programmer, don't expect the program to load and run the very first time. It seldom happens, even in professional circles. Three or four debugs with consequent reassembly are probably typical for a short program of a hundred statements. An alternative to reassembling, by the way, might be "patching" the program after it is loaded. Once errors in logic are found, patches can be put in by using the debug package, or by hand (from the control panel); the patches might range from changing a constant from 5 to 6 to substituting a "jump" for an instruction and jumping out to an unused area where twenty instructions or so are added. The ease with which you patch your program is really a function of the ease of reassembly of your program, as well as other factors.

DOCUMENTATION

Once your program has been debugged and is running properly, why not spend a little time on documentation? If you have written a few notes on how the program works, formalize them now and file them away. At some later time you might want to pass the program on to a fellow hobbyist, and it's nice to be able to give him instructions on exactly how to operate it. (It is amazing that even the larger minicomputer companies invariably omit some very basic instructions—for example, what character terminates an input of a string of characters in a particular program.)

As you write more and more programs, your thoughts and approaches to design, flowcharting, coding, debugging, and documentation will invariably change. You will find a comfortable approach for yourself and your system. This chapter is meant only to provide some basic guidelines.

CHAPTER

8

Microcomputer Profiles

This chapter describes microprocessor chips and the microcomputers that are built around them. While there are literally dozens of microprocessor chips available today, only a small number have been used for hobbyist-oriented microcomputers, and not too many more have been incorporated into general-purpose microcomputers. Most of the latter have been microcomputers specifically geared to manufacturers' program development systems. With these, a volume chip user can develop firmware and software for the microprocessor chip to be used in his special-purpose system (firmware is the part of a system between hardware and software—generally it's a program burned into read-only memories). The program development microcomputers are relatively expensive and quite often do not have frills such as higher-level languages, although they are trending in that direction.

Hobbyist microcomputers at this date fall primarily into four categories: those built on the Intel 8080 microprocessor chip, those built on the Motorola MC-6800, those built on the Fairchild F8, and those which are built on the MOS Technology MCS6502. An earlier chip, the Intel 8008, was used in one hobbyist computer, the Scelbi-8B, but this microcomputer is no longer being manufactured. In most cases, the manufacturers have used the basic chip instruction set and added a front, a control panel, a power supply, printed-circuit boards, and other amenities to produce a "stand-alone" microcomputer. In most cases, the microcomputer manufacturer has also added more software, some going as far as operating systems and higher-level languages. Prices range from about $250 on up.

The Intel 8080, Motorola MC6800, Fairchild F8, and MOS Technology MCS6502 are discussed in this chapter along with microcomputers that use these chips as a base. Since there are a number of 8008-based microcomputers in existence, and since this chip is the granddaddy of them all, the Intel Corporation 8008 CPU chip is also described.

HISTORY OF MICROPROCESSORS

In 1971, Intel Corporation produced a four-bit microprocessor chip known as the Intel 4004. It was a four-bit device, working with data in four-bit slices, with a rather limited instruction set, but it was the forerunner of all of today's devices. The 4004 was followed by the Intel 8008, an eight-bit device that was a great improvement over the 4004. Other microprocessor chips and chip "sets" soon followed, including the Intel 8080, Motorola MC6800, Fairchild F8, and MOS Technology MCS6502, which are considered "third generation" microprocessor chips, being faster in operational speed and wider in data-handling capability than earlier devices. Earlier chips were produced using PMOS LSI technology, which describes the semiconductor techniques used to fabricate the chip. The 4004 and 8008 are of this type. NMOS chips, exemplified by such chips as the 8080, MC6800, F8, and MC6502, operate at speeds more than twice those of their PMOS counterparts. Current NMOS technology permits speeds of about 2 microseconds per cycle, with an instruction being performed in 2 to 10 or 12 microseconds. Data widths have increased from 4 to 16 bits in some cases.

Future developments will undoubtedly bring faster speeds and wider data buses. Speeds of 300 nanoseconds are predicted in several years. Another trend is towards production of chip "sets," or families of devices that are compatible with one another as far as interfacing signals and power-supply requirements. In addition, prices will continue to drop. Currently, one manufacturer offers an MC6800 pin-compatible microprocessor for about $20—quite a change from the $100,000 minicomputer of ten years ago!

INTEL 8008 CHIP DESCRIPTION

The 8008, manufactured by Intel Corporation, is a p-channel silicon-gate MOS CPU chip that can handle

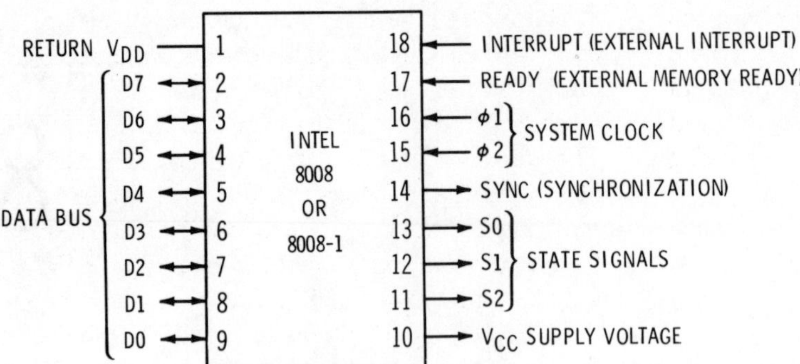

Fig. 8-1. 8008 pin configuration.

data in eight-bit parallel form and address up to 16K bytes of external memory. It has 48 instructions and contains an eight-bit accumulator, six eight-bit data registers, four flags, and eight 14-bit address registers (stack). It has single-level interrupt capability. Instruction cycle times are 12.5 microseconds (8008-1) or 20 microseconds (8008). Its instruction set is a subset of that of the more powerful Intel 8080 microprocessor described in the next section.

Physical Features and Architecture

The 8008 is an 18-pin chip with the pin configuration shown in Fig. 8-1. The basic architecture of the chip is shown in Fig. 8-2. Eight data lines, D7 through D0, input and output data from the chip, working from a data bus buffer on the chip. Eight-bit scratchpad registers are working registers and contain seven registers designated A (accumulator), B, C, D, E, H, L. Registers H and L are used to address external memory; H holds the high-order bits of the address, and L contains the low-order bits. An address stack contains eight 14-bit registers for holding eight addresses for subroutine execution. When a subroutine is called by a CALL instruction, the content of the program counter is saved in the stack. (This is similar to a "Jump to Subroutine" used by minicomputers, except that the stack is used.) When the subroutine is finished, a RETURN instruction causes the CPU to "pop" the stack (get the next address

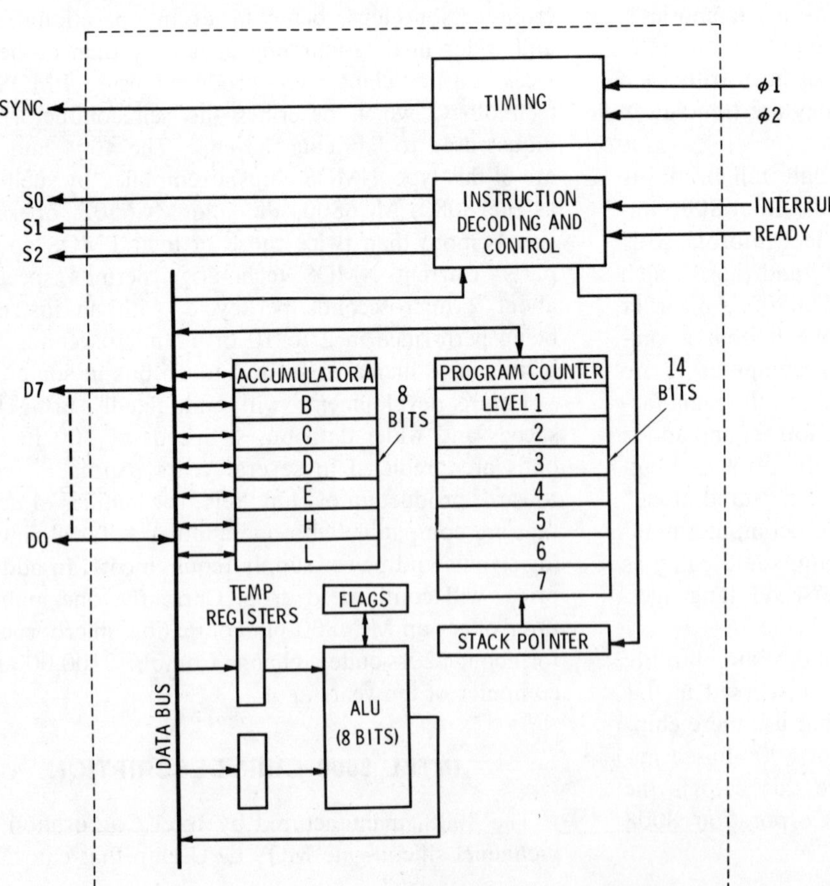

Fig. 8-2. 8008 architecture.

from the stack) and load the program counter with the 14-bit address retrieved. Using the stack, it is possible to nest subroutines to seven levels. A 14-bit program counter is the first word in the stack (top of stack) and performs the same function as other computers, holding the address of the current location.

The ALU (*A*rithmetic *L*ogic *U*nit) portion of the 8008 performs all arithmetic and logical operations. The ALU uses the two temporary registers; they are not available to the programmer. Four control bits, designated C (carry), Z (zero), S (sign), and P (parity), however, are set as a result of arithmetic or logical operations and can be tested under program control. The remainder of the chip is devoted to instruction decoding and timing and control. Two clocks, at 500 kHz (500,000 pulses per second), must be supplied to the chip from external circuitry. Three *state* bits, S0, S1, and S2, define CPU states, indicating to external circuitry what phase of the instruction cycle the CPU is in. A SYNC signal indicates which clock cycle (ϕ1 or ϕ2) the CPU is in. The remaining two lines, READY and INTERRUPT, are external signals supplied to the chip. If the external memory being used is slower than the CPU, the READY line will be low and the CPU will go into "WAIT" state S0S1S2 = 000_2 until the READY line comes true. The INTERRUPT signal is used to signal the CPU of an external interrupt signal which sets state T11 (S0S1S2 = 011_2). At this point, a CALL subroutine instruction can be "jammed" onto the data lines by external circuitry, which will result in the interrupt routine being executed (more about that later).

Instruction Execution

Because memory and peripheral devices are external to the chip and because there are only eight data lines, these data lines are "time-shared," passing the current instruction address out in two phases (states), reading in the current instruction in another state, and passing data in another state, among other things. It is obvious that many states are required to execute an instruction. The ANA B instruction, for example, computes the logical AND of scratchpad register B with accumulator A. The instruction cycle required is shown in Fig. 8-3.

During T1, the eight least significant bits of the address go out on D7 through D0. External circuitry knows that an address is there since the state is 010_2. During T2, the six high-order bits go out on D5–D0. The state is now 001_2. Two control bits, D7 and D6, also appear, indicating (by 00) that this is a memory read. During T3, the instruction is fetched from external memory, which has placed the one byte of the instruction on data type lines D7 through D0 and brought up the READY signal. During T4 and T5, the AND operation is performed. The entire cycle takes 12.5 microseconds in an 8008-1 chip. Since the 8008 also uses two- and three-byte instructions that are memory reference instructions, these might take several *cycles* (each cycle with several states), resulting in execution times as long as 27.5 microseconds for instructions like a JMP (jump). Note that in the 8008 a great deal of control circuitry is external to the chip. Memory, memory timing, peripheral address decoding, and CPU clock generation are all external.

Instruction Repertoire

The instruction set of the 8008 may be divided into five groups:

- Index Register instructions.
- Accumulator Group instructions.
- Program Counter and Stack Control instructions.
- I/O instructions.
- Machine instructions.

The Index Register instruction group includes five 1-byte instructions and two 2-byte instructions. (See Table 8-1.) MOV R1,R2 (*Move R*2 to *R*1) is a one-byte instruction. It moves the contents of the source register to the destination register. MOV R,M (*Move Memory* to *R*, one-byte) loads scratchpad register R with the contents of the memory location pointed to by the H and L registers, treated together as a 14-bit address. For example, MOV A,M would load the accumulator with the contents of the memory location pointed to by H,L. MOV M,R (*Move R* to *M*emory, one-byte) stores the contents of scratchpad register R in the memory location pointed to by H,L. MVI R (*Move Immediate R*, two-byte) loads scratchpad register R with the

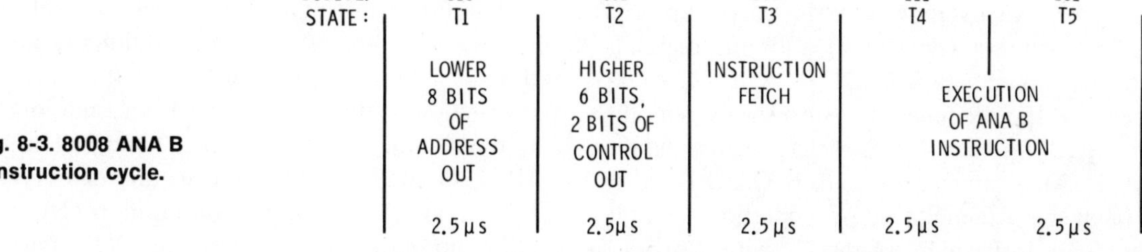

Fig. 8-3. 8008 ANA B instruction cycle.

Table 8-1. Index Register Instructions

MNEMONIC	INSTRUCTION	FORMAT 76543210	DESCRIPTION	EXECUTION TIME* (STATES)
MOV R1,R2	MOVE R2 TO R1	11 R2 R1	(R2) → R1	5
MOV R,M	MOVE MEMORY TO R	11 R 111	(M)** → R	8
MOV M,R	MOVE TO MEMORY	11111 R	(R) → M**	7
MVI R	MOVE IMMEDIATE TO R	00 R 110 B ←——→ B	$BBBBBBBB_2$ → R	8
MVI M	MOVE IMMEDIATE TO M	00111110 B ←——→ B	$BBBBBBBB_2$ → M**	9
INR R	INCREMENT R	00 R 000	(R) + 1 → R Z, S, P	5
DCR	DECREMENT R	00 R 001	(R) − 1 → R Z, S, P	5

* 2.5 μs/STATE.
** M = ADDRESS IN (H, L).

second byte of the instruction. It is an "immediate" instruction, as discussed in earlier chapters. MVI M (*Mov*e *I*mmediate *M,* two-byte) loads the memory location pointed to by H,L with the second byte of the instruction. INR R (*Inc*rement *R,* one-byte) increments scratchpad register R by one; DCR R (*Dec*rement *R,* one-byte) decrements scratchpad register R by one. INR and DCR set the ALU flags by the result of the operation (zero, sign, and parity).

The Accumulator Group instructions (Table 8-2) are used to perform arithmetic and logical operations upon the scratchpad accumulator and another scratchpad register, a memory location, or any immediate operand. All of the flag flip-flops are affected except in the case of "rotate" instructions, which affect only the carry. The ADD instruction adds the contents of R, M, or immediate data B (ADD R, ADD M, or ADI) to the accumulator. An overflow sets the carry flip-flop. The ADC instruction (*Ad*d *C*arry) adds the contents of R, M, or immediate data B (ADC R, ADC M, ACI) plus the carry to the accumulator. An overflow sets the carry. The SUB instruction (*Sub*tract) subtracts the contents of R, M, or immediate data B (SUB R, SUB M, SUI) from the accumulator. An underflow sets the carry. The SBB instruction (*Sub*tract with *B*orrow) subtracts the contents of R, M, or immediate data B (SBB R, SBB M, SBI) from the accumulator, setting the carry with underflow. The preceding instructions are useful for double-precision arithmetic.

The ANA (*An*d *A*) instruction ANDs the contents of R, M, or immediate data B (ANA R, ANA M, ANI) with the accumulator. The XRA (E*x*clusive o*r* *A*) instruction ORs the contents of R, M, or immediate data B with the contents of the accumulator. The CMP (*Comp*are) instruction compares the contents of R, M, or immediate data with the accumulator, leaving the contents of the accumulator unchanged. There are four rotate instructions. RLC (*R*otate Accumulator *L*eft *C*arry) and RRC (*R*otate Accumulator *R*ight *C*arry) rotate the accumulator contents left or right one bit position to the carry. RAL (*R*otate *A*ccumulator *L*eft) and RAR (*R*otate *A*ccumulator *R*ight) bypass the carry while shifting left or right one bit position (see diagrams in Description column of Table 8-2).

The Program Counter and Stack Control instructions (Table 8-3) are used to unconditionally jump, conditionally jump, or "pop" or "push" the stack. The JMP instruction (*Jump,* three-byte) unconditionally jumps to the memory address in bytes 2 and 3. The JNC, JNZ, JP, JPO conditionally jump to the memory address in bytes 2 and 3 if the condition flip-flop (NC = no carry, NZ = no zero, P = sign positive, PO = parity odd) is false. JC, JZ, JM, JPE conditionally jump to the memory address in bytes 2 and 3 if the condition flip-flop

Table 8-2. Accumulator Group Instructions

MNEMONIC	INSTRUCTION	FORMAT 76543210	DESCRIPTION	EXECUTION TIME (STATES)*
ADD R	ADD REGISTER TO A	10000 R	(R) + (A) → A OVERFLOW → C	5
ADD M	ADD MEMORY TO A	10000111	(M)** + (A) → A OVERFLOW → C	8
ADI	ADD IMMEDIATE TO A	00000100 B ←——→ B	$BBBBBBBB_2$ + (A) → A OVERFLOW → C	8
ADC R	ADD REGISTER TO A WITH CARRY	10001 R	(R) + (A) + C → A OVERFLOW → C	5
ADC M	ADD MEMORY TO A WITH CARRY	10001111	(M)** + (A) + C → A OVERFLOW → C	8
ACI	ADD IMMEDIATE TO A WITH CARRY	00001100 B ←——→ B	$BBBBBBBB_2$ + (A) → A OVERFLOW → C	8
SUB R	SUBTRACT REGISTER FROM A	10010 R	(A) — (R) → A UNDERFLOW → C	5
SUB M	SUBTRACT MEMORY FROM A	10010111	(A) — (M)** → A UNDERFLOW → C	8
SUI	SUBTRACT IMMEDIATE FROM A	00010100 B ←——→ B	(A) — $BBBBBBBB_2$ → A UNDERFLOW → C	8
SBB R	SUBTRACT REGISTER FROM A WITH BORROW	10011 R	(A) — (R) — C → A UNDERFLOW → C	5
SBB M	SUBTRACT MEMORY FROM A WITH BORROW	10011111	(A) — (M)** — C → A UNDERFLOW → C	8
SBI	SUBTRACT IMMEDIATE FROM A WITH BORROW	00011100 B ←——→ B	(A) — $BBBBBBBB_2$ — C → A UNDERFLOW → C	8
ANA R	AND REGISTER WITH A	10100 R	(R) AND (A) → A	5
ANA M	AND MEMORY WITH A	10100111	(M)** AND (A) → A	8
ANI	AND IMMEDIATE WITH A	00100100 B ←——→ B	$BBBBBBBB_2$ AND (A) → A	8
XRA R	EXCLUSIVE-OR REGISTER WITH A	10101 R	(R) XOR (A) → A	5
XRA M	EXCLUSIVE-OR MEMORY WITH A	10101111	(M)** XOR (A) → A	8

Table 8-2—Continued

MNEMONIC	INSTRUCTION	FORMAT 7 6 5 4 3 2 1 0	DESCRIPTION	EXECUTION TIME (STATES)*
XRI	EXCLUSIVE-OR IMMEDIATE WITH A	0 0 1 0 1 1 0 0 B ←——→ B	$BBBBBBBB_2$ XOR (A) → A	8
ORA R	OR REGISTER WITH A	1 0 1 1 0 R	(R) OR (A) → A	5
ORA M	OR MEMORY WITH A	1 0 1 1 0 1 1 1	(M)** OR (A) → A	8
ORI	OR IMMEDIATE WITH A	0 0 1 1 0 1 0 0 B ←——→ B	$BBBBBBBB_2$ OR (A) → A	8
CMP R	COMPARE REGISTER WITH A	1 0 1 1 1 R	(A) — (R) FLAG FLIP-FLOPS	5
CMP M	COMPARE MEMORY WITH A	1 0 1 1 1 1 1 1	(A) — (M)** FLAG FLIP-FLOPS	8
CPI	COMPARE IMMEDIATE WITH A	0 0 1 1 1 1 0 0 B ←——→ B	(A) — $BBBBBBBB_2$ FLAG FLIP-FLOPS	8
RAL	ROTATE A LEFT	0 0 0 0 0 0 1 0	ROTATE A LEFT 1 BIT, A7 → A0 AND C	5
RAR	ROTATE A RIGHT	0 0 0 0 1 0 1 0	ROTATE A RIGHT 1 BIT, A0 → A7 AND C	5
RLC	ROTATE A LEFT THROUGH CARRY	0 0 0 1 0 0 1 0	ROTATE A LEFT 1 BIT, A7 → C C → A0	5
RRC	ROTATE A RIGHT THROUGH CARRY	0 0 0 1 1 0 1 0	ROTATE A RIGHT 1 BIT, A0 → C C → A7	5

* 2.5 μs/STATE.
** M = ADDRESS IN (H, L).

(C = carry, Z = zero, M = sign is minus, PE = parity even) is true.

The remainder of the instructions in this group reference the stack in the 8008 chip. The stack is simply a table of eight entries. A pointer to the stack points to one of the eight locations. If another address is added to the stack, it is "pushed" into the stack. If several addresses are pushed, the pointer is adjusted to point to the next available "slot." When an address is "pulled" (sometimes "popped"), the address is transferred and the pointer is adjusted to point to the next address. This "push-down" stack may be thought of as a dinner-plate stacker seen in restaurants. Dinner plates can be stacked one on top of another. As each is added, the stack is pushed down. If plates are taken off, the stack is pulled up. The last dinner plate put on the stack is the first one taken off. A stack of this type is called a "LIFO" stack for "last-in, first-out."

The CALL instruction unconditionally jumps to the location in bytes 2 and 3, assumed to be a subroutine terminated by the *RET*urn instruction. The current content of the program counter is pushed into the stack. The CNC, CNZ, CP, and CPO operate the same as JNC, JNZ, JP, and JPO, except that a branch results in the contents of the program counter being pushed into the stack. The CC, CZ, CM, and CPE operate the same as JC, JZ, JM, and JPE, except that the program counter is again pushed into the stack if the branch is made. The RET (*Ret*urn) instruction unconditionally "pops" or "pulls" the last address in the stack and loads

Table 8-3. Program Counter and Stack Control Instructions

MNEMONIC	INSTRUCTION	FORMAT** 7 6 5 4 3 2 1 0	DESCRIPTION	EXECUTION TIME* (STATES)
JMP	JUMP UNCONDITIONAL	0 1 XXX 1 0 0 ADDLS XX ADDMS	JUMP TO (ADDMS, ADDLS)	11
JNC,JNZ, JP,JPO	JUMP ON NO CARRY, NO ZERO, POSITIVE, PARITY ODD	0 1 0 M 0 0 0 ADDLS XX ADDMS	JUMP IF CONDITION TO (ADDMS, ADDLS)	9/11
JC,JZ, JM,JPE	JUMP ON CARRY, ZERO, MINUS, PARITY EVEN	0 1 1 M 0 0 0 ADDLS XX ADDMS	JUMP IF CONDITION TO (ADDMS, ADDLS)	9/11
CALL	CALL UNCONDITIONAL	0 1 XXX 1 1 0 ADDLS XX ADDMS	JUMP TO ADDMS, ADDLS (PC) → STACK	11
CNC,CNZ, CP,CPO	CALL ON NO CARRY, NO ZERO, POSITIVE, PARITY ODD	0 1 0 M 0 1 0 ADDLS XX ADDMS	JUMP IF CONDITION TO (ADDMS, ADDLS) AND (PC) → STACK	9/11
CC,CZ, CM,CPE	CALL ON CARRY, ZERO, MINUS, PARITY EVEN	0 1 1 M 0 1 0 ADDLS XX ADDMS	JUMP IF CONDITION TO (ADDMS, ADDLS) AND (PC) → STACK	9/11
RET	RETURN	0 0 XXX 1 1 1	(LAST STACK) → PC	5
RNC,RNZ, RP,RPO	RETURN ON NO CARRY, NO ZERO, POSITIVE, PARITY ODD	0 0 0 M 0 1 1	(LAST STACK) → PC IF CONDITION MET	3/5
RC,RZ, RM,RPE	RETURN ON CARRY, ZERO, MINUS, PARITY EVEN	0 0 1 M 0 1 1	(LAST STACK) → PC IF CONDITION MET	3/5
RST	RESTART	0 0 AAA 1 0 1	JUMP TO LOCATION $AAAOOO_2$ AND (PC) → STACK	5

X = DON'T CARE.
* 2.5 μs/STATE.
** M = 00 FOR C, NC; 01 FOR Z, NZ; 10 FOR P, M; 11 FOR PO, PE.

it into the program counter, returning to the instruction after the CNC, CNZ, CALL, or similar instruction. Eight additional instructions *conditionally* return by popping the stack if a condition is met. These are RNC, RNZ, RP, RPO, RC, RZ, RM, and RPE in which the suffix after the "R" has the same meaning as in previous instructions. The RST instruction (*Rest*art) calls the subroutine at location AAA000 where AAA is specified in the instruction word itself and pushes the program counter contents into the stack.

The Input/Output instructions (Table 8-4) consist of two instructions, appropriately labeled IN and OUT. IN reads the contents of one of eight input ports to the accumulator, while OUT writes the contents of the accumulator into one of eight output ports. The eight output/input ports are external ports, and the instructions serve only to notify an external device that this is an input or output operation.

There is only one instruction in the Machine Instruction group, HLT (*H*a*lt*). It causes the CPU to enter the "STOPPED" state ($S0S1S2 = 110_2$), where it remains until interrupted.

Programming Considerations

The 8008 has a fairly comprehensive instruction set. However, it suffers from the small number of pins on the chip. Because of the number of pins, data and addresses have to share an eight-bit bus, resulting in a large number of states per instruction and subsequent long instruction times. Also, the method of addressing memory relies on the H and L registers only (except for a few instructions). To address consecutive data, H and

Table 8-4. I/O Instructions and Machine Instructions

MNEMONIC	INSTRUCTION	FORMAT 7 6 5 4 3 2 1 0	DESCRIPTION	EXECUTION TIME (STATES)
IN	INPUT	0 1 0 0 MMM 1	(INPUT PORT)$_{MMM}$ → A	8
OUT	OUTPUT	0 1 RRMMM 1	(A) → OUTPUT PORT$_{MMM}$	6
HLT	HALT	0 0 0 0 0 0 0 X	STOPS CPU UNTIL INTERRUPTED	4

L (or at least L) must be incremented prior to each memory access. This is quite inconvenient. To move data from one block in memory to another requires quite a large number of instructions, putting the updated source address in H and L, fetching the data, putting the updated destination address in H and L, storing the data, and so forth. The 8008, it appears, is very outdated by the 8080 and other microprocessors, although it deserves a great deal of respect for being the forerunner and innovator in the whole microprocessor marketplace.

INTEL 8080 CHIP DESCRIPTION

The 8080, manufactured by Intel Corporation, is an n-channel silicon-gate MOS CPU chip. The 8080 is an outgrowth of its 8-bit predecessor, the Intel 8008 and includes the instruction set of the 8008 as a subset. Like the 8008, the 8080 handles data in eight-bit bytes. Up to 64K eight-bit bytes can be addressed externally to addition, the address lines are separate lines rather than being time-shared with the data lines. The 8080 has 111 instructions. The CPU contains seven 8-bit data registers accessible by the program. Four flag bits can be tested for the results of arithmetic and logical operations. The program counter is a 16-bit address register, as it is a 16-bit stack pointer. Unlike the 8008, the stack pointer in this case points to an external memory stack. The ALU portion of the chip provides decimal arithmetic capability in addition to normal arithmetic and logical operations.

Physical Features and Architecture

The 8080 is a 40-pin chip. The basic architecture is shown in Fig. 8-4. Eight data lines (D7–D0) input and output data to and from a register on the chip (data bus buffer/latch). Scratchpad registers are eight-bit and designated A, B, C, D, E, H, and L. Registers H and L are used to address external memory, H holding the the chip, contrasted with 16K bytes for the 8008. In eight high-order address bits and L holding the eight low-order address bits. The 16-bit stack pointer addresses external memory, enabling any number of nested subroutines rather than the eight allowed in the 8008. The program counter is 16-bit to permit addressing 64K bytes. Address lines (A15–A0) come out of the chip from an address buffer and hold either a memory address for instructions or data or an I/O device number (8 bits). Status information is output at the beginning of each instruction cycle over D7–D0 to indicate what the address lines represent.

Referring to Fig. 8-5, note that as in the 8008, there are two clock signals, $\phi 1$ and $\phi 2$, with a frequency of 2 MHz (2 million pulses per second). The SNYC output signal indicates to external logical when the CPU is beginning each cycle. A DBIN (Data Bus In) signal is an output signal indicating when the data bus is in the input mode. READY performs the same function as the READY in the 8008. It is an external signal from memory, indicating that the external memory is ready with data. It can also be used to stop the CPU by putting it in a WAIT state. When this is done or if external memory is not READY, the WAIT line from the CPU goes high. The $\overline{WR}$ (not WR) signal is used as an output to indicate when data on the data bus is available for a memory write or I/O output control.

HOLD is an external signal applied to enable an external device to gain control of the 8080 address and data bus. A HLDA (*Hold A*cknowledge) is brought up in response when the CPU enters the HOLD mode. INTE (*Int*errupt *E*nable) is an output indicating that the CPU is interruptible. At this time, the external INT (*Int*errupt) signal can be brought up to interrupt the CPU. The last signal, RESET, clears the program counter and restarts the CPU at location 0.

The ALU is similar to the ALU of the 8008, performing arithmetic and logical operations. The same flags—carry, zero, sign, and parity—are set as the result of ALU operations. In addition, limited decimal arithmetic can be performed by the ALU. The remainder of

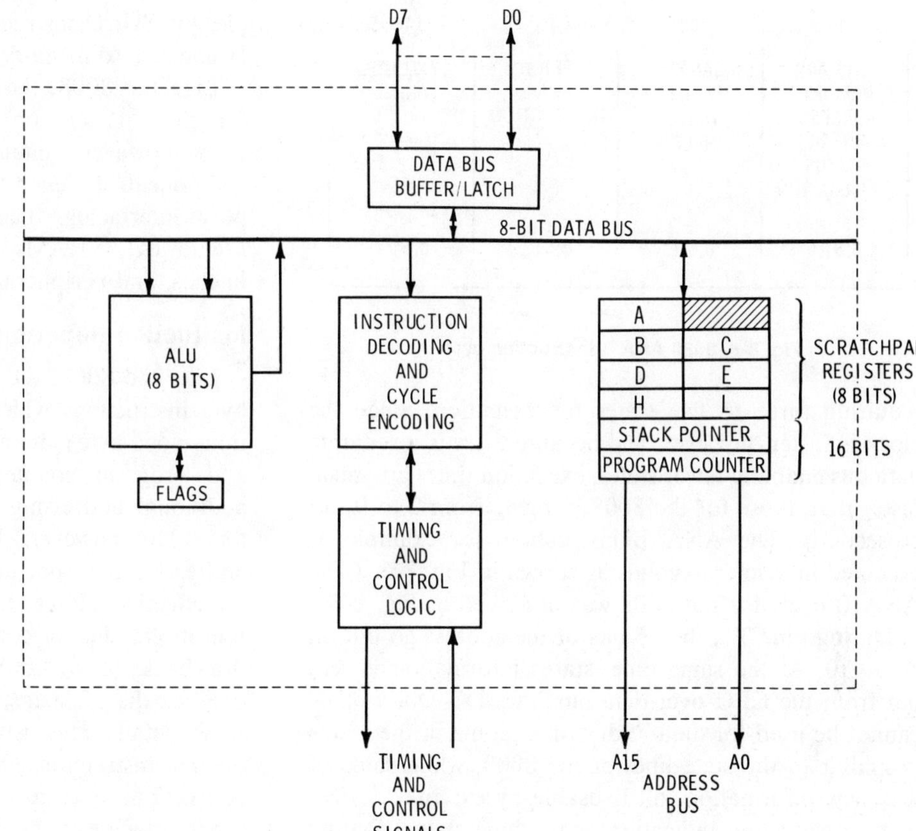

Fig. 8-4. 8080 architecture.

the chip is the expected Timing and Control Logic, which generates or decodes the above control signals, instruction decoding circuits, and some temporary registers used in implementing the instructions only.

Instruction Execution

As in the 8008, one, two, or three cycles may be required for instruction execution, each machine cycle

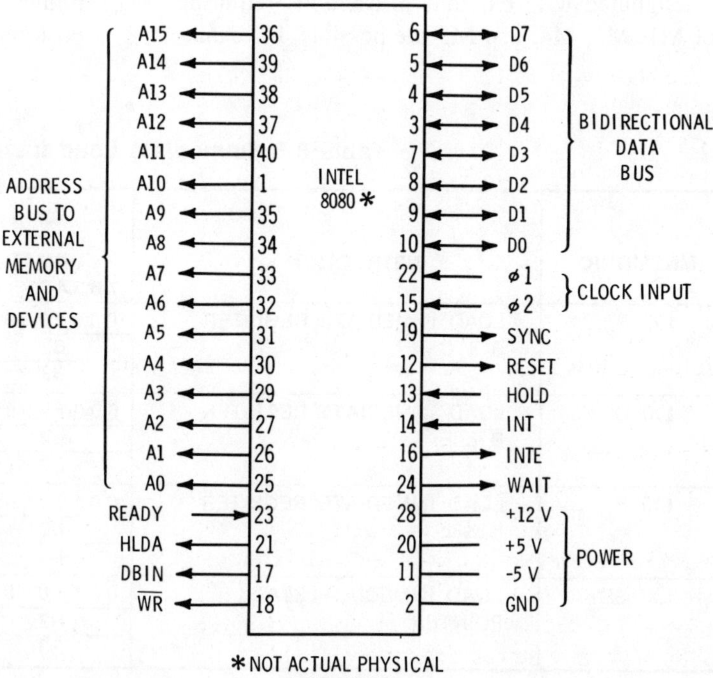

Fig. 8-5. 8080 pin configuration.

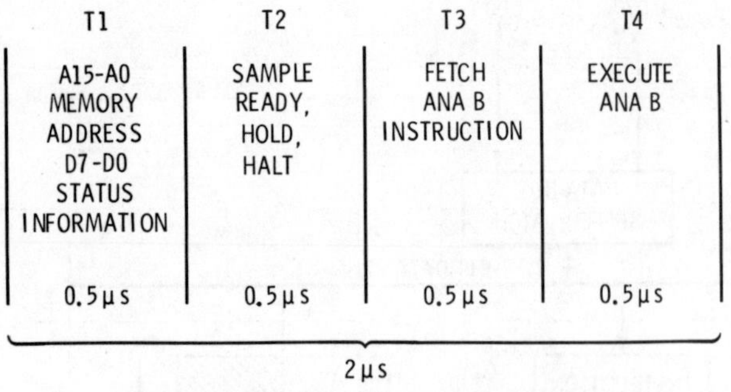

T1	T2	T3	T4
A15-A0 MEMORY ADDRESS D7-D0 STATUS INFORMATION	SAMPLE READY, HOLD, HALT	FETCH ANA B INSTRUCTION	EXECUTE ANA B
0.5μs	0.5μs	0.5μs	0.5μs

2μs

Fig. 8-6. 8080 ANA B instruction cycle.

requiring three to five states for execution. Since the clock is faster, however, and because there is a separate data bus enabling fewer states, execution times are much faster than those for the 8008, ranging from 2 to 9 microseconds. The ANA B instruction, for example, is executed in 2 microseconds as shown in Fig. 8-6. (The ANA B cycle for the 8008 was described in Fig. 8-3.)

During time T1, the 16 bits of the address go out on A15–A0. At the same time, status information is sent out from the CPU over data bus lines D7–D0, as they cannot be used for data at this time. Some of the status is similar to the state lines of the 8008, while some of it is new information; all is usable by external devices or memory as an indication of machine status. During T2, the CPU samples the READY, HOLD, and WAIT inputs. If READY is true and there is no HOLD or WAIT, the CPU enters T3. At T3 (actually before), the external memory puts the ANA B instruction on data lines D7–D0. The instruction is then read in and decoded. At T4, the instruction is executed and T1 is enabled. Note that this instruction requires one cycle T1–T4 designated M1, but that instructions requiring cycles of M1, M3, M4, and M5 are possible, for example, the SHLD instruction which stores the contents of H and L into memory.

Like the 8008, the 8080 requires external circuitry for clock generation, memory timing, and so forth. Intel, however, manufactures a number of standard components designed primarily for the 8080 which simplify interfacing. These include ROMs (*R*ead-*O*nly *M*emories), RAMs (*R*andom-*A*ccess *M*emories), latches, and peripheral interfaces.

Instruction Repertoire

Like the 8008, the 8080 has one-, two-, and three-byte instructions which are register-to-register instructions (one-byte), immediate mode or I/O instructions, and program counter instructions (three-byte). An additional addressing mode has been implemented in the 8080, however. This is direct addressing. Direct addressing does not utilize the H, L registers but takes the effective address from bytes 2 and 3 of the instruction itself. This, of course, overcomes one of the major drawbacks of the 8008 instruction set.

Since the 8008 instruction set has been discussed in some detail previously, this section will describe only the new instructions implemented in the 8080. All 8008 instructions operate the same in software, except that the interfacing to the chip is, of course, radically different. The 8008 instructions discussed are described in Tables 8-5 through 8-7.

The remaining 43 instructions in the 8080 greatly expand the basic 8008 instruction set. For discussion purposes, they are arbitrarily divided into the following groups:

Immediate Load.
Push and Pop.

Table 8-5. Immediate Load Instructions

MNEMONIC	INSTRUCTION	FORMAT 76543210	DESCRIPTION	EXECUTION TIME* (STATES)
LXI B	LOAD IMMEDIATE REGISTER B & C	00000001 B2 B3	B2 → B B3 → C	10
LXI D	LOAD IMMEDIATE REGISTER D & E	00010001 B2 B3	B2 → D B3 → E	10
LXI H	LOAD IMMEDIATE REGISTER H & L	00100001 B2 B3	B2 → H B3 → L	10
LXI SP	LOAD IMMEDIATE STACK POINTER	00110001 B2 B3	B2 → SP_{15-8} B3 → SP_{7-0}	10

* .5 μs PER STATE.

Table 8-6. Push and Pop Instructions

MNEMONIC	INSTRUCTION	FORMAT 76543210	DESCRIPTION	EXECUTION TIME* (STATES)
PUSH B	PUSH REGISTERS B & C ON STACK	11000101	(B, C) → (NEXT STACK)	3
PUSH D	PUSH REGISTERS D & E ON STACK	11010101	(D, E) → (NEXT STACK)	3
PUSH H	PUSH REGISTERS H & L ON STACK	11100101	(H, L) → (NEXT STACK)	3
PUSH PSW	PUSH A AND FLAGS ON STACK	11110101	(A, FLAGS) → (NEXT STACK)	3
POP B	POP REGISTERS B & C OFF STACK	11000001	(LAST STACK) → B, C	3
POP D	POP REGISTERS D & E OFF STACK	11010001	(LAST STACK) → D, E	3
POP H	POP REGISTERS H & L OFF STACK	11100001	(LAST STACK) → H, L	3
POP PSW	POP A AND FLAGS OFF STACK	11110001	(LAST STACK) → A, FLAGS	3

* .5 μs PER STATE.

Direct Load/Store.
Double Register.
Indirect Load/Store.
Accumulator/Carry.
Store/Load H/L.
Interrupts.
NOP.

The Immediate Load group (three-byte instructions) loads two bytes in the instruction word into B and C, D and E, H and L, or the stack pointer. This is the same as the 8008 move immediate instructions except that it loads two bytes into two registers, treated as a register "pair." LXI B loads B and C, LXI D loads D and E, LXI H loads H and L, and LXI SP loads the stack pointer. These are useful for loading addresses as they handle 16 bits of data. The four immediate loads are shown in Table 8-5.

The Push and Pop instructions are one-byte instructions that push register pairs and pop register pairs from the stack. The eight instructions are shown in Table 8-6. These are useful for saving scratchpad register contents and flag status on interrupts and restoring them at the end of interrupts or for saving registers for subroutine calls. In these instructions the register pairs are B and C, D and E, H and L, and A and flags. PUSH B, PUSH

Table 8-7. Direct Load/Store Instructions

MNEMONIC	INSTRUCTION	FORMAT 76543210	DESCRIPTION	EXECUTION TIME (STATES)
STA	STORE A DIRECT	00110010 B2 B3	(A) → MEMORY LOCATION DEFINED BY B2,B3	4
LDA	LOAD A DIRECT	00111010 B2 B3	(MEMORY LOCATION) → A	4

D, PUSH H, PUSH PSW push B, C; D, E; H, L; and A, flags, respectively. POP B, POP D, POP H, and POP PSW pop (or "pull") B, C; D, E; H, L; and A, flags, respectively.

The Direct Load/Store instructions (three bytes) either store the contents of the accumulator in the memory address specified by bytes 2 and 3 in the instruction (STA B2,B3) or load A with the contents of the memory address specified in bytes 2 and 3. Table 8-7 shows the Direct Load/Store instructions.

The Double Register group treats register pairs again. (See Table 8-8.) Register pairs may be added to H and L, exchanged with H and L, or incremented. The object, of course, is to modify the contents of H and L, which are used as a memory address pointer. XCHG (E*x*c*h*ang*e*) exchanges register pair D,E with H,L. XTHL (E*x*change *T*op of Stack with *H,L*) exchanges the two bytes from the top of stack with H,L. SPHL (*S*tack *P*ointer from *H,L*) moves the contents of H,L to the stack pointer register. PCHL (*P*rogram *C*ounter from *H,L*) moves the contents of H,L to the program counter. Four add instructions add register pairs to the H,L registers. DAD B adds B and C to H and L. DAD D adds D and E to H and L. DAD H adds H and L to H and L, effectively doubling the contents, or doing a double-precision left shift. DAD SP adds the stack pointer contents to H and L. All the above additions are double-precision, that is 16-bit additions, rather than two separate 8-bit additions where a lower-order carry is not added into the higher-order 8 bits. The remaining instructions in this group increment and decrement register pairs, performing double-precision operations once more. INX B, INX D, INX H, and INX SP increment B,C; D,E; H,L; and stack pointer, respectively. DCX B, DCX D, DCX H, and DCX SP decrement B,C; D,E; H,L; and stack pointer, respectively.

The Indirect Load/Store instructions use register pairs, B,C and D,E to load or store the contents of the accumulator. (See Table 8-9.) The register pair in this case is treated as an address register identical to H,L. STAX B (*St*ore *A* Indirect to *B*) stores (A) using B,C as a memory address, while STAX D (*St*ore *A* Indirect to *D*) uses D,E as a memory address. LDAX B and LDAX D load A in the same fashion.

The Accumulator/Carry instructions (Table 8-10) complement the contents of A (CMA: *Com*plement *A*) or the carry (CMC: *Com*plement *C*arry), set the carry (STC: *Set C*arry) or "decimal adjust" the contents of A. The last instruction, DAA (*D*ecimal *A*djust *A*), permits decimal subtraction or addition. DAA treats bits 7 through 4 as a binary-coded-decimal (bcd) digit and bits 3 through 0 as a second lower-order bcd digit. If an add or subtract of two decimal operands is desired, the actual addition or subtraction in the ALU is in binary. DAA adjusts the result to give a true bcd result. For example, the two hexadecimal operands 48_{16} and 19_{16} actually represent *decimal* 48 and 19 if the numbers are known to be in bcd format. If the numbers are added in binary fashion, however, the result is 61_{16}, instead of the desired 67_{16}, the correct result for bcd addition. DAA adjusts the result by adding 6 to the least significant bcd digit. The rule that DAA follows is that if the least significant bcd digit (3–0) is greater than 9_{16} or if a carry from bit 3 was present, 6 is added to bits 3 through 0. If the most significant bcd digit (7–4) is greater than 9_{16} or if a carry from bit 7 was present, 6 is added to bits 7 through 4. This adjusts any results to give two true bcd digits in A.

Store/Load H,L instructions are 3-byte instructions that store register pair H,L into the memory location specified in bytes 2 and 3 of the instruction. In the SHLD (*S*tore *H,L D*irect), L is stored in the memory location and H is stored in the memory location + 1. In LHLD (*L*oad *H,L D*irect), L is loaded with the contents of the memory location and H is loaded with the contents of the memory location + 1. These two instructions are shown in Table 8-11.

Two instructions are used for interrupts, EI (*E*nable *I*nterrupts) and DI (*D*isable *I*nterrupts). They set or reset an interrupt-enable flip-flop whose output becomes the INTE signal. No external interrupts are allowed when INTE is reset. The last instruction, NOP (*N*o *Op*eration) does nothing except take up space, which may be used for patching or other purposes at a later time. Table 8-12 shows these instructions.

Programming Considerations

The 8080 has a large instruction set geared basically towards single accumulator operations and stack manipulation. Contrasting its instruction set with the PDP-8, for example, it is obvious that the 8080 has a much more versatile instruction set. The additional instructions added to the 8008 base make indexing more efficient and also eliminate the need for updating the H and L registers' memory addressing. The 8080 is generally regarded as a "third-generation" microprocessor chip, and is a distinct improvement over its predecessor, the second-generation 8008.

Microcomputers Based on the Intel 8080

The original hobbyist computer, the MITS Altair 8800, is illustrated in Fig. 8-7. MITS offers an attractive package for the microcomputer, a wide variety of memory and hardware options and various types of peripheral devices as shown in Chart 8-1. Two of the more interesting peripherals are a 32-character matrix display and a tv camera. The display allows 32 characters to be displayed on a "self-scan" or dot-matrix panel, while 256 to 1024 characters can be held in an internal memory. The unit incorporates an acoustic

Table 8-8. Double Register Instructions

MNEMONIC	INSTRUCTION	FORMAT 76543210	DESCRIPTION	EXECUTION TIME* (STATES)
XCHG	EXCHANGE D & E, H & L REGISTERS	11101011	(D,E) ↔ (H,L)	4
XTHL	EXCHANGE TOP OF STACK, H & L	11100011	(NEXT STACK) ↔ (H,L)	18
SPHL	H & L TO STACK POINTER	11111001	(H,L) → SP	5
PCHL	H & L TO PROGRAM COUNTER	11101001	(H,L) → PC	5
DAD B	ADD B & C TO H & L	00001001	(H,L) + (B,C) → H,L	10
DAD D	ADD D & E TO H & L	00011001	(H,L) + (D,E) → H,L	10
DAD H	ADD H & L TO H & L	00101001	(H,L) + (H,L) → H,L	10
DAD SP	ADD STACK POINTER TO H & L	00111001	(H,L) + (SP) → H,L OVERFLOW → CARRY	10
INX B	INCREMENT B & C	00000011	(B,C) + 1 → B,C	5
INX D	INCREMENT D & E	00010011	(D,E) + 1 → D,E	5
INX H	INCREMENT H & L	00100011	(H,L) + 1 → D,E	5
INX SP	INCREMENT STACK POINTER	00110011	(SP) + 1 → SP	5
DCX B	DECREMENT B & C	00001011	(B,C) − 1 → D,E	5
DCX D	DECREMENT D & E	00011011	(DE) − 1 → D,E	5
DCX H	DECREMENT H & L	00101011	(H,L) − 1 → H,L	5
DCX SP	DECREMENT STACK POINTER	00111011	(SP) − 1 → SP	5

* .5 μs/STATE.

Table 8-9. Indirect Load/Store Instructions

MNEMONIC	INSTRUCTION	FORMAT 76543210	DESCRIPTION	EXECUTION TIME* (STATES)
STAX B	STORE A INDIRECT	00000010	(A) → MEMORY EA DEFINED BY (B,C)	7
STAX D	STORE A INDIRECT	00010010	(A) → MEMORY EA DEFINED BY (D,E)	7
LDAX B	LOAD A INDIRECT	00001010	MEMORY → A EA DEFINED BY (B,C)	7
LDAX D	LOAD A INDIRECT	00011010	MEMORY → A EA DEFINED BY (D,E)	7

* .5 μs PER STATE.

Table 8-10. Accumulator/Carry Instructions

MNEMONIC	INSTRUCTION	FORMAT 76543210	DESCRIPTION	EXECUTION TIME* (STATES)
CMA	COMPLEMENT A	00101111	$(\overline{A}) \rightarrow A$	4
STC	SET CARRY	00110111	1 → CARRY	4
CMC	COMPLEMENT CARRY	00111111	$\overline{CARRY} \rightarrow CARRY$	4
DAA	DECIMAL ADJUST A	00100111	(SEE TEXT)	4

* .5 μs PER STATE.

Table 8-11. Store/Load H,L Instructions

MNEMONIC	INSTRUCTION	FORMAT 76543210	DESCRIPTION	EXECUTION TIME* (STATES)
SHLD	STORE H & L DIRECT	00100010 B2 B3	(H,L) → MEMORY LOCATION DEFINED BY B2,B3	16
LHLD	LOAD H & L DIRECT	00101010 B2 B3	(MEMORY) → H,L MEMORY DEFINED BY B2,B3	16

* .5 μs PER STATE.

Table 8-12. Interrupt and NOP Instructions

MNEMONIC	INSTRUCTION	FORMAT 7 6 5 4 3 2 1 0	DESCRIPTION	EXECUTION TIME* (STATES)
EI	ENABLE INTERRUPTS	1 1 1 1 1 0 1 1		4
DI	DISABLE INTERRUPTS	1 1 1 1 0 0 1 1		4
NOP	NO OPERATION	0 0 0 0 0 0 0 0		4

* .5 μs PER STATE.

coupler or audio cassette play/record with 110- and 300-baud rates. The tv camera, which Altair calls "Cyclops," is a digital, solid-state camera that outputs a 32-by-32 matrix of picture elements. The 1024 "pixels" provide shading of 16 gray levels. By using the camera, a real-time image is digitized for storage or processing—imagine a burglar alarm system that compares the current image with the previous and detects changes in shading, for example.

Software includes assembler, text editor, system monitor, and interpretive BASIC. An accounting applications package, disc operating system, and debugging package are also offered.

The 8800 has spawned a number of companies that manufacture plug-to-plug compatible modules for the Altair 8800. Processor Technology of Berkeley, California, for example, manufactures 4K 8-bit–byte static RAM memory modules that will plug right into the 8800. They provide 520-nanosecond speeds. The same company offers a television interface that provides sixteen 64-character lines of alphanumeric characters for display on a standard tv. Polymorphic Systems of Goleta, California, offers the same type of television interface, along with analog-to-digital and digital-to-analog interface boards. These are but a few of the companies offering 8800 products; more will be found at any hobbyist club or in advertisements in computer hobbyist or electronics magazines.

Another manufacturer using the 8080 microprocessor chip as a base is IMS Associates of San Leandro, California. Their IMSAI 8080 system uses compatible plug-in boards. A full line of hardware options is offered as shown in Chart 8-2. An inexpensive, 32-character-per-line matrix printer is one of their standard peripherals. It will work with either the IMSAI 8080 or the Altair 8800. Other peripherals include floppy disc drives, cassette interfaces, television interfaces, a 30-character-per-second printer, a 300-line-per-minute printer, and a 50-megabyte moving-head disc! The IMSAI 8080 is shown in Fig. 8-8.

MOTOROLA MC6800 CHIP DESCRIPTION

The MC6800, manufactured by Motorola, Inc., is an n-channel MOS CPU chip. It is an 8-bit parallel microprocessor with an addressing capability of 64K

Fig. 8-7. MITS Altair 8800.

Courtesy MITS

Chart 8-1. Microcomputer Specifications of MITS Altair 8800

Mainframe	
Microprocessor chip used:	Intel 8080
System clock:	2 MHz
Power supply:	+8, +16, −16 volts
Number of I/O slots:	3 extra slots in basic configuration
Control panel type:	full panel
Construction:	Pc board
Other:	
Memory	
Static memory:	Speed: 850 ns Increment size: 1024 bytes
Dynamic memory:	Speed: 300 ns Increment size: 4096 bytes
Erasable programmable:	Speed: 1 μs Increment size: 256 bytes
Shared memory:	
Memory limits:	Minimum: 1024 Maximum: 64K bytes
Other:	
Mainframe Options	
Real-time clock:	Yes, 100 μs, 1000 μs, 10 ms, 100 ms
Rack mount:	
Expander card/chassis:	Expander board provided, expander chassis available
DMA:	Yes—controls eight I/O cards at 300K bytes/s
Other:	
Peripheral Devices	
Teletype:	ASR-33 purchasable from MITS
Serial I/O (RS232):	Tty, TTL, and RS-232, up to 25,000 band
Cassette recorder if:	Yes—modulator/demodulator
Character printer:	
Line printer:	80 columns, 5×7 matrix, 100 chars/second
Alphanumeric crt:	
Television interface:	
Floppy disc:	Yes—single drive
Other disc:	
Parallel I/O board:	Yes—standard TTL
Vectored interrupts:	Yes—8 levels
PROM programmer:	Yes
Other manufacturers:	See text
Other:	32-char display with coupler or cassette interface; "Cyclops" tv camera
Software	
Assembler:	Yes
Editor:	Yes
Debug:	Yes
Other utilities:	
BASIC:	4K, 8K versions
Extended BASIC:	Yes
FORTRAN:	No
Other compilers:	
Operating systems:	DOS
Application programs:	Extended Engineering/Accounting
User's groups:	Yes
Other:	
Miscellaneous	
Extender board:	Yes
Documentation:	Thorough
Other:	Cooling fan, prototype board, connectors
Pricing	
Minimum system:	Under $535 kit, under $775 assembled

Chart 8-2. Microcomputer Specifications of IMSAI 8080

Mainframe		
Microprocessor chip used:	Intel 8080A	
System clock:	2 MHz	
Power supply:	28 amps at ±5 volts, 13 amps at +18, −18 volts	
Number of I/O slots:	6, expandable to 22	
Control panel type:	Full panel	
Construction:	Printed circuit	
Other:		
Memory		
Static memory:	Speed: 500 ns	Increment size: 1024 bytes, 4096 bytes
Dynamic memory:	Speed:	Increment size:
Erasable programmable:	Speed: 1 μs	Increment size: 2048 bytes
Shared memory:		
Memory limits:	Minimum: 1024	Maximum: 64K
Other:		
Mainframe Options		
Real-time clock:	.1, .2, 1, 2, 10, 20, 100, 200, 1000 ms	
Rack mount:		
Expander card/chassis:	Yes, 4 to 16 slots	
DMA:		
Other:		
Peripheral Devices		
Teletype:		
Serial I/O (RS232):	RS232, TTL, 75 to 56,000 baud; two channels available	
Cassette recorder if:	Yes—HIT system	
Character printer:	30 char/s, plot made, 132-char line	
Line printer:	125 lines/min, 32 char/line, 5×7 matrix	
Alphanumeric crt:		
Television interface:	Available. Full color alphanumeric and graphics	
Floppy disc:	Single-drive, interface, handles up to 4 drives	
Other disc:	50-megabyte movable-arm disc	
Parallel I/O board:	1 port or 4 ports, input and output	
Vectored interrupts:	8 vectored	
PROM programmer:		
Other manufacturers:		
Other:	300 line/min line printer	
Software		
Assembler:		
Editor:		
Debug:		
Other utilities:		
BASIC:	Yes, 4K, 8K, 12K	
Extended BASIC:	To be developed	
FORTRAN:	To be developed	
Other compilers:	PL/M to be developed	
Operating systems:	Disc operating system	
Application programs:		
User's groups:		
Other:		
Miscellaneous		
Extender board:	Yes	
Documentation:	Thorough	
Other:	Cooling fan	
Pricing		
Minimum system:	Under $600 kit, $950 assembled	

Courtesy IMS Associates, Inc.

Fig. 8-8. IMSAI 8080.

8-bit words (bytes). It is part of a chip set of other parts designed primarily for the MC6800. Many other semiconductor manufacturers "second-source" or copy the chip, producing pin-compatible and software-compatible duplicates. The CPU portion, called the MC-6800 Microprocessing Unit (MPU), has an instruction repertoire of 72 instructions. The MPU has two 8-bit accumulators, a 16-bit index register, a 16-bit program counter, a 16-bit stack pointer, and an 8-bit condition codes register. It has three vectored interrupts and DMA capability. Instruction times vary from 2 to 12 μs.

Physical Features and Architecture

Motorola calls their MC6800 chip an "MPU" for microprocessing unit. The MPU is a 40-pin chip as shown in Fig. 8-9, with the basic architecture illustrated in Fig. 8-10. There are eight data lines designated D7–D0. Sixteen address lines, A15–A0, enable addressing of 64K of external memory or I/O devices. Signals $\phi1$ and $\phi2$ are external two-phase clock signals provided to the chip. Signal $\phi2$ is also routed to external memory or devices to synchronize decoding of address codes. $\overline{\text{RESET}}$ is an external signal supplied to the chip that resets and starts the MPU. It is essentially a vectored interrupt. An interrupt request line, $\overline{\text{IRQ}}$, signals the MPU of an external interrupt which causes a vectored interrupt if an interrupt flag within the MPU is enabled. A nonmaskable interrupt, $\overline{\text{NMI}}$, generates a third type of interrupt regardless of the state of the interrupt flag; it is usually used for detection of power loss. A fourth interrupt, software interrupt, is generated by execution of an SWI instruction.

Two signals, R/W (*R*ead/*W*rite) and VMA (*V*alid *M*emory *A*ddress), are used to inform external devices that a memory or I/O device address is present on address lines A15–A0 and whether a read or write is specified. DBE (*D*ata *B*us *E*nable) and TSC (*T*hree *S*tate *C*ontrol) are external control lines for the data bus and address bus, respectively. TSC can be used to effect a DMA transfer by inhibiting microprocessor-unit access to the address bus and control of the read/write line.

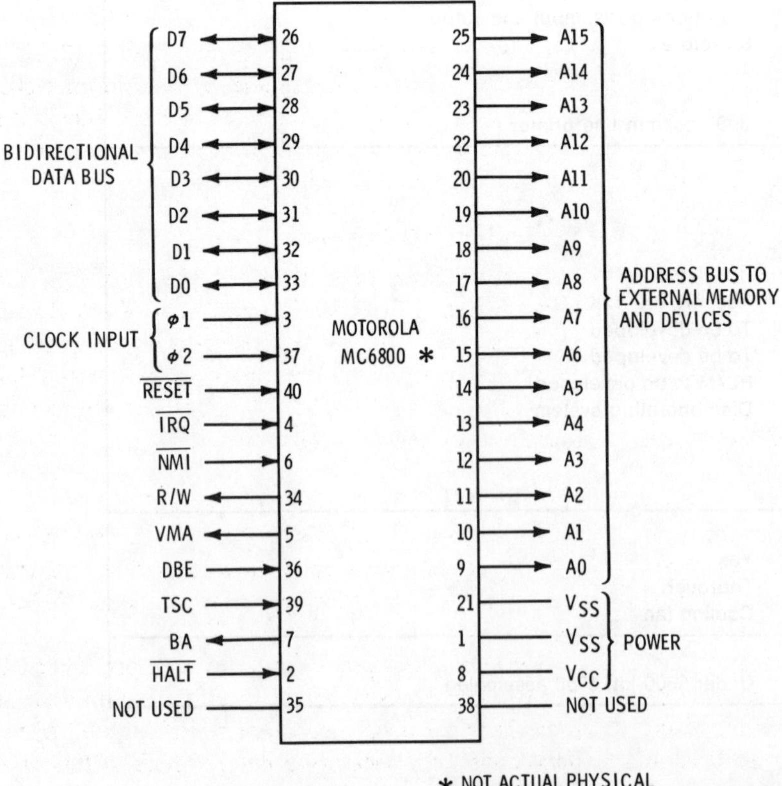

Fig. 8-9. MC6800 pin configuration.

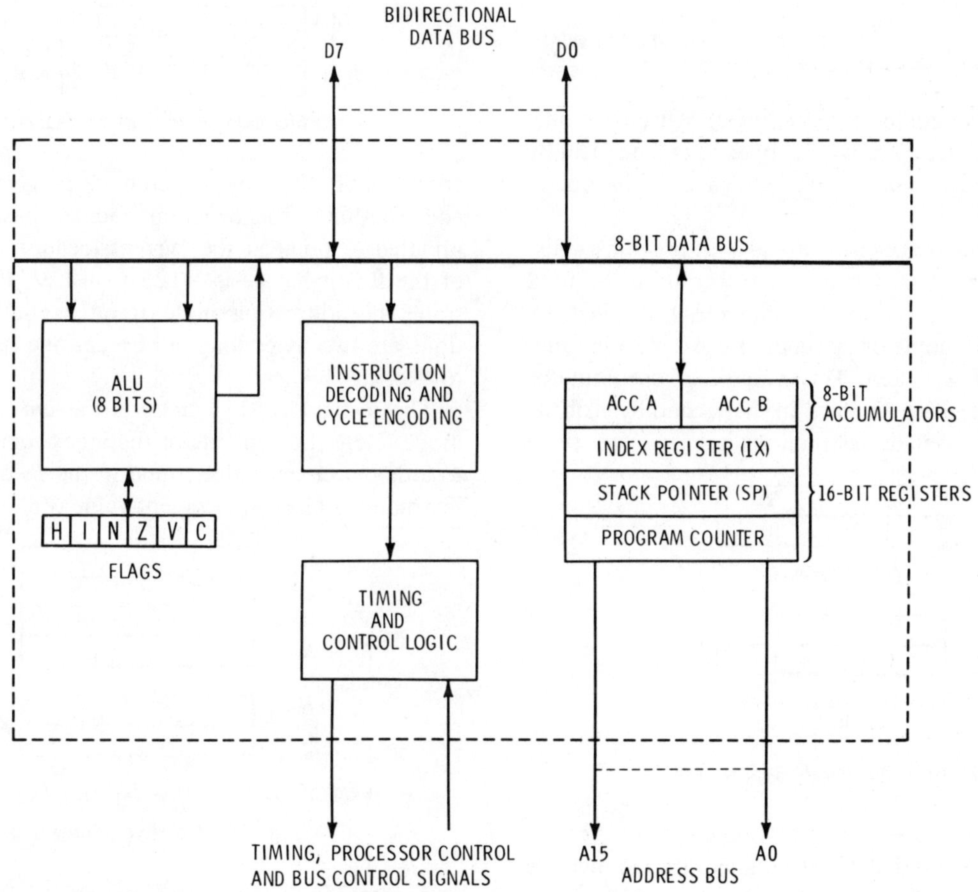

Fig. 8-10. MC6800 architecture.

$\overline{\text{HALT}}$ is an external signal used to stop processing in the MPU. The response to the halt is the bus available signal from the MPU, caused either by the $\overline{\text{HALT}}$ or by execution of a WAIT instruction.

Within the MPU, the programmer has access to four registers: two accumulators designated ACCA and ACCB, an index register (IX), and a stack pointer register (SP). The accumulators are 8-bit registers, while the other registers are 16-bit registers. A 16-bit program counter is used to control program sequence.

A condition codes register is not so much a register, but a collection of flag bits that can be tested for various conditions caused by execution of arithmetic and logical instructions. There are six flag bits designated H, I, N, Z, V, and C. Flag bit H is a "half-carry," and is set whenever a carry from bit position 3 results from an ADD instruction. Flag bit I is the interrupt mask used to enable or disable external interrupts. It can be set or reset by two instructions, or set (disabled) by a hardware or software interrupt. Flag bit N is a negative flag, set whenever the result sign (bit position 7) is set, and cleared when the result is 0. Flag bit Z is set if the result is 0 or is reset if the result is not zero. Flag bit V is an "overflow" bit. It is set if arithmetic overflow resulted from the arithmetic operation. An example of this would be attempting to add -120_{10} and -120_{10}. The result of -240_{10} is too large to be held in an eight-bit signed value and the V flag would be set. The last flag bit is the C bit, which is the usual carry from the most significant bit position of a result.

Instruction Execution

The minimum cycle time for the MC6800 is one microsecond. Instruction lengths range from 2 cycles, or 2 microseconds, for a register-to-register operation to 12 cycles, or 12 microseconds, for a software interrupt. The average number of cycles per instruction is perhaps 5 cycles, or 5 microseconds.

Addressing Modes

Instructions for the MC6800 use several types of addressing. Motorola calls them "inherent," "immediate," "direct," "extended," "relative," and "indexed" addressing.

Inherent addressing is similar to a "short" instruction discussed previously. All of the information necessary to perform the operation can be specified in a one-word instruction (one memory access), which in this case is one 8-bit byte. Fig. 8-11 shows an instruction of this type, an INX (*In*crement Inde*x* Register) instruction,

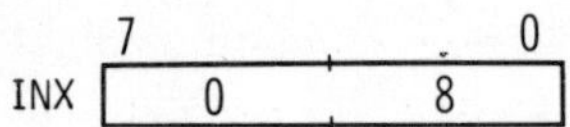

Fig. 8-11. Inherent addressing.

which bumps the contents of the index register by one. This type of instruction is one byte long and usually takes two cycles, sometimes four, and occasionally more.

Immediate addressing is identical with previously discussed immediate instructions. The operand to be used in the instruction execution is contained in the instruction itself. An example of this is the LDAB #16 instruction shown in Fig. 8-12A. This would load accumulator B with the value 16, contained in the second byte of the instruction. Immediate instructions are two or three

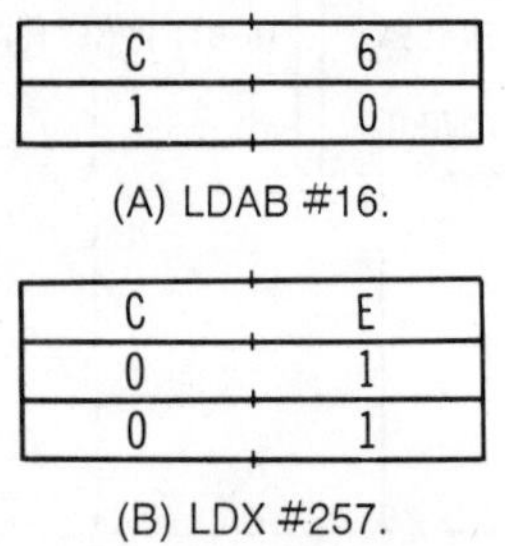

Fig. 8-12. Immediate addressing.

bytes long and take two or three MPU cycles to execute. For two-byte immediate instructions, the immediate value is an operand in the range 0 to 255. For three-byte immediate instructions, the operand is a 16-bit unsigned integer value (0 to 65,535).

Direct addressing uses the one-byte operand field of the instruction to specify a direct address somewhere in locations 0 to 255. An example of this is shown in Fig. 8-13 where the EORA (*E*xclusive *OR A*) instruction addresses memory location 100_{10}. Direct addressing instructions are all two bytes long and take three to five

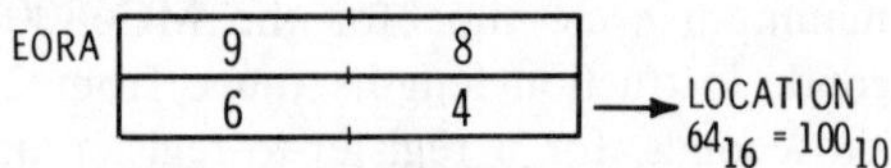

Fig. 8-13. Direct addressing.

cycles to complete. The direct addressing mode is similar to a "page 0" addressing mode in minicomputers.

The MPU uses an *extended addressing* mode to directly address memory locations beyond location 255. Here the direct address, of course, is specified in two bytes to permit addressing up to 64K of memory. Extended addressing instructions are three bytes long and take from four to six cycles to execute. Fig. 8-14 shows an example of extended addressing.

Relative addressing is identical to "floating-page" relative addressing used in many minicomputers. The second byte of the instruction specifies an eight-bit signed displacement value which is added to the current

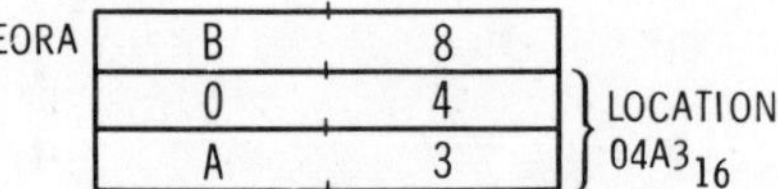

Fig. 8-14. Extended addressing.

contents of the program counter to give the effective address. Since the program counter has already been updated to point at the current location +2, the range of the floating page is −125 to +129. Fig. 8-15 illustrates this addressing mode. Relative addressing instructions are two bytes long; all except one take four cycles to execute.

The last addressing mode is the *indexed addressing* mode. Here the contents of the index register are added to a displacement value found in the second byte of the instruction. The displacement value is an unsigned value

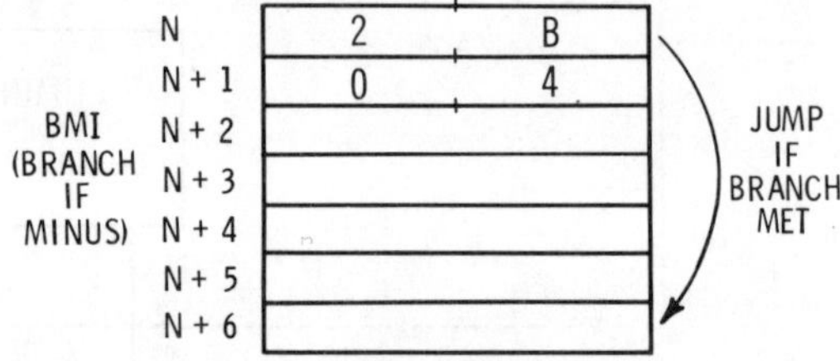

Fig. 8-15. Relative addressing.

from 0 to 255. The instruction ADDA 20,X is shown in Fig. 8-16. Indexed addressing instructions are two bytes long and take five to seven cycles to execute.

The six instruction modes of the MC6800 are not unlike addressing in most minicomputers, except that only one mode is possible per instruction. While a Data General Nova instruction could specify addressing that is relative forward, indexed, and indirect, the MC6800 could specify only one of the three types at a time.

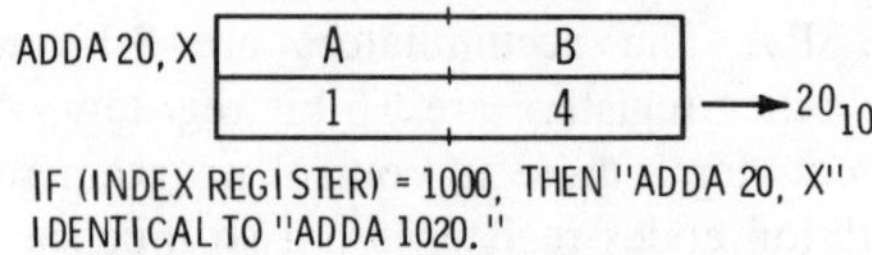

Fig. 8-16. Indexed addressing mode.

Instruction Repertoire

The instructions of the MC6800 may be divided into four groups:

- Accumulator and Memory instructions.
- Index Register and Stack instructions.
- Jump and Branch instructions.
- Conditions Code Register.

Not all of the instructions permit every addressing mode. There are 72 unique instructions, and to permit all addressing modes would require 72 times 6, or 432, unique codes while only a byte (permitting 256) is available for operation codes. In addition, some addressing modes are meaningless for certain instructions, for instance, an inherent LDAA (*L*oad *A*ccumulator) or an immediate INX (*In*crement Inde*x* Register). Altogether there are 197 separate instructions when addressing modes are considered.

The Accumulator and Memory instructions (shown in Tables 8-13 through 8-16) are separated into four subgroups: Arithmetic, Logic, Data Test, and Data Handling instructions.

Add instructions ADDA, ADDB, and ABA add the contents of A and memory, B and memory, or A and B together, respectively, and put the result in the A accumulator. (See Table 8-13.) Add with carry (ADCA, ADCB) instructions add the contents A and memory or B and memory in similar fashion. Three subtracts (SUBA, SUBB, SBA) are similar to the adds except, of course, for the operation. Two subtracts with carry perform in the same fashion. There are three "Negate" instructions (NEG, NEGA, NEGB) that take the two's complement of either a number in memory (NEG), the A register (NEGA), or the B register (NEGB), and put the result back in the source. The DAA instruction (*D*ecimal *A*djust *A*) operates the same as the DAA in the Intel 8080—the result of an arithmetic operation is adjusted to a bcd number by a test of the carry and half-carry.

Logic instructions (Table 8-14) implement an AND, one's complement, exclusive OR, or inclusive OR. ANDA and ANDB AND memory and the A or B register, with the result going to A or B. The exclusive OR (EORA, EORB) and inclusive OR (ORA, ORB) perform their functions similarly. The one's complement instructions (COM, COMA, COMB) perform a one's complement on either memory, A, or B, with the result going into the source.

Data Test instructions (Table 8-15) test A, B, and memory data, and set most of the condition codes except H and I. Registers A and B and memory are left unchanged. Bit Test (BITA, BITB) AND A and memory for the test. A Compare (CMPA, CMPB, and CBA) instruction compares (A − memory), (B − memory), or (A − B), and sets the condition codes. Test, Zero, or Minus (TST, TSTA, TSTB) tests memory, A, or B, and sets condition codes N and Z accordingly.

Data Handling instructions (Table 8-16) include clears, decrements, increments, loads/stores, and shifts. Clear (CLR, CLRA, CLRB) clears memory, A, or B. Decrement (DEC, DECA, DECB) and increment (INC, INCA, INCB) subtract or add one to memory, A, or B. Load Accumulator (LDAA, LDAB) and Store Accumulator (STAA, STAB) load or store A and B. Transfer Accumulator (TAB, TBA) allows transfers from A to B or B to A. Push Data (PSHA, PSHB) pushes (A) or (B) into the external stack in memory defined by the SP (stack pointer) register. The SP register is decremented by one in order to point to the next entry in the stack. Pull Data (PULA, PULB) increments the SP register and transfers the next stack byte to either A or B.

The remaining Data Handling instructions are shifts, operating either on memory, A, or B. (See Fig. 8-17.) The first shift performs a one-bit rotate through the carry either right or left (ROR, RORA, RORB, ROL, ROLA, ROLB). The second type performs a one-bit arithmetic shift (preserving the sign on a right shift). The bit shifted out goes to the carry, and either right or left shifts are performed (ASR, ASRA, ASRB, ASL, ASLA, ASLB). The third type is a logical shift right (LSR, LSRA, LSRB). Note that an arithmetic shift left is the same as a logical shift left.

The Index Register and Stack instructions, as the name indicates, are concerned with loading, storing, or adjusting the index and SP registers. Table 8-17 shows the instructions in this group. Compare Index Register (CPX) compares the 16-bit value in IX with a memory value and sets the N, Z, and V condition codes accordingly. Decrement Index Register (DEX) and Decrement Stack Pointer (DES) subtract one from the IX and SP registers, respectively. Increment Index Register and Increment Stack Pointer (INX and INS) add one. The IX and SP registers can be loaded (LDX, LDS), stored (STX, STS), and transferred to each other (TXS, TSX). All of the above instructions work with 16-bit data values.

Jump and Branch instructions, the third group, are either conditional or unconditional jumps, or subroutine and interrupt calls or returns. All "branch" instructions

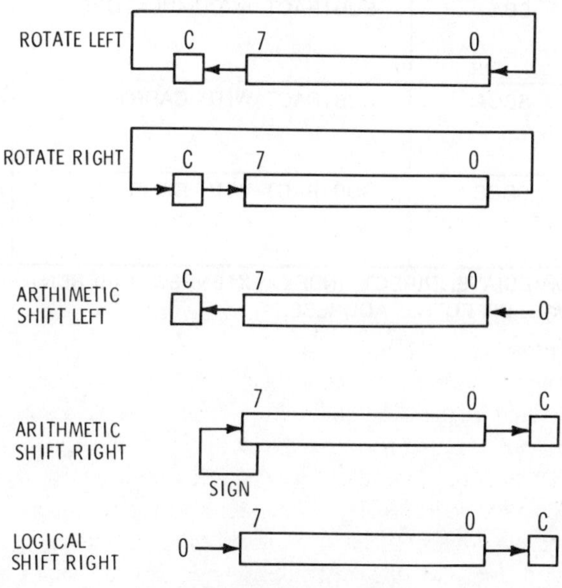

Fig. 8-17. Shift instructions.

Table 8-13. Arithmetic Instructions

MNEMONIC	INSTRUCTION	FORMAT* I	D	I	E	I	DESCRIPTION**	EXECUTION TIME
ADDA	ADD A	✓	✓	✓	✓		(A) + (M) → A CC = CONDITION CODES	
ADDB	ADD B	✓	✓	✓	✓		(B) + (M) → B CC	
ABA	ADD ACCUMULATORS					✓	(A) + (B) → A CC	
ADCA	ADD WITH CARRY A	✓	✓	✓	✓		(A) + (M) + (C) → A CC	
ADCB	ADD WITH CARRY B	✓	✓	✓	✓		(B) + (M) + (C) → B CC	
NEG	NEGATE			✓	✓		—(M) → M CC	
NEGA	NEGATE A					✓	—(A) → A CC	
NEGB	NEGATE A					✓	—(B) → B CC	
DAA	DECIMAL ADJUST A					✓	(SEE TEXT) CC	
SUBA	SUBTRACT A	✓	✓	✓	✓		(A) — (M) → A CC	
SUBB	SUBTRACT B	✓	✓	✓	✓		(B) — (M) → B CC	
SBA	SUBTRACT ACCUMULATORS					✓	(A) — (B) → A CC	
SBCA	SUBTRACT WITH CARRY A	✓	✓	✓	✓		(A) — (M) — (C) → A CC	
SBCB	SUBTRACT WITH CARRY B	✓	✓	✓	✓		(B) — (M) — (C) → B CC	

* IMMEDIATE, DIRECT, INDEX, EXTENDED, INHERENT.
** M = EFFECTIVE ADDRESS.

Table 8-14. Logic Instructions

MNEMONIC	INSTRUCTION	FORMAT* I	D	I	E	I	DESCRIPTION**	EXECUTION TIME
ANDA	AND A	✓	✓	✓	✓		(A) AND (M) → A CC	
ANDB	AND B	✓	✓	✓	✓		(B) AND (M) → B CC	
COM	ONE'S COMPLEMENT			✓	✓		—(M) → M CC	
COMA	ONE'S COMPLEMENT A					✓	—(A) → A CC	
COMB	ONE'S COMPLEMENT B					✓	—(B) → B CC	
EORA	EXCLUSIVE-OR A	✓	✓	✓	✓		(A) XOR (M) → A CC	
EORB	EXCLUSIVE-OR B	✓	✓	✓	✓		(B) XOR (M) → B CC	
ORA	INCLUSIVE-OR A	✓	✓	✓	✓		(A) OR (M) → A CC	
ORB	INCLUSIVE-OR B	✓	✓	✓	✓		(B) OR (M) → B CC	

* IMMEDIATE, DIRECT, INDEX, EXTENDED, INHERENT.
** M = EFFECTIVE ADDRESS.

are relative addressing only. These instructions are shown in Table 8-18. The relative branch instructions branch unconditionally (BRA, *Br*anch *A*lways) or conditionally on carry clear, carry set, zero, less than zero, greater than or equal to zero, greater than zero, higher, less than or equal to zero, lower or same, less than zero, minus, not zero, overflow clear, overflow set, or plus (BCC, BCS, BEQ, BGE, BGT, BHI, BLE, BLS, BLT, BMI, BNE, BVC, BVS, BPL).

A Branch to Subroutine (BSR) instruction stores the contents of the program counter in the stack (two bytes) and decrements the stack by two in order to point to the next slot (see Fig. 8-18).

The JMP instruction is the usual unconditional *jump,* but the Jump to Subroutine (JSR) acts the same as the BSR instruction. BSR can only be a relative addressing type instruction, however, while JSR may specify indexed or extended addressing.

The NOP instruction does nothing. NOPs are used to "waste" an instruction for certain timing requirements (rare) or to save space for later patching to a program.

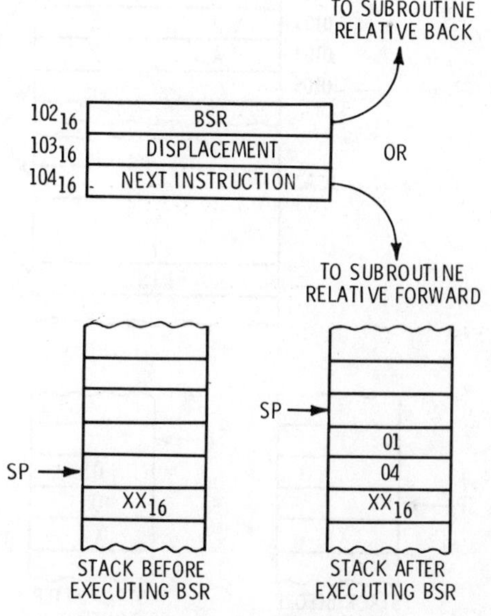

Fig. 8-18. BSR instruction action.

Table 8-15. Data Test Instructions

MNEMONIC	INSTRUCTION	FORMAT* I	D	I	E	I	DESCRIPTION**	EXECUTION TIME
BITA	BIT TEST A	✓	✓	✓	✓		(A) AND (M) CC	
BITB	BIT TEST B	✓	✓	✓	✓		(B) AND (M) CC	
CMPA	COMPARE A	✓	✓	✓	✓		(A) — (M) CC	
CMPB	COMPARE B	✓	✓	✓	✓		(B) — (M) CC	
CBA	COMPARE ACCUMULATORS					✓	(A) — (B) CC	
TST	TEST, ZERO, OR MINUS			✓	✓		TEST (M) CC	
TSTA	TEST, ZERO, OR MINUS A					✓	TEST (A) CC	
TSTB	TEST, ZERO, OR MINUS B					✓	TEST (B) CC	

* IMMEDIATE, DIRECT, INDEXED, EXTENDED, INHERENT.
** M = EFFECTIVE ADDRESS.

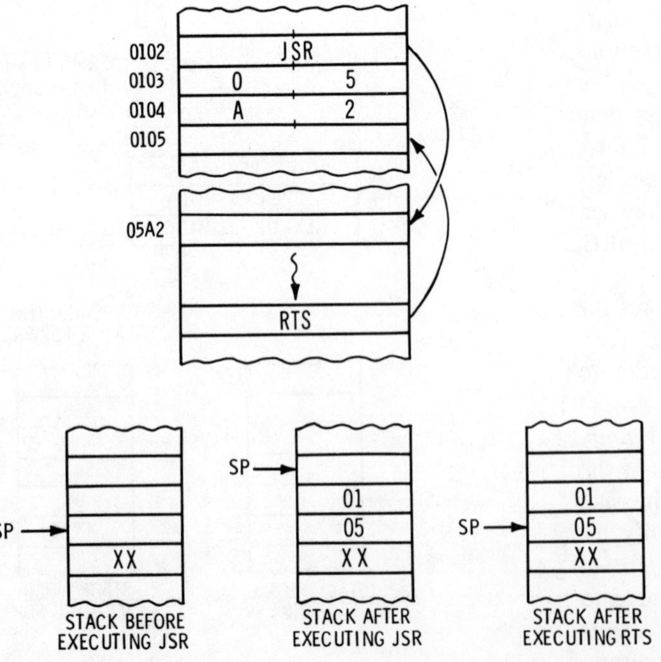

Fig. 8-19. RTS instruction action.

Table 8-16. Data Handling Instructions

MNEMONIC	INSTRUCTION	FORMAT* I	D	I	E	I	DESCRIPTION**	EXECUTION TIME
CLR	CLEAR			✓	✓		0 → M CC	
CLRA	CLEAR A					✓	0 → A CC	
CLRB	CLEAR B					✓	0 → B CC	
DEC	DECREMENT			✓	✓		(M) − 1 → M CC	
DECA	DECREMENT A					✓	(A) − 1 → A CC	
DECB	DECREMENT B					✓	(B) − 1 → B CC	
INC	INCREMENT			✓	✓		(M) + 1 → M CC	
INCA	INCREMENT A					✓	(A) + 1 → A CC	
INCB	INCREMENT B					✓	(B) + 1 → B CC	
LDAA	LOAD ACCUMULATOR A	✓	✓	✓	✓		(M) → A	
LDAB	LOAD ACCUMULATOR B	✓	✓	✓	✓		(M) → B	
PSHA	PUSH DATA A					✓	(A) → NEXT STACK (SP) − 1 → SP	
PSHB	PUSH DATA B					✓	(B) → NEXT STACK (SP) − 1 → SP	
PULA	PULL DATA A					✓	(SP) + 1 → SP (LAST STACK) → A	
PULB	PULL DATA B					✓	(SP) + 1 → SP (LAST STACK) → B	
ROL	ROTATE LEFT			✓	✓		(SEE TEXT)	
ROLA	ROTATE LEFT A					✓	(SEE TEXT)	

Table 8-16—Continued

MNEMONIC	INSTRUCTION	FORMAT* I	D	I	E	I	DESCRIPTION**	EXECUTION TIME
ROLB	ROTATE LEFT B					✓	(SEE TEXT)	
ROR	ROTATE RIGHT			✓	✓		(SEE TEXT)	
RORA	ROTATE RIGHT A					✓	(SEE TEXT)	
RORB	ROTATE RIGHT B					✓	(SEE TEXT)	
ASL	SHIFT LEFT ARITHMETIC			✓	✓		(SEE TEXT)	
ASLA	SHIFT LEFT ARITHMETIC A					✓	(SEE TEXT)	
ALSB	SHIFT LEFT ARITHMETIC B					✓	(SEE TEXT)	
ASR	SHIFT RIGHT ARITHMETIC			✓	✓		(SEE TEXT)	
ASRA	SHIFT RIGHT ARITHMETIC A					✓	(SEE TEXT)	
ASRB	SHIFT RIGHT ARITHMETIC B					✓	(SEE TEXT)	
LSR	LOGICAL SHIFT RIGHT			✓	✓		(SEE TEXT)	
LSRA	LOGICAL SHIFT RIGHT A					✓	(SEE TEXT)	
LSRB	LOGICAL SHIFT RIGHT B					✓	(SEE TEXT)	
STAA	STORE ACCUMULATOR A		✓	✓	✓		(A) → M CC	
STAB	STORE ACCUMULATOR B		✓	✓	✓		(B) → M CC	
TAB	TRANSFER ACCUMULATORS					✓	(A) → B CC	
TBA	TRANSFER ACCUMULATORS					✓	(B) → A CC	

* IMMEDIATE, DIRECT, INDEXED, EXTENDED, INHERENT.
** M = EFFECTIVE ADDRESS.

Table 8-17. Index Register and Stack Instructions

MNEMONIC	INSTRUCTION	FORMAT* I	D	I	E	I	DESCRIPTION**	EXECUTION TIME
CPX	COMPARE INDEX REGISTER	✓	✓	✓	✓		(IX) – (M,M + 1) CC	
DEX	DECREMENT INDEX REGISTER					✓	(IX) – 1 → IX	
DES	DECREMENT STACK POINTER					✓	(SP) – 1 → SP	
INX	INCREMENT INDEX REGISTER					✓	(IX) + 1 → IX	
INS	INCREMENT STACK POINTER					✓	(SP) + 1 → SP	
LDX	LOAD INDEX REGISTER	✓	✓	✓	✓		(M,M + 1) → 1X	
LDS	LOAD STACK POINTER	✓	✓	✓	✓		(M,M + 1) → SP	
STX	STORE INDEX REGISTER		✓	✓	✓		(IX) → M,M + 1	
STS	STORE STACK POINTER		✓	✓	✓		(SP) → M,M, + 1	
TXS	INDEX REGISTER TO STACK POINTER					✓	(IX) – 1 → SP	
TSX	STACK POINTER TO INDEX REGISTER					✓	(SP) + 1 → IX	

* IMMEDIATE, DIRECT, INDEXED, EXTENDED, INHERENT.
** M = EFFECTIVE ADDRESS.

Return from Subroutine (RTS) reverses the operation that BSR or JSR implemented. It retrieves two bytes from the stack and stores them into the program counter, effectively jumping back to the next instruction in sequence after the BSR or JSR (see Fig. 8-19).

To understand the return from interrupt, it is necessary to understand the actions performed during a *s*oft*w*are *i*nterrupt (SWI), an external hardware interrupt, or a nonmaskable interrupt. The first occurs after execution of the SWI instruction. The second always occurs (cannot be masked) after receipt of an external signal. The second can occur if the interrupt mask bit I is not set and an external interrupt occurs. When the interrupt occurs, the current "environment" is pushed into the stack as shown in Fig. 8-20. These seven bytes define the entire status of the system at the interrupted point. At the end of the interrupt routine, these registers and condition codes may be restored to enable the program to take up once again from the interrupted point. After the environment has been pushed into the stack, two

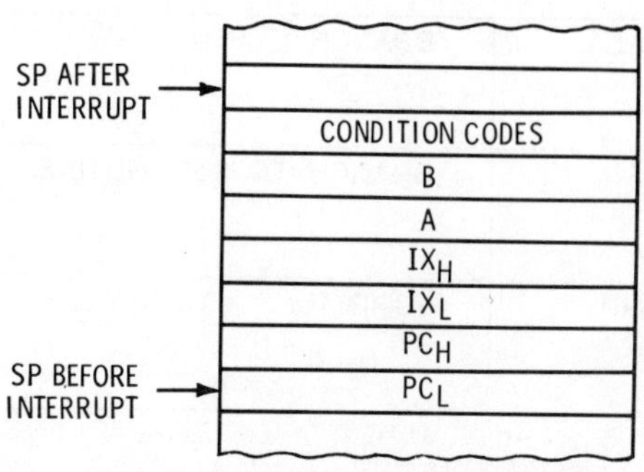

Fig. 8-20. Interrupt stack action.

Table 8-18. Jump and Branch Instructions

MNEMONIC	INSTRUCTION	FORMAT*				DESCRIPTION**	EXECUTION TIME
		R	I	E	I		
BRA	BRANCH ALWAYS	✓				SELF-EXPLANATORY	
BCC	BRANCH IF CARRY CLEAR	✓				SELF-EXPLANATORY	
BCS	BRANCH IF CARRY SET	✓				SELF-EXPLANATORY	
BEQ	BRANCH IF = ZERO	✓				SELF-EXPLANATORY	
BGE	BRANCH IF ≥ ZERO	✓				SELF-EXPLANATORY	
BGT	BRANCH IF > ZERO	✓				SELF-EXPLANATORY	
BHI	BRANCH IF HIGHER	✓				SELF-EXPLANATORY	
BLE	BRANCH IF ≤ ZERO	✓				SELF-EXPLANATORY	
BLS	BRANCH IF LOWER OR SAME	✓				SELF-EXPLANATORY	
BLT	BRANCH IF < ZERO	✓				SELF-EXPLANATORY	
BMI	BRANCH IF MINUS	✓				SELF-EXPLANATORY	
BNE	BRANCH IF NOT EQUAL ZERO	✓				SELF-EXPLANATORY	
BVC	BRANCH IF OVERFLOW CLEAR	✓				SELF-EXPLANATORY	
BVS	BRANCH IF OVERFLOW SET	✓				SELF-EXPLANATORY	
BPL	BRANCH IF PLUS	✓				SELF-EXPLANATORY	
BSR	BRANCH TO SUBROUTINE	✓				(SEE TEXT)	
JMP	JUMP			✓	✓	(M) → PC	

Table 8-18—Continued

MNEMONIC	INSTRUCTION	FORMAT*	DESCRIPTION	EXECUTION TIME
JSR	JUMP TO SUBROUTINE	✓ ✓ (INDEXED, EXTENDED)	(SEE TEXT)	
NOP	NO OPERATION	✓ (INHERENT)	SELF-EXPLANATORY	
RTI	RETURN FROM INTERRUPT	✓ (INHERENT)	(SEE TEXT)	
RTS	RETURN FROM SUBROUTINE	✓ (INHERENT)	(SEE TEXT)	
SWI	SOFTWARE INTERRUPT	✓ (INHERENT)	(SEE TEXT)	
WAI	WAIT FOR INTERRUPT	✓ (INHERENT)	(SEE TEXT)	

* RELATIVE, INDEXED, EXTENDED, INHERENT.
** M = EFFECTIVE ADDRESS.

bytes are fetched from a specified vector location. These two bytes define the address of the interrupt routine and are jammed into the program counter to cause a transfer to one of four routines (for a hardware interrupt, software interrupt, nonmaskable interrupt, or restart). Addresses $FFF8_{16}$ through $FFFF_{16}$ define the vector locations as shown in Fig. 8-21. Previous to the transfer, the interrupt mask bit I is set to disable further interrupts.

When the interrupt has been processed, the last instruction to be executed in the interrupt routine is an RTI instruction (*Ret*urn From *I*nterrupt). The RTI retrieves the seven locations, stores the registers and condition codes, and transfers control back to the next instruction after the interruption. See Fig. 8-22.

The remaining instruction in the Jump and Branch group of instructions is the *Wa*it For *I*nterrupt (WAI).

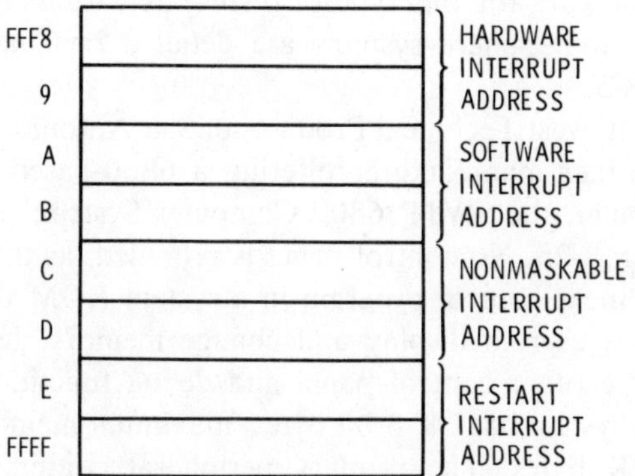

Fig. 8-21. Interrupt vectors.

WAI causes the CPU to enter a wait state, which is essentially the same as a Halt instruction in other machines. The only way the wait state can be exited is by an external hardware interrupt which causes a transfer to the hardware interrupt routine.

The last group of instructions affect the condition codes register. See Table 8-19. The carry (C), interrupt mask (I), and overflow (V) can all be cleared (CLC, CLI, CLV) or set (SEC, SEI, SEV) by instructions in this group. In addition, the six bits of the condition

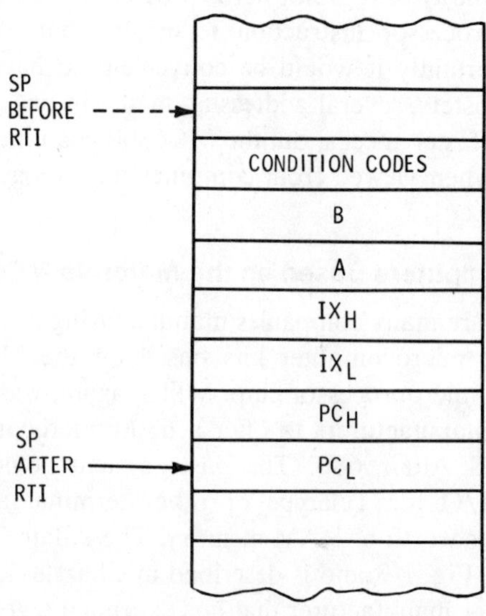

Fig. 8-22. RTI action.

Table 8-19. Condition Code Register Instructions

MNEMONIC	INSTRUCTION	FORMAT (IMPLIED)	DESCRIPTION	EXECUTION TIME
CLC	CLEAR CARRY	✓	0→C	
CLI	CLEAR INTERRUPT MASK	✓	0→I	
CLV	CLEAR OVERFLOW	✓	0→V	
SEC	SET CARRY	✓	1→C	
SEI	SET INTERRUPT MASK	✓	1→I	
SEV	SET OVERFLOW	✓	1→V	
TAP	ACCUMULATOR A TO CONDITION CODES	✓	(A)→CC	
TPA	CONDITION CODES TO A	✓	(CC)→A	

codes register can be loaded from the accumulator (TAP) or stored in the accumulator (TPA).

Programming Considerations

The instruction set of the MC6800 is the most versatile of all of the microprocessor chips discussed so far. With so many instructions, code may be "hand-tailored" to optimize memory or speed or reach some trade-off between the two. It is not hard to be enthusiastic about a microprocessor instruction repertoire that offers so much. Certainly it would be convenient to have additional registers, several addressing modes in one instruction, and faster speeds, but the MC6800 is an incredible bargain when viewed from computer technology of ten years ago.

Microcomputers Based on the Motorola MC6800

There are many companies manufacturing microcomputers or microcomputer kits based on the Motorola MC6800 microprocessor chip. MITS, again, was one of the first manufacturers to offer a 6800 microcomputer, the MITS Altair 680. The basic system comes with built-in I/O for Teletype or other terminal and 1K 8-bit bytes worth of RAM memory. The Altair 680 was shown in Fig. 1-3 and is described in Chart 8-3.

Another manufacturer that has expended a great deal of effort on producing a quality 6800-based microcomputer is Sphere, Inc., of Bountiful, Utah. The Sphere 310 (formerly Sphere I) System is shown in Fig. 8-23. In a minimum configuration, it comes with 4K 8-bit bytes of RAM memory and an alphanumeric keyboard. The Micro-Sphere 200 System, shown in Fig. 8-24, is a somewhat different packaging of the same basic unit, except that the upper memory limit is 8K bytes. Sphere offers a wide variety of options and peripheral devices for its systems. Peripherals include a cassette interface, floppy disc, and 65-line-per-minute printer. Cathode-ray tube displays include an interface to a standard tv that displays 16 lines by 32 characters, and an interface that provides a matrix display of 128 by 128 dots. The latter is usable for real-time display work (although the software for this type of display is extremely complex. Both Sphere systems are detailed in Charts 8-4 and 8-5.

Southwest Technical Products of San Antonio, Texas, is another manufacturer offering a 6800-based microcomputer, the SWTP 6800 Computer System, pictured in Fig. 8-25. No control panel is provided, as there is a permanent control program in a system ROM that enables a user to display and change memory data and provide other control panel and debug functions. The basic system has 2K 8-bit bytes; maximum memory size is 32K bytes. The primary peripheral equipment offered is the SWTP CT-1024 Television Terminal Sys-

Chart 8-3. Microcomputer Specifications of MITS Altair 680

Mainframe		
Microprocessor chip used:	Motorola MC6800	
System clock:	500 kHz	
Power supply:	+5 volts, −16 volts, +16 volts	
Number of I/O slots:		
Control panel type:	Full control panel	
Construction:	Printed-circuit boards	
Other:		
Memory		
Static memory:	Speed: 850 ns	Increment size: 1024 bytes
Dynamic memory:	Speed:	Increment size:
Erasable programmable:	Speed: 1 μs	Increment size: 256 bytes
Shared memory:		
Memory limits:	Minimum: 1024 bytes	Maximum: 64K
Other:		
Mainframe Options		
Real-time clock:		
Rack mount:		
Expander card/chassis:		
DMA:		
Other:		
Peripheral Devices		
Teletype:	ASR-33	
Serial I/O (RS232):	Built-in RS232 or current loop	
Cassette recorder if:	See MITS Altair 8800	
Character printer:	See MITS Altair 8800	
Line printer:	See MITS Altair 8800	
Alphanumeric crt:	See MITS Altair 8800	
Television interface:	See MITS Altair 8800	
Floppy disc:	See MITS Altair 8800	
Other disc:		
Parallel I/O board:		
Vectored interrupts:		
PROM programmer:		
Other manufacturers:		
Other:	Five-level Baudot interface	
Software		
Assembler:	Yes	
Editor:	Yes	
Debug:	Yes	
Other utilities:	PROM monitor	
BASIC:	Yes	
Extended BASIC:		
FORTRAN:		
Other compilers:		
Operating systems:		
Application programs:		
User's groups:	Yes	
Other:		
Miscellaneous		
Extender board:		
Documentation:	Thorough	
Other:	Cooling fan	
Pricing		
Minimum system:	Under $470 kit	

Courtesy Sphere Corp.

Fig. 8-23. Sphere 310 system with peripherals.

tem, which was shown in Fig. 5-12. The CT-1024 provides a display of 16 lines of 32 characters on a standard tv and can be interfaced to the SWTP 6800 in serial or parallel fashion (with the appropriate option). Chart 8-6 describes the SWTP 6800 in detail. Another peripheral device available is a 40-character-per-line alphanumeric printer at a very attractive price (about $250).

The last manufacturer producing a hobbyist microcomputer based on the MC6800 is WaveMate of Gardena, California. WaveMate's Jupiter II system is represented as the "world's finest microcomputer system" in terms of construction, quality control of parts, and reliability, and it may well be. The Jupiter II system is somewhat more expensive than competing microcomputer systems, however. It is up to the potential purchaser to determine how much these benefits are worth to him. Peripheral devices include a 1024-character tv terminal, dual read/write cassette with motor controls, dual floppy disc drives, and other standard I/O devices. Software includes a 2K-byte ROM monitor (there is no extensive control panel), assembler, text editor, and BASIC interpreter. Fig. 8-26 shows the Jupiter II system, and Chart 8-7 describes the system in detail.

FAIRCHILD F8 CHIP DESCRIPTION

The F8, manufactured by Fairchild, Inc., as an n-channel MOS chip set oriented towards an eight-bit data bus. Unlike other chips discussed in this chapter, the F8 requires at least two chips to make up a CPU: the 3850 CPU chip proper and the 3851 Program Storage Unit (PSU). The PSU contains many CPU registers, such as the program counter, stack register, and data counter (pointer), in addition to 1024 bytes of ROM. It also contains interrupt logic. A completely function-

Courtesy Sphere Corp.

Fig. 8-24. Micro-Sphere 200 system.

Chart 8-4. Microcomputer Specifications of Sphere 310

Mainframe	
Microprocessor chip used:	Motorola MC6800
System clock:	1 MHz
Power supply:	5 volts @ 5 amperes, 12 volts @ 3 amperes, –5 volts @ 85 mA
Number of I/O slots:	
Control panel type:	No console—ROM monitor
Construction:	Printed-circuit board
Other:	
Memory	
Static memory:	Speed: Increment size:
Dynamic memory:	Speed: 300 ns Increment size: 4096 bytes
Erasable programmable:	Speed: 1 μs Increment size: 1024 bytes
Shared memory:	
Memory limits:	Minimum: 4K+1K ROM Maximum: 64K
Other:	
Mainframe Options	
Real-time clock:	Yes
Rack mount:	
Expander card/chassis:	
DMA:	
Other:	
Peripheral Devices	
Teletype:	Not offered
Serial I/O (RS232):	Yes, EIA, TTL, current loop, 110 to 9600 baud
Cassette recorder if:	Yes, modem, 300 baud
Character printer:	
Line printer:	65 lines/min (110 Hz), 5×7 matrix
Alphanumeric crt:	
Television interface:	Yes, 16 lines at 32 char/line, 80 × 25 character interface
Floppy disc:	Single, up to 4 on one controller
Other disc:	
Parallel I/O board:	
Vectored interrupts:	
PROM programmer:	
Other manufacturers:	
Other:	
Software	
Assembler:	Yes
Editor:	Yes
Debug:	Yes
Other utilities:	ROM controller
BASIC:	Yes, 4K, 8K, 12K versions
Extended BASIC:	Yes
FORTRAN:	
Other compilers:	
Operating systems:	Yes, FDOS (Flexible Disc O.S.)
Application programs:	Yes, from user's group
User's groups:	Yes
Other:	
Miscellaneous	
Extender board:	
Documentation:	Thorough
Other:	Cable assemblies
Pricing	
Minimum system:	Under $1020 kit, $1600 assembled

Chart 8-5. Microcomputer Specifications of Micro-Sphere 200

Mainframe		
Microprocessor chip used:	Motorola 6800	
System clock:	1 MHz	
Power supply:		
Number of I/O slots:		
Control panel type:	No console—ROM monitor	
Construction:	Printed-circuit board	
Other:		
Memory		
Static memory:	Speed:	Increment size:
Dynamic memory:	Speed: 300 ns	Increment size: 4096 bytes
Erasable programmable:	Speed:	Increment size:
Shared memory:		
Memory limits:	Minimum: 4K	Maximum: 8K
Other:		
Mainframe Options		
Real-time clock:		
Rack mount:		
Expander card/chassis:		
DMA:		
Other:		
Peripheral Devices		
Teletype:	Not offered	
Serial I/O (RS232):	Yes, EIA, TTL, current loop, 110 to 9600 baud	
Cassette recorder if:	Yes, modem 300-baud	
Character printer:		
Line printer:		
Alphanumeric crt:		
Television interface:	Yes, 128×128 dot matrix	
Floppy disc:		
Other disc:		
Parallel I/O board:		
Vectored interrupts:		
PROM programmer:		
Other manufacturers:		
Other:		
Software		
Assembler:	Yes	
Editor:	Yes	
Debug:	Yes	
Other utilities:	ROM monitor	
BASIC:	Yes	
Extended BASIC:	Yes	
FORTRAN:		
Other compilers:		
Operating systems:	SCOS (Sphere Cassette Operating System)	
Application programs:	Yes	
User's groups:	Yes	
Other:		
Miscellaneous		
Extender board:		
Documentation:	Thorough	
Other:		
Pricing		
Minimum system:	Under $800 for 4K, SCOS, games package, cassette interface, tv interface and tv, keyboard	

(A) Exterior view, of cabinet.

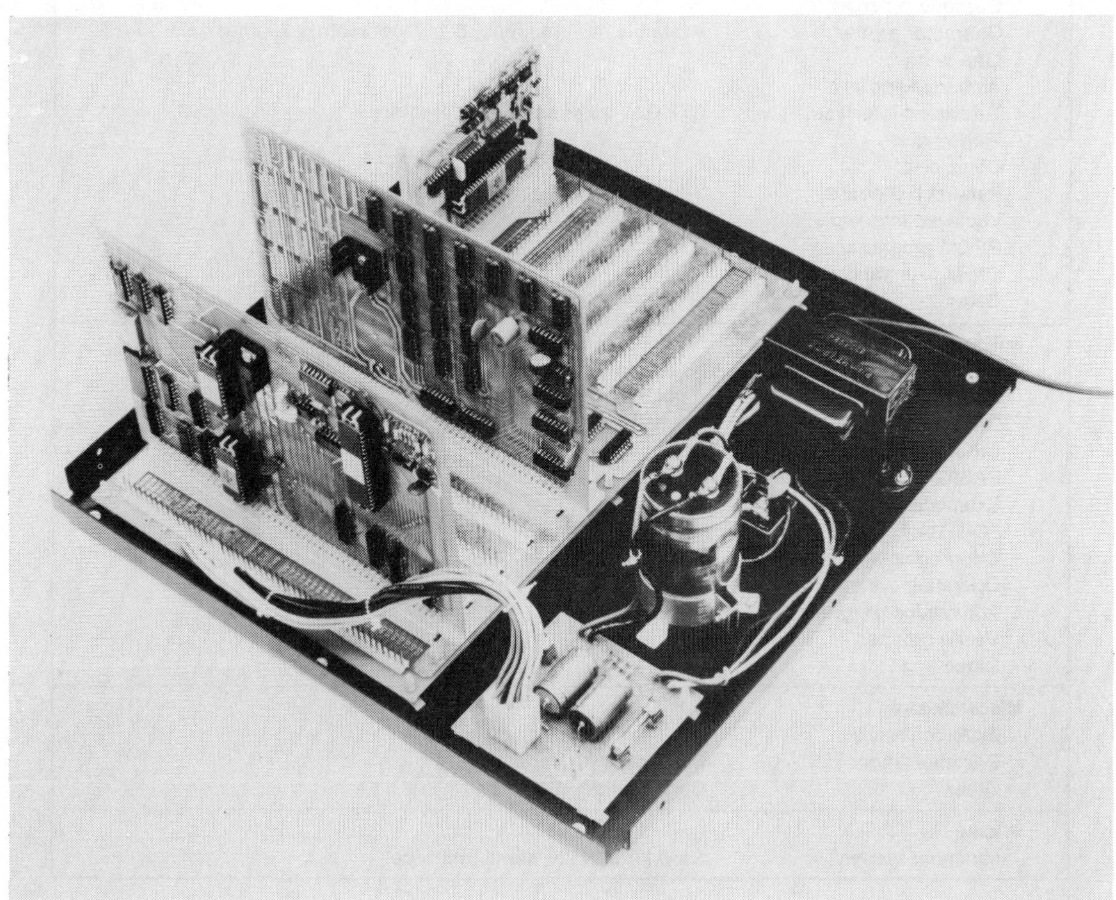

(B) Interior view, with cover removed.

Courtesy Southwest Technical Products

Fig. 8-25. SWTP 6800 computer system.

Chart 8-6. Microcomputer Specifications of SWTP 6800

Mainframe	
Microprocessor chip used:	Motorola MC6800
System clock:	1 MHz
Power supply:	7 volts, ±12 volts
Number of I/O slots:	
Control panel type:	No console, ROM monitor
Construction:	Printed-circuit board
Other:	
Memory	
Static memory:	Speed: Increment size: 2048 bytes
Dynamic memory:	Speed: Increment size:
Erasable programmable:	Speed: Increment size:
Shared memory:	
Memory limits:	Minimum: 2K Maximum: 64K
Other:	
Mainframe Options	
Real-time clock:	
Rack mount:	
Expander card/chassis:	
DMA:	
Other:	
Peripheral Devices	
Teletype:	Not offered
Serial I/O (RS232):	RS232, TTL, current loop, 110–1200 baud
Cassette recorder if:	
Character printer:	Available. 40 char/line, 5 × 7 dot matrix, 75 lines/min
Line printer:	
Alphanumeric crt:	
Television interface:	CT-1024, 16 lines at 32 characters
Floppy disc:	
Other disc:	
Parallel I/O board:	Yes—uses Motorola PIA
Vectored interrupts:	
PROM programmer:	
Other manufacturers:	
Other:	GT-6144 graphics terminal
Software	
Assembler:	Available
Editor:	Available
Debug:	Yes
Other utilities:	ROM monitor
BASIC:	
Extended BASIC:	
FORTRAN:	
Other compilers:	
Operating systems:	
Application programs:	
User's groups:	
Other:	
Miscellaneous	
Extender board:	
Documentation:	Motorola's foremost part
Other:	Connectors
Pricing	
Minimum system:	$450 kit with 2K, serial interface

Chart 8-7. Microcomputer Specifications of WaveMate Jupiter II

Mainframe	
Microprocessor chip used:	Motorola M6800
System clock:	1 MHz
Power supply:	+5 volts @ 5 A, +12 volts @ 2 A, +26 volts @ 100 mA, −5 V @ 1 A, −12 V @ 1 A
Number of I/O slots:	8 modules basic
Control panel type:	Minimum ROM monitor
Construction:	Wire-wrap boards
Other:	
Memory	
Static memory:	Speed: 500 ns Increment size: 1024
Dynamic memory:	Speed: 500 ns Increment size: 4096
Erasable programmable:	Speed: 500 ns Increment size: 1024
Shared memory:	
Memory limits:	Minimum: 2K bytes (ROM) Maximum: 64K bytes
Other:	
Mainframe Options	
Real-time clock:	60 Hz with tv interface
Rack mount:	Yes—standard
Expander card/chassis:	Yes—adds 8 slots
DMA:	Yes
Other:	
Peripheral Devices	
Teletype:	
Serial I/O (RS232):	Yes, 16 selectable baud rates
Cassette recorder if:	Available
Character printer:	Selectric I/O interface
Line printer:	
Alphanumeric crt:	
Television interface:	Available. 64 chars/line at 32 lines, graphics
Floppy disc:	In development
Other disc:	
Parallel I/O board:	Yes, two or four channels
Vectored interrupts:	8 vectored interrupts
PROM programmer:	Available
Other manufacturers:	
Other:	
Software	
Assembler:	Yes, requires 8K
Editor:	Yes, requires 8K
Debug:	Yes
Other utilities:	ROM monitor, 2K bytes
BASIC:	Yes
Extended BASIC:	
FORTRAN:	
Other compilers:	
Operating systems:	Monitor
Application programs:	
User's groups:	Yes, active
Other:	
Miscellaneous	
Extender board:	Yes
Documentation:	Thorough, includes Motorola documentation
Other:	Tools, sockets, universal module
Pricing	
Minimum system:	Under $1500 for 8K, serial interface, rack mount, tools

ing microprocessor can be made by the 3850 and 3851, although only 64 bytes of RAM would be available.

Additional RAM requires another chip, the 3852 or 3853 Memory Interface. It provides up to 64K-byte addressing of external RAM storage. In fact, then it requires at least three chips and external RAM to provide a workable system. However, as usual with third-generation microprocessor systems, the three components are still very inexpensive (under $100 in quantity) so that there is really not too much difference between implementing the CPU and addressing functions on three chips versus only one chip.

The CPU chip contains 64 bytes of RAM (called *scratchpad*), an accumulator, instruction decoding, and the ALU. Several of the CPU scratchpad registers are "dedicated" to communicating with the registers on the PSU. The F8 has a 2-microsecond cycle time and about 70 instructions in the usual one-, two-, and three-byte format. One external interrupt per PSU is provided (multiple PSUs for additional ROM may be used). There is also an internal interrupt. DMA capability is provided by adding another chip, the 3854 Direct Memory Access.

Physical Features and Architecture

Fig. 8-27 shows a functional block diagram of a three-chip version of the F8. All communication between chips is done via an eight-bit bidirectional data bus.

The 3850 CPU chip contains an eight-bit accumulator and sixty-four 8-bit scratchpad registers. The first 16 of these are directly addressable, and data can be passed to and from these and the accumulator by scratchpad register instructions. The other 48 are addressable "indirectly" by a six-bit ISAR (*I*ndirect *S*cr*a*tchpad *R*egister). The ISAR may be loaded by or stored in the accumulator or may be loaded directly by immediate data. When the ISAR is used to indirectly address one of the 48 registers, it may be set up to automatically increment by one, decrement by one, or remain unchanged after the execution of the instruction. Using the increment feature, for example, successive addresses of scratchpad registers 16_{10}–63_{10} could be made without modifying the ISAR under program control in between the addresses. Scratchpad registers 9 through 15 are "dedicated" or "linked" to other system registers. In fact, these registers hold data to permit transfers between system component parts, the 3850 CPU chip, the 3851 ROM, and memory interfaces. Scratchpad register 9 is associated with the status register (on the CPU chip), registers 10 and 11 are associated with the data counter (on the ROM and Memory Interface), registers 12 and 13 are associated with the program counter (ROM and Memory Interface), and registers 14 and 15 are linked to the stack register (ROM and Memory Interface). The additional CPU registers are described below.

The status register is a collection of flag bits representing the interrupt control bit, overflow, zero, carry, and sign. The latter four are set as the result of CPU operations. The interrupt control bit may be set under program control to enable or disable interrupts.

The data counter (on the ROM and Memory Interface) is a 16-bit register used to "indirectly" address

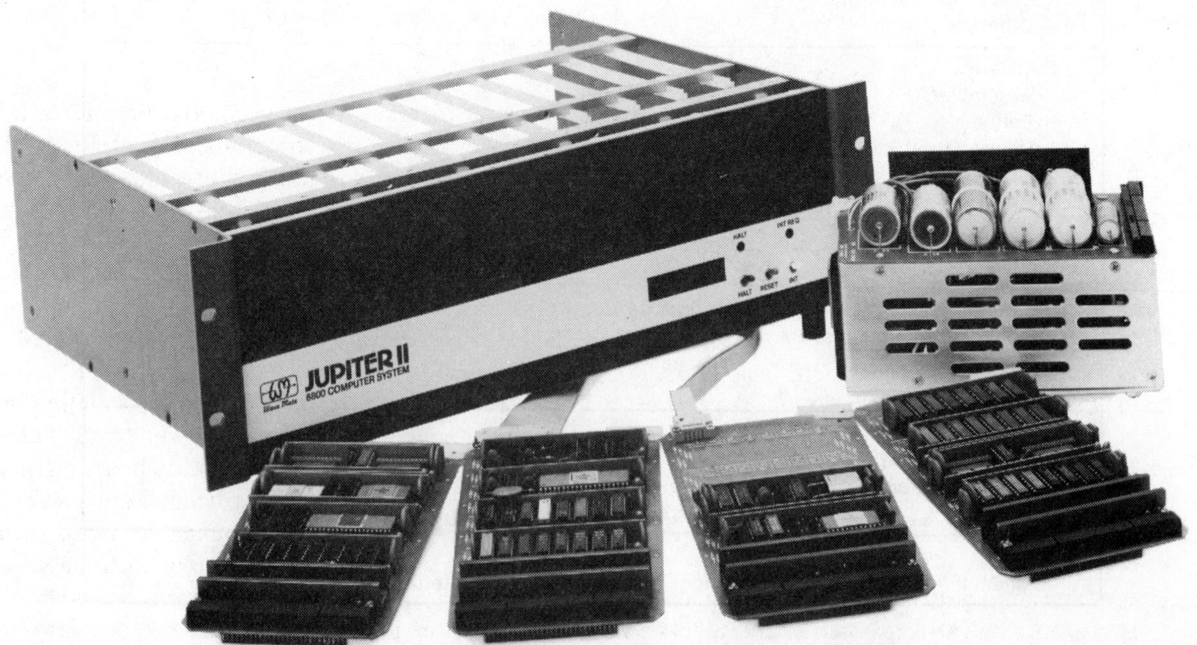

Courtesy WaveMate Computers and Systems

Fig. 8-26. WaveMate Jupiter II system.

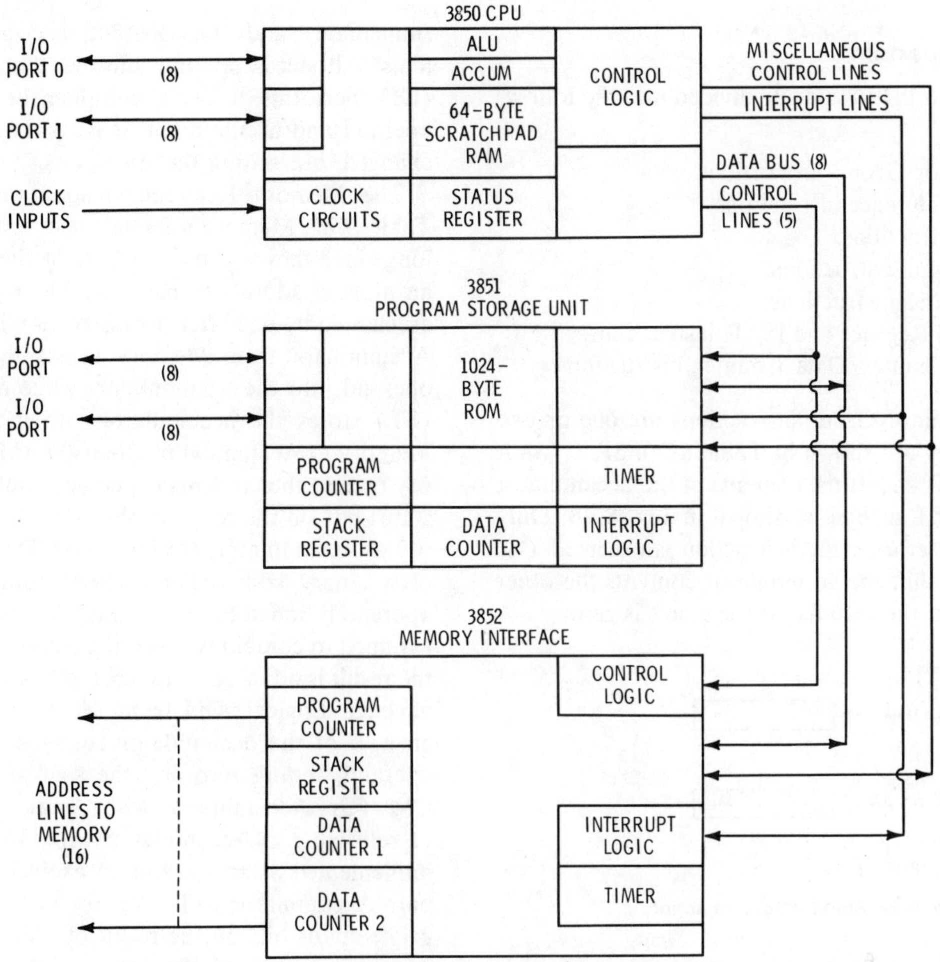

Fig. 8-27. F8 architecture.

64K bytes of memory data. This means that any time a memory reference instruction is executed, the operand location is specified by the contents of the data counter, similar to the H and L registers of the 8008. The data counter is automatically incremented by one after each memory reference instruction. To access a table of sequential data, no adjustment of the data counter would have to be made between the memory interface instructions. To access random (noncontiguous) data, the data counter would have to be set up before each access. Only one of two data counters on the Memory Interface is "active" at any time.

The program counter (on the ROM and Memory Interface) is a 16-bit register that performs the expected control function. The stack register (on the ROM and Memory Interface) is a 16-bit register that does not do what one would expect it to. It is essentially a one-level stack that saves the address of the program counter when a call to subroutine (PK or PJ) is made and then restores the return address when a return from subroutine (POP) is executed. The stack register is also loaded with the program counter during interrupts. The remaining logic in the CPU is concerned with buffering data, decoding instructions, and performing arithmetic and logical functions (ALU).

Instruction Execution

The minimum cycle time for the F8 with a 2-MHz system clock is 2 microseconds. The shortest instructions (accumulator type) are executed in 1 cycle, or 2 microseconds. The longest instruction execution is 6 cycles, or 12 microseconds, and the "average" is around 5 to 6 microseconds.

The F8 instructions are one, two, and three bytes in length. The addressing modes are straightforward. Data are transferred between CPU registers either by instructions that have an implicit register definition in the operating code (what Motorola would call "inherent" addressing) or by a specified scratchpad register address. Memory reference instructions are one-byte instructions and use the data counter to access memory. Branch instructions are relative-type instructions specifying a branch back 128 locations or forward 127. Accumulator immediate instructions are also implemented where an eight-bit operand is contained in the instruction itself.

Instruction Repertoire

Instructions in the F8 may be divided into the following groups:

- Accumulator Group instructions.
- Memory Reference instructions.
- Branch instructions.
- Input/Output instructions.
- Miscellaneous instructions.
- Scratchpad Register and ISAR instructions.
- Program Counter/Data Counter instructions.

The Accumulator Group instructions are one or two bytes long. They are shown in Table 8-20. SR 1 (*S*hift *R*ight 1) and SR 4 shift the contents of the accumulator right for one or four bits, as shown in Fig. 8-28. Only the zero flag is set after the instruction is executed (!). SL 1 and SL 4 shift the accumulator contents the other direction and set the zero flag if the result is zero.

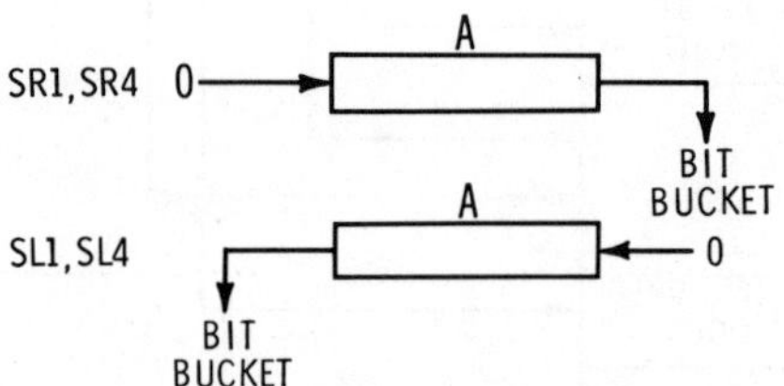

Fig. 8-28. Shift instruction action.

The COM (*Com*plement Accumulator) instruction performs the one's complement on the contents of the accumulator. The zero and sign bits of status are set after the operation. The LNK (*Link* Carry to Accumulator) adds the contents of the carry bit to the current accumulator contents. All status bits (overflow, zero, carry, and sign) are affected after the instruction has been executed. The INC instruction (*Inc*rement Accumulator) increments the accumulator by one and changes all status bits accordingly. LIS (*L*oad *I*mmediate *S*hort) loads a four-bit immediate value into accumulator bits 3–0. Bits 7–4 are set to zero. *Cl*ear Accumulator (CLR) zeroes the accumulator. No status bits are changed for either LIS or CLR. All of the above instructions are one-byte instructions.

The remaining six Accumulator Group instructions are two bytes in length and have an immediate operand as the second byte. The operand is loaded by a *L*oad *I*mmediate instruction (LI). The A*n*d *I*mmediate (NI) ANDs the operand with the contents of the accumulator and sets the zero and sign flags accordingly. The *O*r *I*mmediate (OI) logically ORs the operand and accumulator contents and sets the zero and sign flags on the result. XI (E*x*clusive or *I*mmediate) performs an exclusive OR of the operand and accumulator contents, setting the zero and sign flags if required. AI (*A*dd *I*mmediate) adds the operand and accumulator contents. All status bits are affected. *C*ompare *I*mmediate (CI) performs a two's complement subtract of the operand and accumulator, leaving the accumulator unchanged, but setting the status bits.

The Memory Reference instructions are shown in Table 8-21. Memory reference instructions are one byte long since they use the contents of the data counter as an indirect address to memory. The data counter is incremented by one after the instruction is executed. *L*oad Accumulator from *M*emory (LM) loads the memory operand into the accumulator, while *St*ore to Memory (ST) stores the accumulator into memory. The *A*dd *M*emory to Accumulator, Binary, (AM) adds the memory byte to the contents of the accumulator and sets the status bits on the result of the addition. The *A*dd *M*emory to Accumulator, *D*ecimal, (AMD) is a combination of a binary add and a decimal adjust. The memory operand is added to the accumulator. Both operands are assumed to contain two bcd digits. After the binary add, the result is adjusted to two bcd digits. All status bits are affected. Logical A*n*d from *M*emory (NM) performs an AND of the accumulator contents and the memory operand, setting zero and the sign, if appropriate. An OM (*O*r Accumulator with *M*emory) and an XM (E*x*clusive *O*r Accumulator with *M*emory) are also implemented as an OR and an exclusive OR. The *C*ompare Accumulator with *M*emory (CM) sets the appropriate status bits on the result of (Memory Operand − Accumulator) but, of course, leaves the accumulator contents unchanged.

The Scratchpad Register instructions are shown in Table 8-22. Eight of these transfer data between registers 12, 13, 14, and 15 and the accumulator. These are: LR A,KU; LR A,KL; LR A,QU; LR A,QL; LR KU,A; LR KL,A; LR QU,A; and LR QL,A. Instructions KU, KL, QU, and QL correspond to registers 12, 13, 14, and 15, respectively. (K is the associated program counter register, Q is the associated stack register, U is upper and L is lower.) The destination register is first. Two additional inherent-type instructions transfer data between the status register W and register 9. These are LR W,J and LR J,W with the destination register written first.

Data may also be transferred between the accumulator and any of the other 64 scratchpad registers. The format of the two loads for these transfers is shown in Fig. 8-29. If R is 0 through 11, the scratchpad register addressed is register 0 through 11. If R is 12, the scratchpad address is taken from the ISAR register. If R

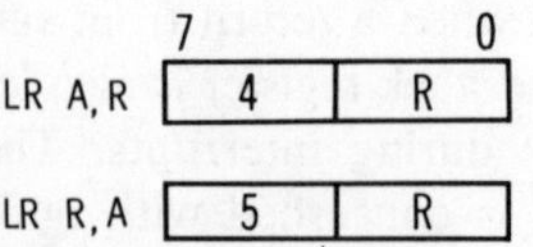

Fig. 8-29. Scratchpad/ accumulator loads.

Table 8-20. Accumulator Group Instructions

MNEMONIC	INSTRUCTION	FORMAT 76543210	DESCRIPTION	EXECUTION TIME* (CYCLES)
SR 1	SHIFT RIGHT 1	00010010	SHIFT ACC RIGHT 1 BIT LOGICAL Z	1
SR 4	SHIFT RIGHT 4	00010100	SHIFT ACC RIGHT 4 BITS LOGICAL Z	1
SL 1	SHIFT LEFT 1	00010011	SHIFT ACC LEFT 1 BIT LOGICAL Z	1
SL 4	SHIFT LEFT 4	00010101	SHIFT ACC LEFT 4 BITS LOGICAL Z	1
COM	COMPLEMENT ACC	00011000	—(ACC) → ACC Z, S	1
LNK	ADD CARRY TO ACC	00011001	(ACC) + (C) → ACC STATUS	1
INC	INCREMENT ACC	00011111	(ACC) + 1 → ACC STATUS	1
LIS	LOAD IMMEDIATE SHORT	0111 | I	1 → ACC_{3-0} 0 → ACC_{7-4}	1
CLR	CLEAR ACC	01110000	0 → ACC	1
LI	LOAD IMMEDIATE	00100000 I	I → ACC Z,S	2.5
NI	AND IMMEDIATE	00100001 I	(ACC) AND I → ACC	2.5
OI	OR IMMEDIATE	00100010 I	(ACC) OR I → ACC Z,S	2.5
XI	EXCLUSIVE-OR IMMEDIATE	00100011 I	(ACC) EXCLUSIVE-OR I → ACC Z,S	2.5
AI	ADD IMMEDIATE	00100100 I	(ACC) + I → ACC STATUS	2.5
C1	COMPARE IMMEDIATE	00100101 I	I — (ACC) STATUS	2.5

* 2 μs/CYCLE.

Table 8-21. Memory Reference Instructions

MNEMONIC	INSTRUCTION	FORMAT 76543210	DESCRIPTION**	EXECUTION TIME* (CYCLES)
LM	LOAD ACC	00010110	(EA) → ACC; (DC) + 1 → DC	2.5
ST	STORE ACC	00010111	(ACC) → EA; (DC) + 1 → DC	2.5
AM	ADD MEMORY TO ACC	10001000	(ACC) + (EA) → ACC; (DC) + 1 → DC STATUS	2.5
AMD	ADD MEMORY TO ACC, DECIMAL	10001001	(ACC) + (EA) → ACC DECIMAL; (DC) + 2 → DC STATUS	2.5
NM	AND ACC WITH MEMORY	10001010	(ACC) AND (EA) → ACC (DC) + 1 → DC Z,S	2.5
OM	OR ACC WITH MEMORY	10001011	(ACC) OR (EA) → ACC (DC) + 1 → DC Z,S	2.5
XM	EXCLUSIVE-OR ACC WITH MEMORY	10001100	(ACC) XOR (EA) → ACC (DC) + 1 → DC Z,S	2.5
CM	COMPARE ACC WITH MEMORY	10001101	(EA) — (AAC) (DC) + 1 → DC STATUS	2.5

* 2 μs/CYCLE.
** (DC) = EFFECTIVE ADDRESS.

Table 8-22. Scratchpad Register Instructions

MNEMONIC	INSTRUCTION	FORMAT 76543210	DESCRIPTION**	EXECUTION TIME* (CYCLES)
LR A,R	LOAD ACC FROM REGISTER	0100 R	(R) → ACC	1
LR R,A	LOAD REGISTER FROM ACC	0101 R	(AC) → R	1
LR A,KU	LOAD ACC FROM REGISTER 12	00000000	(R12) → ACC	1
LR A,KL	LOAD ACC FROM REGISTER 13	00000001	(R13) → ACC	1
LR A,QU	LOAD ACC FROM REGISTER 14	00000010	(R14) → ACC	1

Table 8-22—Continued

MNEMONIC	INSTRUCTION	FORMAT 76543210	DESCRIPTION**	EXECUTION TIME* (CYCLES)
LR A,QL	LOAD ACC FROM REGISTER 15	00000011	(R15) → ACC	1
LR KU,A	LOAD REGISTER 12 FROM ACC	00000100	(ACC) → R12	1
LR KL,A	LOAD REGISTER 13 FROM ACC	00000101	(ACC) → R13	1
LR QU,A	LOAD REGISTER 14 FROM ACC	00000110	(ACC) → R14	1
LR QL,A	LOAD REGISTER 15 FROM ACC	00000111	(ACC) → R15	1
LR W,J	LOAD STATUS REGISTER FROM REG 9	00011101	(R9) → STATUS	2
LR J,W	LOAD REG 9 FROM STATUS REGISTER	00011110	(STATUS) → R9	1
AS R	ADD SCRATCHPAD, BINARY	1100 R	(ACC) + (R) → ACC STATUS	1
ASD R	ADD SCRATCHPAD, DECIMAL	1101 R	(ACC) + (R) → ACC DECIMAL STATUS	2
NS R	AND SCRATCHPAD	1111 R	(ACC) AND (R) → ACC Z,S	1
XS R	EXCLUSIVE-OR SCRATCHPAD	1110 R	(AC) XOR (R) → ACC	1
DS R	DECREMENT SCRATCHPAD	0011 R	(R) − 1 → R STATUS	1.5
LR A,IS	LOAD ACC FROM ISAR	00001010	(ISAR) → ACC	1
LR IS,A	LOAD ISAR FROM ACC	00001011	(ACC) → ISAR	1
LISU	LOAD ISAR UPPER HALF IMMEDIATE	01100 I	1 → $ISAR_{5-3}$	1
LISL	LOAD ISAR LOWER HALF IMMEDIATE	01101 I	I → $ISAR_{2-0}$	1

* 2 μs/CYCLE.

** ACCESS SCRATCHPAD VIA ISAR.

Table 8-23. Branch Instructions

MNEMONIC	INSTRUCTION	FORMAT 76543210	DESCRIPTION	EXECUTION TIME* (CYCLES)
BR	BRANCH RELATIVE	10010000 D	(PC) + D → PC	3.5
JMP	JUMP IMMEDIATE	00101001 D1 D2	(D1,D2) → PC	5.5
BT	BRANCH IF TEST TRUE	1000 M D	(STATUS) OR M → RESULT IF RESULT ≠ 0, (PC) + D → PC	3.0/3.5
BP	BRANCH IF POSITIVE	10000001 D	(PC) + D → PC IF POSITIVE SIGN	3.0/3.5
BC	BRANCH IF CARRY	10000010 D	(PC) + D → PC IF CARRY	3.0/3.5
BZ	BRANCH IF ZERO	10000100 D	(PC) + D → PC IF ZERO	3.0/3.5
BRO	BRANCH IF TEST FALSE	1001 M D	(STATUS) OR M → RESULT IF RESULT ≠ 0, (PC) + D → PC	3.0/3.5
BM	BRANCH IF MINUS	10010001 D	(PC) + D → PC IF SIGN SET	3.0/3.5
BNC	BRANCH IF NO CARRY	10010010 D	(PC) + D → PC IF NO CARRY	3.0/3.5
BNZ	BRANCH IF NONZERO	10010100 D	(PC) + D → PC IF NOT ZERO	3.0/3.5
BNO	BRANCH IF NO OVERFLOW	10011000 D	(PC) + D → PC IF OVF = 0	3.0/3.5
BR7	BRANCH IF (ISARL) ≠ 7	10001111 D	(PC) + D → PC IF (ISARL) NOT EQUAL TO 7	2.0/2.5

* 2 μs/CYCLE.

is 13, the scratchpad address is taken from the ISAR register, and the ISAR is incremented after the data are accessed. If R is 14, the same transfer is made but the ISAR is decremented. R=15 is an assigned address. With the above 12 instructions, data can be transferred from the accumulator to 16 scratchpad registers directly and to all scratchpad registers indirectly through the ISAR.

Five additional instructions allow a binary add, decimal add, AND, and exclusive OR of a scratchpad register with the accumulator or a decrement of a scratchpad register (AS, ASD, NS, XS, DS). The format of these instructions is similar to that shown in Fig. 8-29; the R value has the same meaning, addressing 0 through 11 directly or the remainder through the ISAR.

The ISAR may be loaded by a *L*oad *IS*AR *U*pper Half Immediate (LISU) instruction and a *L*oad *IS*AR *L*ower Half Immediate (LISL) instruction, which load a three-bit immediate operand into the designated three bits of the six-bit ISAR. The ISAR may also be loaded by a Load ISAR from Accumulator (LR IS,A) instruction or transferred to the accumulator by an LR A,IS instruction. In these cases, six bits are transferred.

Branch instructions are shown in Table 8-23. JMP (Branch Immediate) is a special three-byte instruction that causes an unconditional jump to the direct address

Table 8-24. Program Counter/Data Counter Instructions

MNEMONIC	INSTRUCTION	FORMAT 76543210	DESCRIPTION	EXECUTION TIME* (CYCLES)
LR K,P	LOAD K REGISTER FROM STACK REGISTER	00001000	(STACK REG) → R12, R13	4
LR P,K	LOAD STACK REGISTER FROM K REGISTER	00001001	(R12, R13) → STACK REGISTER	4
LR PO,Q	LOAD PC FROM Q REGISTER	00001101	(R14, R15) → PC	4
PK	PUSH K	00001100	(PC) → STACK REGISTER (R12, R13) → PC	4
PI	PUSH IMMEDIATE	00101000 I1 I2	(PC) → STACK REGISTER I1, I2 → PC	4
POP	POP FROM STACK	00011100	(STACK REGISTER) → PC	2
LR Q,DC	LOAD Q REG FROM DC	00001110	(DC) → R14, R15	4
LR DC,Q	LOAD DC FROM Q REG	00001111	(R14, R15) → DC	4
LR H,DC	LOAD H REG FROM DC	00010001	(DC) → R10, R11	4
LR DC,H	LOAD DC FROM H REG	00010000	(R10, R11) → DC	4
ADC	ADD ACC TO DATA COUNTER	10001110	(DC) + (ACC) → DC	2.5
DCI	LOAD DATA COUNTER IMMEDIATE	00101010 I1 I2	I1, I2 → DC	6
XDC	EXCHANGE DATA COUNTERS	00101100	EXCHANGE DC_0 AND DC_1 (CERTAIN CONFIGURATIONS ONLY)	2

* 2 μs/CYCLE.

contained in the second and third bytes of the instruction. An unfortunate side effect of the jump is that the accumulator is used as temporary storage in the implementation of the instruction and that its previous contents are, in programming language, clobbered. The re-

```
        LISL    4       LOAD ISAR
        LISU    3       WITH 28
        CLR             CLEAR ACCUMULATOR
LOOP    AS              ADD AND INCREMENT
        BR7     LOOP    ISAR
```

Fig. 8-30. ISAR example.

maining instructions in the Branch group are all branch relative-type instructions; these branch up to 127_8 locations back or 128_8 locations forward from the current instruction by the usual method of adding the two's complement displacement found in the second operand to the contents of the program counter. The program counter during this instruction points to the second byte of the instruction, hence the 128_8 forward and 127_8 back.

Branches can be made conditionally on positive, carry, zero, minus, no carry, nonzero, and no overflow

—BP, BC, BZ, BM, BNC, BNZ, and BNO, respectively. There are also *B*ranch if Test *T*rue (BT) and *B*ranch if Test False (BR0) instructions which branch if the status flags *and* a four-bit mask field result in a nonzero or zero condition, respectively. A second unconditional branch is implemented in the BR (*B*ranch *R*elative) instruction, which allows a branch within the floating page. The last branch is the *B*ranch if (ISARL)≠7 instruction (BR7). This instruction branches if the three least significant bits of the indirect scratchpad address register (ISARL) are not equal to 7. This allows a form of indexing when working with the scratchpad registers. If the ISAR is set to automatically increment, then groups of eight or fewer registers may automatically be addressed with an automatic branch on the last register. An illustration of this case is shown in Fig. 8-30, where scratchpad locations 28, 29, 30, and 31 are added together.

The Program Counter/Data Counter instructions are shown in Table 8-24. Load K Register from Stack Register (LR K,P) transfers the 16 bits of the stack register to scratchpad registers 12 and 13. The content of the stack register is typically the address of the interrupted location directly after the interrupt occurs. Therefore, this instruction should normally be used to obtain the return address for use after the interrupt has been processed. The LR P,K instruction (Load Stack Register from K Register) is the reverse operation, loading the contents of scratchpad registers 12 and 13 into the external stack register. The stack register will then be set up for a POP instruction (see below).

The LR PO,Q (Load Program Counter from Q Register) instruction loads the contents of scratchpad registers 14 and 15 into the external program counter, causing an unconditional branch to that location. It can be used to perform indirect branches or can be used in place of an LR P,K and POP.

The PK (*P*ush *K*) instruction transfers the contents of the program counter to the stack register and transfers the contents of scratchpad registers 12 and 13 to the program counter. It is a way of doing a subroutine call to an address in 12 and 13 and saving the return address in the stack register. The PI (*P*ush *I*mmediate) instruction performs the same function, pushing the contents of the PC to the stack register, except that a 16-bit immediate value is loaded into the program counter. It is another call to subroutine. The POP instruction (*Pop* from Stack) pops the contents of the stack register to the program counter, causing a return from interrupt or subroutine, depending upon what is in the stack register. The program counter instructions are rather unusual when compared with the stack instructions of the 8008, 8080, and 6800. The difference is that the stack register of the F8 is not a stack pointer but is somewhat like a one-word stack whose contents must be read out and transferred to a second open-ended stack in memory to truly perform a stack operation.

The Data Counter instructions allow the 16-bit contents of the external data counter to be transferred to scratchpad registers 10 and 11, or 14 and 15, or the reverse. Instructions LR Q,DC; LR DC,Q; LR H,DC; and LR DC,H transfer data to or from Q (14 and 15) and H(10 and 11); the destination register is written first. These instructions allow the contents of the data counter to be changed for memory reference addressing. ADC (*A*dd ACC to *D*ata *C*ounter) adds the contents of the accumulator and the data counter and puts the results in the data counter, allowing data counter address to be changed by -128_{10} to $+127_{10}$ locations. DCI (Load *D*ata *C*ounter *I*mmediate) loads the data counter with the 16-bit immediate value in the second and third bytes of the instruction, permitting still another way of modifying the data counter.

The Input/Output instructions are shown in Table 8-25. These instructions transfer data between the accumulator and an I/O port. Up to 256 ports can be implemented by using various F8 system components. Some port addresses are dedicated; for example, address OC_{16} is the upper eight bits of the interrupt vector, while OF_{16} is a Timer, pulsed every 31 clock cycles. There are two eight-bit I/O ports on the CPU chip with dedicated addresses 00_{16} and 01_{16}. These are essentially latch registers. Either a read or a write may be done to each of the ports. INS (*In*put *S*hort Address) reads the contents of I/O port 0 through 15 into the accumulator. The second four bits of the instruction specify the port address. OUTS (*Out*put *S*hort Address) outputs the contents of the accumulator to the I/O port whose address is in the second four bits of the instruction. The IN and OUT instructions perform the same operations, except that a long address of eight bits is used to enable addressing ports 4 through 255.

Miscellaneous instructions are shown in Table 8-26. DI (*D*isable *I*nterrupt) and EI (*E*nable *I*nterrupt) control the interrupt mask in the status register, controlling external interrupts. NOP (*N*o *Op*eration), like all NOPs, does nothing.

Programming Considerations

The F8 has a fairly comprehensive instruction set and is yet another approach to a third-generation microprocessor chip. As mentioned earlier, the program counter architecture is oriented towards tables of consecutive data. In cases where table data have to be processed and several immediate results have to be stored, the F8 should do well. The larger number of scratchpad registers can be used to advantage as directly addressable storage. Accessing random data, however, still has the same problems as in the 8008—a memory

Table 8-25. Input/Output Instructions

MNEMONIC	INSTRUCTION	FORMAT 76543210	DESCRIPTION	EXECUTION TIME* (CYCLES)
INS	INPUT PORT SHORT	1010 I	PORT$_I$ → ACC Z, S	4
IN	INPUT PORT	00100110 I	PORT$_I$ → ACC Z, S	4
OUTS	OUTPUT TO PORT SHORT	1011 I	(ACC) → PORT$_I$	4
OUT	OUTPUT TO PORT	00100111 I	(ACC) → PORT$_I$	4

* 2 μs/CYCLE.

address pointer (data counter) must be set up each time a nonconsecutive data byte is to be accessed.

Microcomputers Based on the Fairchild F8 Chip

Systems Research, Inc., of Salt Lake City, Utah, offers a microcomputer based on the Fairchild F8 microprocessor chip set. The SRI-500 is illustrated in Fig. 8-31. A ROM control program provides control panel and debug functions. Peripherals include a cassette interface and a video interface that provides a display of 16 lines of 32 characters each. Chart 8-8 describes the system in detail.

MOS TECHNOLOGY MCS6502 CHIP DESCRIPTION

The MCS6502, manufactured by MOS Technology, Inc., is an 8-bit parallel microprocessor similar to the Motorola MC6800. As a matter of fact, one of the other members of the MSC650X family, the MCS6501, is *pin*-compatible (but not instruction-compatible) with the MC6800. The MCS6502 can address 64K 8-bit words (bytes). It has 55 instruction types, but many of these have several types of addressing modes, and the actual number of instructions is closer to 150. The architecture of the CPU chip provides one 8-bit accumulator, two 8-bit index registers, a 16-bit program counter, and an 8-bit stack pointer. One of the interesting features of the chip is the "on-board" clock, requiring only three external components to generate clock signals. Minimum instruction speeds of the MCS6502 are 2 microseconds; maximum instruction speeds are 7 microseconds, with the average instruction speed being about 4 microseconds.

Physical Features and Architecture

The MCS6502 pin layout is shown in Fig. 8-32. The architecture of the chip is shown in Fig. 8-33. Eight data lines are designated DB7 through DB0. Sixteen address lines, AB15 through AB0, enable addressing of 64K

Table 8-26. Miscellaneous Instructions

MNEMONIC	INSTRUCTION	FORMAT 76543210	DESCRIPTION	EXECUTION TIME* (CYCLES)
DI	DISABLE INTERRUPT	00011010		2
EI	ENABLE INTERRUPT	00011011		2
NOP	NO OPERATION	00101011		1

* 2 μs/CYCLE.

Courtesy Systems Research, Inc.

Fig. 8-31. Systems Research SRI-500.

bytes of memory. Pins 39, 37, and 3 are connected to the three external components (resistor, capacitor, and buffer) that determine the clock signal frequency. Signal $\overline{\text{RES}}$ is an externally supplied signal that resets or starts the microprocessor from a power-down condition. After six clock cycles, the CPU loads the program counter from external memory locations $FFFC_{16}$ and $FFFD_{16}$ (start location). An interrupt request line ($\overline{\text{IRQ}}$) indicates that there is an external interrupt pending, causing a vectored interrupt if an interrupt mask flag in the CPU is not set. A third type of interrupt ($\overline{\text{RES}}$ is essentially a vectored interrupt), $\overline{\text{NMI}}$, nonmaskable interrupt, causes an interrupt regardless of the state of the interrupt mask flag. Typically, $\overline{\text{NMI}}$ would be used for power failure detection.

Signal R/W (Read/Write) is used to signal an external device or memory of a read or write operation. Signal RDY is an external signal that allows single cycling

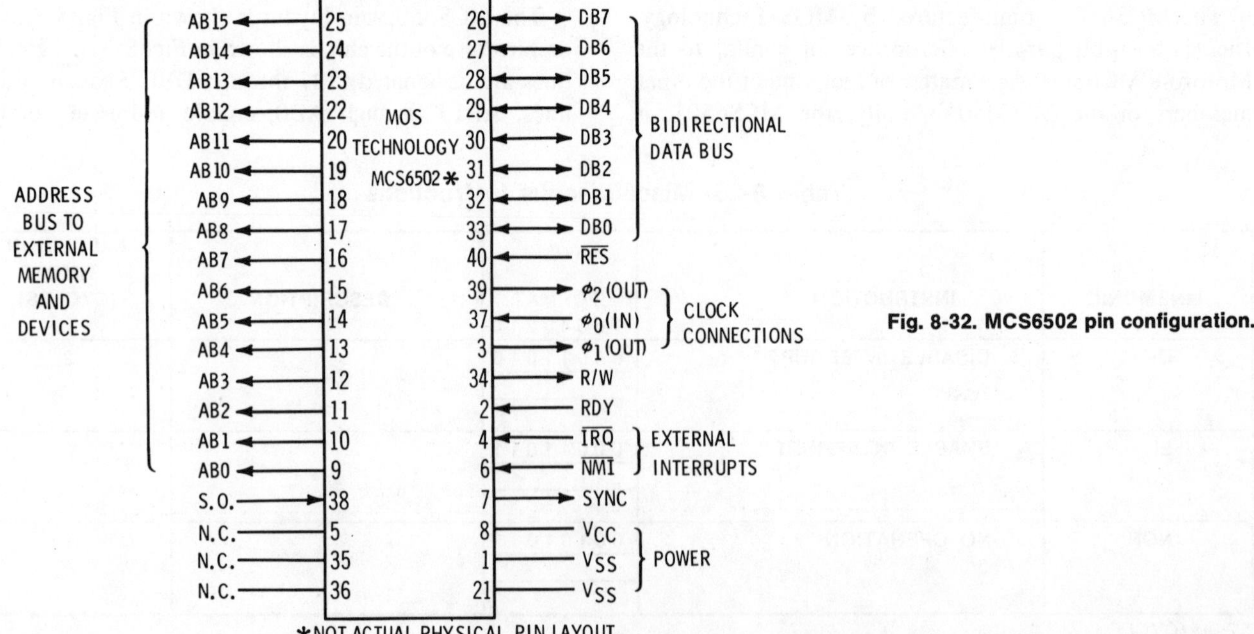

Fig. 8-32. MCS6502 pin configuration.

Chart 8-8. Microcomputer Specifications of Systems Research SRI-500

Mainframe	
Microprocessor chip used:	Fairchild F8
System clock:	1 MHz
Power supply:	+5, +12, −12 regulated
Number of I/O slots:	
Control panel type:	No console, ROM monitor
Construction:	Printed-circuit board
Other:	
Memory	
Static memory:	Speed: Increment size: 1024
Dynamic memory:	Speed: Increment size:
Erasable programmable:	Speed: Increment size:
Shared memory:	
Memory limits:	Minimum: 1024 Maximum: 64K
Other:	
Mainframe Options	
Real-time clock:	
Rack mount:	
Expander card/chassis:	
DMA:	
Other:	
Peripheral Devices	
Teletype:	None offered
Serial I/O (RS232):	RS-232
Cassette recorder if:	Yes
Character printer:	
Line printer:	
Alphanumeric crt:	
Television interface:	Yes, 16 lines of 32 characters each
Floppy disc:	
Other disc:	
Parallel I/O board:	
Vectored interrupts:	
PROM programmer:	
Other manufacturers:	
Other:	
Software	
Assembler:	
Editor:	
Debug:	Yes
Other utilities:	ROM monitor
BASIC:	
Extended BASIC:	
FORTRAN:	
Other compilers:	
Operating systems:	
Application programs:	
User's groups:	
Other:	
Miscellaneous	
Extender board:	
Documentation:	
Other:	
Pricing	
Minimum system:	Under $350 for CPU board alone, assembled

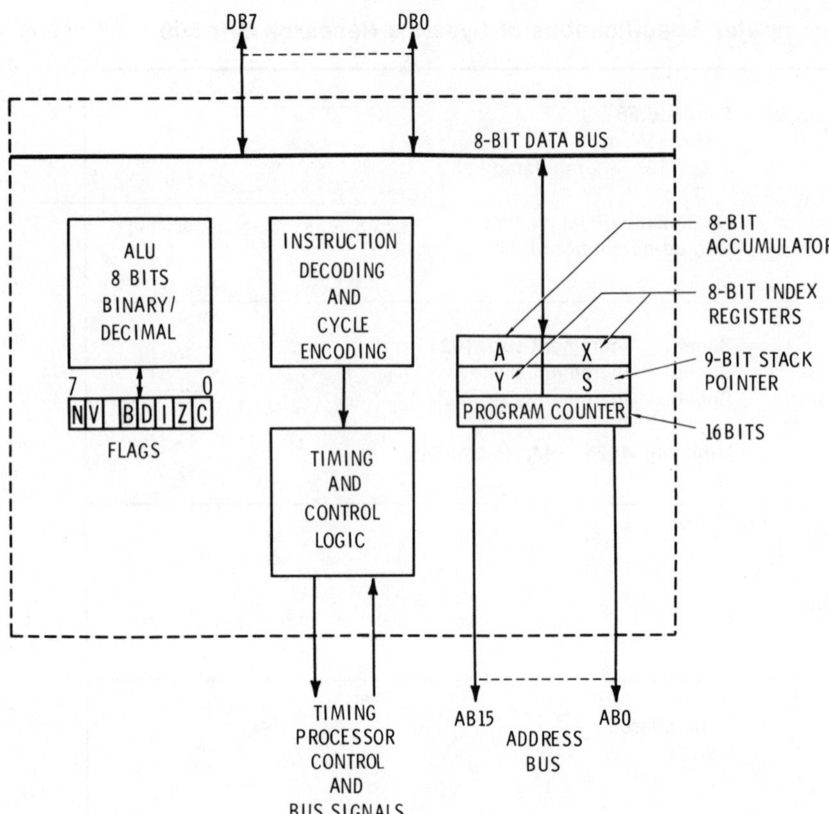

Fig. 8-33. MCS6502 architecture.

of the microprocessor on all cycles except write cycles. This is essentially a way to interface the MCS6502 to low-speed memory devices. The SYNC signal is used to indicate when the CPU is doing an operation code fetch (first cycle of every instruction). An external device can then stop the CPU by the RDY line, permitting single instruction execution. Signal S.O. (Set Overflow Flag) is an externally generated signal allowing control of the overflow flag of the status code register. The remaining pins either are power-supply inputs (V_{SS}, V_{CC}) or are not connections.

In the CPU the programmer has access to five registers. (See Fig. 8-33.) There is one 8-bit accumulator (A). Unlike the MC6800, the MCS6502 has two *8-bit* index registers (X and Y), allowing for indexed addressing over a 256-byte block. The program counter (PCH, PCL) has 16 bits to provide complete addressing of 64K bytes of memory. The stack pointer (S) is a nine-bit register (bit 8=1) which allows for only a 128-byte stack that is located in locations 100_{16} through $1FF_{16}$.

The processor status register (P) has seven flags. Flags N (bit 7, *N*egative), V (bit 6, O*v*erflow), Z (bit 1, *Z*ero), and C (bit 0, *C*arry) are set after arithmetic operations for the appropriate condition. Flag B (bit 4, *B*reak) is set if a BRK instruction has been executed. The BRK instruction provides a software interrupt (see below). Flag I (bit 2, *I*RQ Disable) is used to enable or disable external interrupt requests. Flag D (bit 3, *D*ecimal) is set when the decimal mode of the CPU is in force (see below).

Instruction Execution

The minimum cycle time for the MCS6502 is 1 microsecond. Instruction times range from 2 to 7 microseconds, corresponding to cycle lengths of 2 to 7 cycles. Shorter instructions include instructions that address zero page (locations 0 through FF) and immediate instruction. Longer instructions, of course, involve stack operations.

Addressing Modes

There are 13 addressing modes for the MCS6502, but don't despair; they are not that difficult and there is some duplication because of the two index registers. MOS Technology, Inc., calls them "immediate," "absolute," "zero page," "accumulator," "implied," "indexed," "indirect X," "indexed indirect Y," "Z page X," "Z page Y," "absolute X," "absolute Y," "relative," and "indirect." Operation codes for all instructions are in the first byte.

Immediate addressing is identical with MC6800 immediate addressing. The operand to be used in the instructions is contained in the instruction itself. Immediate instructions are two bytes long and take 2 cycles (2 microseconds). See Fig. 8-34.

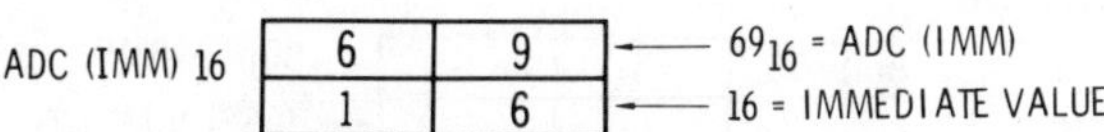

Fig. 8-34. Immediate addressing.

Absolute addressing (Fig. 8-35) is the same as "extended" addressing in the MC6800. The instructions are three bytes long and can address any memory location by the two-byte operand of the instruction. Absolute instructions take from 3 to 6 microseconds to execute.

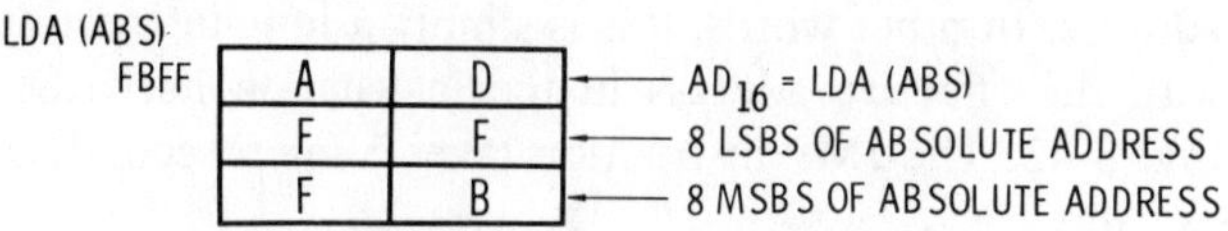

Fig. 8-35. Absolute addressing.

Zero page addressing is identical with the "direct" addressing used in the MC6800. The operand is located in locations 0 through FF_{16}, the zero page. Zero page type instructions take 3 to 5 microseconds to execute (Fig. 8-36).

EOR (ZPA) FE | 4 | 5 | ← 45_{16} = EOR (ZPA)
| F | E | ← ZERO PAGE ADDRESS

Fig. 8-36. Zero page addressing.

Accumulator instructions (Fig. 8-37) perform shifts on the contents of the accumulator and are one-byte instructions taking 2 microseconds for execution. Implied addressing is similar to the MC6800's inherent addressing in which all the information necessary to specify the operation can be held in one byte, such as CLI (*Cl*ear *I* flag). See Fig. 8-38.

ASL (ACC) | 0 | A | ← $0A_{16}$ = ASL (ACC)

Fig. 8-37. Accumulator addressing.

There are two indirect index-type addressing modes, indexed-indirect X and indexed-indirect Y, which are identical except for the index register used. Here the effective address is obtained by adding the contents of the index register to the displacement value found in the second byte of the instruction. The result points to a page 0 location which the instruction uses as an indirect address to find the operand (the page 0 location and the page 0 location plus 1 are treated as a 16-bit indirect address, ordered least significant 8 bits, most significant 8 bits). If X contained $A0_{16}$, and an instruction of LDA (Load A) with a displacement of $0B_{16}$ was executed, the effective address would be AB_{16}. If the contents of AB_{16} and AC_{16} were 02_{16} and 01_{16}, respectively, the accumulator would be loaded with the 8-bit operand at 102_{16}. Weird? Well, not unprecedented, if we look at the Computer Automation instruction set.* Of course, this instruction may be used simply as an indirect to page 0 displacement if the index register contains 0. Instructions of this type take 5 or 6 microseconds. See Fig. 8-39.

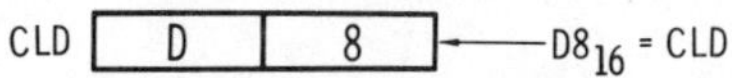

Fig. 8-38. Implied addressing.

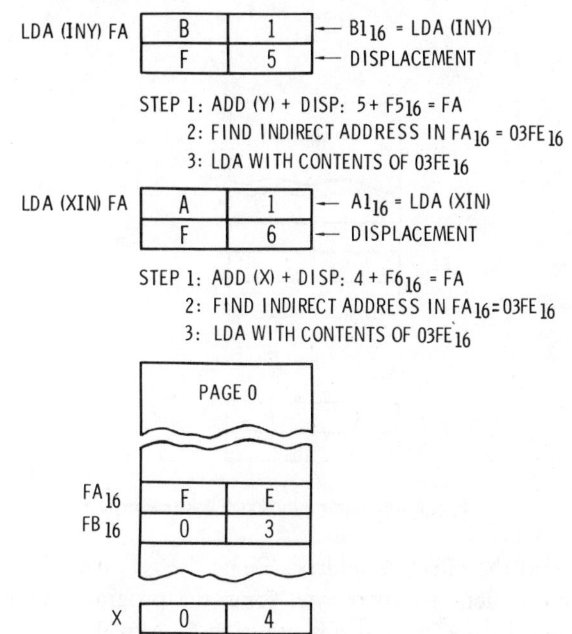

Fig. 8-39. Indirect indexed addressing.

The Z page X and the Z page Y addressing types (Fig. 8-40) are similar to the preceding, except that the addressing is not indirect. The contents of the specified index register are added to the displacement found in the second byte of the instruction to form a page 0 operand address. Instruction execution times are from 4 to 6 microseconds.

Instructions ABS,X and ABS,Y (Fig. 8-41) are also indexed addressing modes. Here the effective address is a 16-bit value obtained by adding the contents of the specified index register to bytes 2 and 3 of the three-byte instruction. Hence, any location in memory from L through $L+255_{10}$ can be addressed with any given ABS,X or ABS,Y instruction, allowing for "indexing through" tables of 256 bytes with one instruction. Instruction execution times are from 4 to 7 microseconds.

The relative addressing mode (Fig. 8-42) is identical with the MC6800 relative addressing. The second byte of the instruction, treated as an eight-bit *signed* value, is added to the current contents of the program counter

* See Chap. 9.

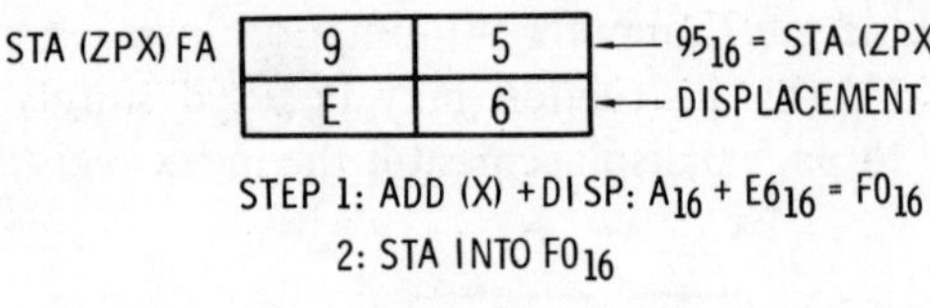

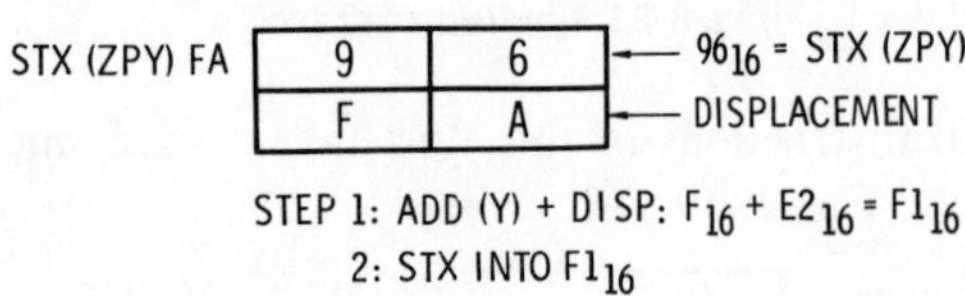

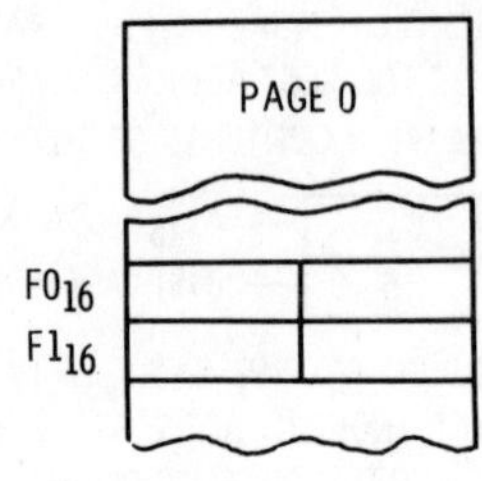

Fig. 8-40. Z page indexed addressing.

to find the effective address. Since the relative-addressing instruction is two bytes long, the program counter points to the current address plus 2, providing for an effective address of from −126 to +129. This addressing mode is used only in conditional branch type instructions.

The last addressing group is the indirect addressing (!) mode used for the JMP (*Jump*) instruction. Here the jump address is found by fetching the memory loca-

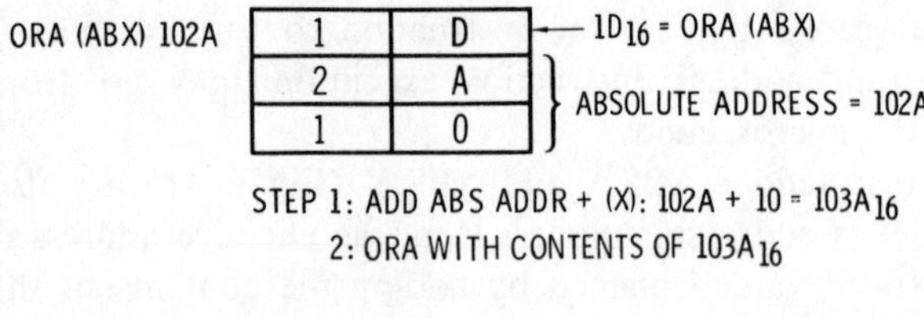

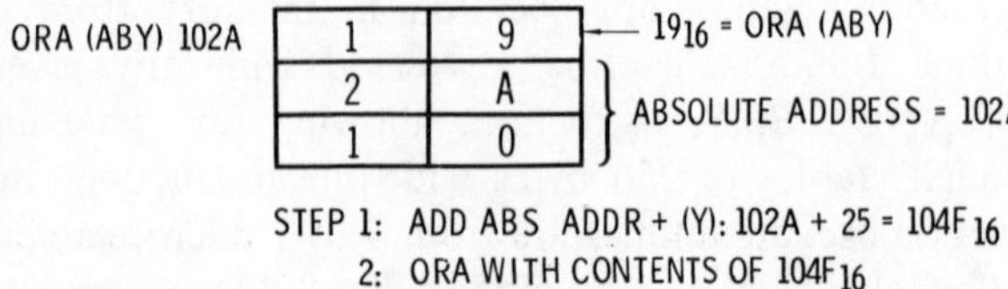

Fig. 8-41. Absolute indexed addressing.

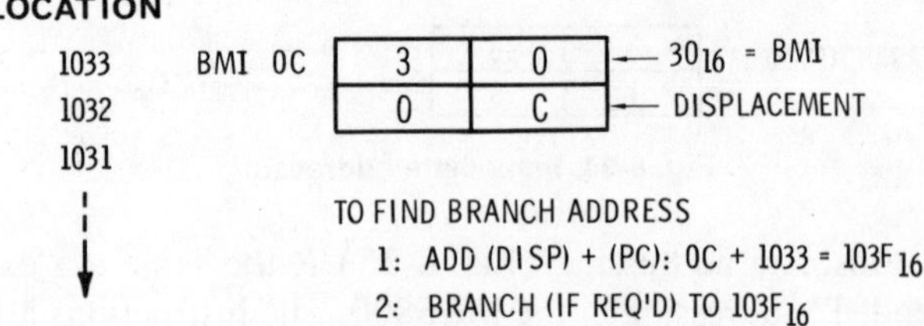

Fig. 8-42. Relative addressing.

tion found in bytes 2 and 3 of the instruction (ordered low and high, respectively) and using this as an indirect address. In other words, this is simply a long instruction with the effective address in the instruction itself! See Fig. 8-43. The JMP instruction takes 5 microseconds to execute.

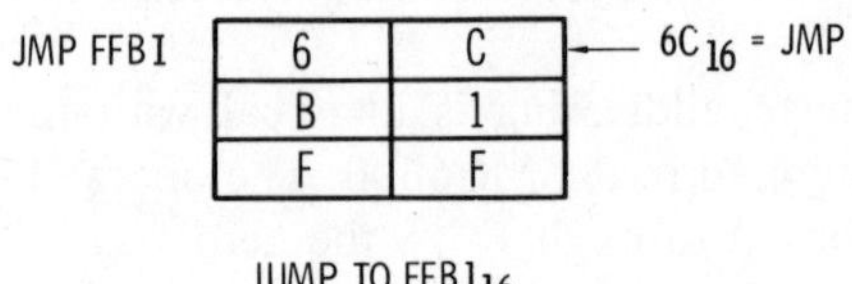

Fig. 8-43. Indirect addressing.

Instruction Repertoire

The instruction set of the MCS6502 may be divided into ten groups:

- Load and Store instructions.
- Transfer instructions.
- Arithmetic and Logical instructions.
- Shift instructions.
- Increment/Decrement instructions.
- Compare instructions.
- Branch instructions.
- Processor Status Register instructions.
- Stack instructions.
- NOP.

Not all of the instructions permit all addressing modes, of course. Some addressing modes would be meaningless for certain instructions, and there are not enough bits in the op code byte (byte 1) to represent all combinations. Table 8-27 lists a cross reference of instructions and addressing modes.

Load and Store instructions are shown in Table 8-28. Instructions LDA (*Load Accumulator*), LDX (*Load X* Index), and LDY (*Load Y* Index) load the appropriate eight-bit register with the eight-bit operand. Instructions STA (*Store Accumulator*), STX (*Store X* Index), and STY (*Store Y* Index) store the appropriate register into the specified memory location.

The Transfer instruction group is essentially a load/store group. (See Table 8-29.) The contents of the accumulator can be stored in X or Y by TAX (*Transfer A* to Index *X*) or TAY (*Transfer A* to Index *Y*). The contents of X and Y can be loaded into the accu-

Table 8-27. MCS6502 Addressing Modes

	IMMED	ABS	ZPG	ACCUM	IMPLD	INDX	INDY	ZPGX	ZPGY	ABSX	ABSY	REL	INDIR
ADC	X	X	X			X	X	X		X	X		
AND	X	X	X			X	X	X		X	X		
ASL		X	X	X				X		X			
BCC												X	
BCS												X	
BEQ												X	
BIT		X	X										
BMI												X	
BNE												X	
BPL												X	
BRK					X								
BVC												X	
BVS												X	
CLC					X								
CLD					X								
CLI					X								
CLV					X								
CMP	X	X	X			X	X	X		X	X		
CPX	X	X	X										
CPY	X	X	X										
DEC		X	X					X		X			
DEX					X								
DEY					X								
EOR	X	X	X			X	X	X		X	X		
INC		X	X					X		X			
INX					X								
INY					X								
JMP		X											
JSR		X											
LDA	X	X	X			X	X	X		X			
LDX	X	X	X								X		
LDY	X	X	X					X		X			
LSR		X	X	X				X		X			
NOP					X								
ORA	X	X	X			X	X	X		X	X		
PHA					X								
PHP					X								
PLA					X								
PLP					X								
ROL		X	X	X				X		X			
RTI					X								
RTS					X								
SBC	X	X	X			X	X	X		X	X		
SEC					X								
SED					X								
SEI					X								
STA		X	X			X	X	X		X	X		
STX		X	X										
STY		X	X					X					
TAX					X								
TAY					X								
TSX					X								
TXA					X								
TXS					X								
TYA					X								

Table 8-28. Load and Store Instructions

MNEMONIC	INSTRUCTION	FORMAT* 76543210	DESCRIPTION	EXECUTION TIME
LDA	LOAD ACCUMULATOR WITH MEMORY		(M) → A	
LDX	LOAD INDEX X WITH MEMORY		(M) → X	
LDY	LOAD INDEX Y WITH MEMORY		(M) → Y	
STA	STORE ACCUMULATOR IN MEMORY		(A) → M	
STX	STORE INDEX X IN MEMORY		(X) → M	
STY	STORE INDEX Y IN MEMORY		(Y) → M	

* SEE TABLE 8-27.

mulator by TXA and TYA [*T*ransfer *X* (or *Y*) to *A*ccumulator]. Likewise, the stack pointer can be switched with the X index register by the instructions TSX and TXS (*T*ransfer *S*tack to *X* and *T*ransfer *X* to *S*tack).

The next group, the Arithmetic and Logical instructions, shown in Table 8-30, is also straightforward. An operand can be added or subtracted from the accumulator with borrow or carry by ADC (*Ad*d Memory to Accumulator with *C*arry) or SBC (*S*u*b*tract Memory from Accumulator with Borrow). If the D bit of the condition codes is set, the add or subtract will be a bcd decimal operation rather than a binary add or subtract. Logical functions of ANDing, exclusive ORing, and inclusive ORing are implemented by AND, EOR, and ORA, respectively.

Table 8-29. Transfer Instructions

MNEMONIC	INSTRUCTION	FORMAT* 76543210	DESCRIPTION	EXECUTION TIME
TAX	TRANSFER A TO INDEX X		(A) → X N, Z	
TAY	TRANSFER A TO INDEX Y		(A) → Y N, Z	
TXA	TRANSFER X TO ACCUMULATOR		(X) → A N, Z	
TYA	TRANSFER Y TO ACCUMULATOR		(Y) → A N, Z	
TSX	TRANSFER STACK POINTER TO INDEX X		(S) → X N, Z	
TXS	TRANSFER X INDEX TO STACK POINTER		(X) → S	

* SEE TABLE 8-27.

Table 8-30. Arithmetic and Logical Instructions

MNEMONIC	INSTRUCTION	FORMAT* 76543210	DESCRIPTION	EXECUTION TIME
ADC	ADD MEMORY TO ACCUMULATOR WITH CARRY		(A) + (M) + C → A N, Z, C, V	
SBC	SUBTRACT MEMORY FROM ACCUMULATOR WITH BORROW		(A) − (M) − C → A N, Z, C, V	
AND	AND MEMORY WITH ACCUMULATOR		(A) EOR (M) → A N, Z	
EOR	EXCLUSIVE-OR MEMORY WITH ACCUMULATOR		(A) EOR (M) → A N, Z	
ORA	OR MEMORY WITH ACCUMULATOR		(A) OR (M) → A N, Z	

* SEE TABLE 8-27.

Three shift instructions are shown in Table 8-31 and Fig. 8-44. Instruction ASL (*A*rithmetic *S*hift *L*eft) shifts the contents of the accumulator or memory operand left one bit position, with bit 7 going into the carry and bit 0 being reset. Instruction LSR (*L*ogical *S*hift *R*ight) shifts the contents of the accumulator or memory operand one bit position right, with bit 0 going into the carry and bit 7 being reset. Instruction ROL (*Ro*-

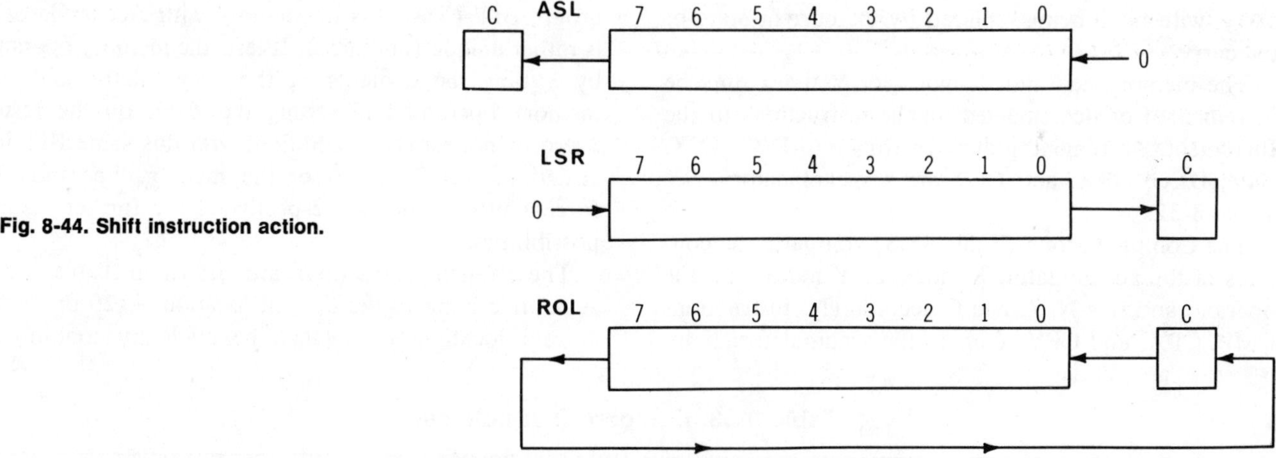

Fig. 8-44. Shift instruction action.

Table 8-31. Shift Instructions

MNEMONIC	INSTRUCTION	FORMAT* 76543210	DESCRIPTION	EXECUTION TIME
ASL	ARITHMETIC SHIFT LEFT		(SEE TEXT)	
LSR	LOGICAL SHIFT RIGHT		(SEE TEXT)	
ROL	ROTATE ONE BIT LEFT		(SEE TEXT)	

* SEE TABLE 8-27.

Table 8-32. Increment/Decrement Instructions

MNEMONIC	INSTRUCTION	FORMAT* 76543210	DESCRIPTION	EXECUTION TIME
INC	INCREMENT MEMORY BY ONE		(M) + 1 → M N, Z	
INX	INCREMENT INDEX X BY ONE		(X) + 1 → X N, Z	
INY	INCREMENT INDEX Y BY ONE		(Y) + 1 → Y N, Z	
DEC	DECREMENT MEMORY BY ONE		(M) − 1 → M N, Z	
DEX	DECREMENT INDEX X BY ONE		(X) − 1 → X N, Z	
DEY	DECREMENT INDEX Y BY ONE		(Y) − 1 → Y N, Z	

* SEE TABLE 8-27.

tate *O*ne Bit *L*eft) rotates the contents of the accumulator or memory operand left one bit. Bit 7 replaces the carry, with bit 0 being replaced by the current state of the carry.

The memory operand, X index, or Y index may be incremented or decremented by the instructions in the Increment/Decrement group. Instructions INC, INX, INY, DEC, DEX, and DEY are self-explanatory. See Table 8-32.

The Compare group (Table 8-33) compares the contents of the accumulator, X index, or Y index with the operand and sets N, Z, and C accordingly. Instructions CMP, CPX, and CPY compare the accumulator, X index, and Y index [*Comp*are Memory and Accumulator (X Index or Y Index)]. A fourth instruction of this group, BIT (Test *Bit*s in Memory with Accumulator), is rather unique (and nice). It tests the memory operand by ANDing the contents of the accumulator and the memory operand and setting the Z bit on the result (zero or nonzero). In addition, with this same BIT instruction, bits 7 and 6 of the memory operand are forced into N and V, respectively, for further testing possibilities.

The Branch instructions are shown in Table 8-34. A relative jump to the current location −126 or to the current location + 129 can be made by conditional

Table 8-33. Compare Instructions

MNEMONIC	INSTRUCTION	FORMAT* 76543210	DESCRIPTION	EXECUTION TIME
CMP	COMPARE MEMORY AND ACCUMULATOR		(A) — (M) N, Z, C	
CPX	COMPARE MEMORY AND INDEX X		(X) — (M) N, Z, C	
CPY	COMPARE MEMORY AND INDEX Y		(Y) — (M) N, Z, C	
BIT	TEST BITS IN MEMORY WITH ACCUMULATOR		(A) AND (M) Z SET ON RESULT (M7) → N, (M6) → V	

* SEE TABLE 8-27.

Table 8-34. Branch Instructions

MNEMONIC	INSTRUCTION	FORMAT* 76543210	DESCRIPTION	EXECUTION TIME
BCC	BRANCH ON CARRY CLEAR		SELF-EXPLANATORY	
BCS	BRANCH ON CARRY SET		SELF-EXPLANATORY	
BEQ	BRANCH ON RESULT ZERO		SELF-EXPLANATORY	
BMI	BRANCH ON RESULT MINUS		SELF-EXPLANATORY	
BNE	BRANCH ON RESULT NOT ZERO		SELF-EXPLANATORY	
BPL	BRANCH ON RESULT PLUS		SELF-EXPLANATORY	
BVC	BRANCH ON OVERFLOW CLEAR		SELF-EXPLANATORY	
BVS	BRANCH ON OVERFLOW SET		SELF-EXPLANATORY	
JMP	JUMP TO NEW LOCATION		SELF-EXPLANATORY	

* SEE TABLE 8-27.

branches based on C=0, C=1, Z=1, N=1, Z=0, N=0, O=0, O=1 by BCC, BCS, BEQ, BMI, BNE, BPL, BVC, or BVS, respectively (*B*ranch on *C*arry *C*lear, *C*arry *S*et, *Eq*ual, *Mi*nus, *N*ot *E*qual, *Pl*us, O*v*erflow *C*lear, O*v*erflow *S*et). The last instruction of the Branch instruction group is a conditional jump (JMP) to a new location.

The next group of instructions is concerned with the processor status register. See Table 8-35. The C bit, D bit, I bit, or V bit may be cleared by a CLC, CLD, CLI, or CLV (*Cl*ear *C, D, I,* or *V*) instruction. Instruction SEC, SED, or SEI (*Se*t *C, D,* or *I*) sets those bits of the processor status register. The BRK instruction sets the B bit and causes a software interrupt which results in the stack action that is described in the following paragraph.

An MCS6502 interrupt can be caused by an external interrupt (IRQ), nonmaskable interrupt (NMI), or software interrupt (BRK instruction). The only difference in the three is that the interrupt vector is different; that is, control is transferred to three separate addresses. On the interrupt, the most significant eight bits of the P register (PCH) are pushed into the next stack location, L. The stack pointer is decremented by one, and the contents of the lower eight bits of the P register (PCL) are pushed into the next stack location. The stack pointer is again decremented, and the contents of the processor status register are pushed into the next stack location (L-2). The stack pointer is decremented by one again in preparation for the next storage. A JSR (*J*ump to New Location *S*aving *R*eturn Address) instruction (which we might suspect could also stand for *J*ump to *S*ub*r*outine) pushes only the P counter into the stack. The *Ret*urn From *I*nterrupt (RTI) and *Ret*urn From *S*ubroutine (RTS) instructions retrieve the stack contents in the proper order. In addition to the automatic stack actions of the interrupts (JSR, RTI, and RTS), the accumulator and processor status register can be pulled or pushed to the stack by the *P*us*h A*ccumulator on Stack (PHA), *P*u*l*l *A*ccumulator from Stack (PLA), *P*us*h P*rocessor Status on Stack (PHP), and *P*u*l*l *P*rocessor Status from Stack (PLP) instructions. The preceding instructions are shown in Table 8-36 and Fig. 8-45.

Table 8-35. Processor Status Register Instructions

MNEMONIC	INSTRUCTION	FORMAT* 76543210	DESCRIPTION	EXECUTION TIME
CLC	CLEAR CARRY FLAG		0→ C	
CLD	CLEAR DECIMAL MODE		0→ D	
CLI	CLEAR INTERRUPT DISABLE BIT		0→ I	
CLV	CLEAR OVERFLOW FLAG		0→ V	
SEC	SET CARRY FLAG		1→ C	
SED	SET DECIMAL MODE		1→ D	
SEI	SET INTERRUPT DISABLE STATUS		1→ I	
BRK	FORCE BREAK		1→ I INTERRUPT ACTION, SEE TEXT	

* SEE TABLE 8-27.

Table 8-36. Stack Instructions

MNEMONIC	INSTRUCTION	FORMAT* 76543210	DESCRIPTION	EXECUTION TIME
JSR	JUMP TO NEW LOCATION SAVING RETURN ADDRESS		SEE TEXT	
RTI	RETURN FROM INTERRUPT		SEE TEXT	
RTS	RETURN FROM SUBROUTINE		SEE TEXT	
PHA	PUSH ACCUMULATOR ON STACK		SEE TEXT	
PHP	PUSH PROCESSOR STATUS ON STACK		SEE TEXT	
PLA	PULL ACCUMULATOR FROM STACK		SEE TEXT	
PLP	PULL PROCESSOR STATUS FROM STACK		SEE TEXT	

* SEE TABLE 8-27.

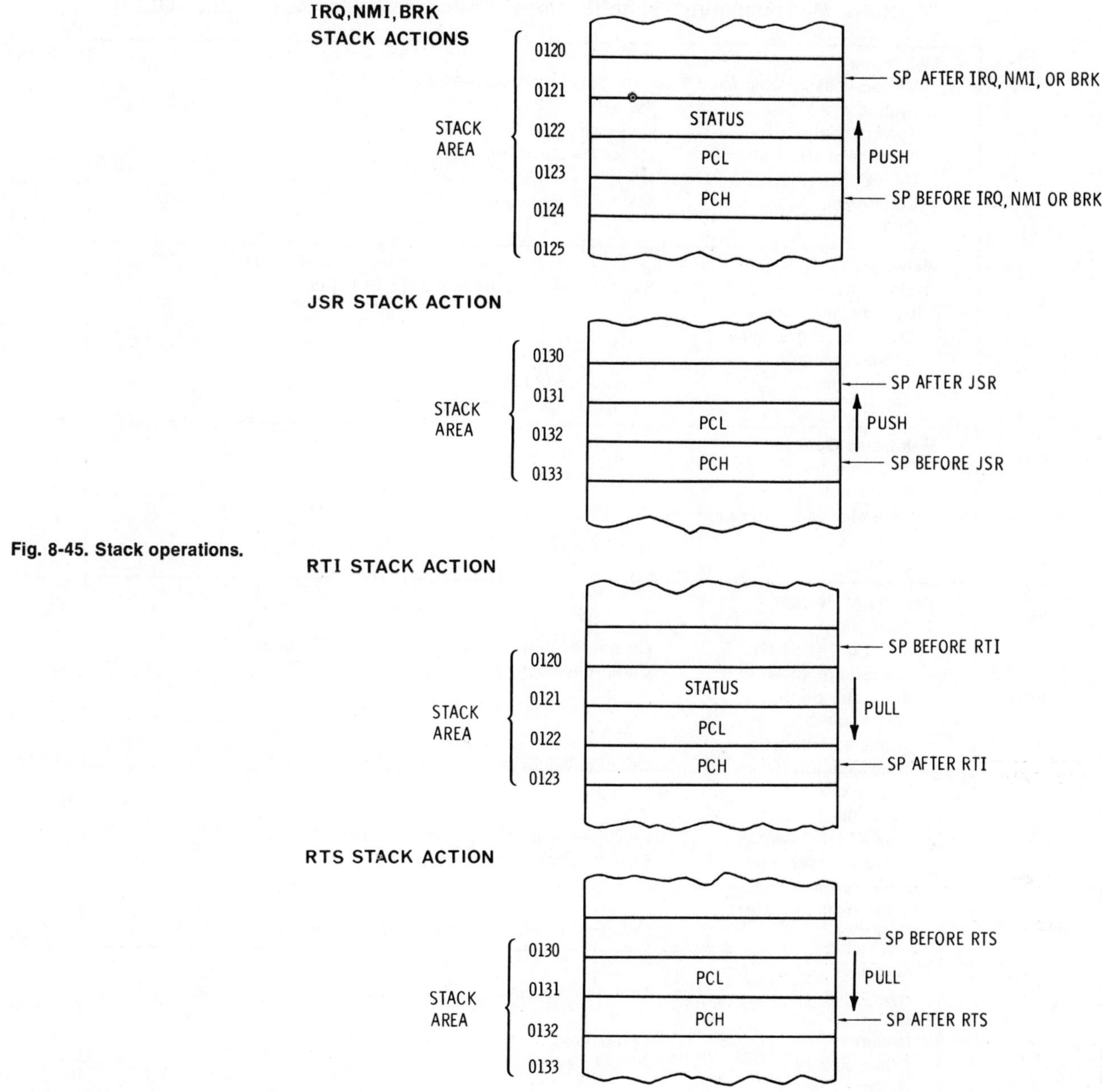

Fig. 8-45. Stack operations.

The last and certainly the least instruction is the lowly NOP instruction, which doesn't deserve a table. It is op code EA_{16}, a one-byte instruction taking 2 microseconds.

Microcomputers Based on the MCS6502

There are several companies manufacturing microcomputers or microcomputer kits based on the MOS Technology MCS6502. Probably the first was the "JOLT" kit from Microcomputer Associates, Inc., which offers a series of modular 4¼ × 7-inch cards containing the CPU, RAM, I/O, and so forth. (See Fig. 8-46.) The basic memory card offers 4096 bytes of static RAM with 1-microsecond access time and on-board "decoding." The I/O card provides two PIA (peripheral interface adapters), thirty-two I/O lines, four interrupt lines, and on-board decoding. Also offered are power supplies, cables, connectors, and a blank "universal" card for construction of other types of interfaces. Chart 8-9 describes the JOLT microcomputer in detail.

Another company offering a neat little package based on the MCS6502 is the EBKA 6502 Familiarizer, shown in Fig. 8-47. The unique thing about this kit (also available in assembled form) is that it does not require a terminal, since it has an on-board hexadecimal and control keyboard and a two-hexadecimal digit display. The usual monitor program in PROM enables the user to load, run, debug, and modify programs. One-K bytes of RAM are also included in the basic unit. Pro-

Chart 8-9. Microcomputer Specifications of Microcomputer Associates JOLT

Mainframe	
Microprocessor chip used:	MOS Technology MCS6502
System clock:	750 kHz
Power supply:	Optional
Number of I/O slots:	Modular—cards are stacked
Control panel type:	None
Construction:	4¼″ × 7″ pc boards
Other:	
Memory	
Static memory:	Speed: 1 μs Increment size: 4K bytes
Dynamic memory:	
Erasable programmable:	
Shared memory:	
Memory limits:	Minimum: 512 bytes Maximum: 32K bytes
Other:	1K-byte ROM for monitor
Mainframe Options	
Real-time clock:	
Rack mount:	
Expander card/chassis:	
DMA:	
Other:	
Peripheral Devices	
Teletype:	
Serial I/O (RS232):	On-board interface. Adjusts from 110-300 baud
Cassette recorder if:	Under development
Character printer:	
Line printer:	
Alphanumeric crt:	
Television interface:	Under development
Floppy disc:	
Other disc:	
Parallel I/O board:	Available 32 programmable I/O lines
Vectored interrupts:	64 bytes: interrupt vector
PROM programmer:	
Other manufacturers:	
Other:	Universal blank card. Cables, connectors, etc.
Software	
Assembler:	Under development
Editor:	
Debug:	In monitor
Other utilities:	PROM monitor
BASIC:	
Extended BASIC:	
FORTRAN:	
Other compilers:	
Operating systems:	
Application programs:	
User's groups:	
Other:	
Miscellaneous	
Extender board:	
Documentation:	Excellent
Other:	
Pricing	
Minimum system:	CPU board, $159

Chart 8-10. Microcomputer Specifications of EBKA Familiarizer

Mainframe	
Microprocessor chip used:	MOS Technology MCS6502
System clock:	400 kHz
Power supply:	User-supplied, requires +5 V at 1.2 A, −9 V at 50 mA
Number of I/O slots:	Not applicable
Control panel type:	Hex keyboard, 2 hex digit display on board
Construction:	Single board
Other:	
Memory	
Static memory:	Speed: 650 ns
Dynamic memory:	
Erasable programmable:	Speed: 1 μs Increment size: 256 bytes
Shared memory:	
Memory limits:	Minimum: 1K-byte RAM Maximum: 1K-byte RAM
Other:	256 bytes of monitor, expandable to 1K bytes
Mainframe Options	
Real-time clock:	
Rack mount:	
Expander card/chassis:	Under development
DMA:	
Other:	
Peripheral Devices	
Teletype:	
Serial I/O (RS232):	Under development
Cassette recorder if:	Under development
Character printer:	
Line printer:	
Alphanumeric crt:	
Television interface:	Under development
Floppy disc:	
Other disc:	
Parallel I/O board:	8-bit input port, 8-bit output port
Vectored interrupts:	
PROM programmer:	Under development
Other manufacturers:	
Other:	4 × 4 dot matrix "Scoreboard"
Software	
Assembler:	Under development
Editor:	Under development
Debug:	In monitor program
Other utilities:	
BASIC:	
Extended BASIC:	
FORTRAN:	
Other compilers:	
Operating systems:	
Application programs:	
User's groups:	
Other:	
Miscellaneous	
Extender board:	
Documentation:	Good, MOS Technology manuals
Other:	
Pricing	
Minimum system:	$229

Chart 8-11. Microcomputer Specifications of MOS Technology KIM-1

Mainframe	
Microprocessor chip used:	MOS Technology MCS6502
System clock:	
Power supply:	User-supplied 5 V, 1 A; +12 V, 50 mA
Number of I/O slots:	
Control panel type:	Keyboard on pc board
Construction:	Pc board
Other:	
Memory	
Static memory:	Speed: 1 μs Increment size: 1K
Dynamic memory:	
Erasable programmable:	
Shared memory:	
Memory limits:	Minimum: 1K-byte RAM Maximum: 4K-byte on-board
Other:	2048-byte ROM monitor program
Mainframe Options	
Real-time clock:	
Rack mount:	
Expander card/chassis:	
DMA:	
Other:	
Peripheral Devices	
Teletype:	On-board
Serial I/O (RS232):	On-board
Cassette recorder if:	On-board
Character printer:	
Line printer:	
Alphanumeric crt:	
Television interface:	
Floppy disc:	
Other disc:	
Parallel I/O board:	15 bidirectional I/O lines
Vectored interrupts:	
PROM programmer:	
Other manufacturers:	
Other:	Interval timer on-board. Six hex-digit display and keyboard on board
Software	
Assembler:	
Editor:	
Debug:	In monitor
Other utilities:	Cassette file manager in monitor
BASIC:	
Extended BASIC:	
FORTRAN:	
Other compilers:	
Operating systems:	
Application programs:	
User's groups:	
Other:	
Miscellaneous	
Extender board:	
Documentation:	Excellent
Other:	90-day warranty
Pricing	
Minimum system:	$250 assembled

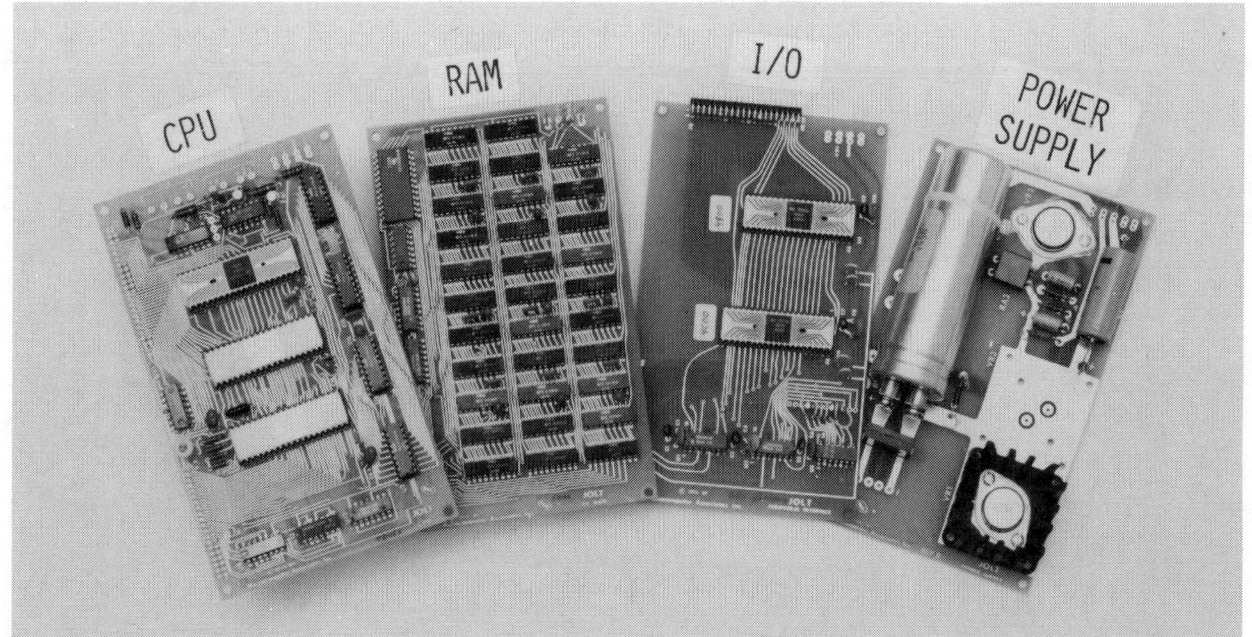

Courtesy Microcomputer Associates, Inc.

Fig. 8-46. Microcomputer Associates' JOLT.

Courtesy EBKA Industries, Inc.

Fig. 8-47. EBKA 6502 Familiarizer.

vision is made for an additional 768 bytes of PROM (the monitor takes 256 bytes). The kit is complete with all parts and documentation and, with the addition of a power supply, it is "ready to run." Chart 8-10 gives the specifications on this EBKA 6502 Familiarizer microcomputer.

The third microcomputer based on the MCS6502 is one from the manufacturer itself, the MOS Technology KIM-1. (See Fig. 8-48). Not offered as a kit, the board is a completely assembled, warranted microcomputer with keyboard and 6-hexadecimal digit display. One-K bytes of RAM are included, along with a monitor program in 2K bytes of ROM. Built in on the board is a complete audio cassette interface and a serial terminal interface! Also included are 15 bidirectional I/O interface lines. The only user-supplied items required to run the system are an optional cassette recorder and a power supply. Chart 8-11 lists the specifications of the MOS Technology KIM-1.

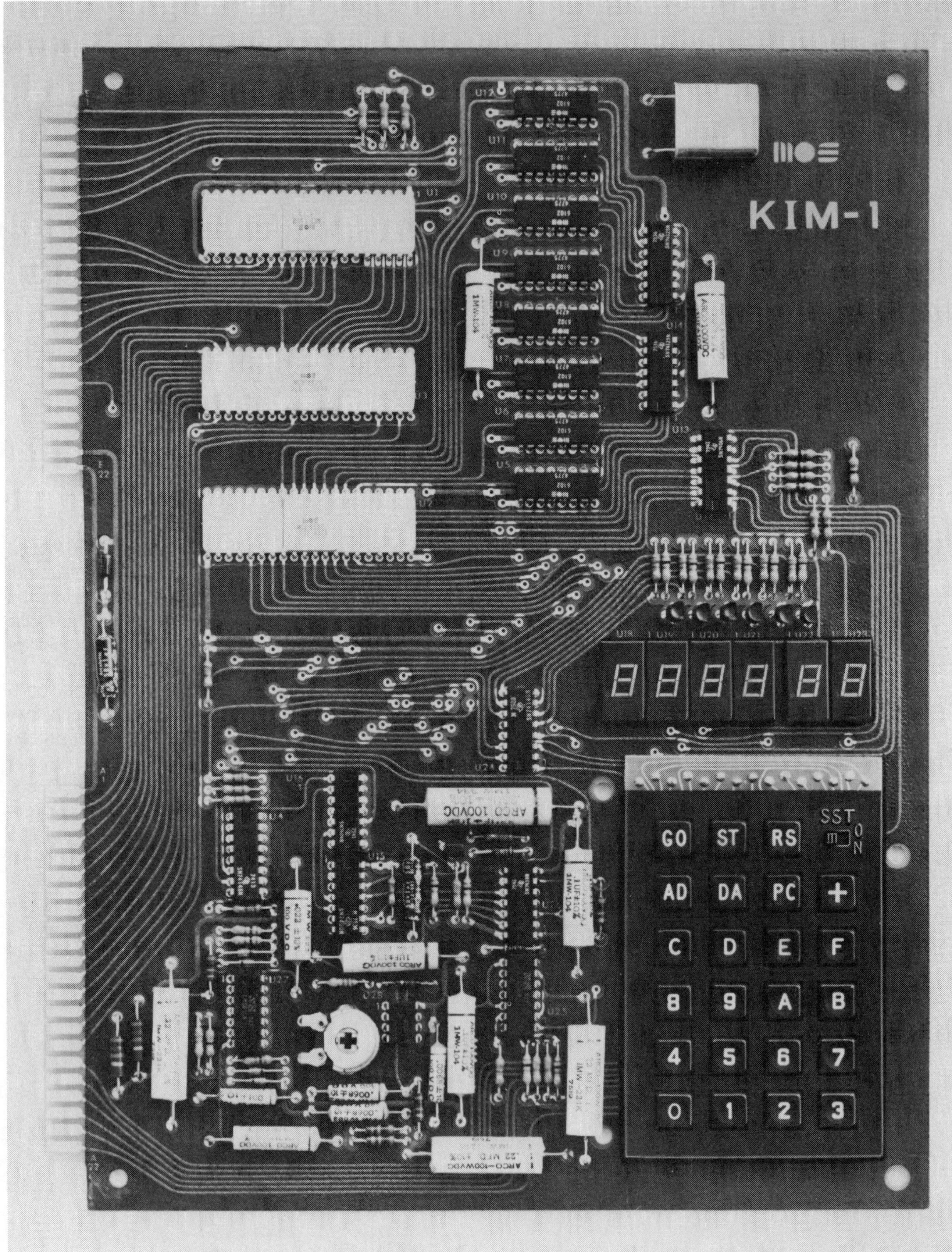

Courtesy MOS Technology, Inc.

Fig. 8-48. MOS Technology KIM-1 microcomputer.

CHAPTER

9

Minicomputer Profiles

This chapter describes some of the most popular minicomputers at the low end of the price scale. The minicomputers discussed here range in price from about $1500 to $3500 with 4K words of memory and no peripherals. Many can be bought used at considerable savings. Bear in mind that prices for new equipment will drop even further with coming advancements in LSI technology.

Disregarding their higher prices in comparison with microcomputers for the moment, let's consider some of the advantages of minicomputers over their smaller relatives. For one thing, software is generally more complete. Diagnostic programs exist where there may be none at all in a microcomputer system. Usually, many higher-level language, utility, and applications programs are available. Another advantage is that a wide range of peripherals are offered. They *are* expensive but are in the same range as microcomputer peripherals, since in many cases they are the same unit. In a large system configuration with many peripherals, the cost of the CPU becomes less and less significant. A third advantage of minicomputers is that currently most minicomputers are more powerful than microcomputers in instruction speeds, data bus width, ALU width, and DMA capability. A fourth advantage is the superior factory support that minicomputer manufacturers can give over microcomputer manufacturers, who may have minimal support or none at all.

Minicomputers from four companies are discussed in detail in this chapter. The minicomputers chosen are meant to be a sampling of inexpensive models of well-known manufacturers. There are many other manufacturers with models in this price range, of course, and the last part of this chapter gives a listing of most of the models with their characteristics and prices.

DIGITAL EQUIPMENT CORP.

Digital Equipment Corp. is the largest minicomputer manufacturer in the world and has been in business since 1957. The PDP-8 was one of the first minicomputers ever produced. It was introduced in 1964, and since that time various versions of the PDP-8 have been produced, including the PDP-8/S, the PDP-8/I, the PDP-8/L, the PDP-8/E, the PDP-8/M, and the PDP-8/F. Differences between the models are minimal, and the instruction sets are the same except that some later models have new microprogrammed instructions. Recently, DEC introduced the PDP-11 minicomputer. In a minimum configuration, the PDP-11/05 is somewhat attractive to the hobbyist. Also available is a PDP-11 on a board, the LSI-11, for roughly $1000. The following discussion of the PDP-8 is based on the newest version of the PDP-8, the PDP-8/A (Fig. 9-1), but for the most part should apply to all models in the PDP-8 series, including other manufacturers' microcomputers that emulate the PDP-8.

PDP-8 Architecture

The architecture of the PDP-8 is shown in Fig. 9-2. Basic memory (core or semiconductor) consists of 4K 12-bit words, provided by three plug-in modules. Additional 4K or 8K word increments of memory may be added to provide up to 32K words of core memory in some models. However, a memory size about 4K words requires a "memory extension" option to increase the addressing capability of the machine, as the basic addressing capability is 4K. Memory cycle time in the PDP-8/A is 1.5 microseconds. The CPU portion consists of one accumulator (A) and a multiplier quotient (MQ) register. The later is implemented principally for an optional hardware multiply and divide, but it is also usable as a second accumulator. A one-bit flag, called the "link" (L), is used for arithmetic testing. Other registers in the CPU are not available to the programmer and are the usual program counter and other registers used in implementing the instructions.

Arithmetic operations in the CPU are 12-bit two's complement. Input/output (I/O) is performed either under programmed I/O, which permits a maximum

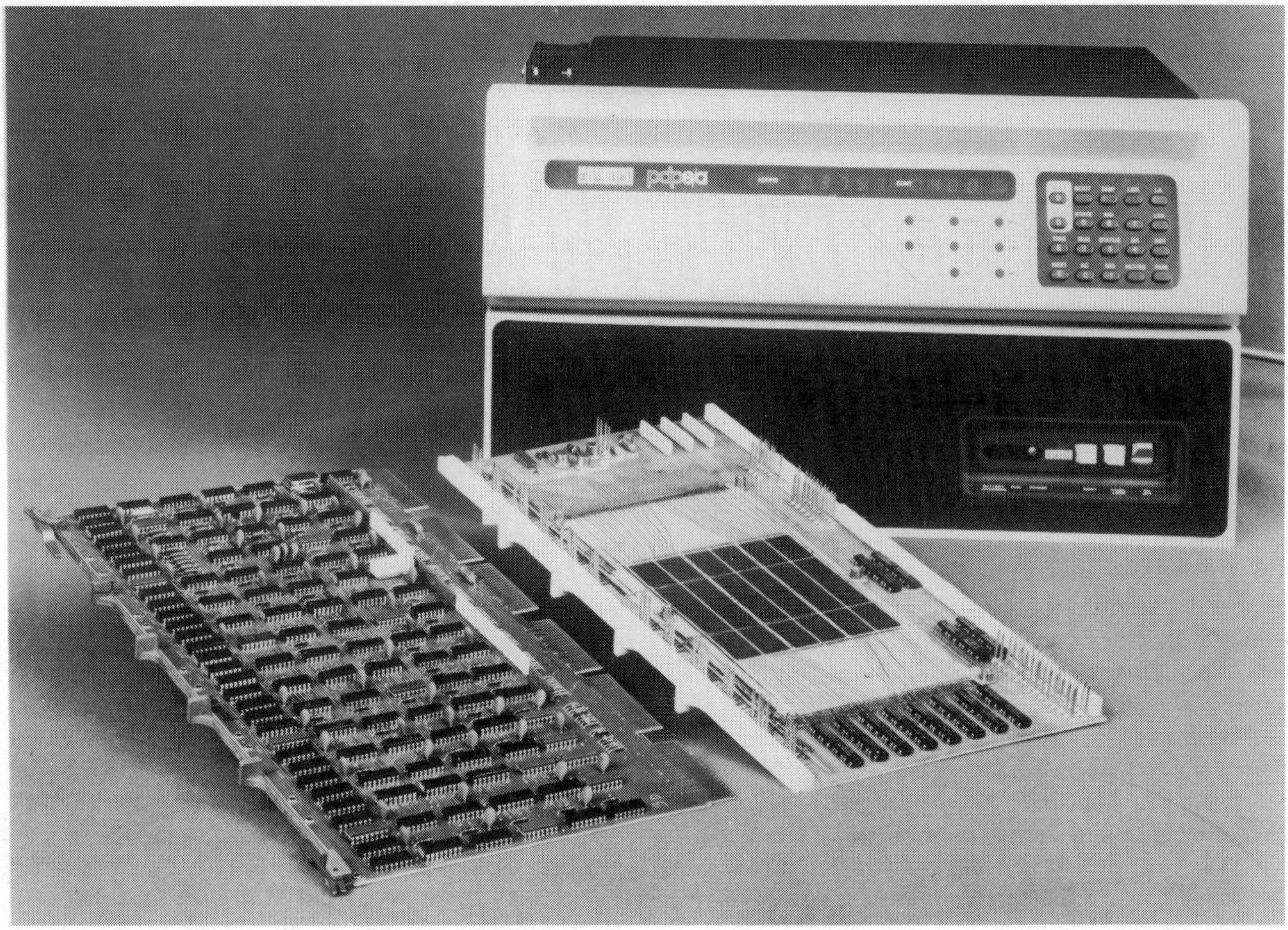

Courtesy Digital Equipment Corp.

Fig. 9-1. Digital Equipment Corp. PDP-8/A minicomputer.

data transfer rate of about 120,000 bytes per second, or under DMA, with a maximum transfer rate of 660,000 words per second. Programmed I/O transfers 12 bits between the A register and an external device. Up to 64 device addresses are possible. The DMA, called a "data break" by Digital Equipment Corp., allows a transfer of up to 4K 12-bit words at a time. Data-break control logic is implemented within the device controller

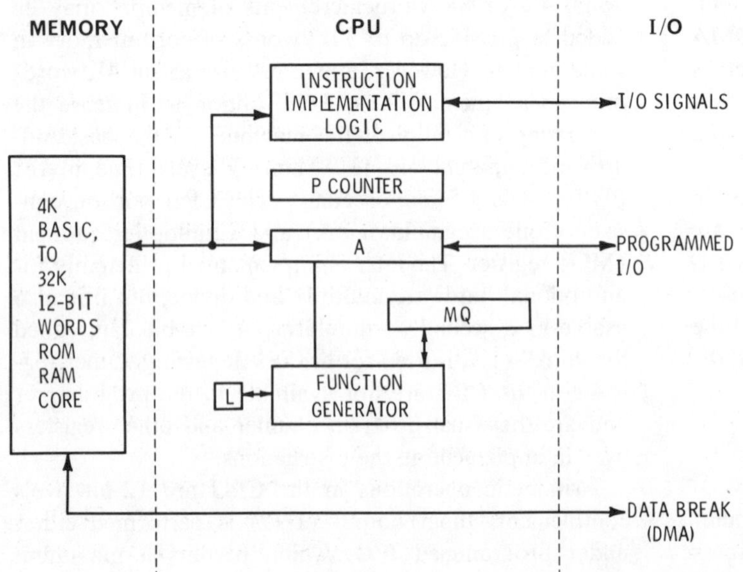

Fig. 9-2. PDP-8 architecture.

and consists of the usual address counter, word counter, and control circuitry.

The interrupt system is a single-level type: An interrupt causes execution of the instruction in location 00001_8 which is a jump to the interrupt service routine. The interrupted location is stored in location 00000_8.

Physical Features

Most PDP-8 chassis are available in either a table-top or rack-mounting configuration. The basic dimensions are 10½ inches high by 24 inches deep by 19 inches wide to fit standard racks. Some of the earlier models are quite a bit larger; the PDP-8/I, for example, is 8½ inches high by 31 inches deep by 30 inches wide, with an auxiliary power-supply chassis (table-top version). The PDP-8/A has 10 slots in the semiconductor memory version and 12 I/O slots in the core memory version available for I/O interfaces or memory—additional expansion capability is provided by an optional expansion chassis.

Primary or standard options are provided on printed-circuit modules which plug into the I/O slots. Primary options include such necessities as tty controller, front panel control, and parallel I/O module. Standard options include other controllers and memory extension. All modules plug into slots that interface to a back plane etched-circuit board that DEC calls an Omnibus. Standard peripherals are connected by cable to modules that plug into the Omnibus.

Instruction Set

The instruction set of the PDP-8 may be divided into the following groups:

- Memory Reference instructions.
- Input/Output instructions.
- Operate instructions.

The memory of the PDP-8 is divided into 4K-word blocks called "memory fields." A minimum-configuration PDP-8 has 4K of memory and only one field. Additional memory and fields may be obtained by adding a memory extension option. Transfers to a different field are then performed by executing special instructions which load a special addressing register called the "instruction field register." This really converts the program counter from 12 bits to 15 bits to enable addressing of 32K words of memory. Our discussion will be confined to only one field and the addressing within that field. Within each field, the 4096 locations are numbered in octal from 0000 to 7777_8. The 4096 locations are further subdivided into 32 pages of 128 words each, numbered from 0 to 37_8 The page subdivision is shown in Fig. 9-3.

The Memory Reference instruction format is shown in Fig. 9-4. The first three bits are the operation code. The next bit is an address mode bit specifying direct or indirect addressing. The next bit is a page bit specifying page 0 or the current page. Bits 5 through 11 specify a displacement. If bit 3 and bit 4 are not set, the instruction references 1 of the 128 locations in page 0 as specified by the displacement in bits 5 through 11. If bit 3 is not set but bit 4 is set, the "current page" mode is indicated, and the effective address is the location within the current page as specified by bits 5 through 11. If, for example, the current instruction is at 1112_8, the current page is page 4 (0–177=page 0, 200–377=page 1, 400–577=page 2, 600–777=page 3, 1000–1177=page 4). If the page mode was set and the displacement field held 140_8, the addressed instruction would be 1000_8 (start of page 4) + $140_8 = 1140_8$. Note that this is not a floating page machine; the displacement actually represents a displacement from the start of the current page rather than from the current instruction.

If bit 3 is set and bit 4 is not set, the effective address is the contents of the page 0 location specified by bits 5 through 11. If bits 3 and 4 are both set, the effective address is the contents of the current page location specified by bits 5 through 11. The possible addressing modes for Memory Reference instructions are shown in Fig. 9-5.

A somewhat unusual but very handy feature of the PDP-8 is the auto-index feature. If a Memory Reference instruction indirectly references locations 10_8 through 17_8 of page 0, or of any field, the content of the location is first incremented by one. This enables these locations to be pointers to consecutive data. If the data are accessed in order, the auto increment automatically bumps the pointer to the next word of data when the pointer is indirectly addressed.

Table 9-1 lists the Memory Reference instructions. The AND (Logical *and*) instruction ANDs the contents of the effective address with the contents of the accumulator and puts the result in the accumulator. TAD (*T*wos' Complement *Ad*d) adds the contents of the effective address with the contents of the accumulator and puts the result in the accumulator. ISZ (*I*ncrement and *S*kip if *Z*ero) increments the content of the effective address by one and replaces it in the effective address. If the result is zero, the next instruction in sequence is skipped. DCA (*D*eposit and *C*lear the *A*ccumulator) stores the contents of the accumulator in the effective address and sets the accumulator to zero. JMS (*Ju*m*p* to *S*ubroutine) stores the contents of the program counter (next location) in the effective address. The CPU then jumps to the effective address plus one. JMP (*Jump*) jumps to the effective address.

Input/Output Instructions—The format of Input/Output transfer (IOT) instructions is shown in Fig. 9-6. Bits 0 through 2 are a 6. Bits 3 through 8 are a device selection code or device address. Bits 9 through 11

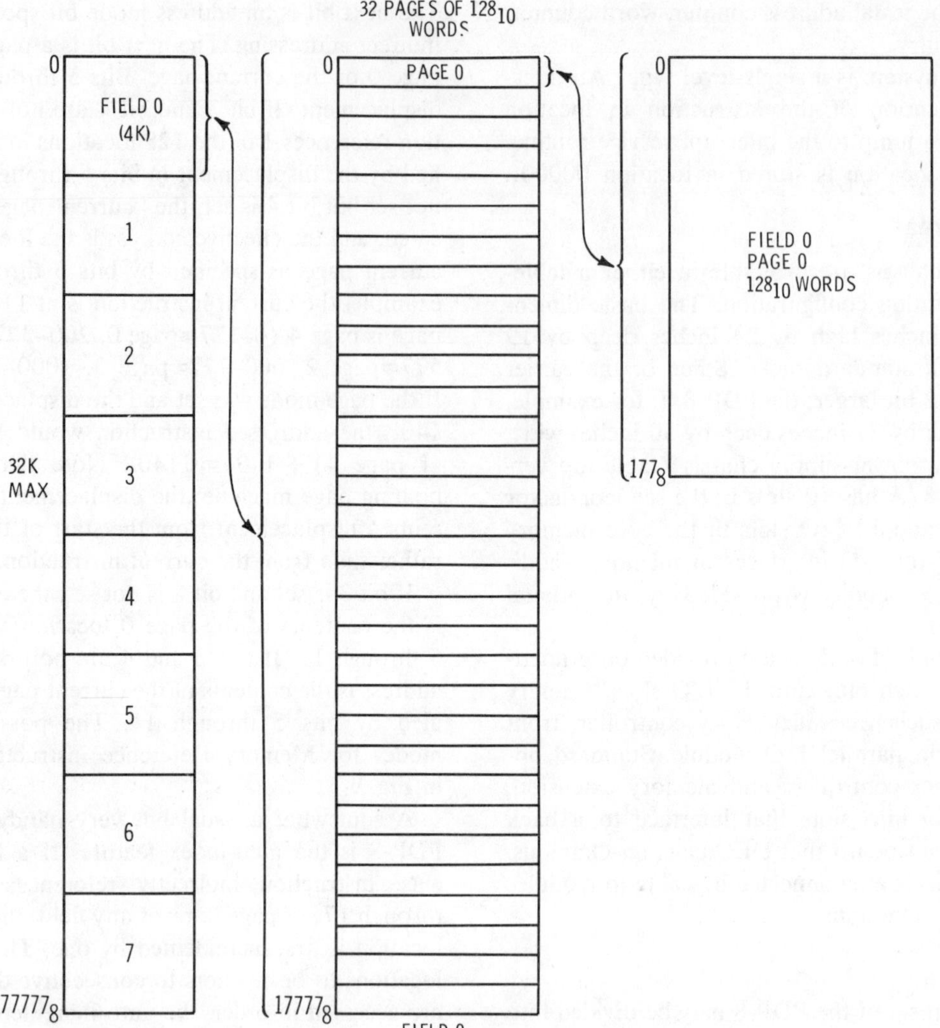

Fig. 9-3. PDP-8 memory mapping.

specify the operation that the device is to perform. An IOT instruction with a value of 6014_8, for instance, would load one character (code 4) from device 1, the paper-tape reader. If the device address is 00_8, an IOT instruction will issue special commands to the interrupt system to enable or disable interrupts, test for interrupts, and so forth. Most PDP-8 I/O devices maintain only one bit of status, a busy-done flip-flop (or flag) indicating whether the device is ready for the next data transfer. The flag may be set or reset or tested under program control by an IOT instruction. Other IOT instructions enable transfer of 12 bits of data to or from the device and accumulator (or program counter).

Operate Instructions—Operate instructions are further subdivided into three groups: 1, 2, and 3. Group 1 Operate instructions perform logical operations upon the accumulator and link (one-bit flag). Group 2 Operate instructions test the contents of the accumulator and link. Group 3 Operate instructions perform logical op-

0 2 3 4 5 11
OP | I | P | PAGE ADDRESS
PAGE BIT 0 = PAGE 0
1 = CURRENT PAGE
ADDRESS MODE BIT
0 = DIRECT
1 = INDIRECT

Fig. 9-4. Memory Reference instruction format.

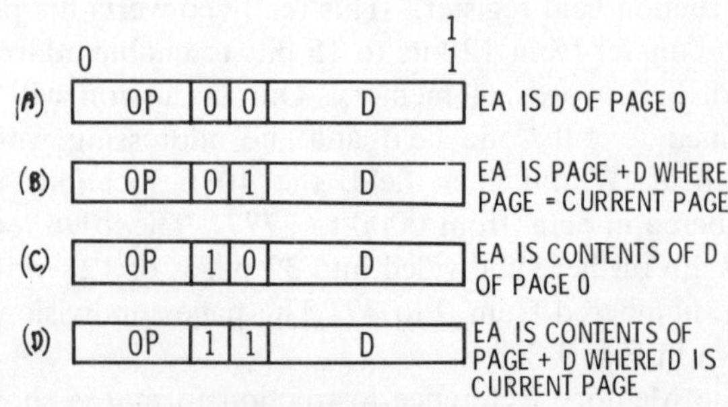

Fig. 9-5. Memory Reference addressing modes.

Table 9-1. Memory Reference Instructions

MNEMONIC	INSTRUCTION	FORMAT (bits 0 1 2 3 4 5 6 7 8 9 10 11)	DESCRIPTION	EXECUTION TIME* (μs)
AND	LOGICAL AND	0 0 0 | IP | D 0XXX8	(EA) AND (A) → A	3.0
TAD	TWO'S COMPLEMENT ADD	0 0 1 | IP | D 1XXX8	(EA) + (A) → A (L̄) → L IF CARRY	3.0
ISZ	INCREMENT AND SKIP IF ZERO	0 1 0 | IP | D 2XXX8	(EA) + 1 → EA IF (EA) = 0, (PC) + 1 → PC	3.0
DCA	DEPOSIT AND CLEAR ACCUMULATOR	0 1 1 | IP | D 3XXX8	(A) → EA 0 → A	3.0
JMS	JUMP TO SUBROUTINE	1 0 0 | IP | D 4XXX8	(PC) → EA EA + 1 → PC	3.0
JMP	JUMP	1 0 1 | IP | D 5XXX8	EA → PC	3.0

* PDP-8/A WITH CORE MEMORY.

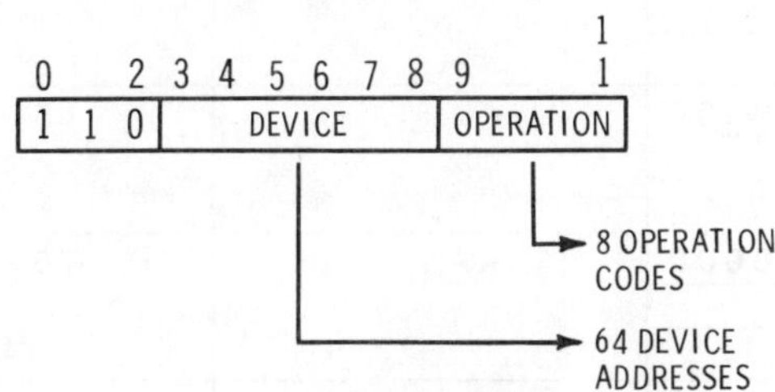

Fig. 9-6. Input/Output instruction format.

erations between the accumulator and MQ (multiplier quotient) register.

Group 1 Operate instructions have the format shown in Fig. 9-7. Bits 0 through 3 are 1110_2. Bits 4 through 11 are "microprogrammed"; that is, the different bit positions represent different actions to be taken in the CPU logic when the instruction is executed. By setting the proper bits, the user may form his own useful combinations of instructions. Setting bits 7 and 11, for example, will complement and increment the accumulator (two's complement). Some combinations may be redundant or meaningless, and others are not allowed (setting more than one bit in bit positions 8, 9, and 10). The commonly used microinstructions in group 1 are shown in Table 9-2.

NOP (*N*o *Op*eration) does nothing. IAC (*I*ncrement *A*ccumulator) increments the contents of the accumulator by one. BSW (*B*yte *Sw*ap) swaps the six least significant bits of the accumulator with the six most significant bits, as shown in Fig. 9-18. RAL (*R*otate *A*ccumulator *L*eft) shifts the accumulator and link left one bit as shown in the figure. RTL (*R*otate *T*wo *L*eft) is the same as two RAL instructions (two shifts). RAR (*R*otate *A*ccumulator *R*ight) shifts the accumulator and

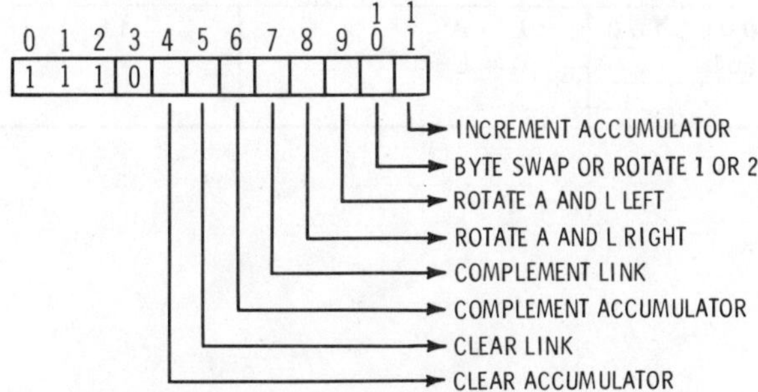

Fig. 9-7. Group 1 Operate instruction format.

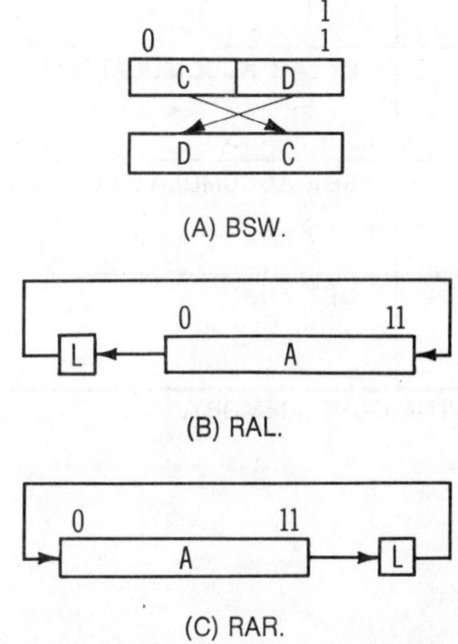

Fig. 9-8. BSW and Rotate instructions.

Table 9-2. Group 1 Operate Instructions

MNEMONIC	INSTRUCTION	FORMAT 1 1 0 1 2 3 4 5 6 7 8 9 0 1	DESCRIPTION	EXECUTION TIME* (μs)
NOP	NO OPERATION	1 1 1 0 0 0 0 0 0 0 0 0 7000_8	DOES NOTHING	1.5
IAC	INCREMENT ACCUMULATOR	1 1 1 0 0 0 0 0 0 0 0 1 7001_8	$(A) + 1 \rightarrow A$ $(\overline{L}) \rightarrow L$ IF CARRY	1.5
BSW	BYTE SWAP	1 1 1 0 0 0 0 0 0 0 1 0 7002_8	$A_{0-5} \leftrightarrow A_{6-11}$	1.5
RAL	ROTATE ACCUMULATOR LEFT	1 1 1 0 0 0 0 0 0 1 0 0 7004_8	$A_{1-11} \rightarrow A_{0-10}$ $A_0 \rightarrow L$ $L \rightarrow A_{11}$	1.5
RTL	ROTATE TWO LEFT	1 1 1 0 0 0 0 0 0 1 1 0 7006_8	TWO RALS	1.5
RAR	ROTATE ACCUMULATOR RIGHT	1 1 1 0 0 0 0 0 1 0 0 0 7010_8	$A_{0-10} \rightarrow A_{1-11}$ $L \rightarrow A_0$ $A_{11} \rightarrow L$	1.5
RTR	ROTATE TWO RIGHT	1 1 1 0 0 0 0 0 1 0 1 0 7012_8	TWO RARS	1.5
CML	COMPLEMENT LINK	1 1 1 0 0 0 0 1 0 0 0 0 7020_8	$(\overline{L}) \rightarrow L$	1.5
CMA	COMPLEMENT ACCUMULATOR	1 1 1 0 0 0 1 0 0 0 0 0 7040_8	$(\overline{A}) \rightarrow A$	1.5
CIA	COMPLEMENT AND INCREMENT ACCUMULATOR	1 1 1 0 0 0 1 0 0 0 0 1 7041_8	$(\overline{A}) + 1 \rightarrow A$ $(-(A) \rightarrow A)$	1.5
CLL	CLEAR LINK	1 1 1 0 0 1 0 0 0 0 0 0 7010_8	$0 \rightarrow L$	1.5
STL	SET LINK	1 1 1 0 0 1 0 1 0 0 0 0 7120_8	$1 \rightarrow L$	1.5
CLA	CLEAR ACCUMULATOR	1 1 1 0 1 0 0 0 0 0 0 0 7200_8	$0 \rightarrow A$	1.5
STA	SET ACCUMULATOR	1 1 1 0 1 0 1 0 0 0 0 0 7240_8	$7777_8 \rightarrow A$	1.5
GLK	GET LINK	1 1 1 0 1 0 0 0 0 1 0 0 7204_8	$L \rightarrow A$ $0 \rightarrow L$	1.5

* PDP-8/A WITH CORE MEMORY.

link right one bit as shown. RTR (*R*otate *T*wo *R*ight) is equivalent to two RAR instructions (two shifts). CML (*Com*plement *L*ink) complements the state of the link (0 to 1 and 1 to 0). CMA (*Com*plement *A*ccumulator) complements the contents of the accumulator (one's complement). CIA (*C*omplement and *I*ncrement *A*ccumulator) performs the two's complement upon the contents of the accumulator. CLL (*Cl*ear *L*ink) clears the link with 0. CLA (*C*lear *A*ccumulator) clears the accumulator. STA (*Set A*ccumulator) sets the accumulator to all ones. GLK (*G*et the *Link*) clears the accumulator, puts the link into bit position 11 of the accumulator, and clears the link.

Group 2 Operate instructions have the format shown in Fig. 9-9. Bits 0 through 3 and bit 11 are 11110_2, respectively. Bits 4 through 10 define microprogramming functions. Many combinations of skips and other functions may be done. For example, a skip microinstruction may be programmed with a CLA, clear accumulator. However, the commonly used group 2 microinstructions are shown in Table 9-3.

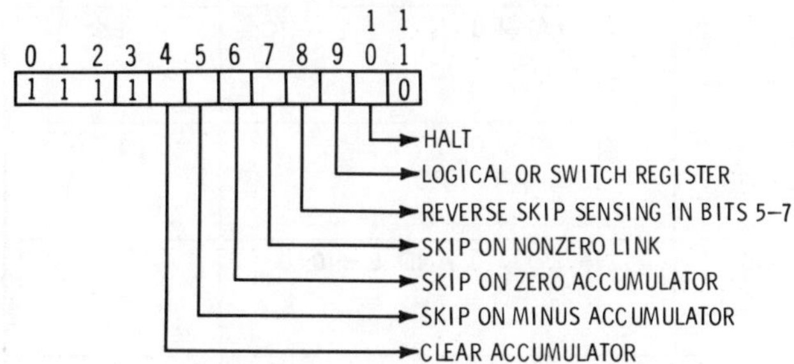

Fig. 9-9. Group 2 Operate instruction format.

The format of group 3 Operate instructions is shown in Fig. 9-10. Bits 0 through 3 and bit 11 are ones. Bits 4, 5, and 7 define microoperations. Commonly used microinstructions are shown in Table 9-4. CLA (*Cl*ear *A*ccumulator) is self-explanatory. MQL (*M*ultiplier *Q*uotient *L*oad) stores the accumulator into the MQ register. The accumulator is cleared. MQA (*M*ultiplier *Q*uotient into *A*ccumulator) ORs the contents of the MQ and A and loads the result into the accumulator. SWP (*Swap* Accumulator and Multiplier Quotient) exchanges the contents of A and MQ. CAM (*C*lear *A*ccumulator and *M*ultiplier Quotient) clears both the A and MQ registers.

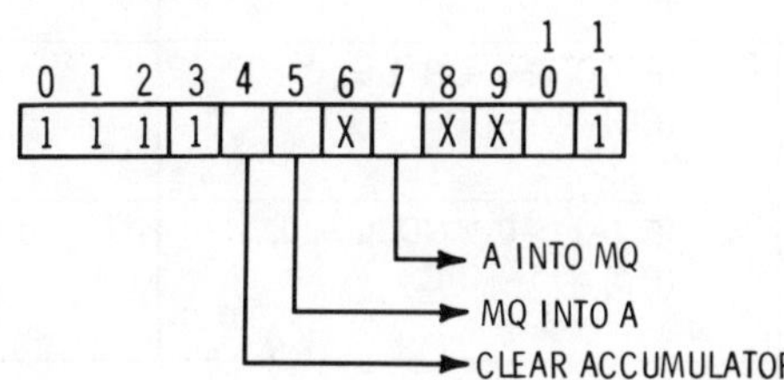

Fig. 9-10. Group 3 Operate instruction format.

Special Instructions—Special instructions include instructions for the PDP-8 interrupt system and options. The Extended Arithmetic Element for the PDP-8 enables a hardware multiply/divide and multiple shifts. The Memory Extension option has special instructions to permit addressing beyond field 0. There are also instructions associated with the Memory Parity, Real-Time Clock, and Power-Fail options.

Peripherals

The peripheral devices offered for the PDP-8 are listed in Chart 9-1, along with speeds and special features.

Software

Digital Equipment Corp. offers a huge amount of software for the PDP-8 since the machine has been available for such a long time. Their handbook on the PDP-8 indicates that more than a thousand programs are available to every PDP-8 user. Assemblers offered are a two-pass "PAL III" assembler, a "macro" assembler (4K memory version available), and an extended-assembler, among others. FORTRAN IV and BASIC are offered along with many of DEC's own higher-level languages, including a language similar to COBOL. Text editors and other utility programs are offered. Operating systems include OS/8, which runs in 8K of memory and at least one DEC tape unit (small magnetic tape). More-powerful operating systems for larger configurations are available. Many application programs, especially scientific packages, are available.

Price and Availability

A PDP-8/A with 4K words of core memory costs under $2000. A PDP-8 on a board, called the KIT-8A, is about $500. Used equipment is readily available at about 50 percent of the current purchase price for a similar configuration.

DATA GENERAL CORPORATION

Data General Corp. has been in the minicomputer business since 1968. It has manufactured a line of 16-bit minicomputers, starting with the DGC Nova computer and continuing with various versions of the Nova. All versions of the Nova utilize the same basic instruction repertoire. Recent developments include the Nova 3, an inexpensive Nova version that uses MOS memory or core memory, and the "Eclipse" computer, a new computer that has a great deal more capability than the older Novas at a subsequently higher cost, and most recently the MicroNova, a Nova based on a Nova-compatible microprocessor chip.

Data General Corp. computers have been popular computers since their inception, and many are available

Table 9-3. Group 2 Operate Instructions

MNEMONIC	INSTRUCTION	FORMAT 1 1 0 1 2 3 4 5 6 7 8 9 0 1	DESCRIPTION	EXECUTION TIME* (μs)
HLT	HALT	1 1 1 1 0 0 0 0 0 0 1 0 7402_8	HALTS CPU	1.5
OSR	LOGICAL OR WITH SWITCH REGISTER	1 1 1 1 0 0 0 0 0 1 0 0 7404_8	(SR) OR (A) → A	1.5
SKP	SKIP	1 1 1 1 0 0 0 0 1 0 0 0 7410_8	(PC) + 1 → PC	1.5
SNL	SKIP ON NONZERO LINK	1 1 1 1 0 0 0 1 0 0 0 0 7420_8	IF L = 1, (PC) + 1 → PC	1.5
SZL	SKIP ON ZERO LINK	1 1 1 1 0 0 0 1 1 0 0 0 7430_8	IF L = 0, (PC) + 1 → PC	1.5
SZA	SKIP ON ZERO ACCUMULATOR	1 1 1 1 0 0 1 0 0 0 0 0 7440_8	IF (A) = 0, (PC) + 1 → PC	1.5
SNA	SKIP ON NONZERO ACCUMULATOR	1 1 1 1 0 0 1 0 1 0 0 0 7450_8	IF (A) ≠ 0, (PC) + 1 → PC	1.5
SZA SNL	SEE ABOVE	1 1 1 1 0 0 1 1 0 0 0 0 7460_8	IF (A) = 0 OR L = 1, (PC) + 1 → PC	1.5
SNA SZL	SEE ABOVE	1 1 1 1 0 0 1 1 1 0 0 0 7470_8	IF (A) ≠ 0 AND L = 0, (PC) + 1 → PC	1.5
SMA	SKIP ON MINUS ACCUMULATOR	1 1 1 1 0 1 0 0 0 0 0 0 7500_8	IF (A) < 0, (PC) + 1 → PC	1.5
SPA	SKIP ON POSITIVE ACCUMULATOR	1 1 1 1 0 1 0 0 1 0 0 0 7510_8	IF (A) ≥ 0, (PC) + 1 → PC	1.5
SMA SNL	SEE ABOVE	1 1 1 1 0 1 0 1 0 0 0 0 7520_8	IF A < 0 OR L = 1, (PC) + 1 → PC	1.5
SPA SZL	SEE ABOVE	1 1 1 1 0 1 0 1 1 0 0 0 7530_8	IF (A) ≥ 0 AND L = 0, (PC) + 1 → PC	1.5
SMA SZA	SEE ABOVE	1 1 1 1 0 1 1 0 0 0 0 0 7540_8	IF (A) ≤ 0, (PC) + 1 → PC	1.5
SPA SNA	SEE ABOVE	1 1 1 1 0 1 1 0 1 0 0 0 7550_8	IF (A) > 0, (PC) + 1 → PC	1.5
SMA SZA SNL	SEE ABOVE	1 1 1 1 0 1 1 1 0 0 0 0 7560_8	IF (A) ≤ 0 OR L = 0, (PC) + 1 → PC	1.5
SPA SNA SZL	SEE ABOVE	1 1 1 1 0 1 1 1 1 0 0 0 7570_8	IF (A) > 0 AND L = 0, (PC) + 1 → PC	1.5
CLA	CLEAR ACCUMULATOR	1 1 1 1 1 0 0 0 0 0 0 0 7600_8	0 → A	1.5

* PDP-8/A WITH CORE MEMORY.

Table 9-4. Group 3 Operate Instructions

MNEMONIC	INSTRUCTION	FORMAT 1 1 0 1 2 3 4 5 6 7 8 9 0 1	DESCRIPTION	EXECUTION TIME* (μs)
CLA	CLEAR ACCUMULATOR	1 1 1 1 1 0 0 0 0 0 0 1 7601_8	0 → A	1.5
MQL	MULTIPLIER QUOTIENT LOAD	1 1 1 1 0 0 0 1 0 0 0 1 7421_8	(A) → MQ 0 → A	1.5
MQA	MULTIPLIER QUOTIENT INTO ACCUMULATOR	1 1 1 1 0 1 0 1 0 0 0 1 7501_8	(MQ) OR (A) → A	1.5
SWP	SWAP ACCUMULATOR AND MULTIPLIER QUOTIENT	1 1 1 1 0 1 0 1 0 0 0 1 7521_8	(A) ↔ (MQ)	1.5
CAM	CLEAR ACCUMULATOR AND MULTIPLIER QUOTIENT	1 1 1 1 1 0 0 1 0 0 0 1 7621_8	0 → A 0 → MQ	1.5

* PDP-8/A WITH CORE MEMORY.

on the used computer market. This discussion will cover all DGC minicomputers with the exception of the newer Eclipse. Models implicitly covered in the discussion are the Nova, Supernova, Supernova SC (semiconductor memory), Nova 800, Nova 1200, Nova 820, Nova 840, Nova 1210, Nova 1220, Nova 1230, Nova 2/4, Nova 2/10, Nova 3, and MicroNova, ranked loosely in order of appearance.

All of the above Novas look alike as far as their instruction repertoire, with the exception of the Nova 3, which has additional "stack" and "trap" instructions. The differences in the various models lie mainly in memory cycle time, physical size and number of card slots, and implementation of the instruction set in the CPU. The Nova 8XX series model has 800-nanosecond core memory. The 12XX series has 1.2-microsecond core memory. The Supernova SC has a 300-nanosecond semiconductor memory. Nova 2's have 800- or 1000-nanosecond memory cycle times. The Nova 3 memory cycle times are 800 nanoseconds and 1 microsecond for core and 700 nanoseconds for MOS semiconductor memory. Generally, the higher the suffix in the model number ("30" in 1230 or "10" in 2/10, for example) the more subassembly slots that are available for memory, I/O controllers, and other plug-in boards. The Nova 2/4 has four slots, for instance, while the Nova 1230, or "jumbo," has 17 subassembly slots. Expander chassis for additional subassemblies are an option. Fig. 9-11 shows a Nova 3/4.

Nova Architecture

The architecture of the Nova series is shown in Fig. 9-12. Memory comes in 4K, 8K, or 16K increments of 16-bit words up to 32K of core or semiconductor memory. Addressing of memory is on a word basis. Data words are transferred from memory to CPU via four accumulators, AC0–AC3, each 16 bits long. Arithmetic operations are performed register-to-register from one accumulator to another. Hardware operations in the CPU are 16-bit two's complement. A carry flip-flop is

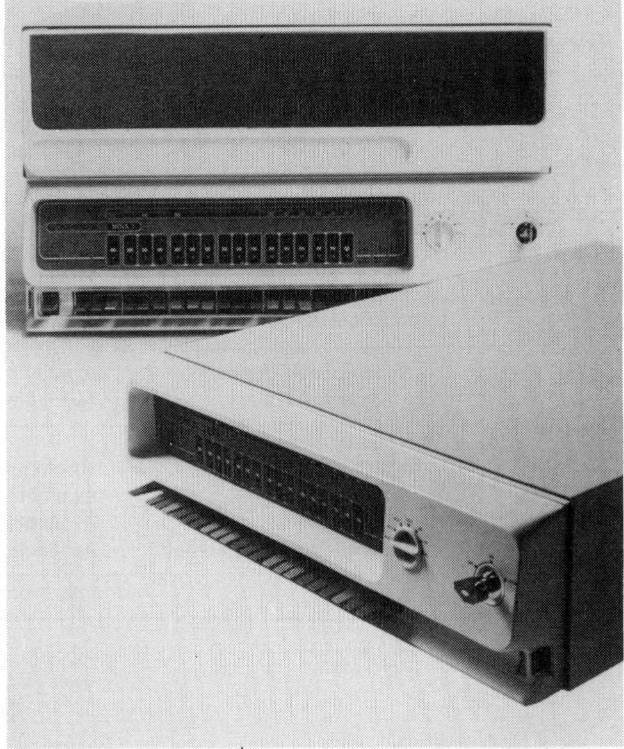

Courtesy Data General Corp.

Fig. 9-11. Data General Corp. Nova 3 minicomputer.

Chart 9-1. Peripheral Options and CPU Options for PDP-8/A

CPU/Memory Options	
Turnkey (minimum) console:	Available
Full console:	Available
Power-fail safe:	Available
Automatic bootstrap:	Available. Uses one of several ROMs
Real-time clock:	Available. 100 Hz (10 ms). Others available.
Additional selector channel:	
Semiconductor memory:	RAM, ROM, or PROM available, RAM is 2.4 μs.
Core memory:	Available. 1.5 μs for PDP-8/A
Memory protection:	"Timeshare" option has user/executive modes
Memory expansion:	Up to 32K 12-bit words
Hardware multiply/divide:	Available as option with other "extended" instructions
Other:	Floating-point hardware
Teletype	
Tty—33:	Available
Tty (other):	
Tty modification kit:	Available
Other terminals:	DEC writer. 30 Hz, 7×7 dot matrix printer
CRT	
Alphanumeric display:	VT50 video display. 12 lines × 80 characters
Graphic display:	Available
Oscilloscope control:	Available
Printer Plotter	
Line printer:	Available
Plotter:	Available for Calcomp incremental plotter
Card Reader	
Card reader:	200 cards/min
Paper Tape	
Paper tape reader:	300 chars/s
Paper tape punch:	Reader/punch available. Punch is 50 chars/s
Magnetic Tape	
Audio cassette tape:	
Cassette tape:	Dual "Philips-type" cassette. 560 bytes/s
Cartridge tape:	
Reel-to-reel tape:	DEC tape. One or two drives. 8325 words/s, also 7- and 9-track tape drives available
Magnetic Disc	
Fixed head:	Available
Movable head:	1.6-megaword capacity. 120K words/s
Floppy disc:	
Communications	
Asynchronous interface:	For tty or other device. 110-9600 baud
Synchronous interface:	Available
Modem control:	Available
Special-Purpose Interfaces	
ADC:	16 channels of input/board (multiplexed)
DAC:	Available
Relay driver:	Available
General-purpose parallel:	Available. Includes interrupt 50 words/s
Other	Interprocessor communications

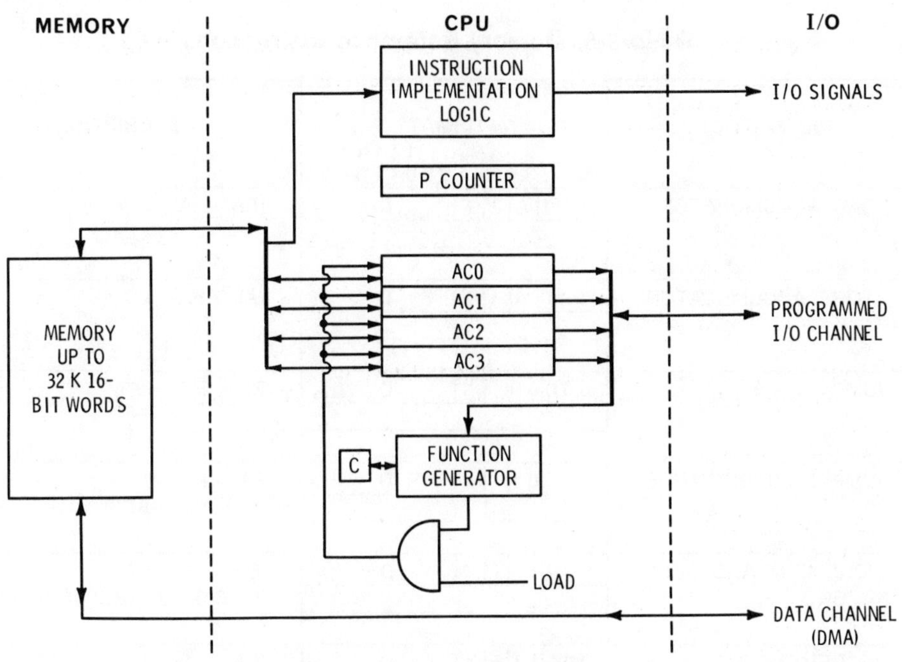

Fig. 9-12. Nova series architecture.

set by the results of register-to-register operations and can be tested for conditional skipping.

Input/output is performed under either programmed I/O or DMA. In the former case, up to 16 bits at a time may be transferred between CPU accumulators and external devices. In the DMA case, up to one million 16-bit words or so per second may be transferred between an external device and memory through a "data channel" to memory. The DMA control logic is implemented in the appropriate controller (disc, magnetic tape, etc.) rather than having a "block transfer" controller or selector channel within the CPU itself. Up to 64 different I/O addresses are possible. Among the CPU options are real-time clock, power-fail safe, multiply/divide, and memory mapping and protect.

Physical Features

Nova chassis vary from 5¼ inches to 10½ inches in height, and mount in standard 19-inch racks. The number of I/O slots in the chassis varies from 4 to 17. The CPU comes on a single 15-inch printed-circuit board. Memory on a single 15-inch printed-circuit board varies from 4K words to 16K words. Controllers and CPU options are contained on either a separate printed-circuit board or a portion of a pc board. Standard peripherals such as tty and paper-tape equipment plug into either a set of dedicated back panel pins, paddle boards from the back panel, or dedicated plugs, depending on the model of the Nova.

Instruction Set

The instructions of the Nova computers are divided into the following groups:

- Memory Reference instructions.
- Arithmetic and Logical instructions.
- Input/Output instructions.
- Special instructions.

Memory Reference Instructions—Memory Reference instructions and jump instructions use the same type of instruction format as that shown in Fig. 9-13. Bits 0 through 4 are the operation code and possible register. Bits 5 through 15 specify the memory location accessed or used in the jump. If bits 6 and 7 are 0 and bit 5 is zero, the effective address (EA) is in page 0 as specified by the D field. Since there are eight bits in the D field, 256_{10} locations in page 0 can be specified. If bit 5 is 0 and bits 6 and 7 are 01_2, relative addressing is denoted. The D field is then treated as an eight-bit signed displacement to be added to the contents of the program counter to give the effective address. The D field can hold -200_8 (-128_{10}) to $+177_8$ (127_{10}), and the floating page is therefore 256 words (back 128, forward 127, and the current location).

If bit 5 is 0 and bits 6 and 7 are 10_2 or 11_2, indexed addressing is in effect. The effective address is determined by adding the contents of accumulator 2 (bits

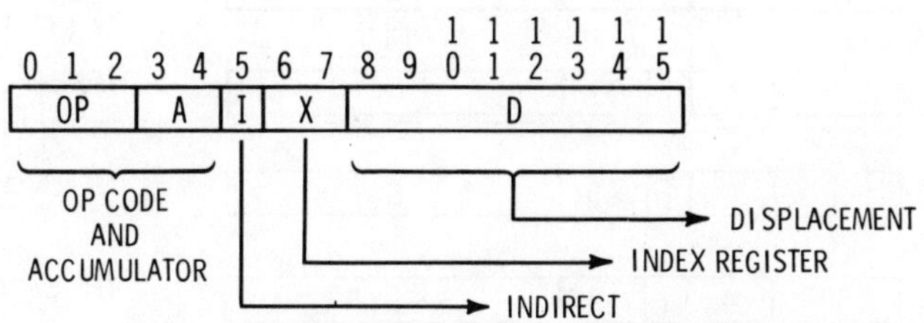

Fig. 9-13. Memory Reference instruction format.

Table 9-5. Memory Reference Instructions

MNEMONIC	INSTRUCTION	FORMAT (bits 0 1 2 3 4 5 6 7 8 9 10 11 12 13 14 15)	DESCRIPTION	EXECUTION TIME* (μs)
LDA	LOAD ACCUMULATOR	001 A I X D	(EA) → A	1.6/2.4
STA	STORE ACCUMULATOR	010 A I X D	(A) → EA	1.6/2.4
JMP	JUMP	000 00 I X D	EA → PC	.8/1.6
JSR	JUMP TO SUBROUTINE	000 01 I X D	EA → PC (PC) + 1 → AC3	.8/1.6
ISZ	INCREMENT AND SKIP IF ZERO	000 10 I X D	(EA) + 1 → EA IF (EA) = 0, (PC) + 1 → PC	1.8/2.6
DSZ	DECREMENT AND SKIP IF ZERO	000 11 I X D	(EA) − 1 → EA IF (EA) = 0, (PC) + 1 → PC	1.8/2.6

* NOVA 800: FIRST FIGURE, DIRECT ADDRESSING; SECOND, INDIRECT.

6,7 = 10) or accumulator 3 (bits 6,7 = 11) to the D field (treated as an eight-bit signed value). If bit 5 is a one, all of the above applies except that the addressing is indirect. The indirect address is first determined by the above addressing procedures. The contents of this indirect address are then read. If the value read does not have bit 0 set, this value is now the effective address. If bit 0 is set, another memory access is made and the process continues until a memory word is read with bit 0 = 0; that memory word now becomes the effective address. This is *n-level indirect addressing.* There may be *n* words each of which points to another word, which points to another word, and so forth. In practice, it is rare to see more than two levels of indirect address. The possible addressing modes of the Nova Memory Reference instructions are shown in Fig. 9-14.

Table 9-5 shows the Memory Reference instructions. LDA (Load Accumulator) loads the contents of the effective address into accumulator A (0–3). STA (*S*tore *A*ccumulator) stores the contents of accumulator A into the effective address location. ISZ (*I*ncrement and *S*kip If *Z*ero) adds 1 to the contents of the

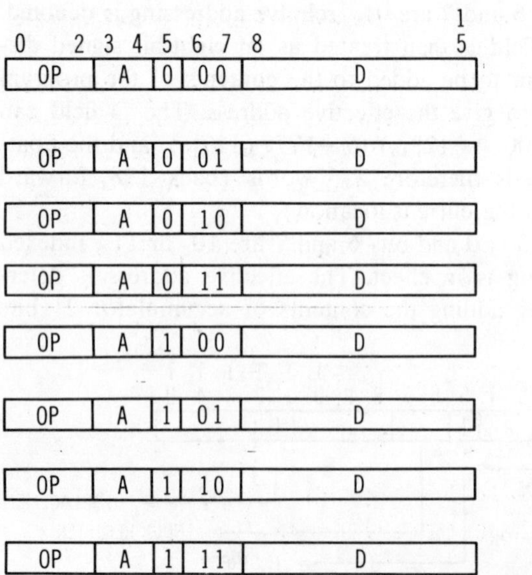

(A) EA is location D of page 0.

(B) EA is (PC)+D.

(C) is (AC2)+D.

(D) EA is (AC3)+D.

(E) EA is *content* of page 0 location D, unless (D) has bit 0 set, in which case another level of indirect addressing is specified, etc.

(F) EA is *content* of location={(PC)+D}, unless content of location has bit 0 set, etc.

(G) EA is *content* of location={(AC2)+D}, unless content of location has bit set, etc.

(H) EA is *content* of location={(AC3)+D}, unless content of location has bit 0 set, etc.

Fig. 9-14. Addressing modes of Memory Reference instructions.

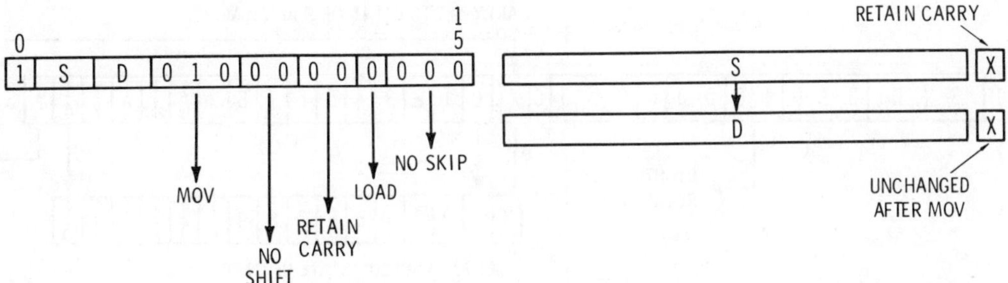

Fig. 9-16. MOV with no other functions.

effective memory address location. If the result is zero, the next instruction in sequence is skipped. DSZ (*De*crement and *S*kip If *Z*ero) works the same as ISZ except that 1 is subtracted from memory. JMP (*Jump*) causes an unconditional jump to the effective memory address. JSR (*J*ump to *S*ub*r*outine) jumps unconditionally to the effective address but stores the contents of the program counter in AC3. Return can thus easily be made to the next instruction in sequence at the end of the subroutine.

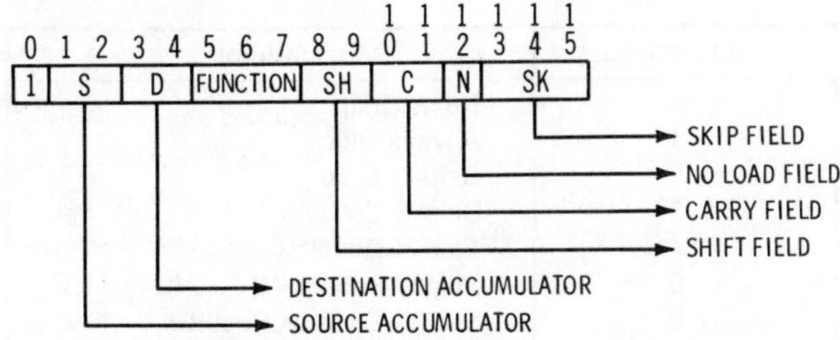

Fig. 9-15. Arithmetic and Logical instruction format.

Arithmetic and Logical Instructions—Arithmetic and Logical instructions perform operations between CPU registers—they do not reference memory. Their format is shown in Fig. 9-15. Bit 0 is always set. An "S" specifies the source accumulator (0–3), and "D" specifies the destination accumulator. The accumulator S may be the same as the D. Bits 5 through 7 are the operation code within the Arithmetic and Logical instruction group. To illustrate the remainder of the fields, consider a MOV (*Move*) instruction. If the MOV is as shown in Fig. 9-16, MOV moves the contents of accumulator S to accumulator D. Period. If the SH field is 01_2, the contents of S are rotated left one bit as shown in Fig. 9-17. The leftmost bit goes into the carry flip-flop and the previous contents of the carry go into bit 15 of the destination accumulator. If the SH field is 10_2, the contents of S are rotated right in similar fashion. See Fig. 9-18. If the SH field is 11_2, the contents of S are "swapped" to the destination register. See Fig. 9-19.

If the C field is 01_2, a zero is put into the carry flip-flop *before* the instruction is performed. If the C field is 10_2, a one is put into the carry flag, and if the C field is 11_2, the complement (inverse) of the carry is used. For example, the previous MOV with SH=10_2 (Fig. 9-18) with the additional code of C=10_2 would result in the operation shown in Fig. 9-20.

If the N bit of the instruction is set, the destination register is not affected (the result is dumped in the bit bucket). The SK field defines a skip condition. After the instruction has been executed, a skip of the next instruction may be performed: always, if C=0, if C≠0, if result=0, if result ≠ 0, if C=0 or result=0, or if C ≠ 0 and result ≠0. The possible skip conditions are shown in Table 9-6.

Needless to say, all of the above microprogrammed fields lead to some weird and wonderful instructions, some even useful. Considering the MOV alone, we can have the combinations shown in Table 9-7, to illustrate a few.

The carry, shift, no-load, and skip fields are in operation for all of the remainder of the Nova Arithmetic and Logical instructions. The other Arithmetic and Logical instructions perform operations from source accumulator to destination accumulator in the same fashion as the MOV. COM (*Com*plement) performs a one's com-

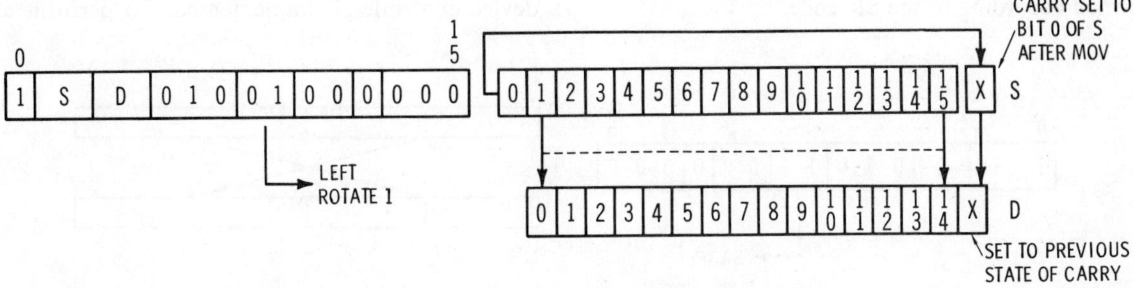

Fig. 9-17. MOV with SH field=01_2.

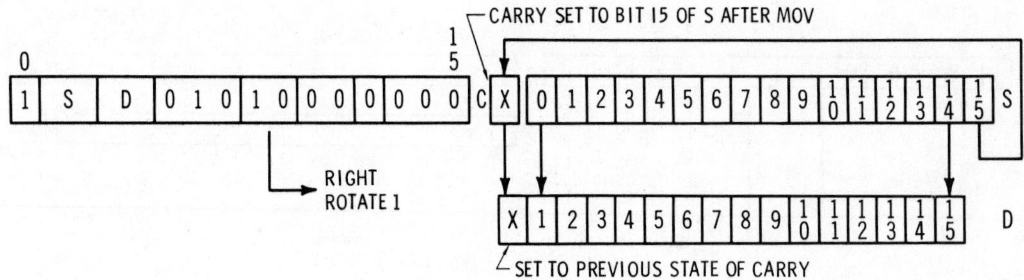

Fig. 9-18. MOV with SH field = 10_2.

plement on the source register data (changes all ones to zeros and all zeros to ones). NEG (*Neg*ate) performs a two's complement. INC (*Inc*rement) increments the contents of the source register. ADC (*Ad*d *C*omplement) adds the one's complement of the source to the contents of the destination register. SUB subtracts the source from the destination. ADD adds the source and destination. AND logically ANDs the source and destination. Note that in all of these functions, the result goes

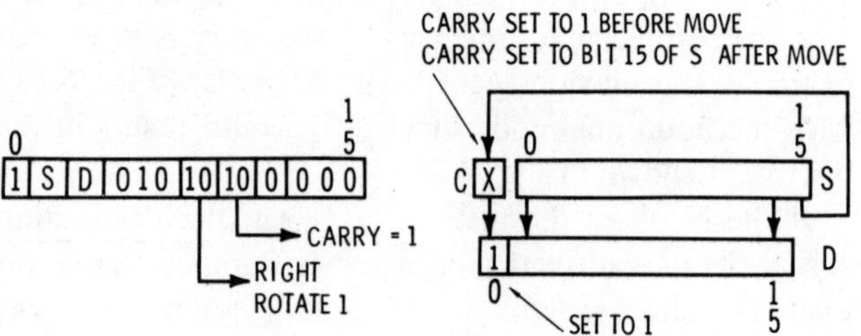

Fig. 9-20. MOV with C field = 10_2.

to the destination register only if the no-load bit is a 0. Table 9-8 lists the Arithmetic and Logical instructions with SH = C = N = SK = 0.

If one or more of the SH, C, N, or SK fields are nonzero, the instruction is implemented as follows:

1. The carry is left alone, set, reset, or complemented according to the state of C.
2. The function is performed on (S), (D), and the current state of C.
3. The result is shifted according to the SH code.
4. If the no-load bit is a 0, the result is sent to the destination register and C.
5. The C and the result are tested and the skip is performed according to the SK code.

Some examples of Arithmetic and Logical instructions with various configurations of SH, C, N, and SK are shown in Table 9-9. Suffice it to say that the Arithmetic and Logical instructions with their microprogrammed fields are sufficient to do most required arithmetic operations in one instruction.

Input/Output Instructions—Input/output device controllers have two flags, Busy and Done, defining the state of the device. If both are clear, the device is idle.

Table 9-6. SK (Skip) Functions

Bits 13–15	SK Condition
0	Never Skip
1	Always Skip
2	Skip if C=0
3	Skip if C≠0
4	Skip if Result= 0
5	Skip if Result≠ 0
6	Skip if C=0 or Result= 0
7	Skip if C≠0 and Result≠ 0

If Busy is set, the device is in operation. When data are available, Busy is reset and Done is set. A third flip-flop in the device controller is set if the device is to interrupt at the end of the I/O operation. The Interrupt flag is set by a special interrupt enable instruction (Mask Out: DOB A, CPU). The Busy and Done flags are partially controlled by two bits in the I/O instruction and partially controlled by the status of the device. Fig. 9-21 shows the format of "Data In" and "Data Out" instructions. Bits 8 and 9 control the Busy, Done flags as shown in Table 9-10, and D is a six-bit device address.

There are three Data In and three Data Out instructions. Which one is used is strictly a function of how the device controller is implemented. To perform an input

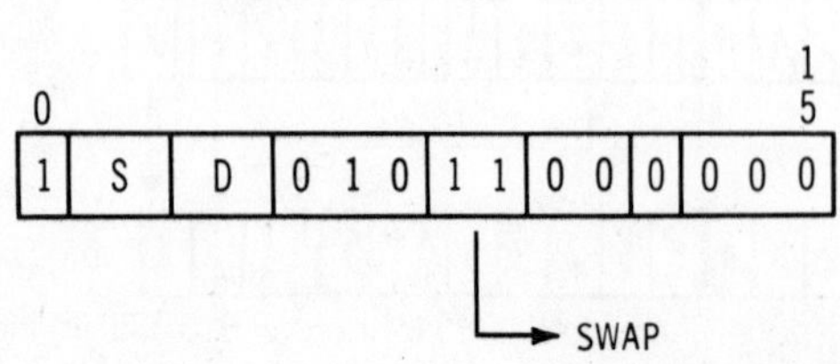

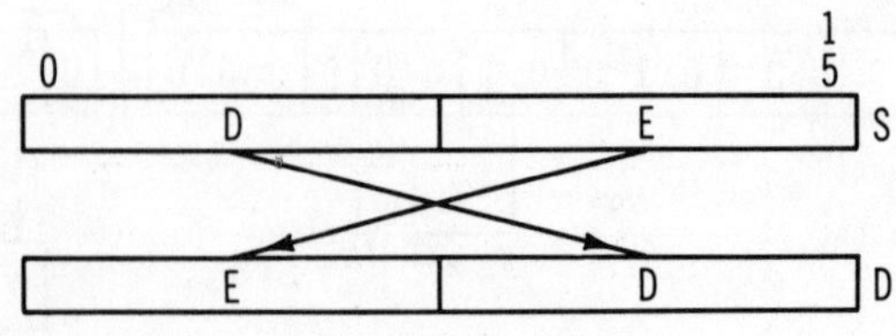

Fig. 9-19. MOV with SH field = 11_2.

Table 9-7. Carry, Shift, No Load, and Skip Functions

Mnemonic	SH	C	N	SK	Result
MOV# 1,1	none	none	yes	none	Does nothing
MOV 1,2	none	none	no	none	(AC1) → AC2
MOVS 1,2	swap	none	no	none	Bits 0–7 of AC1 to bits 8–15 of AC2, and bits 8–15 of AC1 to bits 0–7 of AC1
MOV# 1,1,SZR	none	none	yes	res=0	Tests (AC1) for zero
MOVZL 3,3	left	zero	no	none	(AC3) × 2 → AC3
NOVZR 3,3	right	zero	no	none	(AC3)/2 → AC3
NOVZL 3,3,SNC	left	zero	no	C=1	(AC3) × 2 → AC3, skip if bit 0 of AC3 was set

Table 9-8. Arithmetic and Logical Instructions

MNEMONIC	INSTRUCTION	FORMAT (bits 0 1 2 3 4 5 6 7 8 9 10 11 12 13 14 15)	DESCRIPTION (SH = C = N = SK = 0)	EXECUTION TIME* (μs)
COM	COMPLEMENT	I | S | D | 0 0 0 | SH | C | N | SK	$(\overline{S})$ → D (ONE'S COMPLEMENT)	.8
NEG	NEGATE	I | S | D | 0 0 1 | SH | C | N | SK	TWO'S COMPLEMENT (S) → D	.8
MOV	MOVE	I | S | D | 0 1 0 | SH | C | N | SK	(S) → D	.8
INC	INCREMENT	I | S | D | 0 1 1 | SH | C | N | SK	(S) + 1 → D	.8
ADC	ADD COMPLEMENT	I | S | D | 1 0 0 | SH | C | N | SK	$(\overline{S})$ + (D) → D	.8
SUB	SUBTRACT	I | S | D | 1 0 1 | SH | C | N | SK	(D) − (S) → D	.8
ADD	ADD	I | S | D | 1 1 0 | SH | C | N | SK	(D) + (S) → D	.8
AND	AND	I | S | D | 1 1 1 | SH | C | N | SK	(S) AND (D) → D	.8

* NOVA 800.

Table 9-9. Arithmetic and Logical Examples

Mnemonic	SH	C	N	SK	Result
SUBZL 1,1	left	zero	no	no	1 → AC1 (!!) 0 → C
ADC 3,3	none	none	no	none	all ones → AC3
SUBZ# 1,0,SZC	none	zero	yes	C=0	Skip if AC0 < AC1
ADCZ# 1,0,SZC	none	zero	yes	C=0	Skip if AC0 ≤ AC1

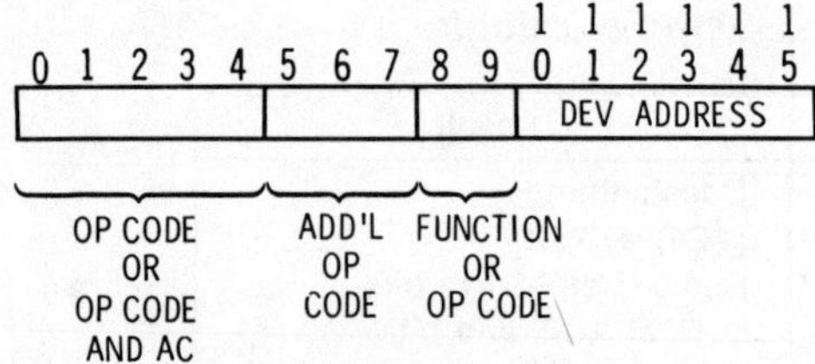

Fig. 9-21. Input/Output instruction format.

Table 9-10. Input/Output Instruction Function Codes

Bits 8–9	Function
00	None
01	Start the device—clear Done, set Busy
10	Clear Busy, Done
11	Special pulse out to device

operation of one byte, for instance, a DIA instruction with the tty address of 10_8 and a function code (bits 8,9) of 01_2 would be done. To set up a DMA operation for magnetic tape, a DOB, DOC, and DOA would be performed to send the address of the buffer, the word count for the transfer, and the function, respectively. The DOA would include a function of 01_2 to start the DMA operation.

Besides the Data In and Data Out instructions, there are four additional instructions to test the state of the device. These are SKPBN (*Skip* if *B*usy is *N*onzero), SKPBZ (*Skip* if *B*usy is *Z*ero), SKPDN (*Skip* if *D*one is *N*onzero), and SKPDZ (*Skip* if *D*one is *Z*ero), and are shown in Table 9-11. A fifth I/O instruction, NIO, does nothing but perform the function specified by bits 8 and 9.

Table 9-11. Input/Output Instructions

MNEMONIC	INSTRUCTION	FORMAT 1 1 1 1 1 1 0 1 2 3 4 5 6 7 8 9 0 1 2 3 4 5	DESCRIPTION	EXECUTION TIME* (μs)
DIA	DATA IN A	0 1 1 | AC | 0 0 1 | F | DEVICE	I/O DATA → AC	2.2
DIB	DATA IN B	0 1 1 | AC | 0 1 1 | F | DEVICE	I/O DATA → AC	2.2
DIC	DATA IN C	0 1 1 | AC | 1 0 1 | F | DEVICE	I/O DATA → AC	2.2
DOA	DATA OUT A	0 1 1 | AC | 0 1 0 | F | DEVICE	(AC) → I/O DEVICE	2.2
DOB	DATA OUT B	0 1 1 | AC | 1 0 0 | F | DEVICE	(AC) → I/O DEVICE	2.2
DOC	DATA OUT C	0 1 1 | AC | 1 1 0 | F | DEVICE	(AC) → I/O DEVICE	2.2
NIO	NO I/O	0 1 1 0 0 | 0 0 0 | F | DEVICE	ONLY FUNCTION CODE APPLIES	2.2
SKPBN	SKIP IF BUSY NONZERO	0 1 1 0 0 | 1 1 1 | 0 0 | DEVICE	IF DEVICE BUSY FLAG = 1, (PC) + 1 → PC	1.4
SKPBZ	SKIP IF BUSY IS ZERO	0 1 1 0 0 | 1 1 1 | 0 1 | DEVICE	IF DEVICE BUSY FLAG = 0, (PC) + 1 → PC	1.4
SKPDN	SKIP IF DONE IS NONZERO	0 1 1 0 0 | 1 1 1 | 1 0 | DEVICE	IF DEVICE DONE FLAG = 1, (PC) + 1 → PC	1.4
SKPDZ	SKIP IF DONE IS ZERO	0 1 1 0 0 | 1 1 1 | 1 1 | DEVICE	IF DEVICE DONE FLAG = 0, (PC) + 1 → PC	1.4

* NOVA 800.

Special Instructions—Special instructions include those to control standard special features (such as the interrupt system) and options (such as multiply/divide). They will not be discussed in detail. Sixteen locations in page 0 are "auto-increment" or "auto-decrement" locations, similar in concept to the PDP-8 auto index. These locations are automatically incremented by one each time they are addressed indirectly. This saves one instruction when those locations are used as pointers to tables and the data in the tables must be addressed sequentially.

Peripherals

The peripheral devices offered are listed in Chart 9-2, along with speeds and special features.

Software

Data General Corp. offers a great deal of software for the Nova series. The basic assembler will run in 4K words and is a two-pass assembler. An "extended" assembler and a "macro" assembler permit user-defined conditional assembly. The editor is a string-oriented editor. Higher-level languages include BASIC, Extended BASIC (with expanded I/O capability for high-speed reader and punch, line printer, and disc), Extended FORTRAN IV, FORTRAN V, and Extended ALGOL. Operating systems include the Stand-Alone Operating System (for magnetic tape or cassette tape), Disc Operating System (DOS), Real Time Operating System (RTOS), and Real Time Disc Operating System (RDOS).

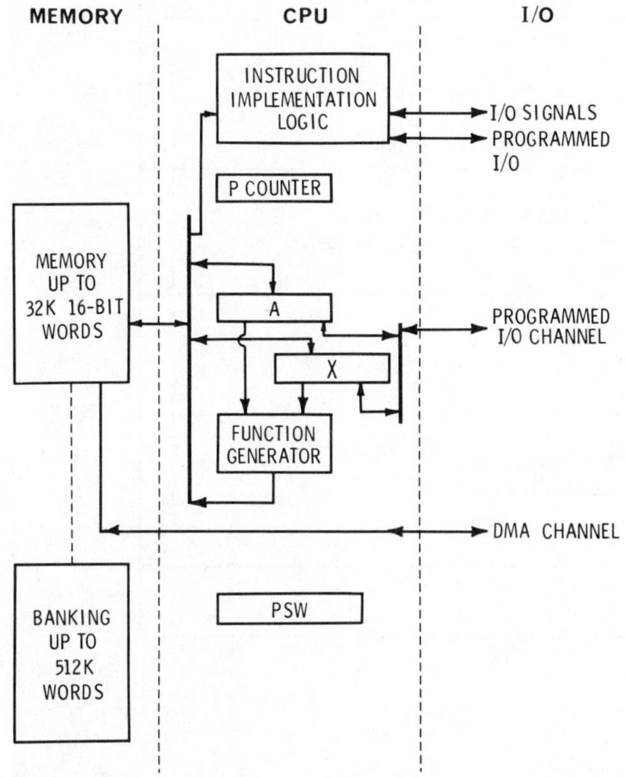

Fig. 9-22. LSI-3/05 architecture.

Price and Availability

Prices for new Data General Equipment start at under $2000 for a MicroNova with nine I/O slots and 4K-word MOS memory. Used equipment appears to be readily available at 40 to 60 percent of the new system cost.

COMPUTER AUTOMATION, INC.

Computer Automation, Inc. (CAI), is one of the larger minicomputer manufacturers and has been in business since about 1968. During that time CAI has introduced several 8-bit and 16-bit models. The latest series of minicomputers is the "LSI" series, including the LSI 2/20 and LSI 2/10, LSI 1-T, LSI-1G, and LSI-3/05. The latest model is the LSI-3/05, which is a 16-bit general-purpose computer with 93 instructions. It is offered in several versions, the least expensive being the "Naked Milli LSI-3/05." This version is the printed-circuit board model sans power supply and panel, and it sells for about $700. The fully packaged model is designated the Alpha LSI-3/05 and sells for under $2000 (see Fig. 1-2 of Chapter 1). Instruction speeds for the LSI-3/05 start at 3.75 microseconds. The LSI-2 series is the most powerful of the models with 188 instructions, including a subset of the LSI-3/05 instructions. Memory speeds are 980 to 1600 nanoseconds. The LSI-1 model has 168 instructions, with core memory and semiconductor memory speeds of 1600 nanoseconds; again, the instruction repertoire is compatible with other models in the LSI series.

Since the LSI-3/05 is the newest and least expensive of all of the CAI minicomputers, the following discussion will describe only the LSI-3/05 subset of instructions.

LSI-3/05 Architecture

The architecture of the LSI-3/05 is shown in Fig. 9-22. The CPU registers include a 16-bit accumulator, designated A, and a 16-bit index register, designated X. Arithmetic is done in two's complement form. An overflow flag (OV) is set whenever there is arithmetic overflow or for other conditions. Arithmetic overflow would occur, for example, in adding two 16-bit values where the result is greater than +32,767 or less than −32,768. Four sense bits from the front panel can be read under program control if they have been set before program execution. A separate sense flag can be set dynamically, that is, while the program is running.

The upper limit of memory is 32K words. However, memory can be extended up to 512K words by mem-

Chart 9-2. Peripheral Options and CPU Options for Nova Series

CPU/Memory Options	
Turnkey (minimum) console:	
Full console:	
Power-fail safe:	Available
Automatic bootstrap:	Available
Real-time clock:	Available. 10-, 100-, 1000-Hz plus line frequency
Additional selector channel:	
Semiconductor memory:	MOS memory 700 ns
Core memory:	800 and 1000 ns
Memory protection:	Available
Memory expansion:	To 128K (Nova 3)
Hardware multiply/divide:	Available
Other:	Floating-point hardware. Memory parity
Teletype	
Tty—33:	Available
Tty (other):	KSR33, KSR35 (10 Hz), ASR-37 (15 Hz)
Tty modification kit:	Available
Other terminals:	
CRT	
Alphanumeric display:	
Graphic display:	
Oscilloscope control:	Available
Printer Plotter	
Line printer:	245 and 356 lines/min. Up to 132 columns
Plotter:	Two types of incremental plotters
Card Reader	
Card reader:	220 or 400 cards per minute
Paper Tape	
Paper tape reader:	300 chars/s
Paper tape punch:	63 chars/s
Magnetic Tape	
Audio cassette tape:	
Cassette tape:	Up to three drives per unit. Philips type
Cartridge tape:	
Reel-to-reel tape:	7-track, 9-track to 120 inches per second
Magnetic Disc	
Fixed head:	64K to 256K 16-bit words. Up to 8/controller
Movable head:	Cartridge or fixed disc. 1.2 to 12.2 megawords
Floppy disc:	Soon to be available
Communications	
Asynchronous interface:	Available
Synchronous interface:	Available
Modem control:	Available. Up to 16 modems (or tty's)
Special-Purpose Interfaces	
ADC:	1 to 128 channels, 8 to 15 bits
DAC:	1 to 32 channels, 8 to 14 bits
Relay driver:	Available
General-purpose parallel:	Available
Other	Multiprocessor (CPU-to-CPU) controller IBM system interface

ory banking. Either byte or word addressing of memory can be performed. Page 0 is 128 locations, and the floating page is 128 words forward and 127 words back. In certain configurations, memory can be interleaved; that is, reads of consecutive instructions will go to separate memory modules, allowing faster effective memory cycle times.

Input/output is performed to or from the A or X registers or directly to memory under DMA control. Multiple DMA controllers are permitted. An "automatic" type of I/O can be performed by the Automatic I/O instruction on an interrupt basis. Transfer rates during this mode are between programmed I/O and DMA transfer rates. Vectored hardware interrupts are implemented along with internal interrupts including a console (control panel) interrupt, real-time clock (optional), and three "traps" (automatic hardware-initiated interrupts) for illegal instructions, nonexistent memory, and power fail.

Physical Features

All chassis in the LSI series are standard 19-inch rack types about 17½ inches deep and 9 inches high. The LSI-3/05 processor board mounts on a larger "motherboard," with additional mounting connectors on the motherboard for memory modules or I/O boards. Either a "Standard" chassis or a "Jumbo" chassis is available. The Jumbo has a larger motherboard with nine pairs of connectors, allowing more plug-in options. The actual LSI-3/05 CPU itself is about 7½ inches by 17 inches in size. The tty cable connects to one of the plug-in modules in the rear of the chassis. The control panel is somewhat unique is that it has a hexadecimal keyboard on the right of the panel. This keyboard replaces the more common data switches on the panel to allow entry of data and addresses. Fig. 9-23 shows the panel.

Instruction Addressing

All instructions are 16 bits long. Memory Reference instructions include scratchpad (page 0), index and byte scratchpad, and word and byte relative. Operands accessed are either 8-bit bytes or 16-bit words. The "byte" mode is set by execution of the Set Byte Mode (SBM) instruction. Once this instruction is executed, the instructions that follow will operate on 8-bit bytes until a Set Word Mode (SWM) instruction changes byte mode to word mode.

Scratchpad instruction format is shown in Fig. 9-24. If the word mode is set, 128 words of page 0 are accessed by the instruction. If the byte mode is set, the first 64 bytes of page 0 can be accessed. The page 0 location is defined by the displacement value D in the instruction. If the I (Indirect) bit is set, the page 0 location points to the word or byte to be accessed. In the byte mode, the byte address format shown in Fig. 9-25 is used. Since 16 bits are needed to specify the byte address, only one level of indirect addressing can be used in the byte mode. (The most significant bit otherwise could be either an indirect flag or part of a valid byte address.) N-level indirect addressing is possible in the word mode (bit 15 is the indirect flag).

The second instruction format is index and byte scratchpad, as shown in Fig. 9-26. If the word mode is set and I=0, the contents of the index register X are added to bits 5 through 0, assumed to be an unsigned displacement of 0 through 63. The result is the effective address. If I=1 for this case, bits 5 through 0 define a page 0 word which is accessed. If bit 15 of this word is set, another indirect level is specified. When the accessed word no longer specifies indirect addressing (bit 15=0), the contents of index register X are added to the final address to yield the effective address. This is called "post" indexing, for obvious reasons. If the byte mode is set and I=0, the displacement value in D (5–0) is added to the contents of the X register in order to get the effective byte address. If I=1, the instruction operates much the same way as in the word mode, except that only one level of indirection is possible.

The third addressing format is word and byte relative format, shown in Fig. 9-27. If the word mode is set and I=0, the effective address is the content of the program counter plus the D field minus 80_{16}. Weird? Not really, at least as far as implementation ease in hardware. The 80_{16} is "excess 128" biasing to simplify address calculation internally. If the effective address is relative back with this scheme, bit 7 is 0; if relative forward, bit 7 is 1. Relative forward 128 and relative back 127 words make up the size of the floating page in this type of addressing. If bit 8 is 1 (indirect), the calculated address is treated as a pointer to the next level of indirection. If the byte mode is set and I=0, only forward addressing of 128 locations is possible—bit 7 is set automatically to a one. If I=1 in byte mode, relative forward and back one-level indirect addressing is permitted, with the address treated as a 16-bit byte address.

The addressing scheme is not as easily understood as that of the PDP-8 or the Nova, but it does offer a great deal of flexibility. A diagram of word and byte addressing is shown in Fig. 9-28.

Instruction Repertoire

The instruction set of the LSI-3/05 (and a portion of other models) consists of the following groups:

- Arithmetic and Logical Memory Reference instructions.
- Data Transfer Memory Reference instructions.
- Program Transfer Memory Reference instructions.
- Immediate instructions.

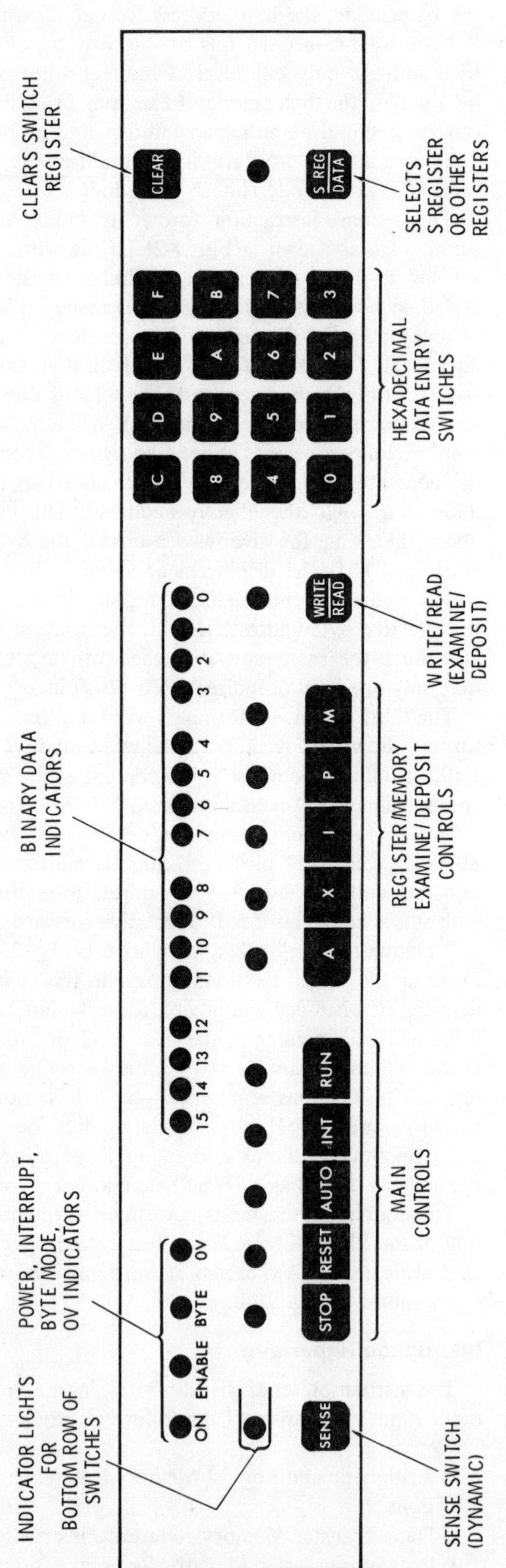

Fig. 9-23. LSI-3/05 control panel.

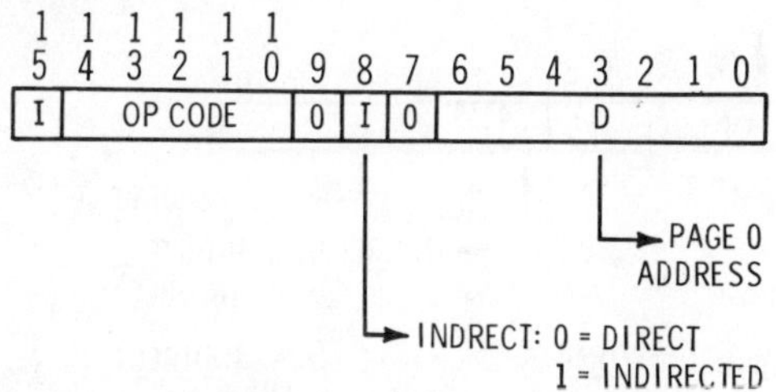

Fig. 9-24. Scratchpad instruction format.

- Conditional Jump instructions.
- Shift instructions.
- Register Change instructions.
- Control instructions.
- Input/Output instructions.

Arithmetic Memory Reference instructions are shown in Table 9-12. For all byte instructions, the byte is treated as a right-justified eight-bit value in bit positions 7 through 0 with zeros in bits 15 through 8 as shown in Fig. 9-29. ADD and ADDB (*Add* and *Add Byte*) add the contents of the effective memory address to the A register and set the overflow flag (OV) if overflow exists. SUB and SUBB (*Sub*tract and *Sub*tract *Byte*) perform a subtract, setting OV if an overflow resulted. AND, IOR, and XOR perform an AND, inclusive OR, and exclusive OR with the contents of the effective ad-

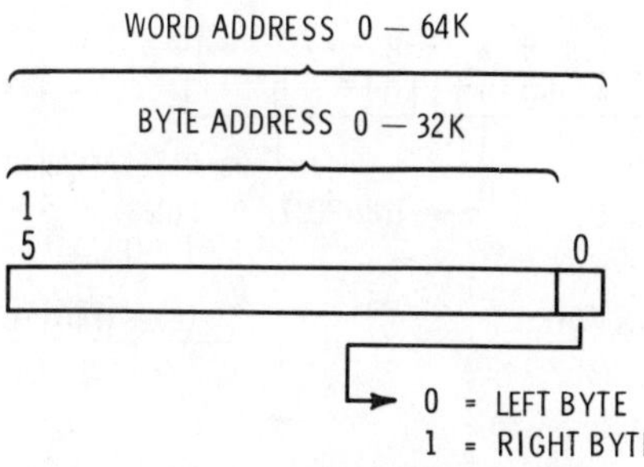

Fig. 9-25. LSI-3/05 byte addressing.

Table 9-12. Arithmetic Memory Reference Instructions

MNEMONIC	INSTRUCTION	FORMAT 111111 5432109876543210	DESCRIPTION	EXECUTION TIME* (μs)
ADD	ADD TO A	1 00010 VARIES	(EA) + (A) → A OV	6.25
ADDB	ADD BYTE TO A	1 00010 VARIES	$(EA)_{BYTE}$ + (A) → A OV	6.25
SUB	SUBTRACT FROM A	1 00011 VARIES	(A) — (EA) → A OV	6.50
SUBB	SUBTRACT BYTE FROM A	1 00011 VARIES	(A) — $(EA)_{BTYE}$ → A OV	6.50
AND	AND TO A	1 00101 VARIES	(EA) AND (A) → A	6.50
ANDB	AND BYTE TO A	1 00101 VARIES	$(EA)_{BYTE}$ AND (A) → A	6.50
IOR	INCLUSIVE-OR TO A	1 01101 VARIES	(EA) OR (A) → A	6.50
IOB	INCLUSIVE-OR BYTE TO A	1 01101 VARIES	$(EA)_{BYTE}$ OR (A) → A	6.50
XOR	EXCLUSIVE-OR TO A	1 00110 VARIES	(EA) XOR (A) → A	6.50
XORB	EXCLUSIVE-OR BYTE TO A	1 00110 VARIES	$(EA)_{BYTE}$ XOR (A) → A	6.50

* FOR CORE MEMORY TO SCRATCHPAD.

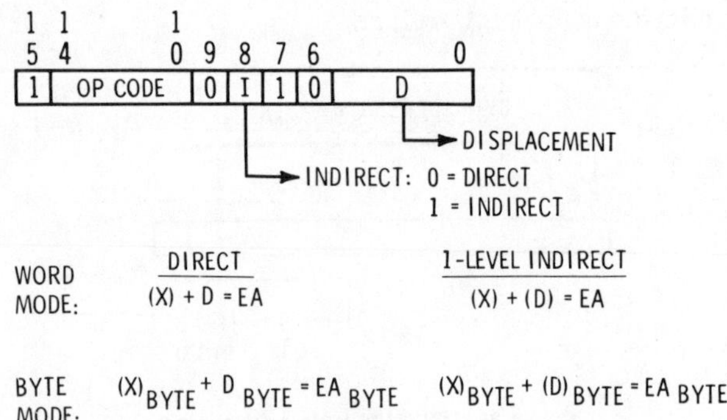

Fig. 9-26. Index and Byte Scratchpad format.

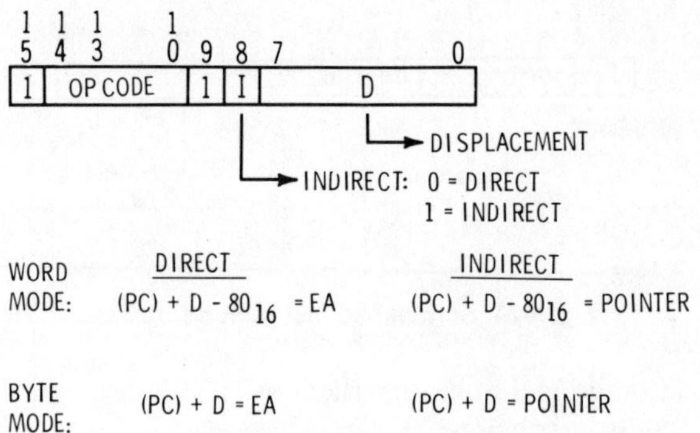

Fig. 9-27. Word and Byte relative format.

dress and (A). ANDB, IORB, and XORB implement the same logical operations but with a byte from the effective address. Because bits 15 through 8 are zeros in the memory operand, ANDB, IORB, and XORB result in zeros in bits 15 through 8 for the ANDB, and no change in the bits for the IORB and XORB.

Data Transfer Memory Reference instructions (Table 9-13) are basically loads and stores of words and bytes. LDA, LDBA, LDX, and LDXB load a memory word (LDA, LDX) into the A and X registers or a memory byte into the A and X registers (LDAB, LDXB). STA, STAB, STX, and STXB store words (STA, STX) or bytes (STAB, STXB) from the A or X registers. Note that a store byte changes only one byte in memory.

Program Transfer Memory Reference instructions are shown in Table 9-14. CMS (*C*ompare *M*emory to A and *S*kip if High or Equal) and CMBS (*C*ompare *M*emory *B*yte and . . .) compare a word or byte from memory to the contents of A. If (A) is greater than the memory operand, a one-word skip occurs. If (A) equals the memory operand, a two-word skip occurs. If (A) is less than the memory operand, no skip occurs. IMS (*I*ncrement *M*emory and *S*kip on Zero Result) increments the contents of the effective address and skips if the contents become 0. OV is set if overflow occurs. JMP (*J*um*p* Unconditional) causes exactly that. JST (*J*ump and *St*ore) causes an unconditional jump to the effective address plus one. The contents of the P register are stored in the effective address.

The Immediate instruction format is shown in Fig. 9-30. The operand, of course, is not fetched from mem-

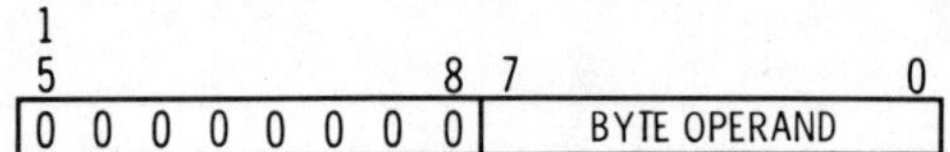

Fig. 9-29. Byte operands.

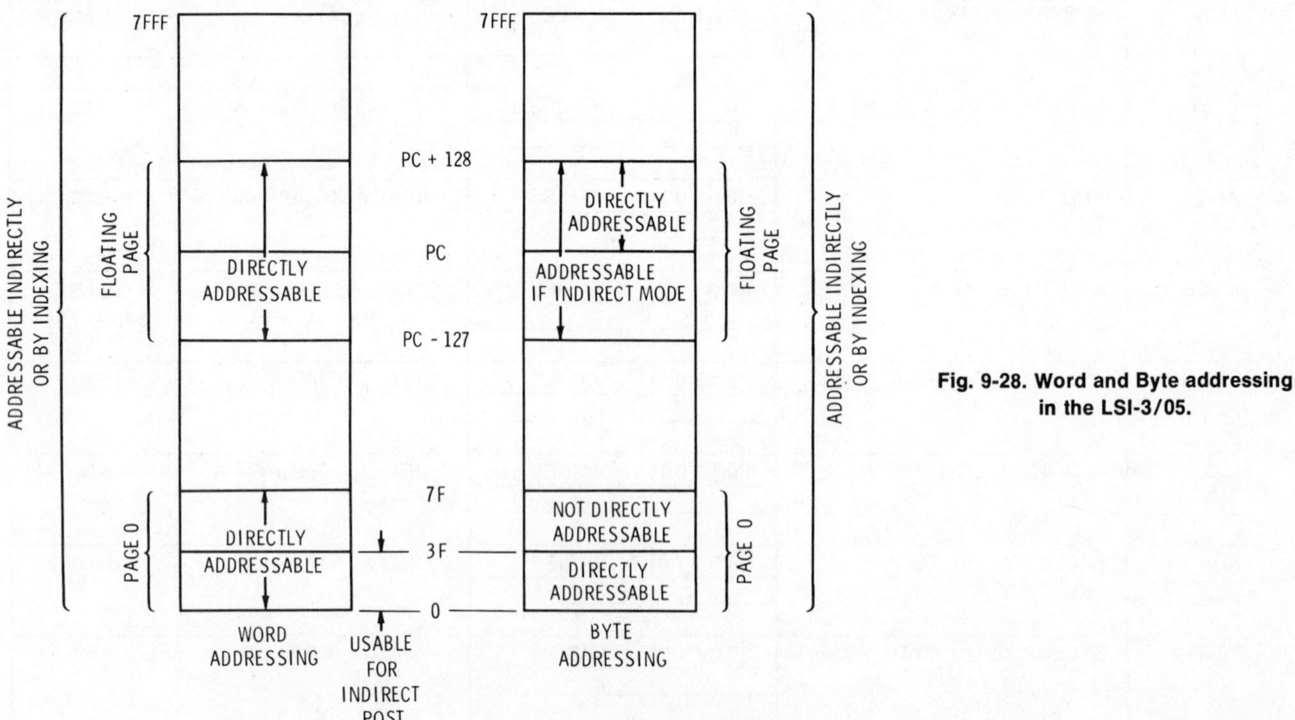

Fig. 9-28. Word and Byte addressing in the LSI-3/05.

Table 9-13. Data Transfer Memory Reference Instructions

MNEMONIC	INSTRUCTION	FORMAT 1 1 1 1 1 1 5 4 3 2 1 0 9 8 7 6 5 4 3 2 1 0	DESCRIPTION	EXECUTION TIME* (μs)
EMA	EXCHANGE MEMORY AND A	1 0 0 1 0 0 VARIES	$(EA) \leftrightarrow A$	8.75
EMAB	EXCHANGE MEMORY BYTE AND A	1 0 0 1 0 0 VARIES	$(EA)_{BYTE} \leftrightarrow A$ $0 \rightarrow A_{15-8}$	8.75
LDA	LOAD A	1 0 0 0 0 0 VARIES	$(EA) \rightarrow A$	5.5
LDAB	LOAD A BYTE	1 0 0 0 0 0 VARIES	$(EA)_{BYTE} \rightarrow A$ $0 \rightarrow A_{15-8}$	5.5
LDX	LOAD X	1 0 1 0 0 0 VARIES	$(EA) \rightarrow X$	5.5
LDXB	LOAD X BYTE	1 0 1 0 0 0 VARIES	$(EA)_{BYTE} \rightarrow X$ $0 \rightarrow X_{15-8}$	5.5
STA	STORE A	1 0 0 0 0 1 VARIES	$(A) \rightarrow EA$	7.75
STAB	STORE A BYTE	1 0 0 0 0 1 VARIES	$(A)_{7-0} \rightarrow EA_{BYTE}$	7.75
STX	STORE X	1 0 1 0 0 1 VARIES	$(X) \rightarrow EA$	7.75
STXB	STORE X BYTE	1 0 1 0 0 1 VARIES	$(X)_{7-0} \rightarrow EA_{BYTE}$	7.75

* FOR CORE MEMORY TO SCRATCHPAD.

ory but is in the instruction itself. Table 9-15 lists the instructions in this group. AAI and AXI (*A*dd to *A* *I*mmediate and *A*dd to *X* *I*mmediate) add the eight-bit immediate value to (A) or (X), setting OV if required. SAI and SXI (*S*ubtract from *A* *I*mmediate and *S*ubtract from *X* *I*mmediate) operate in the same fashion. CAI and CXI (*C*ompare to *A* *I*mmediate and *C*ompare to *X* *I*mmediate) cause a one-word skip if the operand is not equal to (A) or (X). LAP and LXP load the immediate operand into A or X, setting bits 15–8 to zeros. LAM and LXM negate the immediate operand before loading it into A or X.

The Conditional Jump instruction format is shown in Fig. 9-31. These instructions test the sign or contents of A, the contents of X, the OV flag, or the SENSE indicator (console) and perform a jump. Table 9-16 lists these instructions. The jump can be −63 to +64 from

1 1 1 1 1 1
5 4 3 2 1 0 8 7 0
| 0 | 0 | R | 0 | 1 | OP CODE | D |
8 - BIT UNSIGNED IMMEDIATE OPERAND
REGISTER SELECT
0 = A
1 = X

Fig. 9-30. Immediate instruction format.

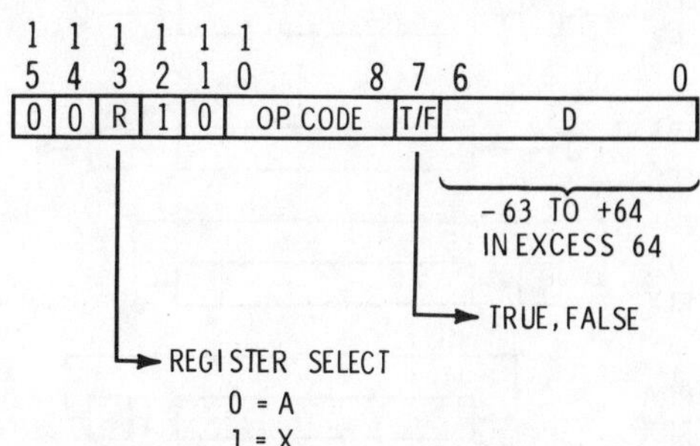

Fig. 9-31. Conditional Jump format.

Table 9-14. Program Transfer Memory Reference Instructions

MNEMONIC	INSTRUCTION	FORMAT 1 1 1 1 1 1 5 4 3 2 1 0 9 8 7 6 5 4 3 2 1 0	DESCRIPTION	EXECUTION TIME* (μs)

CMS	COMPARE MEMORY TO A AND SKIP IF HIGH OR EQUAL	1 0 1 1 1 0 VARIES	COMPARE EA: (A)
			IF (A) > (EA), (PC) + 1 → PC
			IF (A) = (EA), (PC) + 2 → PC
				6.75**

CMSB	COMPARE BYTE AND SKIP IF HIGH OR EQUAL	1 0 1 1 1 0 VARIES	COMPARE $(EA)_{BTYE}$: (A)
			IF (A) > (EA), (PC) + 1 → PC
			IF (A) = (EA), (PC) + 2 → PC
				6.75**

IMS	INCREMENT MEMORY AND SKIP ON ZERO RESULT	1 1 0 1 1 1 VARIES	(EA) + 1 → EA IF (EA) = 0, (PC) + 1 → PC OV	9.75**
JMP	JUMP UNCONDITIONAL	1 0 0 1 1 1 VARIES	EA → PC	6.25
JST	JUMP AND STORE	1 0 1 1 1 1 VARIES	(PC) → EA EA + 1 → PC	9.75

* CORE MEMORY TO SCRATCHPAD.
** NO SKIP.

the current instruction if the condition is met. The A register is tested for greater than zero (JAG), positive (JAP), zero (JAZ), not zero (JAN), less than or equal to zero (JAL), or minus (JAM). The X register is tested for zero or not zero (JXZ, JXN). The SENSE and OV flags are tested for set (JSS, JOS) or reset (JSR, JOR) conditions.

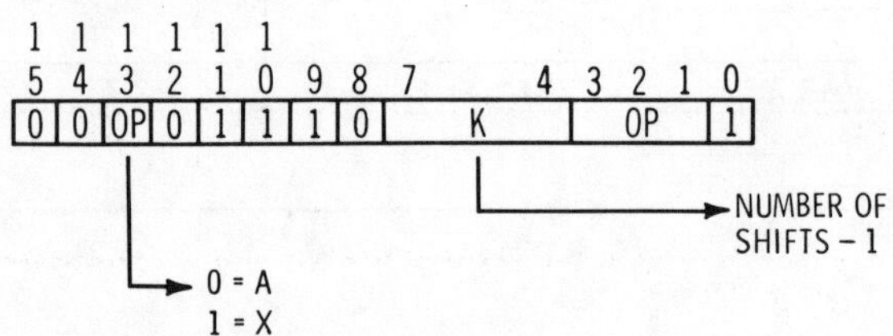

Fig. 9-32. Shift instruction format.

The Shift instruction format is shown in Fig. 9-32. Both A and X can be shifted, and this shift may or may not go through the overflow. Logical and circular shifts may be performed, and more than one shift may be per-

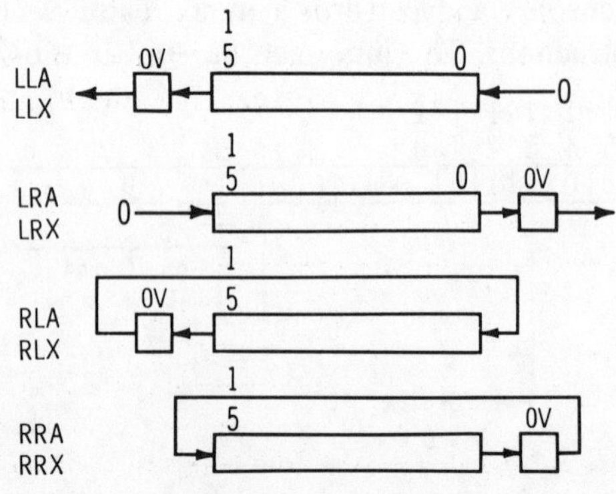

Fig. 9-33. Shift operations.

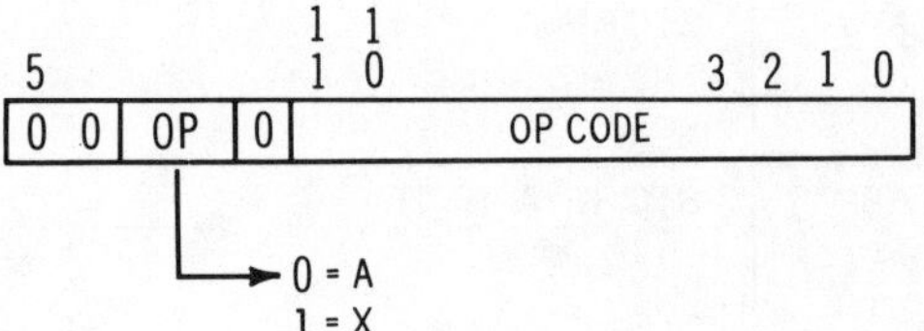

Fig. 9-34. Register Change instruction format.

formed, which is rather unusual for a lower-cost minicomputer. Fig. 9-33 shows the shift operations, and Table 9-17 lists the instructions in this group. LLA and LLX (*L*ogical Shift *L*eft *A* and *L*ogical Shift *L*eft *X*) shift A or X *n* bit positions to the left through the overflow. LRA and LRX perform the same operation to the right. RLA and RLX (*R*otate *A* *L*eft with Overflow and *R*otate *X* *L*eft with Overflow) perform a left circular shift on A or X of *n* bit positions through the OV. RRA and RRX perform a right circular shift in the same fashion.

The Register Change instructions are register-to-register type instructions involving the A register, X register, and OV. Their instruction format is shown in Fig. 9-34. Table 9-18 lists the instructions in this group. NAR (*N*egate *A* *R*egister) and NXR (*N*egate *X* *R*egister) do exactly that, setting OV if overflow occurs. SOV and ROV set or reset the OV flag. TAX (*T*ransfer *A* to *X*), TPX (*T*ransfer *P* to *X*), and TXA (*T*ransfer *X* to *A*) are self-explanatory. NAX (*N*egate *A* to *X*) and NXA (*N*egate *X* to *A*) transfer the two's complement of the source to the destination register, setting OV if overflow occurs. The console data register can be loaded into either the A or X register by an ICA or ICX instruction (*I*nput Console Data to *A*, *X*). Conversely,

Table 9-15. Immediate Instructions

MNEMONIC	INSTRUCTION	FORMAT 1 1 1 1 1 1 5 4 3 2 1 0 9 8 7 6 5 4 3 2 1 0	DESCRIPTION*	EXECUTION TIME** (μs)
AAI	ADD TO A IMMEDIATE	0 0 0 0 1 0 1 1 D	OP + (A) → A OV	5.25
AXI	ADD TO X IMMEDIATE	0 0 1 0 1 0 1 1 D	OP + (X) → X OV	5.25
SAI	SUBTRACT FROM A IMMEDIATE	0 0 0 0 1 0 1 0 D	(A) − OP → A OV	5.25
SXI	SUBTRACT FROM X IMMEDIATE	0 0 1 0 1 0 1 0 D	(X) − OP → X OV	5.25
CAI	COMPARE TO A IMMEDIATE	0 0 0 0 1 1 0 0 D	COMPARE OP: A IF OP ≠(A),(PC) + 1 → PC	5.0***
CXI	COMPARE TO X IMMEDIATE	0 0 1 0 1 1 0 0 D	COMPARE OP: X IF OP ≠ (X),(PC) + 1 → PC	5.0***
LAP	LOAD A POSITIVE IMMEDIATE	0 0 0 0 1 0 0 1 D	OP → A 0 → A_{15-8}	3.75
LXP	LOAD X POSITIVE IMMEDIATE	0 0 1 0 1 0 0 1 D	OP → X 0 → X_{15-8}	3.75
LAM	LOAD A MINUS IMMEDIATE	0 0 0 0 1 0 0 0 D	−OP → A	3.75
LXM	LOAD X MINUS IMMEDIATE	0 0 1 0 1 0 0 0 D	−OP → X	3.75

* OP IS 8-BIT IMMEDIATE OPERAND.
** CORE MEMORY, TO SCRATCHPAD.
*** NO SKIP.

the (A) or (X) can be output to the console data register by OCA or OCX (*O*utput *A, X* to the *C*onsole Data Register). The four bits of the console SENSE register (not the SENSE flag) can be loaded into A or X by an ISA or ISX instruction (*I*nput Console *S*ense Register to *A, X*). The most significant 12 bits of A or X are set to zeros after the transfer.

The instructions in the Control group are used to control status in the CPU (Fig. 9-35). HLT (*Halt*) halts the CPU, while HTR (*H*alt and *R*eset) halts the CPU and generates a system reset signal. SBM and SWM set byte and word modes, respectively.

The CPU has a collection of bits defining the general status of the CPU. Collectively they are known as the *processor status word* (*PSW*) and are shown in Fig. 9-36. OV and Mode have been mentioned. Bit 4 is the console interrupt, bit 5 is the real-time clock interrupt,

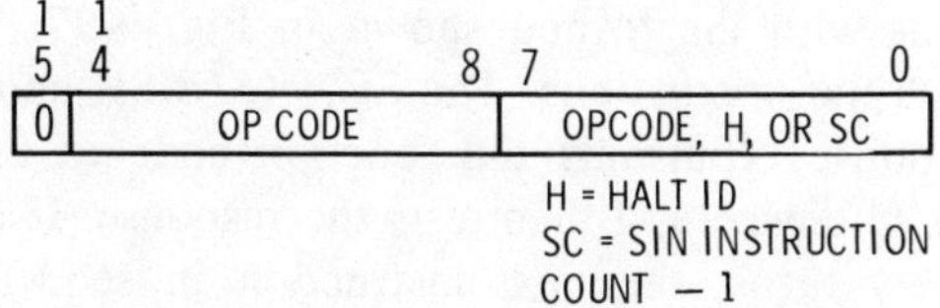

Fig. 9-35. Control instruction format.

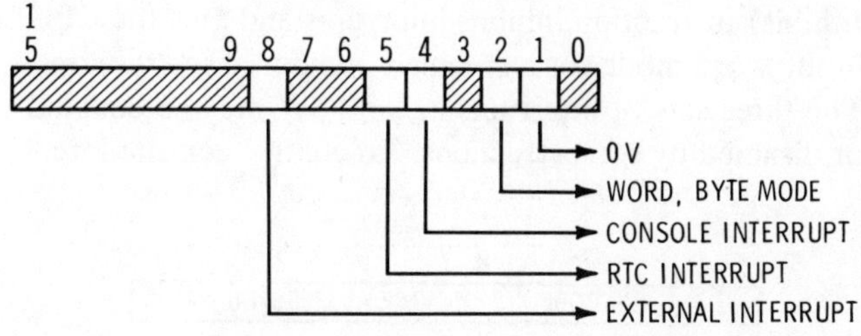

Fig. 9-36. Processor status word.

Table 9-16. Conditional Jump Instructions

MNEMONIC	INSTRUCTION	FORMAT 111111 5432109876543210	DESCRIPTION	EXECUTION TIME* (μs)
JAG	JUMP IF A GREATER THAN ZERO	000101000 D	IF (A) > 0, (PC) + 1 → PC	4.25
JAP	JUMP IF A POSITIVE	000100110 D	IF (A) ≥ 0, (PC) + 1 → PC	4.25
JAZ	JUMP IF A ZERO	000100010 D	IF (A) = 0, (PC) + 1 → PC	4.25
JAN	JUMP IF A NOT ZERO	000100011 D	IF (A) ≠ 0, (PC) + 1 → PC	4.50
JAL	JUMP IF A LESS THAN OR EQUAL TO ZERO	000100101 D	IF A ≤ 0, (PC) + 1 → PC	4.50
JAM	JUMP IF A MINUS	000100111 D	IF A < 0, (PC) + 1 → PC	4.00
JXZ	JUMP IF X ZERO	001100010 D	IF (X) = 0, (PC) + 1 → PC	4.25
JXN	JUMP IF X NOT ZERO	001100011 D	IF (X) ≠ 0, (PC) + 1 → PC	4.50
JSS	JUMP IF SENSE INDICATOR SET	000101100 D	IF SENSE ON, (PC) + 1 → PC	5.5
JSR	JUMP IF SENSE INDICATOR RESET	000101101 D	IF SENSE OFF, (PC) + 1 → PC	4.5
JOS	JUMP IF OVERFLOW SET	001111000 D	IF OV = 1, (PC) + 1 → PC	5.25
JOR	JUMP IF OVERFLOW RESET	001101101 D	IF OV = 0, (PC) + 1 → PC	4.50

* LEAST, CORE MEMORY.

and bit 8 is the external interrupt. The status can be read into the A or X register by SIA or SIX (*S*tatus *I*nput to *A*, *S*tatus *I*nput to *X*) and can be output from A or X by an SOA or SOX instruction. An SIN (*S*tatus *In*hibit) instruction inhibits interrupts and puts the CPU in the word mode for a specified number of instructions. The three sets of interrupts in the PSW may be enabled or disabled by six instructions. To control console interrupts EIN and DIN (*E*nable or *D*isable External *In*terrupt) change bit 8 of the PSW. CIE and CID (*C*onsole *I*nterrupt Enable, *C*onsole *I*nterrupt *D*isable) change bit 4 of the PSW to control console interrupts. RTCE and RTCD control the *R*eal *T*ime *C*lock by bit 5 of the PSW. Table 9-19 shows these instructions.

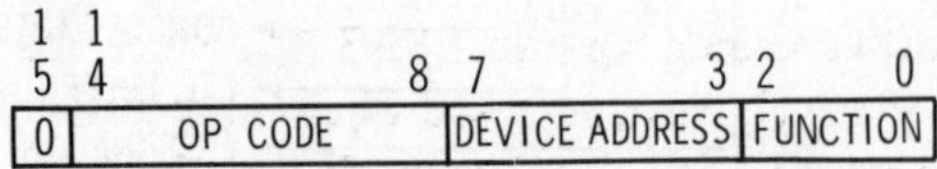

Fig. 9-37. Input/Output instruction format.

The last group of instructions are Input/Output instructions with the format shown in Fig. 9-37. Table 9-20 lists the instructions. The SEN (*SEN*SE and Skip on Response) transmits the function code to the selected I/O device and then tests the response. If a true response returns, the next instruction in sequence is skipped. SEA and SEX (*Se*lect and Present *A*, *Se*lect

Table 9-17. Shift Instructions

MNEMONIC	INSTRUCTION	FORMAT (bits 15 14 13 12 11 10 9 8 7 6 5 4 3 2 1 0)	DESCRIPTION	EXECUTION TIME* (μs)
LLA	LOGICAL SHIFT A LEFT	00001110 K 0001	SEE FIG. 9-43	5.75
LLX	LOGICAL SHIFT X LEFT	00101110 K 0001	SEE FIG. 9-43	5.75
LRA	LOGICAL SHIFT A RIGHT	00001110 K 1001	SEE FIG. 9-43	5.75
LRX	LOGICAL SHIFT X RIGHT	00101110 K 1001	SEE FIG. 9-43	5.75
RLA	ROTATE A LEFT WITH OVERFLOW	00001110 K 0011	SEE FIG. 9-43	5.75
RLX	ROTATE X LEFT WITH OVERFLOW	00101110 K 0011	SEE FIG. 9-43	5.75
RRA	ROTATE A RIGHT WITH OVERFLOW	00001110 K 1011	SEE FIG. 9-43	5.75
RRX	ROTATE X RIGHT WITH OVERFLOW	00101110 K 1011	SEE FIG. 9-43	5.75

* CORE MEMORY, ADD .25 μs/SHIFT.

and Present *X*) transmit the three-bit function code to the selected I/O device along with the Select Control signal. The contents of A or X are then placed on the data bus. Register A or X may contain additional data or control information depending upon the I/O device. There are four input and output instructions. INA and INX transfer 8 or 16 bits of data from the selected I/O device to A or X. OTA and OTX output 8 or 16 bits of data. The Automatic I/O instructions are somewhat unique. They provide a means to output words or bytes (AOT, AOB) from memory or to input words or bytes (AIN, AIB) without CPU intervention, but they do not use DMA. The instruction is placed in an interrupt location along with a negative word count and address pointer. As each word (byte) is transferred, an interrupt occurs and the CPU increments the count and address pointer. At the end of the transfer, the instruction at the interrupt location plus 4 is executed. (See Fig. 9-38.)

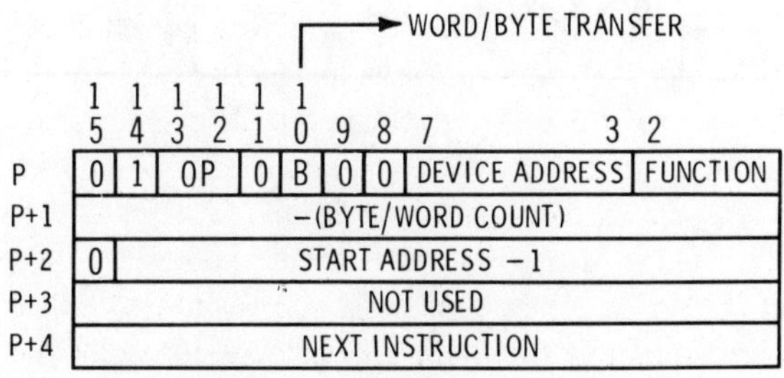

Fig. 9-38. Automatic I/O setup.

Peripherals

The peripheral devices offered for the LSI-3/05 are listed in Chart 9-3 along with speeds and special features.

Software and Availability

Software for the LSI-3/05 includes the Omega conversational assembler/editor, a Real-Time Executive program, loaders, and a set of utilities including a debug package. The utilities are called the AutoMagic Package. A complete set of diagnostic programs for the CPU, memory, and I/O devices is offered. Available but not included in the LSI-3/05 purchase are BASIC, FORTRAN IV, and other software packages. Earlier versions appear to have a more comprehensive set of software, but possibly more development will be done in the software area for the LSI-3/05. Since the LSI-3/05 is relatively new, no used equipment is available, but there may be some earlier models in the LSI-2 and LSI-1 series that are on the market.

Table 9-18. Register Change Instructions

MNEMONIC	INSTRUCTION	FORMAT 111111 5432109876543210	DESCRIPTION	EXECUTION TIME* (μs)
NAR	NEGATE A REGISTER	0000000000000001 0001_{16}	—(A) → A OV	7.0
NXR	NEGATE X REGISTER	0010000000100001 02021_{16}	—(X) → X OV	7.0
SOV	SET OVERFLOW	0000111000010101 $0E15_{16}$	1 → OV	5.5
ROV	RESET OVERFLOW	0000111000010111 $0E17_{16}$	0 → OV	5.5
TAX	TRANSFER A TO X	0010000000000000 2000_{16}	(A) → X	4.75
TPX	TRANSFER P TO X	0010000000010000 2010_{16}	(P) → X	4.75
TXA	TRANSFER X TO A	0000000000100000 0020_{16}	(X) → A	4.75
NAX	NEGATE A TO X	0010000000000001 2001_{16}	—(A) → X OV	7.0
NXA	NEGATE X TO A	0000000000100001 0021_{16}	—(X) → A OV	7.0
ICA	INPUT CONSOLE DATA REGISTER TO A	0000000100000100	(CONSOLE DATA) → A	5.5
ICX	INPUT CONSOLE DATA REGISTER TO X	0010000100000100	(CONSOLE DATA) → X	5.5
OCA	OUTPUT A TO CONSOLE DATA REGISTER	0000010000000100	(A) → CONSOLE DATA	4.75
OCX	OUTPUT X TO CONSOLE DATA REGISTER	0010010000000100	(X) → CONSOLE DATA	4.75
ISA	INPUT CONSOLE SENSE REGISTER TO A	0000000100000001	(CONSOLE SENSE) → A_3-A_0 0 → A_{15}-A_1	5.5
ISX	INPUT CONSOLE SENSE REGISTER TO X	0010000100000001	(CONSOLE SENSE) → X_3-X_0 0 → X_{15}-X_4	5.5

* CORE MEMORY.

Table 9-19. Control Instructions

MNEMONIC	INSTRUCTION	FORMAT 1 1 1 1 1 1 5 4 3 2 1 0 9 8 7 6 5 4 3 2 1 0	DESCRIPTION	EXECUTION TIME* (μs)
HLT	HALT	0 0 0 0 1 1 1 0 0 0 0 0 1 1 0 1 0E0D$_{16}$	HALTS CPU	
HTR	HALT AND RESET	0 0 0 0 0 0 0 0 1 0 0 0 0 0 0 0 0080$_{16}$	HALTS CPU RESETS	
NOP	NO OPERATION	0 0 0 0 0 0 0 0 0 0 0 0 0 0 0 0 0000$_{16}$	NO FUNCTION	4.75
SBM	SET BYTE MODE	0 0 0 0 1 1 1 0 0 0 1 0 0 1 0 1 0E25$_{16}$	SETS BYTE MODE ADDRESSING	5.75
SWM	SET WORD MODE	0 0 0 0 1 1 1 0 0 0 1 0 0 1 1 1 0E27$_{16}$	SETS WORD MODE ADDRESSING	5.75
SIN	STATUS INHIBIT	0 0 0 0 1 1 1 0 N − 1 1 1 1 1 0E0F$_{16}$	INHIBITS INTERRUPTS WORD MODE SET FOR N INSTRUCTIONS	6.25
SIA	STATUS INPUT TO A	0 0 0 0 0 0 0 0 0 0 1 1 0 0 0 0 0030$_{16}$	(PSW) → A	4.75
SIX	STATUS INPUT TO X	0 0 1 0 0 0 0 0 0 0 1 1 0 0 0 0 2030$_{16}$	(PSW) → X	4.75
SOA	STATUS OUTPUT FROM A	0 0 1 1 0 0 0 0 0 0 0 0 0 0 0 0 3000$_{16}$	(A) → PSW	4.75
SOX	STATUS OUTPUT FROM X	0 0 1 1 0 0 0 0 0 0 1 0 0 0 0 0 3020$_{16}$	(X) → PSW	4.75
EIN	ENABLE INTERRUPTS	0 0 0 0 1 1 1 0 1 0 0 0 0 1 0 1 0EB5$_{16}$	1 → PSW_8	7.25
DIN	DISABLE INTERRUPTS	0 0 0 0 1 1 1 0 1 0 0 0 0 1 1 1 0E87$_{16}$	0 → PSW_8	7.25
CIE	CONSOLE INTERRUPT ENABLE	0 0 0 0 1 1 1 0 1 0 0 0 0 1 0 1 0E45$_{16}$	1 → PSW_4	6.25
CID	CONSOLE INTERRUPT DISABLE	0 0 0 0 1 1 1 0 0 1 0 0 0 1 1 1 0E47$_{16}$	0 → PSW_4	6.25
RTCE	REAL-TIME CLOCK ENABLE	0 0 0 0 1 1 1 0 0 1 0 1 0 1 0 1 0E55$_{16}$	1 → PSW_5	6.5
RTCD	REAL-TIME CLOCK DISABLE	0 0 0 0 1 1 1 0 0 1 0 1 0 1 1 1 0E57$_{16}$	0 → PSW_5	6.5

* CORE MEMORY.

Chart 9-3. Peripheral Options and CPU Options for LSI-3/05

CPU/Memory Options	
Turnkey (minimum) console:	Available
Full console:	Available
Power-fail safe:	Standard
Automatic bootstrap:	Standard. Twice line frequency
Real-time clock:	
Additional selector channel:	RAM, ROM, EPROM available
Semiconductor memory:	980 ns to 1200 ns
Core memory:	
Memory protection:	To 512K bytes
Memory expansion:	
Hardware multiply/divide:	
Other:	
Teletype	
Tty—33:	Available
Tty (other):	
Tty modification kit:	Available (Under $100)
Other terminals:	
CRT	
Alphanumeric display:	24 lines by 80 columns
Graphic display:	
Oscilloscope control:	
Printer Plotter	
Line printer:	120 chars/s, 80 columns
Plotter:	
Card Reader	
Card reader:	285 cards/min
Paper Tape	
Paper tape reader:	300 chars/s
Paper tape punch:	Paper-tape reader/punch. Punch is 75 chars/s
Magnetic Tape	
Audio cassette tape:	
Cassette tape:	
Cartridge tape:	
Reel-to-reel tape:	25-ips, 9-track, 7-in reels
Magnetic Disc	
Fixed head:	
Movable head:	4.9M bytes storage, one fixed, one removable
Floppy disc:	Dual floppy disc available
Communications	
Asynchronous interface:	Available
Synchronous interface:	Available
Modem control:	Available
Special-Purpose Interfaces	
ADC:	Available
DAC:	Available
Relay driver:	Available
General-purpose parallel:	Available
Other	

Table 9-20. Input/Output Instructions

MNEMONIC	INSTRUCTION	FORMAT 0 1 2 3 4 5 6 7 8 9 1 1 1 1 1 1 0 1 2 3 4 5	DESCRIPTION	EXECUTION TIME* (μs)
SEN	SENSE AND SKIP ON RESPONSE	0 0 0 0 0 1 1 0 DEV FUN	IF RESPONSE, (PC) + 1 → PC	4.75
SEA	SELECT AND PRESENT A	0 0 0 0 0 1 0 0 DEV FUN	(A) → DATA BUS FUNCTION CODE → I/O	4.75
SEX	SELECT AND PRESENT X	0 0 1 0 0 1 0 0 DEV FUN	(X) → DATA BUS FUNCTION CODE → I/O	4.75
INA	INPUT TO A REGISTER	0 0 0 0 0 0 0 1 DEV FUN	I/O DEVICE → A	5.5
INX	INPUT TO X REGISTER	0 0 1 0 0 0 0 1 DEV FUN	I/O DEVICE → X	5.5
OTA	OUTPUT A REGISTER	0 0 0 0 0 0 1 0 DEV FUN	(A) → I/O DEVICE	4.75
OTX	OUTPUT X REGISTER	0 0 1 0 0 0 1 0 DEV FUN	(X) → I/O DEVICE	4.75
AIB	AUTOMATIC INPUT BYTE TO MEMORY	0 1 0 0 0 1 0 1 DEV FUN	SEE FIG. 9-36	20.0
AIN	AUTOMATIC INPUT WORD TO MEMORY	0 0 0 0 0 1 0 1 DEV FUN	SEE FIG. 9-36	19.75
AOB	AUTOMATIC OUTPUT BYTE FROM MEMORY	0 1 1 0 0 1 0 1 DEV FUN	SEE FIG. 9-36	18.5
AOT	AUTOMATIC OUTPUT WORD FROM MEMORY	0 0 1 0 0 1 0 1 DEV FUN	SEE FIG. 9-36	18.5

* CORE MEMORY.

INTERDATA, INC.

Interdata is another large minicomputer manufacturer, having been in business since 1969. Current models are of two basic types: a 16-bit series oriented toward a 16-bit data bus, designated the 7/16, and a set of 32-bit machines, designated the 7/32 and 8/32. The latest model is a new version of the 7/16 called the 6/16. Earlier models included the Interdata 4 and 5, Interdata 70, 80, and 85. All models are based on the same instruction set, and 16-bit models are upward-compatible with 32-bit machines.

Interdata instructions are similar in format to the IBM 360/370 series, and in general they are a fairly powerful set. Since many manufacturers have been committed to making newer machines downward-compatible with previous models, it certainly helps to have started off with a powerful instruction set initially, and this is Interdata's strongest feature.

The Interdata Model 6/16 discussed here is the newest of the line and is somewhat less expensive than previous models but has about the same capability. The Model 6/16 is shown in Fig. 9-39.

Model 6/16 Architecture

The Model 6/16 architecture is shown in Fig. 9-40. There are 16 general-purpose registers of 16 bits each in the CPU. The registers may be used both for accumulators and index registers. Four condition code flags (C, V, G, and L) represent carry, overflow, greater than zero condition, and less than zero condition, and may be tested under program control for conditional

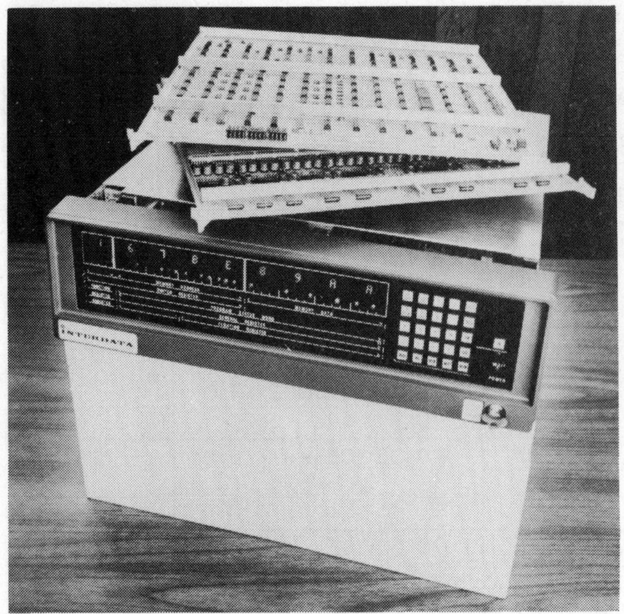

Courtesy Interdata, Inc.

Fig. 9-39. Interdata Model 6/16 minicomputer.

branching. Byte or word arithmetic operations may be performed in the CPU. Memory size is expandable in 8K-byte increments to 64K bytes. The machine is byte oriented, but 16-bit words are accessed from memory. Core memory has a 1-microsecond cycle time, while MOS memory has a 500-nanosecond cycle.

Input/output devices pass data under programmed I/O to CPU registers. A "selector channel" permits DMA operations between high-speed devices and memory at rates up to a million 16-bit words a second. The selector channel is essentially an integral DMA controller which competes with the CPU for memory cycles. Rather than having a separate DMA controller on each I/O interface, the selector channel is a separate entity. Although vectored interrupts are implemented, there is only one external interrupt vector. However, by use of an "automatic I/O" feature, automatic vectoring of external interrupts is possible. The remaining interrupt vectors are used for "trap" types of interrupts, such as illegal instructions or arithmetic faults. These, combined with a "supervisor call" type of interrupt, which puts the machine into a supervisory state, facilitate using the machine in an operating system environment.

Physical Features

The 6/16 is 7 inches high by 26 inches deep with a standard 19-inch rack width. The CPU is on a single board, with memory modules coming in 8K-byte increments on 15-inch printed-circuit boards. The standard chassis comes with eight subassembly slots. Several options come in half-size boards. The control panel is separately priced from the main chassis and comes in either a binary or hexadecimal version or "turnkey" version with minimal controls. The hexadecimal panel is similar

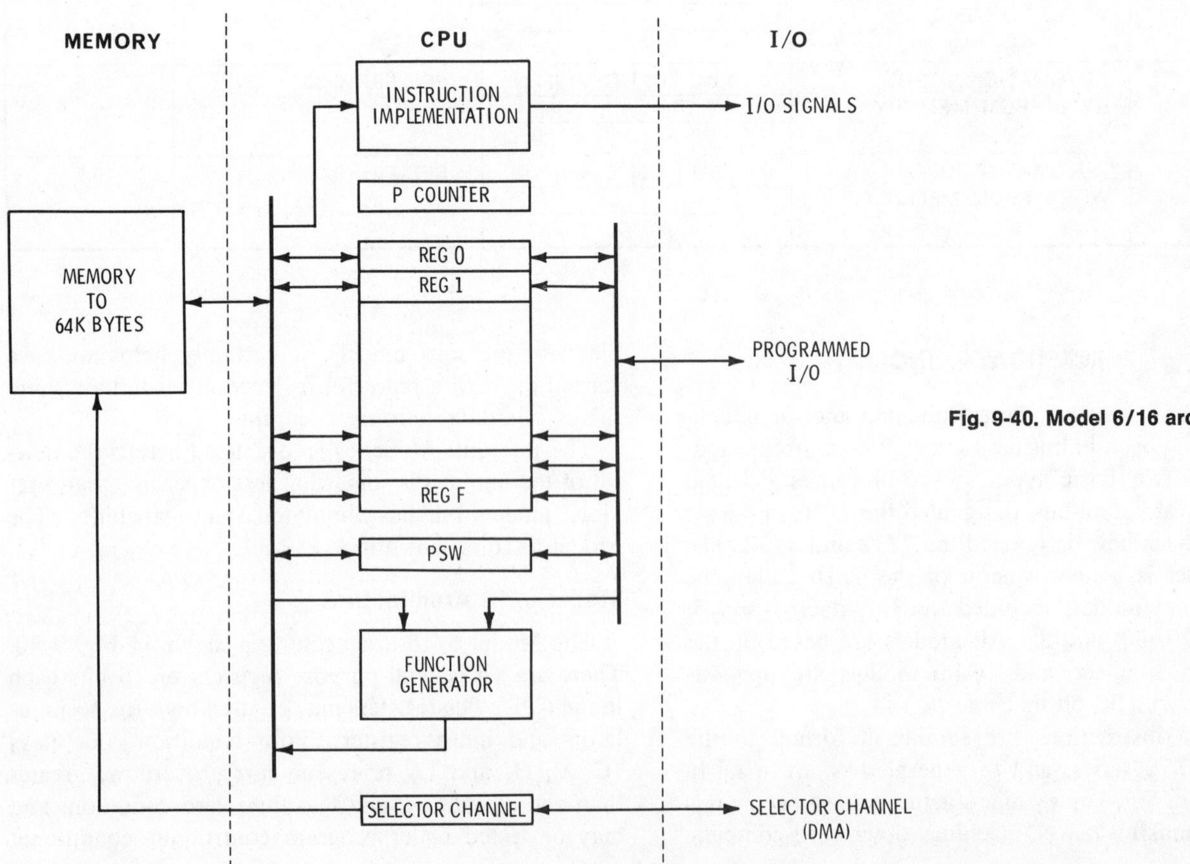

Fig. 9-40. Model 6/16 architecture.

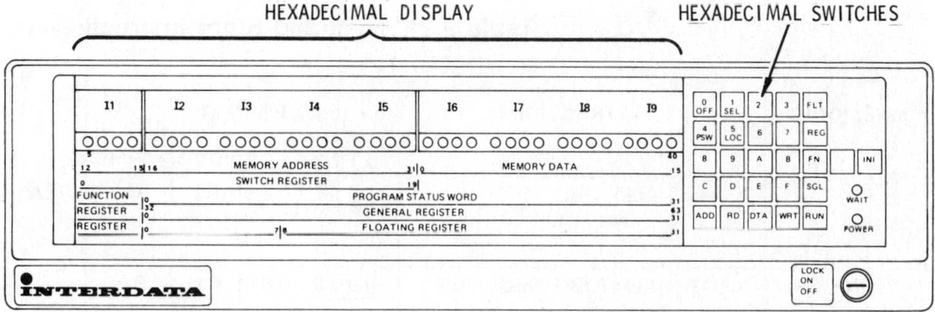

Fig. 9-41. Hexadecimal control panel.

to that of the Computer Automation LSI-3/05 and is shown in Fig. 9-41.

Instruction Formats

There is no indirect addressing in the 6/16, and no need for it since all of the 64K core can be accessed directly. Instruction word sizes are either 16 or 32 bits. The register-to-register instruction format is shown in Fig. 9-42. R1 is the source register (0–15), and R2 is the destination register. The second type of 16-bit instruction is shown in Fig. 9-42B and is called a short format instruction (SF). It is essentially an immediate type instruction with an operand in bits 12 through 15 and with the register operand specified in bits 8 through 11.

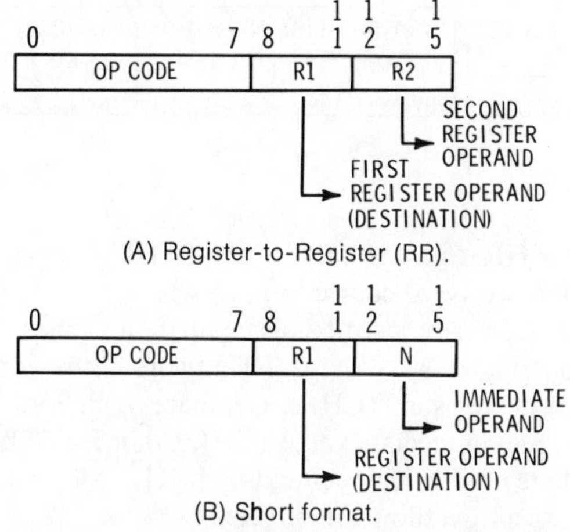

(A) Register-to-Register (RR).

(B) Short format.

Fig. 9-42. Register-to-Register instruction format.

Fig. 9-43 shows the 32-bit instruction formats. The RX type of format allows indexing using CPU registers. The effective address is computed by adding the contents of the index register specified in X2 to the displacement value in A2. R1 specifies an operand in a CPU register. The second type of long instruction is a register immediate (RI) type. Here R1 contains one operand and the second operand is computed by adding the contents of X2 to the value found in the immediate field, I2.

Data Formats

In the 6/16 data are organized in three ways: eight-bit bytes called, logically enough, *bytes,* 16-bit values called *halfwords* (reflecting the IBM approach), and 32-bit

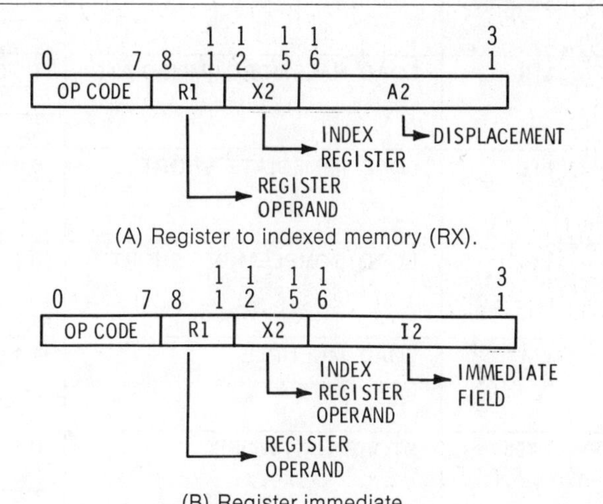

(A) Register to indexed memory (RX).

(B) Register immediate.

Fig. 9-43. Thirty-two-bit instruction format.

values called *fullwords.* Most instructions involve either bytes or halfwords.

Instruction Repertoire

Instructions in the 6/16 may be divided into the following groups:

- Load and Store instructions.
- Fixed-Point Arithmetic instructions.
- Logical instructions.
- Shift and Rotate instructions.
- Byte Processing instructions.
- Conditional branches.
- System Control instructions.
- Input/Output instructions.

Load and Store instructions (Table 9-21) involve halfword (16-bit) operands. LH (*L*oad *H*alfword) loads a 16-bit value into a CPU register. LHR (*L*oad *H*alfword *R*egister) transfers the contents of R2 to R1. LHI (*L*oad *H*alfword *I*mmediate) loads R1 with the 16-bit immediate value. LIS (*L*oad *I*mmediate *S*hort) loads R1 with the four-bit value found in the immediate field. Higher-order bits are set to 0. LCS (*L*oad *C*omplement *S*hort) loads the two's complement of the four-bit immediate value into R1 (1001_2 becomes $111111111111\ 0111_2$). LM (*L*oad *M*ultiple) loads up to 16 registers with a block of data in memory. R1 specifies the starting register. If R1=0, for instance, R0 through RF are

Table 9-21. Load and Store Instructions

MNEMONIC	INSTRUCTION	FORMAT (bits 0–15)	DESCRIPTION	EXECUTION TIME* (μs)
LH	LOAD HALFWORD	10001000 | R1 | X2 A2	(EA) → R1 CC	3.0
LHR	LOAD HALFWORD REGISTER	00001000 | R1 | R2	(R2) → R1 CC	1.0
LHI	LOAD HALFWORD IMMEDIATE	11001000 | R1 | X2 I2	I2 + (X2) → R1 CC	2.0
LIS	LOAD IMMEDIATE SHORT	00100100 | R1 | N	N → R1 CC	1.0
LCS	LOAD COMPLEMENT SHORT	00100101 | R1 | N	− N → R1	1.0
LM	LOAD MULTIPLE	11010001 | R1 | X2 A2	(EA) — (EA + N) → R1 — R1 + N	2.75 + 1.0 × N**
STH	STORE HALFWORD	01000000 | R1 | X2 A2	(R1) → EA	3.75
STM	STORE MULTIPLE	11010000 | R1 | X2 A2	(R1) — (R1 + N) → EA — EA + N	2.75 + 1.0 × N**

* 1.0-μs CORE MEMORY.
** N = NUMBER OF REGISTERS.

loaded with the contents of the effective address to the effective address plus 31_{10} (byte addressing). If R1 = 8, R8 through RF are loaded with (EA) through (EA +15). STM (*St*ore *M*ultiple) operates in the same fashion as LM, except in reverse, storing the register contents. These are powerful instructions for reentrant coding. *St*ore *H*alfword (STH) stores R1 into the effective address.

Fixed-Point Arithmetic instructions are shown in Table 9-22. AH (*A*dd *H*alfword) adds the memory operand to R1. AHR (*A*dd *H*alfword *R*egister) adds R2 to R1. AHI (*A*dd *H*alfword *I*mmediate) adds the 16-bit immediate operand to (R1). AIS (*A*dd *I*mmediate *S*hort) adds the four immediate bits to the contents of R1. All condition codes are utilized for the above instructions. AHM (*A*dd *H*alfword to *M*emory) performs the same add as AH, except that the result goes to the effective address. Two ACH and ACHR (*A*dd with *C*arry *H*alfword) instructions perform the same operations as AH and AHR, except that the state of the carry is added to the result.

Six Subtract Halfword instructions are implemented in much the same way as the six Add Halfword instructions (there is no Subtract Halfword to Memory). They are SH, SHR, SHI, SIS, SCH, and SCHR. The carry in the latter two is, of course, a borrow.

Three Compare instructions compare a memory location contents (CM, *Com*pare Halfword), the contents of another register (CHR, *C*ompare *H*alfword *Reg*ister), or an immediate value (CHI, *C*ompare *H*alfword *I*mmediate) with the contents of R1. All condition codes except overflow are affected.

Both signed and unsigned multiply and divide instructions are available as options.

Logical instructions are shown in Table 9-23. NH (A*n*d *H*alfword) ANDs a memory operand with (R1) and puts the result into R1. NHR (A*n*d *H*alfword *R*egister) uses a register operand to perform the same function. NHI (A*n*d *H*alfword *I*mmediate) ANDs the immediate operand with R1. The G and L condition codes are affected.

OH (*O*r *H*alfword), OHR (*O*r *H*alfword *R*egister), and OHI (*O*r *H*alfword *I*mmediate) operate in the same fashion as the AND instructions, except that the OR function is performed. Three exclusive OR instructions operate similarly (XHR, XH, XHI). Three Compare instructions (CLH, CLHR,CLHI) operate the same way as the previous Compares except that the

Table 9-22. Fixed-Point Arithmetic Instructions

MNEMONIC	INSTRUCTION	FORMAT 1 1 1 1 1 1 0 1 2 3 4 5 6 7 8 9 0 1 2 3 4 5	DESCRIPTION	EXECUTION TIME* (μs)
AH	ADD HALFWORD	0 1 0 0 1 0 1 0 | R1 | X2 A2	(EA) + (R1) → R1 CC	3.0
AHR	ADD HALFWORD REGISTER	0 0 0 0 1 0 1 0 | R1 | R2	(R1) + (R2) → R1 CC	1.0
AHI	ADD HALFWORD IMMEDIATE	1 1 0 0 1 0 1 0 | R1 | X2 I2	(R1) + I2 + (X2) → R1 CC	2.0
AIS	ADD IMMEDIATE SHORT	0 0 1 0 0 1 1 0 | R1 | N	(R1) + N → R1 CC	1.0
AHM	ADD HALFWORD TO MEMORY	0 1 1 0 0 0 0 1 | R1 | X2 A2	(EA) + (R1) → EA CC	4.25
ACH	ADD WITH CARRY HALFWORD	0 1 0 0 1 1 1 0 | R1 | X2 A2	(EA) + (R1) + C → R1 CC	3.0
ACHR	ADD WITH CARRY HALFWORD REGISTER	0 0 0 0 1 1 1 0 | R1 | R2	(R1) + (R2) + C → R1 CC	1.0
SH	SUBTRACT HALFWORD	0 1 0 0 1 0 1 1 | R1 | X2 A2	(R1) — (EA) → R1 CC	3.0
SHR	SUBTRACT HALFWORD REGISTER	0 0 0 0 1 0 1 1 | R1 | R2	(R1) — (R2) → R1 CC	1.0
SHI	SUBTRACT HALFWORD IMMEDIATE	1 1 0 0 1 0 1 1 | R1 | X2 I2	(R1) — (I2 + (X2)) → R1	2.0
SIS	SUBTRACT IMMEDIATE SHORT	0 0 1 0 0 1 1 1 | R1 | N	(R1) — N → R1 CC	1.0
SCH	SUBTRACT WITH CARRY HALFWORD	0 1 0 0 1 1 1 1 | R1 | X2 A2	(R1) — EA — C → R1 CC	3.0
SCHR	SUBTRACT WITH CARRY HALFWORD REGISTER	0 0 0 0 1 1 1 1 | R1 | R2	(R1) — (R2) — C → R1 CC	1.0
CH	COMPARE HALFWORD	0 1 0 0 1 0 0 1 | R1 | X2 A2	(R1) : (EA) CC	3.0
CHR	COMPARE HALFWORD REGISTER	0 0 0 0 1 0 0 1 | R1 | R2	(R1) : (R2) CC	1.25
CHI	COMPARE HALFWORD IMMEDIATE	1 1 0 0 1 0 0 1 | R1 | X2 I2	(R1) : (I2 + (X2)) CC	2.25

* 1.0-μs CORE MEMORY.

Table 9-23. Logical Instructions

MNEMONIC	INSTRUCTION	FORMAT (bits 0–15)	DESCRIPTION	EXECUTION TIME* (μs)
NH	AND HALFWORD	01000100 | R1 | X2 / A2	(R1) AND (EA) → R1 CC	3.0
NHR	AND HALFWORD REGISTER	00000100 | R1 | R2	(R1) AND (R2) → R1 CC	1.0
NHI	AND HALFWORD REGISTER IMMEDIATE	11000100 | R1 | X2 / I2	(R1) AND (I2 + (X)) → R1 CC	2.0
OH	OR HALFWORD	01000110 | R1 | X2 / A2	(R1) OR (EA) → R1 CC	3.0
OHR	OR HALFWORD REGISTER	00000110 | R1 | R2	(R1) OR (R2) → R1 CC	1.0
OHI	OR HALFWORD IMMEDIATE	11000110 | R1 | X2 / I2	(R1) OR (I2 + (X)) → R1 CC	2.0
XH	EXCLUSIVE-OR HALFWORD	01000111 | R1 | X2 / A2	(R1) XOR (EA) → R1 CC	3.0
XHR	EXCLUSIVE-OR HALFWORD REGISTER	00000111 | R1 | R2	(R1) XOR (R2) → R1 CC	1.0
XHI	EXCLUSIVE-OR HALFWORD IMMEDIATE	11000111 | R1 | X2 / I2	(R1) XOR (I2 + (X2)) → R1 CC	2.0
CLH	COMPARE LOGICAL HALFWORD	01000101 | R1 | X2 / A2	(R1) : (EA) LOGICAL CC	3.0
CLHR	COMPARE LOGICAL HALFWORD REGISTER	00000101 | R1 | R2	(R1) : (R2) LOGICAL CC	1.0
CLHI	COMPARE LOGICAL HALFWORD IMMEDIATE	11000101 | R1 | X2 / I2	(R1) : (I2 + (X2)) LOGICAL CC	2.0
THI	TEST HALFWORD IMMEDIATE	11000011 | R1 | X2 / I2	(R1) AND (I2 + (X2)) CC	2.0

* 1-μs CORE MEMORY.

16-bit operands are treated as unsigned operands. This is useful for comparisons of memory addresses where a valid memory value of $80A5_{16}$ would represent a negative number and give an invalid algebraic comparison result. THI (*T*est *H*alfword *I*mmediate) takes the 16-bit immediate value and ANDs it with the contents of R1. R1 remains unchanged and only condition codes G and L are affected.

There are many types of shifts in the 6/16, but they are variations of the arithmetic shift, logical shift, and circular (rotate) shift performed either right or left and on either one or two registers. They are shown in Table 9-24.

In the *S*hift *L*eft *H*alfword *L*ogical (SLHL) or *S*hift *R*ight *H*alfword *L*ogical (SRHL) instructions, the contents of R1 are shifted left or right the number of bits specified by the contents of the effective address. *S*hift *L*eft *L*ogical *S*hort (SLLS) or its right shift equivalent (SRLS) shift (R1) left or right the number of bits specified in the short immediate value (up to 15). *S*hift *L*eft *L*ogical (SLL) and *S*hift *R*ight *L*ogical (SRL) shift (R1) *and* (R1+1), treated as a 32-bit value, the speci-

Table 9-24. Shift Instructions

MNEMONIC	INSTRUCTION	FORMAT (bits 0 1 2 3 4 5 6 7 8 9 10 11 12 13 14 15)	DESCRIPTION*	EXECUTION TIME** (μs, MINIMUM)
SLL	SHIFT LEFT LOGICAL	11101101 | R1 | X2 I2	SHIFT (R1, R1 + 1) LEFT (I2 + (X2)) PLACES CC	5.0
SRL	SHIFT RIGHT LOGICAL	11101100 | R1 | X2 I2	SHIFT (R1, R1 + 1) RIGHT (I2 + (X2)) PLACES CC	5.25
SLHL	SHIFT LEFT HALFWORD LOGICAL	11001101 | R1 | X2 I2	SHIFT (R1) LEFT (I2 + (X2)) PLACES CC	4.0
SLLS	SHIFT LEFT LOGICAL SHORT	00000001 | R1 | N	SHIFT (R1) LEFT N PLACES CC	2.0
SRHL	SHIFT RIGHT HALFWORD LOGICAL	11001100 | R1 | X2 I2	SHIFT (R1) RIGHT (I2 + (X2)) PLACES CC	4.25
SRLS	SHIFT RIGHT LOGICAL SHORT	10010000 | R1 | N	SHIFT (R1) RIGHT N PLACES CC	2.25
SLA	SHIFT LEFT ARITHMETIC	11101111 | R1 | X2 I2	SHIFT (R1, R1 + 1) LEFT (12 + (X2)) PLACES CC	6.25
SLHA	SHIFT LEFT HALFWORD ARITHMETIC	11001111 | R1 | X2 I2	SHIFT (R1) LEFT (I2 + (X2)) PLACES CC	5.0
SRA	SHIFT RIGHT ARITHMETIC	11101110 | R1 | X2 I2	SHIFT (R1, R1 + 1) RIGHT (I2 + (X2)) PLACES CC	6.25
SRHA	SHIFT RIGHT HALFWORD ARITHMETIC	11001110 | R1 | X2 I2	SHIFT (R1) RIGHT (I2 + (X2)) PLACES CC	5.25
RLL	ROTATE LEFT LOGICAL	11101011 | R1 | X2 I2	ROTATE (R1, R1 + 1) LEFT (I2 + (X2)) PLACES CC	5.25
RRL	ROTATE RIGHT LOGICAL	11101010 | R1 | X2 I2	ROTATE (R1, R1 + 1) RIGHT (I2 + (X2)) PLACES CC	5.25

* SEE FOLLOWING FIGURES.
** 1-μs CORE MEMORY.

fied number of shifts. All condition codes except C are set for the above shifts. These shifts are shown in Fig. 9-44.

There are four arithmetic shift instructions: *S*hift *R*ight or *L*eft *H*alfword *A*rithmetic (SRHA, SLHA) and Shift *R*ight or *L*eft *A*rithmetic (SRA, SLA). The SHRA and SLHA operate only on the contents of R1, while SLA and SRA operate on the double-register pair R1, R1+1, treated as a 32-bit value. As previously mentioned, in an arithmetic shift the sign bit is maintained or propagated during the shift. The number always retains the same sign after the shift. SRHA and SLHA shift (R1) the number of shifts specified by the contents of the effective address. SRA and SLA shift (R1, R1+1) the number of shifts specified. Condition codes G and L are influenced, and V is set to 0. The arithmetic shifts are shown in Fig. 9-45.

There are two rotate shifts: Rotate Right Logical (RRL) and Rotate Left Logical (RLL). Both operate on fullwords (32 bits) and are shown in Fig. 9-46. Condition codes G and L are affected.

The Byte Processing instructions are shown in Table 9-25. *L*oad *B*yte (LB) and *L*oad *B*yte *R*egister (LBR) load the R1 register with the byte operand from mem-

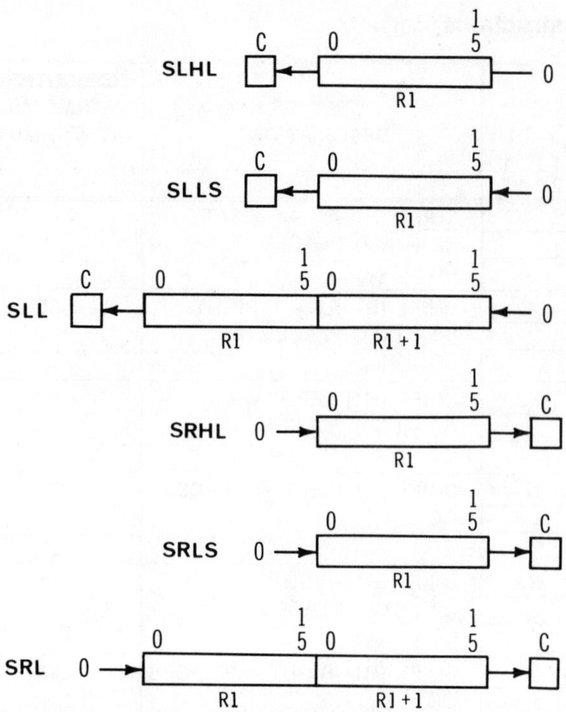

Fig. 9-44. Logical shift implementation.

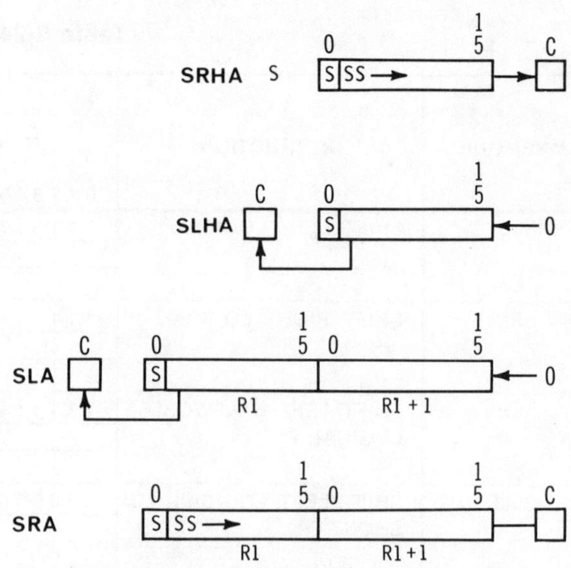

Fig. 9-45. Arithmetic shift implementation.

ory or with bits 8 through 15 of the R2 register. The byte is loaded into bits 8 through 15, and bits 0 through 7 are forced to zeros. *S*tore *B*yte (SB) stores bits 8 through 15 of R1 into the effective address. SBR (*S*tore *B*yte *R*egister) stores bits 8 through 15 of R1 into R2, but does not change bits 0 through 7. *Ex*change *B*yte *R*egister (EXBR) takes the two bytes in R2, swaps them, and stores them into R1. R1 and R2 may be the same register. *C*ompare *L*ogical *B*yte (CLB) compares bits 8 through 15 of R1 to the memory operand and sets condition codes C, G, and L accordingly. The comparison is a logical (unsigned) comparison rather than an arithmetic comparison.

The next group of instructions, the Conditional Branch instructions, are used to test the condition codes. These are shown in Table 9-26. The conditional branches can be subdivided into three groups: branch on true or false, branch and link, and branch on index. Branch on true or false uses a four-bit value, M1, which replaces the R1 field. M1 is a mask that determines which of the four condition codes are to be tested. If $M1 = 0000_2$, no bits are to be tested. If $M1 = 1010_2$, C and G are to be tested. If $M1 = 1111_2$, all codes are to be tested. A branch on false instruction ANDs the M1 value with the contents of the condition codes and then branches if the result is zero. A branch on true instruction ANDs the M1 value with the contents of the condition codes and then branches if one or more bits are set. To test for zero, for example, the M1 field would specify 0011_2 and a branch on false would be programmed. This branch on false would essentially be a branch on zero, since the false condition can be met only if G and L are both zero. The condition that G and L both be 0 specifies that the first operand was neither greater than or less than the second. In practice, it is not necessary to remember the values for the masks for greater than, less than, etc., since the assembler will assemble mnemonics into the proper masks.

*B*ranch on *F*alse *C*ondition (BFC) tests the condition codes in the above fashion and branches to the effective address if the condition is false. *B*ranch on *F*alse *C*ondition *R*egister (BFCR) branches indirectly to the contents of R2 if the M1 condition is met. *B*ranch on *F*alse Condition Backward *S*hort (BFBS) and *B*ranch on *F*alse Condition *F*orward *S*hort (BFFS) use the four-bit N-value to branch forward or backward from the current instruction if the false condition is met. BTC, BTCR, BTBS, and BTFS operate exactly the same as the branch on false instruction except that the true condition causes the branch. An unconditional branch can easily be performed by using $M1 = 000_2$ and a branch on false condition.

*B*ranch *a*nd *L*ink (BAL) and *B*ranch *a*nd *L*ink *R*egister (BALR) unconditionally branch to the effective address (BAL) or address in R2 (BALR), and place the address of the next instruction in sequence in R1.

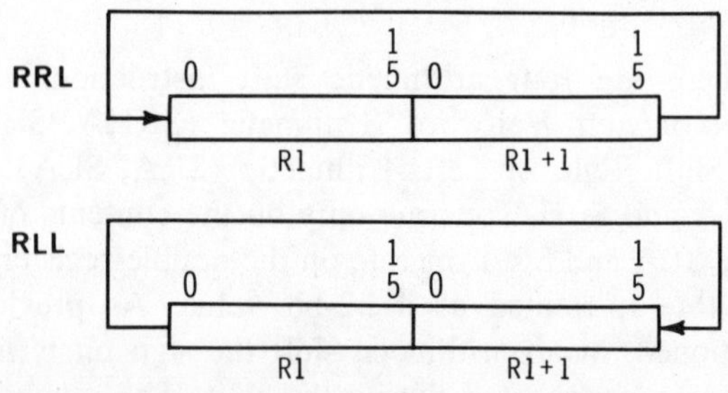

Fig. 9-46. Rotational shift implementation.

Table 9-25. Byte Processing Instructions

MNEMONIC	INSTRUCTION	FORMAT (bits 0–15)	DESCRIPTION	EXECUTION TIME* (μs)
LB	LOAD BYTE	11010011 | R1 | X1 A2	$(EA)_{BYTE} \rightarrow A1_{8-15}$ $0 \rightarrow R1_{0-7}$	3.5
LBR	LOAD BYTE REGISTER	10010011 | R1 | R2	$(R2)_{8-15} \rightarrow R1_{8-15}$ $0 \rightarrow R1_{0-7}$	1.25
EXER	EXCHANGE BYTE REGISTER	10010100 | R1 | R2	$(R2)_{0-7} \rightarrow R1_{8-15}$ $(R2)_{8-15} \rightarrow R1_{0-7}$	1.0
SB	STORE BYTE	11010010 | R1 | X2 A2	$(R1)_{8-15} \rightarrow EA_{BYTE}$	4.5
SBR	STORE BYTE REGISTER	10010010 | R1 | R2	$(R1)_{8-15} \rightarrow R2_{8-15}$	2.0
CLB	COMPARE LOGICAL BYTE	11010100 | R1 | X2 A2	$(R1)_{8-15} : (EA)_{BYTE}$ CC	3.5

* 1-μs CORE MEMORY.

```
R1   FOR RESULT
R2   START
R3   INCREMENT
R4   END

        LIS    R0,0
        LIS    R1,1
        LIS    R2,1
        LHI    R3,100
LOOP    ADR    R1,R0
        BXLE   R2, LOOP
------------------------------
        (R1) = SUM OF NUMBERS
               FROM 1 TO 100
```

Fig. 9-47. BXLE example.

*B*ranch on Inde*x* *L*ow or *E*qual (BXLE) is used to implement an instruction loop. Prior to execution, the register specified by R1 must contain a start index value or memory address. Register R1+1 must contain an increment value, and R1+2 must contain an end value. When the instruction is executed, the increment value (R1+1) is added to the start value (R1) and the result is compared to the end value (R1+2). If (R1) is less than or equal to (R1+2), the branch is performed, if not, the next instruction is executed. This is an extremely powerful instruction for loops, as is shown in Fig. 9-47. *B*ranch on Inde*x* *H*igh (BXH) is set up exactly the same way, but it branches on the inverse.

The remainder of the Conditional Branch instructions are not new instructions but are variations of BFC and BTC with various mask values. Mnemonics in the assembler are provided for branching on zero, not zero, plus, minus, not plus, not minus, carry, overflow, low, not low, equal, and not equal. A NOP can also be implemented by BTC where M1 = 0000_2.

The System Control instructions are basically instructions to load, exchange, or modify the *program status word* (*PSW*). The PSW is a collection of 32 bits which reflect the current state of the machine (see Fig. 9-48). Bits 16 through 31 are the program counter. Bits 12 through 15 are the condition codes. The remainder of the bits enable or disable interrupts (bits 1 through 6), enable or disable the WAIT mode (bit 0), or enable or

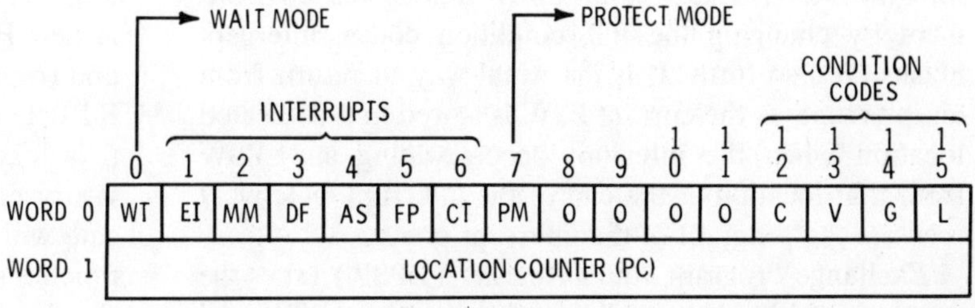

Fig. 9-48. Program status word format.

Table 9-26. Conditional Branch Instructions

MNEMONIC	INSTRUCTION	FORMAT (bits 0 1 2 3 4 5 6 7 8 9 10 11 12 13 14 15)	DESCRIPTION	EXECUTION TIME* (μs)
BFC	BRANCH ON FALSE CONDITION	01000011 | M1 | X2 A2	IF (CC) AND (M1) = 0, (EA) → PC	2.0
BFCR	BRANCH ON FALSE CONDITION REGISTER	00000011 | M1 | R2	IF (CC) AND (M1) = 0, (R2) → PC	1.0
BFBS	BRANCH ON FALSE CONDITION BACKWARD SHORT	00100010 | M1 | N	IF (CC) AND (M1) = 0, (PC) — N → PC	1.0
BFFS	BRANCH ON FALSE CONDITION FORWARD SHORT	00100011 | M1 | N	IF (CC) AND (M1) = 0, (PC) + N → PC	1.0
BTC	BRANCH ON TRUE CONDITION	01000010 | M1 | X2 A2	IF (CC) AND (M1) ≠ 0, (EA) → PC	2.0
BTCR	BRANCH ON TRUE CONDITION REGISTER	00000010 | M1 | R2	IF (CC) AND (M1) ≠ 0, (R2) → PC	1.0
BTBS	BRANCH ON TRUE CONDITION BACKWARD SHORT	00100000 | M1 | N	IF (CC) AND (M1) ≠ 0, (PC) — N → PC	1.0
BTFS	BRANCH ON TRUE CONDITION FORWARD SHORT	00100001 | M1 | N	IF (CC) AND (M1) ≠ 0, (PC) + N → PC	1.0
BAL	BRANCH AND LINK	01000001 | R1 | X2 A2	(PC) → R1 (EA) → PC	2.25
BALR	BRANCH AND LINK REGISTER	00000001 | R1 | R2	(PC) → R1 (R2) → PC	1.25
BXLE	BRANCH ON INDEX LOW OR EQUAL	11000001 | R1 | RX A2	(R1 + 1) + (R1) → R1 IF (R1) ≦ (R1 + 2), EA → PC	3.25
BXH	BRANCH ON INDEX HIGH	11000000 | R1 | RX A2	(R1 + 1) + (R1) → R1 IF (R1) > (R1 + 2), EA → PC	3.25

* 1-μs CORE MEMORY.

disable the protect mode (bit 7). The protect mode is used in operating systems to prevent a user from executing "privileged" instructions such as System Control instructions and I/O. *L*oad *P*rogram *S*tatus *W*ord (LPSW, Table 9-27) loads the fullword from the EA into the PSW. This will instantly change the environment by changing the PC, condition codes, interrupt masks, and so forth. It is the usual way to return from an interrupt, as the current PSW is stored in a dedicated location when the interrupt occurs; doing an LPSW from that location at the end of the interrupt effectively reenters the program at the interrupt point.

*E*xchange *P*rogram *S*tatus *R*egister (EPSR) takes the contents of bits 0 through 15 of the current PSW and stores them in R1. The content of R2 replaces bits 0 through 15 of the PSW. This instruction enables rapid switching of interrupt masks and other flags in the PSW. SVC (*S*uper*v*isor *C*all) is essentially a software interrupt. The effective address is placed in location 94_{16}–95_{16}. The current PSW is saved in locations 96_{16}–99_{16}. A new PSW is loaded from $9A_{16}$ and $9B_{16}$ (bits 0–15) and from one of sixteen PC values in $9C_{16}$ to BB_{16}. The R1 field determines which one of the sixteen, 0 through f, is loaded. The SVC is generally used in the supervisory mode when a user program wishes to communicate with the operating system for I/O service or other functions. The SINT (*S*imulate *Int*errupt) is used to simulate an interrupt signal from an external device

Table 9-27. System Control Instructions

MNEMONIC	INSTRUCTION	FORMAT 111111 0123456789012345	DESCRIPTION	EXECUTION TIME* (μs)
LPSW	LOAD PROGRAM STATUS WORD	11000010 | R1 | X2 A2	(EA, EA + 1) → PSW	5.75
EPSR	EXCHANGE PROGRAM STATUS REGISTER	10010101 | R1 | R2	PSW_{0-15} → R1 R2 → PSW_{0-15}	3.0
SVC	SUPERVISOR CALL	11100001 | R1 | X2 A2	(SEE TEXT)	7.5
SINT	SIMULATE INTERRUPT	11100010 | R1 | X2 I2	(SEE TEXT)	7.5

* 1-μs CORE MEMORY.

whose device number is in bits 8 through 15 of the instruction. The SINT is used to perform the automatic I/O discussed a little further on.

The Input/Output instructions are shown in Table 9-28. The read and write instructions transfer 8, 16, or 64 bits to or from a selected device on the multiplexer bus. *R*ead *D*ata (RD) and *R*ead *D*ata *R*egister (RDR) read in 8 bits from the device addressed by bits 8 through 15 of R1. The byte is stored in memory (RD) or in R2 (RDR). *R*ead *H*alfword (RH) and *R*ead *H*alfword *Register* (RHR) read 16 bits of data from the device specified in R1 and store the data in memory (RH) or R2 (RHR). *R*ead *B*lock (RB) reads 64 bits from the device specified in R1 and stores the 8 bytes of

Table 9-28. Input/Output Instructions

MNEMONIC	INSTRUCTION	FORMAT 111111 0123456789012345	DESCRIPTION	EXECUTION TIME* (μs)
AI	ACKNOWLEDGE INTERRUPT	11011111 | R1 | X2 A2	ADDRESS OF INTERRUPT DEVICE → R1 DEVICE STATUS → EA, CC	6.25
AIR	ACKNOWLEDGE INTERRUPT REGISTER	10011111 | R1 | R2	ADDRESS OF INTERRUPT DEVICE → R1 DEVICE STATUS → R2, CC	3.25
SS	SENSE STATUS	11011101 | R1 | X2 A2	STATUS OF DEVICE → EA, CC $(R1_{8-15})$ = DEVICE ADDRESS	5.5
SSR	SENSE STATUS REGISTER	10011101 | R1 | R2	STATUS OF DEVICE → R2, CC $(R1_{8-15})$ = DEVICE ADDRESS	2.5
OC	OUTPUT COMMAND	11011110 | R1 | X2 A2	$(R1_{8-15})$ = DEVICE ADDRESS $(EA)_{BYTE}$ → DEVICE CC	4.0
OCR	OUTPUT COMMAND REGISTER	10011110 | R1 | R2	$(R1_{8-15})$ = DEVICE ADDRESS $(R2_{8-15})$ → DEVICE CC	2.5
RD	READ DATA	11011011 | R1 | X2 A2	$(R1_{8-15})$ = DEVICE ADDRESS $DEVICE_{BYTE}$ → EA	5.0
RDR	READ DATA REGISTER	10011101 | R1 | R2	$(R1_{8-15})$ = DEVICE ADDRESS $DEVICE_{BTYE}$ → R2 CC	2.5

Table 9-28—Continued

MNEMONIC	INSTRUCTION	FORMAT 111111 0123456789012345	DESCRIPTION	EXECUTION TIME* (μs)
RH	READ HALFWORD	11011001 | R1 | X2 A2	$(R1_{8-15})$ = DEVICE ADDRESS $DEVICE_{WORD}$ → EA CC	6.75
RHR	READ HALFWORD REGISTER	10011001 | R1 | R2	$(R1_{8-15})$ = DEVICE ADDRESS $DEVICE_{WORD}$ → R2	2.75
RB	READ BLOCK	11010111 | R1 | X2 A2	$(R1_{8-15})$ = DEVICE ADDRESS (EA — EA + 3) = BUFFER START, END; $DEVICE_{8\ BYTES}$ → BUFFER	9.0 MIN
RBR	READ BLOCK REGISTER	10010111 | R1 | R2	$(R1_{8-15})$ = DEVICE ADDRESS (R2), (R2 + 1) = BUFFER START, END $DEVICE_{8\ BYTES}$ → BUFFER CC	7.75 MIN
WD	WRITE DATA	11011010 | R1 | X2 A2	$(R1_{8-15})$ = DEVICE ADDRESS $(EA)_{BYTE}$ → DEVICE CC	4.0
WDR	WRITE DATA REGISTER	10011010 | R1 | R2	$(R1_{8-15})$ = DEVICE ADDRESS $(R2_{8-15})$ → DEVICE CC	2.5
WH	WRITE HALFWORD	11011000 | R1 | X2 A2	$(R1_{8-15})$ = DEVICE ADDRESS $(EA)_{WORD}$ → DEVICE CC	4.25
WHR	WRITE HALFWORD REGISTER	10011000 | R1 | R2	$(R1_{8-15})$ = DEVICE ADDRESS (R2) → DEVICE CC	2.75
WB	WRITE BLOCK	11010110 | R1 | X2 A2	$(R1_{8-15})$ = DEVICE ADDRESS (EA — EA + 3) = BUFFER START, END $BUFFER_{8\ BYTES}$ → DEVICE CC	9.0 MIN
WBR	WRITE BLOCK REGISTER	10010110 | R1 | R2	$(R1_{8-15})$ = DEVICE ADDRESS (R2), (R2 + 1) = BUFFER START, END $BUFFER_{8\ BYTES}$ → DEVICE CC	7.75 MIN
AL	AUTOLOAD	11010101 | R1 | X2 A2	(SEE TEXT)	12.75 MIN

* 1-μs CORE MEMORY.

data in the effective address to the effective address plus 7. *R*ead *B*lock *R*egister (RBR) performs the same operation except that (R2) contains the starting address of the data buffer and (R2+1) contains the ending address.

*W*rite *D*ata (WD), *W*rite *D*ata *R*egister (WDR), *W*rite *H*alfword (WH), *W*rite *H*alfword *R*egister (WHR), and *W*rite *B*lock (WB) perform the same way as their equivalent read instructions, except that 8, 16, or 64 bits of data are transmitted to the selected device.

*S*ense *S*tatus (SS) and *S*ense *S*tatus *R*egister (SSR) are used to read device status from the device specified in bits 8 through 15 of R1. An eight-bit status code is transmitted to memory or R2. The four least significant status bits also set the condition codes, for device busy, examine status, and device unavailable. SS and SSR are the usual tests found in other computers for a device ready status.

*O*utput *C*ommand (OC) and *O*utput *C*ommand *R*egister (OCR) transmit an eight-bit command from mem-

Chart 9-4. Peripheral Options and CPU Options for Model 6/16

CPU/Memory Options	
Turnkey (minimum) console:	Available
Full console:	Available. Binary or Hexadecimal
Power-fail safe:	Available
Automatic bootstrap:	Available. Up to 4K bytes
Real-time clock:	Available
Additional selector channel:	Available
Semiconductor memory:	MOS 500 ns } To 64K bytes
Core memory:	1000 ns } To 64K bytes
Memory protection:	Supervisor mode a standard feature
Memory expansion:	
Hardware multiply/divide:	Available
Other:	Memory parity
Teletype	
Tty—33:	Available
Tty (other):	ASR-35
Tty modification kit:	Available
Other terminals:	Carousel 15, 30, and 300 chars/s. To 132 characters
CRT	
Alphanumeric display:	24 lines by 80 characters, 110 to 9600 baud
Graphic display:	1024 × 1024 matrix, alphanumeric mode
Oscilloscope control:	
Printer Plotter	
Line printer:	60 to 600 lines/min
Plotter:	
Card Reader	
Card reader:	400 or 1000 cards/min
Paper Tape	
Paper tape reader:	300 chars/s
Paper tape punch:	Reader/Punch. Punch speed is 75 chars/s
Magnetic Tape	
Audio cassette tape:	
Cassette tape:	INTERTAPE dual cassette system, 1000 chars/s
Cartridge tape:	
Reel-to-reel tape:	7-track, 9-track
Magnetic Disc	
Fixed head:	
Movable head:	2.5M- to 40M-byte cartridge drives
Floppy disc:	
Communications	
Asynchronous interface:	Available
Synchronous interface:	Available
Modem control:	Available
Special-Purpose Interfaces	
ADC:	Available
DAC:	Available
Relay driver:	Available
General-purpose parallel:	Available
Other	IBM system interface

Table 9-29. Low-End Minicomputer Manufacturers

	Full-Size Configurations	Computers on a Board	Word Sizes (Instruction)	Word Sizes (Data)	Memory Speed**	Minimum	Utility Software	BASIC	FORTRAN	Other Compilers	Operating Systems	Pricing*
Computer Automation	✓	✓	16	16	800	4K	G	✓	✓		✓	E
Data General	✓		16	16	800	4K	E	✓	✓	✓	✓	G
Digital Computer Controls	✓		16	16	800	4K	F	✓	✓	✓	✓	G
Digital Equipment	✓	✓	12/ 16	12/ 16	900	4K	E	✓	✓	✓	✓	G
General Automation	✓	✓	12/ 16	12/ 16	800	4K	G	✓	✓		✓	G
Hewlett Packard	✓		16	16	900	4K	G	✓	✓	✓	✓	P
Interdata	✓		16	16	1000	4K	G	✓	✓		✓	F
Microdata	✓		16	16	1000	4K	G	✓	✓	✓	✓	F
Modular Computer Systems	✓		16	16	800	4K	F	✓	✓		✓	F
Prime Computer	✓	✓	16	16	1000	4K	F	✓	✓		✓	G
Texas Instruments	✓		16	16	750	4K	F		✓		✓	G
Varian	✓		16	16	660	4K	G	✓	✓	✓	✓	F

E = Excellent F = Fair
G = Good P = Poor

* Excellent equated to very low prices.
** Core speeds given. Semiconductor may be available.

ory or R2 to the device. *A*cknowledge *I*nterrupt (AI) and *A*cknowledge *I*nterrupt *R*egister (AIR) are used to clear an external interrupt after the interrupt occurs. The address of the device causing the interrupt is put into R1. Eight bits of device status are put into memory (AI) or R2 (AIR).

The Autoload instruction (AL) automatically loads a bootstrap program, starting at location 80_{16} and ending at the location specified by the effective address. The input device number is specified in location 78_{16} with the device command code in 79_{16}. AL is simply a conveniently implemented instruction enabling a byte-oriented load of a bootstrap program from an I/O device.

Peripherals

Peripheral devices offered for the 6/16 and 7/16 series are listed in Chart 9-4, along with speeds and special features.

Software

Software offered for this series of minicomputers are an assembler, interactive text editor, interactive debug, and other utility programs. Interactive FORTRAN, FORTRAN IV, FORTRAN V, BASIC and a macro-assembler called MACROCAL are offered as higher-level languages. Four operating systems are offered and, of course, are dependent upon the configuration. They are Basic Operating System (BOSS), Disc Operating System (DOS), Real-Time Operating System (RTOS), and Mini Real-Time Operating System (OS/16-MT).

Price and Availability

The 6/16 with 8K bytes of MOS memory can be purchased new for around $3000 including hexadecimal console. Used equipment, especially of the Interdata 4 and 5 types, is available, but is not as readily available as PDP-8s and Novas.

OTHER MINICOMPUTER SYSTEMS

Table 9-29 includes manufacturers that sell models for $5000 or less, new. The table is intended to provide a general idea of what is available rather than giving exact specifications. Further information may be obtained by contacting the manufacturers. Minicomputer manufacturers' addresses are listed in Appendix G, p. 221, of this book.

APPENDIX

Powers of 2

$2^0 = 1$	$2^{17} = 131{,}072$	$2^0 = 1.0$
$2^1 = 2$	$2^{18} = 262{,}144$	$2^{-1} = 0.5$
$2^2 = 4$	$2^{19} = 524{,}288$	$2^{-2} = 0.25$
$2^3 = 8$	$2^{20} = 1{,}048{,}576$	$2^{-3} = 0.125$
$2^4 = 16$	$2^{21} = 2{,}097{,}152$	$2^{-4} = 0.0625$
$2^5 = 32$	$2^{22} = 4{,}194{,}304$	$2^{-5} = 0.03125$
$2^6 = 64$	$2^{23} = 8{,}388{,}608$	$2^{-6} = 0.015625$
$2^7 = 128$	$2^{24} = 16{,}777{,}216$	$2^{-7} = 0.0078125$
$2^8 = 256$	$2^{25} = 33{,}554{,}432$	$2^{-8} = 0.0039062$
$2^9 = 512$	$2^{26} = 67{,}108{,}864$	$2^{-9} = 0.0019531$
$2^{10} = 1024$	$2^{27} = 134{,}217{,}728$	$2^{-10} = 0.0009766$
$2^{11} = 2048$	$2^{28} = 268{,}435{,}456$	$2^{-11} = 0.0004883$
$2^{12} = 4096$	$2^{29} = 536{,}870{,}912$	$2^{-12} = 0.0002441$
$2^{13} = 8192$	$2^{30} = 1{,}073{,}741{,}824$	$2^{-13} = 0.0001220$
$2^{14} = 16{,}384$	$2^{31} = 2{,}147{,}483{,}648$	$2^{-14} = 0.0000610$
$2^{15} = 32{,}768$	$2^{32} = 4{,}294{,}967{,}296$	$2^{-15} = 0.0000305$
$2^{16} = 65{,}536$		$2^{-16} = 0.0000153$

40

0100

40

768 128

51

128
2|256

90000

20

16 0000 - 0F

7

2K 6

5

32K 4 53

4(2 s3 + S2)

0 0 81

01

1

128 80

APPENDIX

B

Binary, Octal, Decimal, and Hexadecimal Conversions

N_2	N_8	N_{10}	N_{16}
00000000	000	000	00
00000001	001	001	01
00000010	002	002	02
00000011	003	003	03
00000100	004	004	04
00000101	005	005	05
00000110	006	006	06
00000111	007	007	07
00001000	010	008	08
00001001	011	009	09
00001010	012	010	0A
00001011	013	011	0B
00001100	014	012	0C
00001101	015	013	0D
00001110	016	014	0E
00001111	017	015	0F
00010000	020	016	10
00010001	021	017	11
00010010	022	018	12
00010011	023	019	13
00010100	024	020	14
00010101	025	021	15
00010110	026	022	16
00010111	027	023	17
00011000	030	024	18
00011001	031	025	19
00011010	032	026	1A
00011011	033	027	1B
00011100	034	028	1C
00011101	035	029	1D
00011110	036	030	1E
00011111	037	031	1F
00100000	040	032	20
00100001	041	033	21
00100010	042	034	22
00100011	043	035	23
00100100	044	036	24
00100101	045	037	25
00100110	046	038	26
00100111	047	039	27
00101000	050	040	28
00101001	051	041	29
00101010	052	042	2A
00101011	053	043	2B
00101100	054	044	2C
00101101	055	045	2D
00101110	056	046	2E
00101111	057	047	2F
00110000	060	048	30
00110001	061	049	31
00110010	062	050	32
00110011	063	051	33
00110100	064	052	34
00110101	065	053	35
00110110	066	054	36
00110111	067	055	37
00111000	070	056	38
00111001	071	057	39
00111010	072	058	3A
00111011	073	059	3B
00111100	074	060	3C
00111101	075	061	3D
00111110	076	062	3E
00111111	077	063	3F
01000000	100	064	40
01000001	101	065	41
01000010	102	066	42
01000011	103	067	43
01000100	104	068	44
01000101	105	069	45
01000110	106	070	46
01000111	107	071	47
01001000	110	072	48
01001001	111	073	49
01001010	112	074	4A
01001011	113	075	4B
01001100	114	076	4C
01001101	115	077	4D
01001110	116	078	4E
01001111	117	079	4F
01010000	120	080	50
01010001	121	081	51
01010010	122	082	52
01010011	123	083	53
01010100	124	084	54
01010101	125	085	55
01010110	126	086	56
01010111	127	087	57
01011000	130	088	58
01011001	131	089	59
01011010	132	090	5A
01011011	133	091	5B
01011100	134	092	5C
01011101	135	093	5D
01011110	136	094	5E
01011111	137	095	5F
01100000	140	096	60
01100001	141	097	61
01100010	142	098	62
01100011	143	099	63
01100100	144	100	64
01100101	145	101	65
01100110	146	102	66
01100111	147	103	67
01101000	150	104	68
01101001	151	105	69
01101010	152	106	6A
01101011	153	107	6B
01101100	154	108	6C
01101101	155	109	6D
01101110	156	110	6E
01101111	157	111	6F
01110000	160	112	70
01110001	161	113	71
01110010	162	114	72
01110011	163	115	73
01110100	164	116	74
01110101	165	117	75
01110110	166	118	76
01110111	167	119	77
01111000	170	120	78
01111001	171	121	79
01111010	172	122	7A
01111011	173	123	7B
01111100	174	124	7C
01111101	175	125	7D
01111110	176	126	7E
01111111	177	127	7F
10000000	200	128	80
10000001	201	129	81
10000010	202	130	82
10000011	203	131	83
10000100	204	132	84
10000101	205	133	85
10000110	206	134	86
10000111	207	135	87
10001000	210	136	88
10001001	211	137	89
10001010	212	138	8A
10001011	213	139	8B
10001100	214	140	8C
10001101	215	141	8D
10001110	216	142	8E
10001111	217	143	8F
10010000	220	144	90
10010001	221	145	91
10010010	222	146	92
10010011	223	147	93
10010100	224	148	94
10010101	225	149	95
10010110	226	150	96
10010111	227	151	97

N_2	N_8	N_{10}	N_{16}
10011000	230	152	98
10011001	231	153	99
10011010	232	154	9A
10011011	233	155	9B
10011100	234	156	9C
10011101	235	157	9D
10011110	236	158	9E
10011111	237	159	9F
10100000	240	160	A0
10100001	241	161	A1
10100010	242	162	A2
10100011	243	163	A3
10100100	244	164	A4
10100101	245	165	A5
10100110	246	166	A6
10100111	247	167	A7
10101000	250	168	A8
10101001	251	169	A9
10101010	252	170	AA
10101011	253	171	AB
10101100	254	172	AC
10101101	255	173	AD
10101110	256	174	AE
10101111	257	175	AF
10110000	260	176	B0
10110001	261	177	B1
10110010	262	178	B2
10110011	263	179	B3
10110100	264	180	B4
10110101	265	181	B5
10110110	266	182	B6
10110111	267	183	B7
10111000	270	184	B8
10111001	271	185	B9
10111010	272	186	BA
10111011	273	187	BB
10111100	274	188	BC
10111101	275	189	BD
10111110	276	190	BE
10111111	277	191	BF
11000000	300	192	C0
11000001	301	193	C1
11000010	302	194	C2
11000011	303	195	C3
11000100	304	196	C4
11000101	305	197	C5
11000110	306	198	C6
11000111	307	199	C7
11001000	310	200	C8
11001001	311	201	C9
11001010	312	202	CA
11001011	313	203	CB
11001100	314	204	CC
11001101	315	205	CD
11001110	316	206	CE
11001111	317	207	CF
11010000	320	208	D0
11010001	321	209	D1
11010010	322	210	D2
11010011	323	211	D3
11010100	324	212	D4
11010101	325	213	D5
11010110	326	214	D6
11010111	327	215	D7
11011000	330	216	D8
11011001	331	217	D9
11011010	332	218	DA
11011011	333	219	DB
11011100	334	220	DC
11011101	335	221	DD
11011110	336	222	DE
11011111	337	223	DF
11100000	340	224	E0
11100001	341	225	E1
11100010	342	226	E2
11100011	343	227	E3
11100100	344	228	E4
11100101	345	229	E5
11100110	346	230	E6
11100111	347	231	E7
11101000	350	232	E8
11101001	351	233	E9
11101010	352	234	EA
11101011	353	235	EB
11101100	354	236	EC
11101101	355	237	ED
11101110	356	238	EE
11101111	357	239	EF
11110000	360	240	F0
11110001	361	241	F1
11110010	362	242	F2
11110011	363	243	F3
11110100	364	244	F4
11110101	365	245	F5
11110110	366	246	F6
11110111	367	247	F7
11111000	370	248	F8
11111001	371	249	F9
11111010	372	250	FA
11111011	373	251	FB
11111100	374	252	FC
11111101	375	253	FD
11111110	376	254	FE
11111111	377	255	FF

APPENDIX

C

ASCII Codes

CCC_2 (columns), $RRRR_2$ (rows)

	000	001	010	011	100	101	110	111
0000	NUL	DLE	SP	0	@	P	`	p
0001	SOH	DC1	!	1	A	Q	a	q
0010	STX	DC2	"	2	B	R	b	r
0011	ETX	DC3	#	3	C	S	c	s
0100	EOT	DC4	$	4	D	T	d	t
0101	ENQ	NAK	%	5	E	U	e	u
0110	ACK	SYN	&	6	F	V	f	v
0111	BEL	ETB	'	7	G	W	g	w
1000	BS	CAN	(	8	H	X	h	x
1001	HT	EM	)	9	I	Y	i	y
1010	LF	SUB	*	:	J	Z	j	z
1011	VT	ESC	+	;	K	[	k	{
1100	FF	FS	,	<	L	\	l	|
1101	CR	GS	–	=	M	]	m	}
1110	SO	RS	.	>	N	Λ	n	~
1111	SI	US	/	?	O	___	o	DEL

$RRRR_2$: 0000–1111

SPECIAL COMMUNICATIONS AND CONTROL CHARACTERS EXCEPT FOR LF, CR, ESC.

COMMONLY USED SPECIAL CHARACTERS

NUMERIC

ALPHABETIC (UPPER CASE)

ALPHABETIC (LOWER CASE)

RUB OUT OR DELETE (ALL ONES)

Control Characters

NUL	Null (All Zeros)	DC1	Device Control 1
SOH	Start of Heading	DC2	Device Control 2
STX	Start of Text	DC3	Device Control 3
ETX	End of Text	DC4	Device Control 4
EOT	End of Transmission	NAK	Negative Acknowledgement
ENQ	Enquiry	SYN	Synchronous/Idle
ACK	Acknowledgement	ETB	End of Transmitted Block
BEL	Bell, or Attention Signal	CAN	Cancel (Error in Data)
BS	Backspace	EM	End of Medium
HT	Horizontal Tabulation	SUB	Start of Special Sequence
LF	Line Feed	ESC	Escape
VT	Vertical Tabulation	FS	File Separator
FF	Form Feed	GS	Group Separator
CR	Carriage Return	RS	Record Separator
SO	Shift Out	US	Unit Separator
SI	Shift In	SP	Space
DLE	Data Link Escape	DEL	Delete

To find the character equivalent of a 7-bit binary number, divide the number into $CCC\,RRRR_2$ and look under the respective row RRRR and column CCC.

APPENDIX

D

EBCDIC Codes

Bit Positions

1	2	3	4	5	6	7	8

Bit Positions 1, 2, 3, 4 (columns); Bit Positions 5, 6, 7, 8 (rows)

	0000	0001	0010	0011	0100	0101	0110	0111	1000	1001	1010	1011	1100	1101	1110	1111
0000	NUL	DLE	DS		SP	&	–						{	}	\	0
0001	SOH	DC1	SOS				/		a	j	~		A	J		1
0010	STX	DC2	FS	SYN					b	k	s		B	K	S	2
0011	ETX	TM							c	l	t		C	L	T	3
0100	PF	RES	BYP	PN					d	m	u		D	M	U	4
0101	HT	NL	LF	RS					e	n	v		E	N	V	5
0110	LC	BS	ETB	UC					f	o	w		F	O	W	6
0111	DEL	IL	ESC	EOT					g	p	x		G	P	X	7
1000		CAN							h	q	y		H	Q	Y	8
1001		EM						`	i	r	z		I	R	Z	9
1010	SMM	CC	SM		¢	!	¦	:								|
1011	VT	CU1	CU2	CU3	.	$	,	#								
1100	FF	IFS		DC4	<	*	%	@					⑀		⑁	
1101	CR	IGS	ENQ	NAK	(	)	_	'								
1110	SO	IRS	ACK		+	;	>	=					⑂			
1111	SI	IUS	BEL	SUB	|	¬	?	"								

Special Graphic Characters

- ¢ Cent Sign
- . Period, Decimal Point
- < Less-Than Sign
- (Left Parenthesis
- + Plus Sign
- | Logical OR, Absolute
- & Ampersand
- ! Exclamation Point
- $ Dollar Sign
- * Asterisk
-) Right Parenthesis
- ; Semicoln
- ¬ Logical NOT
- – Minus Sign, Hyphen
- / Slash
- ¦ Logical OR, Absolute
- , Comma
- % Percent
- _ Underscore
- > Greater-Than Sign
- ? Question Mark
- ` Accent Mark
- : Colon
- # Number Sign
- @ At Sign
- ' Prime, Apostrophe
- = Equal Sign
- " Quotation Mark
- ~ Tilde
- { Left Brace
- } Right Brace
- \ Backslash
- | Logical OR, Absolute
- ⑀ Hook
- ⑂ Fork
- ⑁ Chair

Control Characters

NUL Null (All Zeros)
SOH Start of Heading
STX Start of Text
ETX End of Text
PF Punch Off
HT Horizontal Tabulation
LC Lower Case
DEL Delete
SMM Start of Manual Message
VT Vertical Tabulation
FF Form Feed
CR Carriage Return
SO Shift Out

SI Shift In
DLE Data Link Escape
DC1 Device Control 1
DC2 Device Control 2
TM Tape Mark
RES Restore
NL New Line
BS Backspace
IL Idle
CAN Cancel (Error in Data)
EM End of Medium
CC Cursor Control
CU1 Customer Use 1

IFS Interchange File Separator
IGS Interchange Group Separator
IRS Interchange Record Separator
IUS Interchange Unit Separator
DS Digit Select
SOS Start of Significance
FS Field Separator
BYP Bypass
LF Line Feed
ETB End of Transmission Block
ESC Escape
SM Set Mode
CU2 Customer Use 2

ENQ Enquiry
ACK Acknowledgment
BEL Bell, or Attention Signal
SYN Synchronous/Idle
PN Punch On
RS Reader Stop
UC Upper case
EOT End of Transmission
CU3 Customer Use 3
DC4 Device Control 4
NAK Negative Acknowledgement
SUB Substitute
SP Space

APPENDIX

E

Floating-Point Number Representation

Representation:

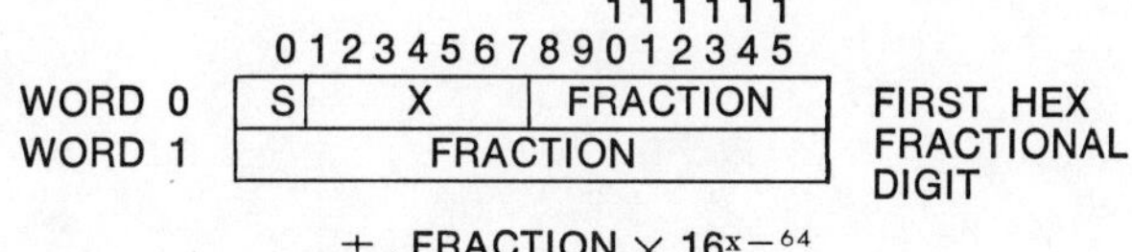

$\pm .\,\text{FRACTION} \times 16^{X-64}$

Example:

0	1 2 3 4 5 6 7	8 9 10 11 12 13 14 15
0	1 0 0 0 0 1 0	1 0 1 1 0 1 1 0
0 1 1 0 0 0 0 0 0 0 0 0 0 0 0 0		

$$+.1011\ 0110\ 0110\ 0000\ 0000\ 0000 \times 16^{100\ 0010_2 - 64_{10}} =$$

$$+.1011\ 0110\ 0110\ 0000\ 0000\ 0000 \times 16^{66-64} =$$

$$+.1011\ 0110\ 0110\ 0000\ 0000\ 0000 \times 16^{2} =$$

$$+.1011\ 0110\ 0110\ 0000\ 0000\ 0000 = 182_{10} + .0110_2 =$$

$$+182 + \frac{0}{2^1} + \frac{1}{2^2} + \frac{1}{2^3} + \frac{0}{2^4} = +182 + .25 + .125 = +182.375$$

Notes:

1. Fraction usually has at least one "1" in the first hex digit position. This is called *normalization.*
2. Sign of fraction is positive if $S = 0$, negative if $S = 1$. Sign of power is determined by sign of $(X - 64)$.
3. $(X - 64)$ allows powers of from $(127 - 64) = +63_{10}$ to $(0 - 64) = -64_{10}$ to be expressed.
4. Layout of two data words may vary from one machine to another, but above layout is common. Sign, fraction $\times\ 16^{X-64}$ form is also more or less standard form.

APPENDIX

Reference Books and Periodicals

PERIODICALS

ACM Computing Surveys
Association for Computing Machinery
1133 Avenue of the Americas
New York, NY 10036

BYTE Magazine
Green Publishing Co.
Peterborough, NH 03485

Computer Decisions
Hayden Publishing Co., Inc.
50 Essex St.
Rochelle Park, NJ 07662

Computer Design
221 Baker Ave.
Concord, MA 01742

Computer
IEEE Computer Society
5855 Naples Plaza
Suite 301
Long Beach, CA 90803

ComputerWorld (weekly newspaper)
797 Washington St.
Newton, MA 02160

Datamation
1801 S. La Cienega Blvd.
Los Angeles, CA 90035

EDN
221 Columbus Ave.
Boston, MA 02116

Electronic Design
Hayden Publishing Co.
50 Essex Street
Rochelle Park, NJ 07662

Modern Data
5 Kane Industrial Dr.
Hudson, MA 01749

Popular Electronics
Ziff-Davis Publishing Co.
One Park Avenue
New York, NY 10016

Radio-Electronics
Gernsback Publications, Inc.
200 Park Avenue South
New York, NY 10003

BOOKS

Albrecht, R. et al. *BASIC*. New York: John Wiley & Sons, Inc., 1973.

Dymax Publishing. *My Computer Likes Me.*

Flores, Ivan. *Computer Software*. Englewood Cliffs, NJ: Prentice-Hall, Inc., 1965.

Foster, Caxton C. *Computer Architecture.* New York: Van Nostrand Reinhold Co., 1970.

Katzan, Harry Jr. *Operating Systems: A Pragmatic Approach.* New York: Van Nostrand Reinhold Co., 1973.

Knuth, Donald E. *The Art of Computer Programming: Vol. 1. Fundamental Algorithms.* Reading, MA: Addison-Wesley Pub. Co., 1968.

Lancaster, Don. *TTL Cookbook.* Indianapolis: Howard W. Sams & Co., Inc., 1974.

McCracken, Daniel D. *A Guide to FORTRAN Programming.* New York: John Wiley & Sons, Inc., 1961.

Texas Instruments, Inc. *The TTL Data Book.* Texas Instruments, Box 5012, Dallas, TX 75222.

APPENDIX

G

Microprocessor, Microcomputer, and Minicomputer Manufacturers

MICROPROCESSOR CHIPS

Advanced Micro Devices
901 Thompson Place
Sunnyvale, CA 94086
(408) 732-2400

American Microsystems (AMI)
3800 Homestead Road
Santa Clara, CA 95051
(408) 246-0330

Electronic Arrays
550 Middlefield Road
Mountain View, CA 94043
(415) 964-4321

Intel Corp.
3065 Bowers Avenue
Santa Clara, CA 95051
(408) 246-7501

Intersil
10900 N. Tantau Avenue
Cupertino, CA 95014
(408) 257-5450

Fairchild Semiconductor
464 Ellis Street
Mountain View, CA 94040
(415) 962-5011

Monolithic Memories
1165 East Arques Avenue
Sunnyvale, CA 94086
(408) 739-3535

Mostek
1215 West Crosby Road
Carrollton, TX 75006
(214) 242-0444

Motorola, Inc.
P.O. Box 20912
5005 E. McDowell Road
Phoenix, AZ 85036
(602) 244-3465

National Semiconductor Corp.
2900 Semiconductor Drive
Santa Clara, CA 95051
(408) 732-5000

NEC Microcomputers, Inc.
Five Militia Drive
Lexington, MA 02173
(617) 862-6410

RCA Corp.
Solid State Division
Somerville, NJ 08776
(201) 722-3200

Rockwell International
Microelectronics Division
3310 Miraloma Avenue
Anaheim, CA 92803
(714) 632-5803

Signetics
811 East Arques Avenue
Sunnyvale, CA 94086
(408) 739-7700

Texas Instruments
P.O. Box 5012
Dallas, TX 75222
(214) 238-3741

Toshiba Transistor Works
1-Komukai
Toshiba-Cho
Kawasaki-Chi, Japan

Transitron
168 Albion Street
Wakefield, MA 01880
(617) 245-4500

Western Digital Corp.
19242 Red Hill Avenue
Newport Beach, CA 92663
(714) 557-3550

MICROCOMPUTERS

Fabri-Tek Computer Systems, Inc.
5901 South Country Road 18
Minneapolis, MN 55436
(612) 935-8811

IMS Associates, Inc.
1922 Republic Avenue
San Leandro, CA 94577
(415) 483-2093

Microcomputer Associates, Inc.
111 Main Street, Department B
Los Altos, CA 94022
(415) 941-1977

MiniMicroMart
1618 James Street
Syracuse, NY 13203
(315) 422-4467

MITS
6328 Linn, N.E.
Albuquerque, NM
(505) 265-7553

PCM Inc.
San Ramon, CA 94583

Prime Computer, Inc.
23 Strathmore Road
Natick, MA 01760
(617) 655-6988

Pro-Log
852 Airport Road
Monterey, CA 93940
(408) 372-4593

R2E Micro-Computers
38 Garden Road
Wellesley Hills, MA 02181
(617) 235-3130

Southwest Technical Products
Box 32040
San Antonio, TX 78284

Sphere Corp.
791 South 500 West #4
Bountiful, UT 84010
(801) 292-8466

Systems Research, Inc.
P.O. Box 151280
Salt Lake City, UT 84115
(801) 942-1093

WaveMate Computers and Systems
1015 West 190th
Gardena, CA 90247
(213) 329-8941

MINICOMPUTERS (SMALLER CONFIGURATIONS)

Computer Automation, Inc.
18651 Von Karman Avenue
Irvine, CA 92715
(714) 833-8830

Data General Corp.
Route 9
Southboro, MA 01772
(617) 485-9100

Datapoint Corp.
9725 Datapoint Drive
San Antonio, TX 78284
(512) 696-4520

Digital Computer Controls
12 Industrial Road
Fairfield, NJ 07006
(201) 575-9100

Digital Equipment Corp.
146 Main Street
Maynard, MA 01754
(617) 897-5111

General Automation, Inc.
1055 S. East Street
Anaheim, CA 92805
(714) 778-4800

Hewlett-Packard Co.
Data Systems Division
11000 Wolfe Road
Cupertino, CA 95014
(408) 257-7000

Interdata, Inc.
2 Crescent Place
Oceanport, NJ 07757
(201) 229-4040

Microdata Corp.
17481 Red Hill Avenue
Irvine, CA 92714
(714) 540-6730

Texas Instruments, Inc.
Digital Systems Division
P.O. Box 1444
Houston, TX 77001
(713) 494-5115

Varian Data Machines
2722 Michelson Drive
Irvine, CA 92713
(714) 833-2400

APPENDIX

H

Directory of Minicomputer Brokers

American Used Computer Corp.
P.O. Box 68
Kenmore Station, Boston, MA 02215
(617) 261-1100

Mini-Computer Exchange
12601 Henrietta Avenue
Sunnyvale, CA 94086
(408) 733-4400

Newman Computer Exchange
3960 Varsity Drive
Ann Arbor, MI 48104
(313) 973-1230

APPENDIX

I

Software Benchmarks

Benchmark I—This benchmark moves one-hundred 16-bit words (one-hundred 12-bit words in the case of the PDP-8) from one block in memory to another block in memory. The blocks are nonoverlapping and are not optimally located (they may cross page boundaries).

BENCHMARK I FOR INTEL 8008-1

	Instruction		Number of Bytes	Time (States)
	MVI	B,DESM	2	8
	MVI	C,DESL	2	8
	MVI	H,SORM	2	8
	MVI	L,SORL	2	8
	MVI	E,200	2	8
LOOP	MOV	A,M	1	8
	MOV	H,D	1	5
	MOV	B,H	1	5
	MOV	D,B	1	5
	MOV	L,D	1	5
	MOV	C,L	1	5
	MOV	D,C	1	5
	MOV	M,A	1	7
	DCR	E	1	5
	JZ	DONE	3	9/11
	MOV	H,D	1	5
	MOV	B,H	1	5
	MOV	D,B	1	5
	MOV	L,D	1	5
	MOV	C,L	1	5
	MOV	D,C	1	5
	INR	L	1	5
	JNC	NXT	3	9/11
	INR	M	1	5
NXT	INR	C	1	5
	JNC	NX2	3	9/11
	INR	B	1	5
NX2	JMP	LOOP	3	11
DONE				
Storage				
None			41	

Timing

100.0 μs initialization
69115.0 μs loop
69215.0 μs total

BENCHMARK I FOR INTEL 8080

	Instruction		Number of Bytes	Time (Cycles)
	MVI	H,200	2	7
	LXI	B,ATAB	3	10
	LXI	D,BTAB	3	10
LOOP	LDAX	B	1	7
	STAX	D	1	7
	INX	B	1	5
	INX	D	1	5
	DCR	H	1	5
	JNZ	LOOP	3	10
Storage				
None			17	

Timing

54 μs initialization
7800 μs loop
7854 μs total

BENCHMARK I FOR INTERDATA 6/16

	Instruction		Number of Bytes	Time (μs)
	XHR	R1,R1	2	1
	LIS	R2,10	2	1
	LIS	R3,90	2	1
LOOP	LM	R6,BLKA,R1	4	12.75
	STM	R6,BLKB,R1	4	12.75
	BXLE	R0,LOOP	4	3.25
Storage				
None			18	

Timing

3 μs initialization
287.5 μs loop
290.5 μs total

BENCHMARK I FOR MOTOROLA MC6800

	Instruction		Number of Bytes	Time (Cycles)
	LDAB	#200	2	2
	LDX	#BLKB	3	3
	STX	BLKBP	2	5
	LDX	#BLKA	3	3
	STX	BLKAP	2	5
LOOP	LDX	BLKAP	2	4
	LDAA	X	2	5
	INX		1	2
	STX	BLKAP	2	5
	LDX	BLKBP	2	4
	STAA	X	2	6
	INX		1	2
	STX	BLKBP	2	5
	DECB		1	2
	BGE	LOOP	2	4
Storage				
BLKAP			2	
BLKAP			2	
			33	

Timing

18 μs initialization
3900 μs loop
3918 μs total

BENCHMARK I FOR FAIRCHILD F8

	Instruction		Number of Bytes	Time (Cycles)
	DCI	TABA	3	6
	LR	Q,DC	1	4
	DCI	TABB	3	6
	LR	H,DC	1	4
	LI	100	2	2.5
	LR	R3,A	1	1
LOOP	LR	DC,Q	1	4
	LM		1	2.5
	LR	Q,DC	1	4
	LR	DC,H	1	4
	ST		1	2.5
	LR	H,DC	1	4
	DS	R3	1	1.5
	BNZ	LOOP	2	3.5/3.0
Storage				
None			12	

Timing

47.0 μs initialization
5200.0 μs loop
5247.0 μs total

BENCHMARK I FOR DEC PDP-8/E

	Instruction		Number of Bytes*	Timing (μs)
	CLA		2	1.2
	TAD	TABA	2	2.6
	DCA	APNT	2	2.6
	TAD	TABB	2	2.6
	DCA	BPNT	2	2.6
	TAD	D101	2	2.6
	DCA	CNT	2	2.6
	CLA		2	1.2
LOOP,	TAD	I APNT	2	3.8
	DCA	I BPNT	2	3.8
	ISZ	CNT	2	2.6
	JMP	LOOP	2	1.2
Storage				
TABA			2	
TABB			2	
CNT			2	
			30 = 23 8-bit bytes	

Timing

18 μs initialization
1140 μs loop
1158 μs total

* 6 bits.

BENCHMARK I FOR CAI LSI-3/05*

	Instruction		Number of Bytes	Time (μs)
	LDA	ATAB	2	5.5
	STA	APNT	2	7.75
	LDA	BTAB	2	5.5
	STA	BPNT	2	7.75
	LDX	DM101	2	5.5
LOOP	LDA	*APNT	2	7.25
	STA	*BPNT	2	9.5
	IMS	APNT	2	9.75
	IMS	BPNT	2	9.75
	AXI	1	2	5.25
	JXN	LOOP	2	5.75
Storage				
APNT			2	
BPNT			2	
ATAB			2	
BTAB			2	
DM101			2	
			34	

Timing

6 μs initialization
4000 μs loop
4006 μs total

* Core memory.

BENCHMARK I FOR NOVA 800

Instruction			Number of Bytes	Time (μs)
	LDA	0,BLKA	2	1.6
	STA	0,20	2	1.6
	LDA	1,BLKB	2	1.6
	STA	1,21	2	1.6
	LDA	2,DM101	2	1.6
LOOP:	LDA	0,@20	2	2.6
	STA	0,@21	2	2.6
	INC	2,2,SZR	2	.8
	JMP	LOOP	2	.8
Storage				
BLKA			2	
BLKB			2	
20			2	
21			2	
DM101			2	
			28	

Timing

8.0 μs initialization
688.0 μs loop
688.0 μs total

BENCHMARK I FOR MOS TECHNOLOGY MCS6502

Instruction			Number of Bytes	Time (Cycles)
	LDX	(IMM) 00	2	2
	LDA	(IMM) 00	2	2
LOOP	LDY	(ABX) BLKA	3	4
	STA	(ABY) BLKB	3	5
	CPX	(IMM) C9	2	2
	BNE	LOOP	2	2
Storage				
None			14	

Timing

4 μs initialization
2600 μs loop
2604 μs total

Benchmark II—This benchmark converts six ASCII characters, assumed to be valid ASCII octal digits 0 through 7, through a contiguous buffer into a 16-bit binary value. Most significant ASCII character is assumed to be 0 or 1.

BENCHMARK II FOR MOTOROLA MC6800

Instruction			Number of Bytes	Time (Cycles)
	LDX	#BUF	3	3
	CLR	MSRES	3	6
	CLR	LSRES	3	6
LOOP	LDAA	X	2	5
	INX		1	4
	ANDA	#7	2	2
	LDAB	LSRES	2	3
	ABA		1	2
	LDAB	MSRES	2	3
	CPX	#BUF+5	3	3
	BEQ	DONE	2	4
	ASLA		1	2
	ROLB		1	2
	ASLA		1	2
	ROLB		1	2
	ASLA		1	2
	ROLB		1	2
	STAA	LSRES	2	4
	STAB	MSRES	2	4
	BRA	LOOP	2	4
DONE				
Storage				
MSRES			2	
LSRES			2	
			38	

Timing

15 μs initialization
276 μs loop
291 μs total

BENCHMARK II FOR MOS TECHNOLOGY MCS6502

Instruction				Number of Bytes	Time (Cycles)
	LDX	(IMM)	00	2	2
	STX	(ZPG)	RESMS	2	3
	STX	(ZPG)	RESLS	2	3
LOOP2	LDA	(ABX)	LIST	3	4
	AND	(IMM)	07	2	2
	CLC			1	2
	ADC	(ZPG)	RESLS	3	2
	INX			1	2
	CPX	(IMM)	07	2	2
	BNE	LOOP1		2	2
	JMP	DONE		3	5
LOOP1	CLC			1	2
	ROL	(ACC)		1	2
	ROL	(ZPG)	RESMS	2	5
	ROL	(ACC)		1	2
	ROL	(ZPG)	RESMS	2	5
	ROL	(ACC)		1	2
	ROL	(ZPG)	RESMS	2	5
	STA	(ZPG)	RESLS	3	2
	JMP	LOOP2		3	3
DONE					
Storage					
None					
				39	

Timing

6 μs initialization
441 μs loop
447 μs total

BENCHMARK II FOR INTEL 8008-1

	Instruction		Number of Bytes	Time (States)
	MVI	H,BUFM	2	8
	MVI	L,BUFL	2	8
	MVI	D,0	2	8
	MVI	C,0	2	8
	MVI	B,6	2	8
LOOP	MOV	A,M	1	8
	ANI	A,7	2	8
	ADD	D	1	5
	MOV	D,A	1	5
	INR	L	1	5
	DCR	B	1	5
	JZ	DONE	3	9/11
	CALL	SHFT	3	11
	CALL	SHFT	3	11
	CALL	SHFT	3	11
	JMP	LOOP	3	11
SHFT	MOV	A,D	1	5
	RLC		1	5
	MOV	D,A	1	5
	MOV	A,C	1	5
	RAL		1	5
	MOV	C,A	1	5
	RET		1	5
Storage				
None				
			39	

Timing

100.0 μs initialization
1667.5 μs loop
1767.5 μs total

BENCHMARK II FOR INTEL 8080

	Instruction		Number of Bytes	Time (Cycles)
	MVI	C,6	2	10
	LXI	H,BUF	3	10
	LXI	D,0	3	10
LOOP	MOV	A,M	1	5
	ANI	7	2	7
	ADD	E	1	4
	MOV	E,A	1	5
	XCHG		1	4
	DCR	C	1	5
	JZ	DONE	3	10
	DAD	H	1	10
	DAD	H	1	10
	DAD	H	1	10
	XCHG		1	4
	INX	H	1	5
	JMP	LOOP	3	10
DONE				
Storage				
None				
			26	

Timing

30 μs initialization
988 μs loop
1018 μs total

BENCHMARK II FOR FAIRCHILD F8

	Instruction		Number of Bytes	Time (Cycles)
	CLR		1	1
	LR	R3,A	1	1
	LR	R4,A	1	1
	LI	6	1	1
	LR	R5,A	1	1
	DCI	BUF	3	6
LOOP	LM		1	2.5
	NI	7	2	2.5
	AS	R4	1	1
	DS	R5	1	1.5
	BZ	DONE	2	3.5
	PI	SHFT	3	4
	PI	SHFT	3	4
	PI	SHFT	3	4
	JMP	LOOP	3	5.5
SHFT	LR	A,R3	1	1
	SL	1	1	1
	LR	R3,A	1	1
	LR	A,R4	1	1
	AS	R4	1	1
	LR	R4,A	1	1
	LR	A,R3	1	1
	LNK		1	1
	LR	R3,A	1	1
	POP		1	2
DONE				
Storage				
None				
			37	

Timing

22 μs initialization
417 μs loop
439 μs total

BENCHMARK II FOR DEC PDP-8/E

	Instruction		*Number of Bytes**	*Time (μs)*
	CLA		2	1.2
	TAD	BUFA	2	2.6
	DCA	BUFP	2	2.6
	TAD	D4	2	2.6
	DCA	CNT	2	2.6
	DCA	VALUE	2	2.6
LOOP,	TAD	MSMSK	2	2.6
	AND	I BUFP	2	3.8
	BSW		2	1.2
	TAD	VALUE	2	2.6
	RTL		2	1.2
	RAL		2	1.2
	DCA	VALUE	2	2.6
	TAD	LSMSK	2	2.6
	AND	I BUFP	2	3.8
	TAD	VALUE	2	2.6
	ISZ	CNT	2	2.6
	JMP	NEXT	2	1.2
	JMP	DONE	2	1.2
NEXT,	RTL		2	1.2
	RAL		2	1.2
	DCA	VALUE	2	2.6
	ISZ	BUFP	2	2.6
	JMP	LOOP	2	1.2
DONE,				
Storage				
BUFA			2	
BUFP			2	
D4			2	
CNT			2	
VALUE			2	
MSMSK			2	
LSMSK			2	
			62 = 47 8-bit bytes	

Timing

14.2 μs initialization
111.6 μs loop
125.8 μs total

* 6-bit bytes.

BENCHMARK II FOR NOVA 800

	Instruction		*Number of Bytes*	*Time (μs)*
	LDA	0,BLKS	2	1.6
	STA	0,20	2	1.6
	LDA	3,DM3	2	1.6
	SUB	0,0	2	.8
NEXT:	LDA	1,@20	2	2.6
	LDA	2,MSMSK	2	1.6
	ANDS	1,2	2	.8
	ADD	2,0	2	.8
	MOVZL	0,0	2	.8
	MOVZL	0,0	2	.8
	MOVZL	0,0	2	.8
	LDA	2,LSMSK	2	1.6
	AND	1,2	2	.8
	ADD	2,0	2	.8
	INC	3,3,SNR	2	1.0
	JMP	DONE	2	.8
	MOVZL	0,0	2	.8
	MOVZL	0,0	2	.8
	MOVZL	0,0	2	.8
	JMP	NEXT	2	.8
DONE				
Storage				
20			2	
BLKS			2	
DM3			2	
LSMSK			2	
MSMSK			2	
			50	

Timing

5.6 μs initialization
53.2 μs loop
58.8 μs total

BENCHMARK II FOR CAI LSI-3/05*

Label	Instruction	Operand	Number of Bytes	Time (μs)
	LDA	BLKE	2	5.5
	STA	BLKP	2	7.75
	LXM	5	2	3.75
	LDA	ZERO	2	5.5
	STA	VALUE	2	7.75
LOOP	LAM	7	2	3.75
	SBM		2	5.75
	ANDB	*@BLKP	2	9.25
	ADD	VALUE	2	6.25
	AXI		2	5.25
	JXN		2	5.25
	JMP	DONE	2	6.25
	LLA	3	2	6.5
	STA	VALUE	2	7.75
	JMP	LOOP	2	6.25
DONE				
Storage				
BLKE			2	
BLKP			2	
VALUE			2	
			36	

Timing

30.25 μs initialization
308.75 μs loop
339.0 μs total

* Core memory.

BENCHMARK II FOR INTERDATA 6/16

Label	Instruction	Operand	Number of Bytes	Time (μs)
	LHI	RA,BUF	4	2
	LIS	RB,1	2	1
	LHI	RC,BUF+5	4	2
	LIS	R3,7	2	1
	XHR	R1,R1	2	1
LOOP	LB	R2,0,RA	4	3.5
	XHR	R3,R2	2	1
	AHR	R2,R1	2	1
	BXH	RA,DONE	4	3.25
	SLLS	R1,3	2	3.8
	BFBS	0,LOOP	2	1
DONE				
Storage				
None				
			30	

Timing

7 μs initialization
81.3 μs loop
88.3 μs total

Benchmark III—This benchmark searches a string of 80 characters for a search character. A "not found" test is implemented. The first occurrence of the character causes a branch out of the routine. All cases assume that the character is found at the 40th byte.

BENCHMARK III FOR INTEL 8008-1

Label	Instruction	Operand	Number of Bytes	Time (States)
	MVI	H,CHRM	2	8
	MVI	L,CHRL	2	8
	MOV	B,M	1	8
	MVI	H,TABM	2	8
	MVI	L,TABL	2	8
	MVI	C,80	2	8
LOOP	MOV	A,M	1	8
	SUB	B	1	5
	JZ	FND	3	9/11
	INR	L	1	5
	JNC	NEXT	3	9/11
	INR	M	1	5
NEXT	DCR	C	1	5
	JNZ	LOOP	3	9/11
NFND				
FND				
Storage				
None				
			25	

Timing

120 μs initialization
5422.5 μs loop
5542.5 μs total

BENCHMARK III FOR INTEL 8080

Label	Instruction	Operand	Number of Bytes	Time (Cycles)
	MVI	D,80	2	10
	LDA	CHAR	3	13
	LXI	H,TAB	3	10
LOOP	MOV	C,M	1	7
	CMP	C	1	4
	JZ	FND	3	10
	INX	H	1	5
	DCR	D	1	5
	JNZ	LOOP	3	10
NFND				
Storage				
None				
			18	

Timing

66 μs initialization
3480 μs loop
3546 μs total

BENCHMARK III FOR MOTOROLA MC6800

Label	Instruction		Number of Bytes	Time (Cycles)
	LDAA	CHAR	3	4
	LDX	#TAB	3	3
LOOP	CMPA	X	2	5
	BEQ	FND	2	4
	INX		1	4
	CPX	#TAB+200	3	3
	BNE	LOOP	2	4
NFND				
FND				
Storage				
None				
			16	

Timing

7 μs initialization
800 μs loop
807 μs total

BENCHMARK III FOR FAIRCHILD F8

Label	Instruction		Number of Cycles	Timing (Cycles)
	DCI	CHAR	3	6
	LM		1	2.5
	DCI	STRNG	3	6
LOOP	CM		1	2.5
	BZ	FND	2	3.5
	DS	R3	1	1.5
	BNZ	LOOP	2	3.5
NFND				
FND				
Storage				
None				
			13	

Timing

29 μs initialization
870 μs loop
899 μs total

BENCHMARK III FOR MOS TECHNOLOGY MCS6502

Label	Instruction			Number of Bytes	Time (Cycles)
	LDA	(ABS)	CHAR	3	4
	LDX	(IMM)	00	2	2
LOOP	CMP	(ABX)	TABLE	4	3
	BEQ	FND		2	2
	INX			1	2
	CPX	(IMM)	51	2	2
	BNE	LOOP		2	2
NFND					
FND					
Storage					
None					
				16	

Timing

6 μs initialization
434 μs loop
440 μs total

BENCHMARK III FOR DEC PDP-8/E

Label	Instruction		Number of Bytes*	Time (μs)
	CLA		2	1.2
	TAD	DM100	2	2.6
	DCA	CNT	2	2.6
	TAD	TAB	2	2.6
	DCA	TABP	2	2.6
LOOP,	TAD	MSMSK	2	2.6
	AND	I TABP	2	3.8
	BSW		2	1.2
	CIA		2	1.2
	TAD	CHAR	2	2.6
	SNA		2	1.2
	JMP	FNDL	2	1.2
	CLA		2	1.2
	TAD	LSMSK	2	2.6
	AND	I TABP	2	3.8
	CIA		2	1.2
	TAD	CHAR	2	2.6
	SNA		2	1.2
	JMP	FNDR	2	1.2
	CLA		2	1.2
	ISZ	TABP	2	2.6
	ISZ	CNT	2	2.6
	JMP	LOOP	2	1.2
Storage				
DM100			2	
CNT			2	
TABP			2	
TAB			2	
MSMSK			2	
LSMSK			2	
			60 = 45 8-bit bytes	

Timing

11.6 μs initialization
657.2 μs loop
668.8 μs total

* 6-bit bytes.

BENCHMARK III FOR INTERDATA 6/16

Label	Instruction		Number of Bytes	Time (μs)
	LB	R1,CHAR	4	3.5
	LHI	RA,TABS	4	2
	LIS	RB,1	2	1
	LHI	RC,TABS+80	4	2
LOOP	CLB	R1,0,RA	4	3.5
	BEQ	FND	2	1
	BXLE	RA,LOOP	4	3.25
NFND				
FND				
Storage				
None				
			24	

Timing

8.5 μs initialization
310.0 μs loop
390.5 μs total

BENCHMARK III FOR NOVA 800

Label	Instruction		Number of Bytes	Time (μs)
	LDA	0,DM40	2	1.6
	STA	0,CNT	2	1.6
	LDA	0,CHAR	2	1.6
	LDA	3,TABL	2	1.6
AGAIN:	INC	3,3	2	1.8
	LDA	1,0,3	2	1.6
	LDA	2,MSMSK	2	1.6
	ANDS	1,2	2	.8
	SUB	2,0,SNR#	2	1.0
	JMP	FNDL	2	.8
	LDA	2,LSMSK	2	1.6
	AND	1,2	2	.8
	SUB	2,0,SZR#	2	.8
	JMP	FNDR	2	.8
	ISZ	CNT	2	1.8
	JMP	AGAIN	2	.8
NFND:				
FNDR:				
FNDL:				
Storage				
TABL			2	
MSMSK			2	
LSMSK			2	
CNT			2	
DM40			2	
			42	

Timing

6.4 μs initialization
246.2 μs loop

252.6 μs total

BENCHMARK III FOR CAI LSI-3/05†

Label	Instruction		Number of Bytes	Time (μs)
	LDA	BUF	2	5.5
	STA	ADDR	2	7.75
	SBM		2	5.75
	LXP	0	2	3.75
	LDAB	CHAR	2	6
LOOP	CMSB	*@ADDR	2	10
	JMP	NXT	2	6.25
	JMP	FND	2	6.25
NXT	AXI	1	2	5.25
	CXI	80	2	5.0
	JMP	NFND	2	6.25
	JMP	LOOP	2	6.25
NFND				
FND				
Storage				
ADDR			2	
BUF			2	
			32	

Timing

28.75 μs initialization
1220.0 μs loop

1248.75 μs total

† Core memory.

APPENDIX

J

Minicomputer and Microcomputer Glossary

accumulator—The main working register(s) of the CPU, many times designated "A."

ADC—Analog-to-digital converter, *which see.*

address bus—A common set of address lines that go to many memory modules and somtimes I/O devices.

ALGOL—A higher-level language that is not used too frequently in minicomputers. *Algo*rithmic *L*anguage.

algorithm—A well-defined procedure for doing something.

ALU—Arithmetic and Logical Unit. Usually refers to the central processing part of a microprocessor chip.

analog computer—A computer representing numbers by voltages that are proportional to the size of the number.

analog-to-digital converter—Peripheral device that converts analog voltages to digital form for input.

AND—A hardware or software operation in which the result is a 1 if all inputs are ones.

AND *gate*—Logic element implementing the AND function.

arithmetic overflow—*See* Overflow.

arithmetic shift—A shift in which the sign of the operand is retained by extension in a right shift or circumvention in a left shift.

array—A matrix of data.

ASCII—Commonly used seven-bit code for representation of alphanumeric and special characters.

assembler program—Program that translates symbolic statements into machine language code.

auto-index—Automatic hardware increment of a memory cell when that cell is used as a pointer to data.

autoload—A hardware option enabling a load of a small bootstrap program.

BASIC—A higher-level language that is one of the easiest to use and understand.

bcd—Binary-coded decimal. Numbers expressed in this form include the digits 0 through 9. Binary 1010_2 through 1111_2 are not allowed.

benchmark—A test program to measure a computer's speed or efficiency.

binary—Name for base-two numbers. Includes two binary digits: 0 and 1.

bit—A *bi*nary digi*t*.

bootstrap—A short program used to load a larger program, usually a more complete loader.

borrow—Analogous to a carry, but for binary subtraction.

breakpoint—A point in the program at which the debug routine gains control during debugging.

buffer—Logic element whose output is the same state as its input. Serves to "buffer" a logic signal or increase its "driving" capability.

bus (or *buss*)—A common set of lines that go to many units or devices.

byte—A collection of bits, usually eight. A convenient grouping for memory addressing and data.

byte addressing—A term used in reference to a 16-bit device that also has the capability of addressing 8 bits of data.

carry—The result of binary addition where the sum exceeds 1, as in $1_2 + 1_2 = 10_2$. The leftmost 1 is a carry to the next bit position.

central processing unit (CPU)—Portion of a computer that controls sequencing, does instruction decoding, and performs arithmetic and logical operations.

chassis—The metal box containing power supplies, control panel, and I/O slots of a computer.

checksum—An 8- or 16-bit value that is a check on validity of a block of data. It is obtained by the addition of all bytes or words of the data, or by some similar algorithm.

chip—A small integrated-circuit package containing many logic elements.

circular shift—A shift in which the rightmost or leftmost bit is shifted into the opposite end of the register.

compiler—A program that compiles a higher-level language into machine language or assembly language output.

complement—Usually refers to one's complement of a number, where all ones are changed to zeros and all zeros to ones.

condition codes—A collection of CPU flag bits usually representing result zero, sign of result, carry, and overflow.

console—Control panel of a computer.

console interrupt—An interrupt generated by pressing a console switch.

control panel—Main panel of a computer with data switches, indicator lights, and so forth.

controller—Usually used in reference to interface logic between an I/O device and the computer.

core memory—Computer memory made up of ferrite cores. Nonvolatile.

cross assembler—Assembler operating in a host computer that assembles programs for another computer.

crt display—Cathode-ray tube display peripheral device. Usually displays lines of characters on the screen, but may display dots or lines.

cycle time—Time of one memory or CPU cycle.

DAC—Digital-to-analog converter, *which see.*

data bus—A common set of data lines that go to many I/O devices and memory.

decimal adjust—The conversion of the result of a binary addition to a binary-coded-decimal number.

decode—To detect a specific configuration of bits.

diagnostic—An error indication is an assembly listing or compilation. A program designed to test and diagnose failures of computer hardware.

digital-to-analog converter—Peripheral device that converts a digital output to an analog voltage.

direct addressing—An addressing mode where the actual address is contained in the instruction itself.

direct memory access—A hardware feature designed to transfer data between memory and a high-speed I/O device.

disc—A random-access I/O device that stores data on a rotating magnetic disc.

DMA—Direct memory access.

double-dabble—A method for easily converting a binary, octal, or hexadecimal number to decimal.

double-precision—Referring to operations with twice the precision of the computer's word size. An 8-bit machine does 16-bit double-precision operations.

drum—A random-access I/O device that stores data on a rotating magnetic drum.

EA—Effective address, *which see.*

EBCDIC—Extended-Binary-Coded Decimal Interchange Code: a code for representing alphanumeric and special characters.

effective address—The memory reference address after the instruction displacement, indexing, and indirect addressing have been considered.

even parity—A parity in which the parity bit is set to a one if the remaining bits total an odd number.

exclusive OR—A hardware or software operation in which the result is one if one input and only one input is 1.

execution—Second part of an instruction cycle, used to decode and implement the instruction.

extender board—A plug-in board used as an extension for another circuit board to facilitate troubleshooting.

fetch—First part of an instruction cycle where the current instruction is "fetched" from memory.

field—A defined area in an instruction or data word that is used to represent a specific function.

file—A collection of records representing some meaningful series of events.

firmware—Usually refers to the contents of a read-only memory which represent a "burned-in" program.

flag—A flip-flop that can be tested under program control.

flip-flop—Logic element that may be set to remember an input signal—in effect, a one-bit memory.

floating-page—A form of addressing in which a fixed number of locations forward and backward from the current instruction may be addressed. Also called Relative Addressing, *which see.*

floating point—A number representation in a computer similar to scientific notation. Alolws very large or small numbers to be held in 32 bits.

floppy disc—A low-cost disc drive in which the medium is a flexible magnetic material.

FORTRAN—A higher-level language oriented toward formulas (*For*mula *Tran*slator) and mathematical functions.

full duplex—A mode of I/O data transfer that permits simultaneous transmission of data in two directions.

gigo—Garbage in, garbage out. An old computer axiom relating to program input and output results.

hard copy—A permanent printed copy.

hardware—Generally used to refer to any computer system components other than the program and paperwork.

hardware interrupt—An interrupt generated by an external interrupt signal.

hexadecimal—Numbers in base 16. Includes the digits 0 through 9, and the letters A through F.

high—Logic one. Active high lines are a one when the logic signal is true; otherwise, they are zero.

higher-level languages—An Englishlike or procedure-oriented language whose statements are compiled into a program to be run on a computer.

immediate addressing—An instruction addressing mode in which the operand is contained in the instruction word itself.

inclusive OR—A hardware or software operation in which the result is a one if any of the inputs are ones.

index register—A CPU register used in determining the effective address of an instruction.

indexed addressing—An instruction addressing mode in which the effective address is calculated by adding the contents of an index register to a displacement value found in the instruction.

indirect addressing—A mode of addressing in which the effective address is contained in another word of memory.

inherent—An instruction addressing mode in the Motorola MC6800 microprocessor that is equivalent to immediate addressing.

input/output—Refers to the transfer of data between CPU and peripheral devices or between memory and peripheral devices.

interface—Logic circuitry that connects one system component to another.

interpreter—A program that translates a machine code or higher-level language into another machine's instructions.

interrupt—An external event that causes transfer of control to a specified location under certain conditions.

inverter—Logic element whose output is the opposite of the input.

K—Refers to a storage capacity of 1024_{10}.

large-scale integration—Refers to integrated-circuit packages with high packing densities.

library—A collection of programs, routines, and files that are stored for future use.

line printer—A printing peripheral device that (usually) prints a line at a time.

literal addressing—An addressing mode in which the operand is inherent in the instruction itself.

loader—A program that loads object programs produced by an assembler or other types of files.

logical comparison—A comparison of two operands without regard to sign.

logical shift—A shift in which bits are lost off the end of a register. They are not rotated, and the sign bit is not maintained in the shift.

loop—A section of code that is repeated more than once before the program proceeds.

low—Logic 0. Active low lines are set to a 0 when the logic signal is true; otherwise, they are a 1.

machine language—Computer programs written in the actual numeric codes that the machine recognizes.

macroassembler—An "extended" assembler that permits user-defined macros, or sets of instructions.

mask—Usually used in reference to the disabling of an interrupt flag.

memory—A set of storage elements, eihter ferrite core, LSI RAM, or hardware registers.

memory bus—A common set of memory lines that go to all memory modules.

memory mapping—A hardware option that enables hardware protection or allocation of memory.

Memory Reference instruction—An instruction that reads or writes (or both) data to or from memory.

microcomputer—A minicomputer having a microprocessor chip or chips as its CPU.

microprocessor—A small CPU on an integrated-circuit chip.

microprogram—An internal CPU program that controls instruction implementation.

minicomputer—An inexpensive (hundreds to thousands of dollars) physically small, general-purpose computer.

mnemonic—An easily remembered name for a code or data.

MPU—Motorola's name for their MC6800 CPU chip. "*M*icro-processing *u*nit."

NAND—Logic element whose output is false when all inputs are true.

NOR—Logic element whose output is false when any input is true.

null character—A character made up of all zeros. Blank tape for paper-tape data.

object format—The output of an assembler in a form suitable for loading by a loader program.

octal—Base 8 numbers. Includes the digits 0 through 7.

odd parity—A parity in which the parity bit is set to a 1 if the total of the remaining bits is even.

omnibus—DEC's PDP-8 bus structure.

one-shot—A logic element that provides a predetermined time delay.

operating system—A central program that supervises, controls, and sequences assemblies, compilations, and loads, and that executes user programs and other tasks.

operand—A unit of data that is to be operated on.

OR *gate*—Logic element whose output is true when any input is true.

overflow—A condition resulting when an arithmetic result is too large to be held in a CPU register or memory. Sometimes sets a flag in the CPU.

page—An arbitrary number of memory words related to the addressing structure of the computer.

page 0 (zero page)—The lowest-value page in a page-oriented computer. Includes locations 0 through *N*, where *N* is the size of the page minus 1.

paper-tape punch—Peripheral device that punches paper tape.

paper-tape reader—Peripheral device that reads nine-level (or other format) paper tape.

parity—A check bit or bits used to validate data.

peripheral devices—Devices connected to a computer for purposes of data storage, printing, or display.

power-fail option—A hardware option that automatically saves volatile registers in core memory if power fails, and then restores them when power returns.

processor status word —See Program status word.

program—A set of computer instructions designed to perform one or more functions.

program counter—Register in the CPU that holds the address of the current instruction.

program status word (PSW)—A collection of flags and the program counter, defining the current status of the machine.

PROM—A read-only memory that can be programmed by electrical pulses. Once programmed, it is read only.

pseudo-operation—An assembler directive that instructs the assembler to perform some function other than generation of an instruction.

RAM—Random-access memory. Usually refers to volatile LSI memory.

real-time—Computer operations performed fast enough to keep up with real-world events, whether they be microseconds or days.

real-time clock—A hardware option to count real time.

register—A high-speed set of flip-flop storage devices.

relative addressing—An addressing mode in which the effective address is determined by the current contents of the program counter plus a displacement value found in the instruction.

ROM—Read-only memory. A "burned-in" memory that can be read but not altered.

rotate—A circular shift.

routine—A subroutine. A collection of instructions frequently used.

scratchpad register—A small, fast storage register.

selector channel—A DMA controller with word count, address, and function registers that control DMA transfers.

sense switch—A control panel switch that may be sensed by a program during execution.

single-step—To execute a program an instruction at a time from the control panel.

software—The programs and documentation in a computer system.

software interrupt—An interrupt generated by a specific instruction as in the MC6800 SWI instruction.

source program—The input to an assembler or compiler.

stack—A fixed or variable-size area in memory where data can be stored on a last-in, first-out basis.

subroutine—A collection of frequently used instructions, such as instructions for multiplying two numbers.

switch register—A register containing the contents of the control panel switches, usually addressable under program control.

Teletype—A peripheral device that includes a printer, keyboard, and optional paper-tape reader and punch.

trap—A hardware-generated interrupt for an abnormal hardware condition, such as a nonexistent instruction.

two's complement—Method of representing data where negative numbers are the complement of their positive value plus one.

utility programs—Support programs such as assemblers, editors, and debug packages.

vectored interrupt—An interrupt that causes a transfer to a unique interrupt location, rather than to a common interrupt location.

volatile—Nonretentive. Usually used in reference to LSI memory, where data are destroyed when power is turned off, as opposed to core, which retains data.

word—One or more bytes. One byte in microcomputers with an eight-bit data bus. Two bytes, or 16 bits, in most minicomputers.

Index

N

O

P